My Story

www.**transworldbooks**.co.uk

JULIA GILLARD

My Story

BANTAM PRESS

LONDON • TORONTO • SYDNEY • AUCKLAND • JOHANNESBURG

TRANSWORLD PUBLISHERS
61–63 Uxbridge Road, London W5 5SA
A Random House Group Company
www.transworldbooks.co.uk

First published in Great Britain
in 2014 by Bantam Press
an imprint of Transworld Publishers

A CIP catalogue record for this book
is available from the British Library.

ISBN 9780593075234

Addresses for Random House Group Ltd companies outside the UK
can be found at: www.randomhouse.co.uk
The Random House Group Ltd Reg. No. 954009

The Random House Group Limited supports the Forest Stewardship Council® (FSC®),
the leading international forest-certification organisation. Our books carrying the
FSC label are printed on FSC®-certified paper. FSC is the only forest-certification
scheme supported by the leading environmental organisations, including Greenpeace.
Our paper procurement policy can be found at www.randomhouse.co.uk/environment

Typeset in Adobe Garamond Pro
Printed and bound in Great Britain by
Clays Ltd, Bungay, Suffolk

For my late father. His love of learning was inspiring,
his belief in me was sustaining.

CONTENTS

SECTION ONE

How I did it

SNAPSHOT

I felt a sense of stillness and loneliness on the walk from Labor's caucus room to my office, having just been voted out of the prime ministership. Around me was anything but stillness. There was the frenzy of the cameras and reporters pushing and shoving to try and get 'the' shot, hear a comment. Good colleagues, loyal colleagues walked with me, yet that did not over-whelm the sense of being isolated in the moment. My wonderful staff lined the corridor to my office, applauding in tribute to me. Caterina Giugovaz, a young woman on my staff who had become a close friend, like a daughter to me, was sobbing as she clapped, her face a picture of misery.

But, apart from the briefest of hugs, I couldn't stop to console her or to be consoled by those who had become so important to me. There was too much more to do this night. Shortly I would walk to the Blue Room, the government's press conference room, and make my final speech as prime minister to the assembled media and the nation.

While prime minister, I had shed tears: tears of sadness for the suffering of Australians hurt by natural disaster, tears of grief at the loss of my father, tears of relief at finally delivering a better way for our nation to embrace people with disabilities. But I was not going to stand before the nation as prime minister and cry for myself. I was not going to let anyone conclude that a woman could not take it. I was not going to give any bastard the satisfaction. I was going to be resilient one more time.

1

Throughout my prime ministership, people would ask me when I met them, 'How do you do it?' They would search my face for clues, wanting to know why I wasn't at home hiding, sobbing, screaming. It was a question I could never answer in such brief moments, often with television cameras rolling and journalists hovering. But at the heart of the answer is resilience – a modern buzzword, yet a term that came to encapsulate so much about my life.

Every leader faces adversity. The prime ministership is a position that affords both the luxury of helping shape the nation's future and the pressure of intense days and audacious scrutiny. The last easy days of prime ministership were probably lived by Robert Menzies during his long sojourns to the United Kingdom. Every prime minister in the modern age must show fortitude in the face of a crushing, constant workload, a relentless, often negative media and many roadblocks to policy change. These pressures are formidable but routine for leaders and I do not focus on them in this section.

What I do recount is what was different for me as a result of Labor Party instability, the uniqueness of a federal minority government and the ways in which gender plays into perceptions of leadership. This section necessarily deals with some hard truths because it is impossible to discuss resilience without explaining why resilience was necessary.

In my view, it is also impossible to be resilient without having a sense of purpose. In section two, I detail the answer to the most essential question of why I did it, the beliefs that drove me.

The taste of politics is always bittersweet because the best and the worst of things are often inextricably woven together. I have endeavoured to convey the complexity of the flavour. But for me, even in the most difficult of times, the sweet – the ability to do the things I so passionately believed would make our nation stronger and fairer – was always the most intense.

1

Becoming the first

'. . . a nation where hard work is rewarded and where the dignity of work is respected; a nation that prides itself on the excellence of its education system, where the government can be relied on to provide high-quality services for all Australians; an Australia that can achieve even greater things in the future'

STATEMENT TO THE AUSTRALIAN PEOPLE ON
THE DAY I BECAME PRIME MINISTER

I BECAME PRIME MINISTER in what felt like a whirlwind on Thursday 24 June 2010. My memories of the day are in fragments, quick glimpses snatched as events propelled me on. Two hours of fitful sleep were not the best foundation for such a momentous day. Fortunately adrenaline kicked in and spurred me into action.

There was no running sheet for 'what would happen when'. No family gathered around me. As if it was just another parliamentary day, I showered and put on the suit I had always intended to wear. But unlike any other day, I walked out the door of my Canberra apartment and into history.

The photographs of me, the nation's first female prime minister, being sworn in that afternoon by the nation's first female Governor-General, Quentin Bryce, document the moment. The necklace I am wearing is an afterthought, borrowed straight from the neck of staff member Sally Tindall. Chatting with Quentin before she officiated at the brief ceremony provided the day's only soothing interlude. I felt enveloped in her warmth.

Other fragments of memory: the stunned journalists at my first press conference; the eerie silence of my first Question Time; receiving my first briefings.

The day ended where it had started, in the apartment. By now I was joined by my partner, Tim Mathieson, Julie Ligeti, the lifetime mate and long-term Labor staffer who shared my Canberra flat with me, and my very good friends Robyn McLeod and her husband, Barry, who had dashed up from Melbourne. We ate Chinese takeaway. It was a hasty meal.

During the preceding hours, I had felt moments of elation, an occasional sense of unreality, a hunger for what was to come, a wistfulness about what might have been. However, in what was to become the pattern of my prime ministership, I quickly turned away from reflections about what had happened to planning for the following day. There was no forensic replay in my mind of how I got here. The circumstances that caused the Australian Labor Party (ALP) to change its leader and make me prime minister were not chewed over with our food.

Much lay behind the explanation I gave to the Australian people in my first press conference as prime minister, that I was now the nation's leader because a good government had lost its way.

Originally Kevin Rudd and I had been heralded as the 'Dream Team'. In 2006, our partnership had started out so brilliantly but perhaps so wrongly. As Labor prepared for the election the following year, it was a do or die moment. If Labor could not unseat John Howard after 11 years, and when he had so badly over-reached with his hated industrial relations policy, Work Choices, when would it ever happen? Australians did want change, I believed, but safe change. Their prevailing mood towards Howard was not one of anger but they were ready to move on from him. Yet if Labor in any way discomforted them, robbed them of their vision of safe change, at the last moment Australians might give Howard one more win. Should the Liberals then manage an orderly transition to the post-Howard generation, they were likely to cement themselves in for an even longer period of government. Every day, I feared that while the political winds were finally favourable for Labor, our leader, Kim Beazley, was not the one to get us there, to give Australians the political permission they needed to change the government.

Government wears you down. Opposition wears you down. Kim had been a long-term server in both, plus he had been quite unwell with an illness that required weeks of bed rest and seemed to rob him of energy.

As Labor's Manager of Opposition Business, responsible for putting together the pack of questions that would be asked at Question Time, I saw Kim daily when parliament sat. Question Time is the lifeblood of Opposition, so getting ready for it requires making the day's most important tactical judgements. Yet I never saw him grab the work of preparing for it, shape it, demand his way about it. Watching this, I worried that the fire to succeed was not burning strongly enough in him. My fear was that in the final ballot box judgement of Australians, Kim would not be chosen.

It was this that led me into discussions with Kevin Rudd about forming an alliance to become the new leadership of the Labor Party. Kevin seemed the embodiment of safe change. Physically a younger version of a Howard-style figure. A family man. A Christian. From a Queensland country town. Fresh, new and 'here to help'. If Labor was to change leader, it had to be to this kind of figure. Kevin in 2006 dramatically lacked the majority support required from our Labor colleagues to become the leader. But in an alliance, he and I would succeed.

Kevin had to be the leader in our alliance because I understood that I was not what Labor needed at that point: a woman, not married, an atheist. I would not be perceived as the embodiment of safe change. In joining forces with Kevin, I accepted the probable consequence that I was unlikely to ever lead the Labor Party. I had not come into parliament with an ambition to do so. When Mark Latham, Labor's leader from 2003 until 2005, imploded and resigned the leadership, I had put my name forward in the subsequent leadership contest to make a point about Labor culture and values, not with any expectation of winning.

But in 2006, my motivations were not all altruistic: in the next Labor government, I wanted to be a key player. I felt frustrated by the tight and seemingly exclusive circle around Kim and thought I could and should do more than I was ever going to be asked to do with him as leader.

That said, the decision to form the so-called Dream Team with Kevin was not an easy one. I was painfully aware of his propensity for anger: when I annoyed him in a parliamentary tactics discussion one day, as the meeting broke up he had stepped into my space to spit menacing, bullying words at me. My long-term staff member Michelle Fitzgerald, who was within earshot, was about to place herself between us when Kevin stormed off. Her protectiveness was not necessary. Kevin would never have done more than speak angry words, but even so the outburst was a red flag. What kind of leader would he be?

Upon deep reflection, I concluded that Kevin's flaws stemmed from a yearning for approval. That the difficulties of his childhood had produced a man who craved attention and the applause of the crowd. It appeared that there was a hole in him that had to be filled by success and the poor substitute for real love that is political homage.

Surely, I reasoned, becoming Labor leader and then prime minister would be enough; the neediness would fall away and the many positive aspects of Kevin's character would come to the fore. After all, he was a man with a sophisticated world view, capable of the most complex policy discussions, a politician who knew how to work the media, a brilliant tactician. He was also capable of surprising acts of thoughtfulness. My friend Michelle O'Byrne told me how after she lost her seat of Bass in the 2004 election, Kevin went to considerable trouble to meet up and console her. He knew from his own loss in the 1996 election, he explained, the terrible feeling that comes when the phone is silent and everyone has moved on from your loss but you.

Was I wrong in my judgement of Kim Beazley in 2006? I fear I may have been, that what I inferred as his lack of interest in the work of Opposition was really a more nuanced understanding of electoral politics than I then possessed. The prospect of losing consumed me, made me desperately anxious. Kim may rightly have judged that we were so likely to win that a quieter biding of time in the lead-up to election day was a better approach than strenuous political exertion.

In politics you never get to run the control test. We will never know what would have happened in a John Howard versus Kim Beazley election or what a Beazley Government might have been like. How long Kim would have stayed. Who would have been his successor.

What I do know is that my decision made the difference. Kevin had spent his years in Opposition assiduously courting factional leaders, particularly the New South Wales Right, and media backers. Even so, none of that calculated work would have made him Labor leader without my intervention. I bear the responsibility for creating his leadership.

In 2007, Kevin was a major electoral asset for Labor; my judgement of his campaign capability and likely acceptance by the electorate was right. But my assessment of how he would perform as leader, in essence what kind of man he was, proved to be dreadfully wrong. There was never enough applause, approval, love. He always craved the next hit of a good poll and the hit after that.

In the year of campaigning in the lead-up to the 2007 election, nothing was lost; indeed so very much was gained through Kevin's quest for popularity. All of us were engaged in that hunt for votes. Kevin worked incredibly hard, and it was awe inspiring. He showed constant tactical agility. He was in his element.

The marketing campaign that turned him into Kevin 07 was masterful. It brought with it the vibe and energy for our victory. It also brought with it expectations that could never be fulfilled: Kevin was human, Kevin 07 was hype. For everyone who becomes a brand, there is a dangerous space between reality and image.

Victory on 24 November 2007 was sweet. Inevitably the presidential style of modern campaigning meant the focus moved from Kevin and me as the Dream Team to Kevin 07. Still, along with Wayne Swan and Lindsay Tanner, I emerged from the campaign as one of the leading players in the federal Labor Party and the government. I was the first woman ever to serve as deputy prime minister. In subsequent months, my parliamentary performances and ministerial work made me undeniably the second most significant player in the government.

I took on the equivalent of double the usual cabinet minister's workload, serving as Minister for Education, Minister for Employment and Workplace Relations and Minister for a newly created coordinating portfolio of Social Inclusion, which aimed to tie together across government all the work done to combat disadvantage. It was at once an onerous load and the exciting opportunity of a lifetime. Since 1998, I had served in Opposition. After nine long years, I was not going to miss my chance to deliver change.

In Opposition, you are in a political speedboat. You can twist, turn and zoom to new locations for political advantage. Kevin was the absolute master of doing things like waking up in Sydney, reading the newspapers, seeing a political advantage in being in Hobart, then jumping on a plane. But government is the *Queen Mary* – huge, powerful, but not agile. The art of being prime minister is in charting a strategic course and using the sheer weight of government to plough through the rough choppy bits. Government requires long-term thinking, process, method. It took some adjustment but I could feel the true power of government and was determined to use it to deliver Labor policy and values, particularly by replacing Work Choices with a fair system and creating new opportunities for working people through a fresh approach to education.

Unfortunately Kevin wanted to still be in a speedboat. His forte was tactics, not strategy. He felt the 'love' of the electorate and enjoyed the deference of those around him but he did not identify his driving purpose for the government he led.

The 2007 election campaign had been premised on two key themes: building for the future and easing people's cost of living. Expectations were high for change, and in the cost-of-living area, unrealistically so. Being empathetic about people's cost-of-living pressures is grist to the mill for Oppositions. But come government, I soon learnt that even when new benefits are provided, people do not conclude that there is more spare cash in their wallet than there used to be. So from the outset, there was considerable work to do and looming political issues as voters' high campaign expectations gave way to day-to-day governing realities.

While the in-tray was already full, Kevin added more. Kevin's guiding doctrines in tactically and artfully managing the ferociously fast media cycle were 'fill the space' and 'kick the can down the road'. The first meant pump so much content into the hands of journalists that bad news about the government or the Opposition's complaints should be crowded out. The second that any issue being reported negatively should be neutralised by some means of postponement, like announcing an inquiry. It was common for a minister to end up the reluctant custodian of a review or prime ministerial promise to take action on a particular problem, with a general instruction to fix it.

Personally I was shielded from the worst excesses of this kind of conduct. By virtue of working together so closely, Kevin and I had formed a genuine personal and political bond, so his conduct towards me was respectful. Largely, and in sharp contrast to other ministers, many of whom suffered micro-management at Kevin's hands, I was able to run my own race. But both of these doctrines raised expectations that the government would be doing more and more. In truth, these patterns of behaviour were more than media management strategies; both were the product of a restlessness that arose because of a lack of definition of the government's core mission.

Even with this flurry of unfocused activity, the government enjoyed a continuing honeymoon and moments of magic. Sitting in the parliament as Kevin delivered our nation's apology to the Stolen Generations was to have a ringside seat at a perfect moment in history.

Day to day, though, Kevin's approach made the exacting work of government so much harder. As mountains of unfinished work kept piling up, huge policy reform agendas were hostage to a haphazard decision-making style: Kevin demanding more and more paperwork, with directives to produce it by punishing deadlines, only for it to never be read or properly responded to. Meetings supposedly called to make decisions would turn into rolling seminars because it was obvious that Kevin had not read any of the papers and he needed to be taken verbally through what was contained in them. At the end of the explanation, he would frequently ask for more papers to be prepared, which also did not get read.

Often ministers and senior public servants cooled their heels for hours waiting for meetings to start or were, with no notice, ordered to be in a different part of Australia for a meeting with the Prime Minister; sometimes that meeting never happened.

While the published opinion polls continued to show that both the government and Kevin were held in high esteem by voters, even during 2008 some troubling signs were appearing in community attitudes. The results of Labor's focus group polling, in which discussions of issues are held with soft voters, echoed the kind of feedback that was coming from community interactions generally. Australians were starting to liken the government to an inexperienced swimmer: plenty of action and flailing of limbs but not much progress being made.

My view remained that Kevin would soon settle into a steadier rhythm and start to take a more strategic approach rather than a media-driven tactical one. Indeed all these matters of Kevin's style and focus still weighed lightly compared to the excitement we all shared about finally being in government and able to enact policies we had dreamt of for so long.

Then the global financial crisis (GFC) broke into our world. It is hard now, in a country that never went into recession, to describe the emotions and pressures of those days. Put simply, the GFC ushered in the unbridled fear that comes from having no ability to predict what might happen next. Our globalised, interconnected, interdependent world had never before faced such a phenomenon. Was Australia about to be hit by bank failures, queues of people wanting to withdraw deposits degenerating into riots, mass unemployment, suicides? It all seemed heart-stoppingly possible.

This was a crisis made for the Kevin Rudd leadership style. Or perhaps Kevin was made for this crisis. In a genuine emergency, no one expects perfect process or deep consultation. No one begrudges pulling an all-nighter to be ready for a meeting the next day. No one chafes against centralised decision-making. Instead everyone wants a leader who will work without rest and push through. Kevin Rudd was that leader, not only in the domestic decisions – on vital matters like providing a timely guarantee to our banks and quick economic stimulus to our economy – but also the international ones. Without Kevin's strident international advocacy, Australia ran a real risk of being locked out of the key global meetings where decisions would be made about how to respond to the crisis. Kevin's work helped ensure that the global body at the centre of the action was the G20, a grouping of major economies where Australia is in the room.

It was high-adrenaline, high-octane politics and Kevin excelled at it. Wayne Swan, a man who always put in extraordinarily hard work, matched Kevin's work rate hour by hour, meeting by meeting, and proved his capability as an economic manager. Jobs were saved, the economy was kept out of recession and credit must go to Kevin for his leadership and our Labor government for its performance during those dark days. Yet as the crisis receded from days of immediate economic peril to days of hard slog to manage the roll-out of stimulus and return to the usual business of governing, Kevin did not adapt; he could not find that steadier rhythm.

It had been appropriate in the short term to have a smaller and more centralised body doing much of the urgent decision-making. The four-person Strategic Priorities and Budget Committee (SPBC) – comprising Kevin, Wayne Swan as Treasurer, Lindsay Tanner as Finance Minister and me as deputy prime minister – was that group. But well beyond the requirement for this kind of nimble, central decision-making structure, Kevin kept the SPBC in operation, using it to supplant cabinet. Even though the absolute crisis days of the GFC had passed, there were 84 meetings of the SPBC in 2009 and 2010.[1]

Other ministers became bit players when invited to attend SPBC. Decisions were taken at SPBC meetings on all facets of government, not just the economic policy required because of the GFC. The agendas became unwieldy, the meeting schedules erratic; the capability of the public service to generate documents in support of decision-making was stretched beyond breaking.

The very calling of items at the meetings became marred by this general mayhem. Stephen Conroy tells the story of waiting all after-noon on an upper floor of the federal government offices in Sydney to be called down to the SPBC meeting in progress in a room floors below. As night rolled in, he became so hungry he thought he would check to see if he had time to nip out and pick up something to eat before his item was reached on the agenda. He took the lift to a darkened meeting room: SPBC had concluded and no one had told him or his staff.

Then there were times when Kevin decided something was more important than attending SPBC. In Kevin's absence, I chaired 14 of these 84 meetings.[2] As Wayne, Lindsay and I worked our way through the agenda, we would do our best to second-guess Kevin's attitudes and which decisions he would accept and not seek to overturn. Other vital meetings, including cabinet itself and its National Security Committee, were treated the same way.

Ministers would complain bitterly and their complaints were not confined to the running of meetings. The prime ministerial paperwork required to authorise ministerial actions routinely went missing. Ministers would be desperately trying to get sign-off on items months old, even items that were in no way controversial. It was impossible for them to plan their diaries or media agendas with any certainty, to know on which days big announcements would be made, because at the last minute their plans were frequently countermanded by Kevin's office.

If the sense of being jostled around and ignored was strong for ministers, it was even worse for caucus members. They no longer had a telephone number to ring that Kevin would answer. Instead his phone was constantly diverted to a staff member. Face to face their contact with him was limited to appearances – often very short ones – at caucus meetings.

In the community, Kevin began to seem like a handyman who starts too many jobs and never finishes any.

My personal relationship with Kevin remained solid and I tried, more and more desperately, to get him to address our political problems. In June 2009, I managed to get him to agree to create a Political Strategy Group (PSG) comprising me, Wayne, John Faulkner, Mark Arbib and Karl Bitar.

It was inconceivable that such a group would not include Wayne, given both his pivotal role in government and his campaign strategy abilities. John Faulkner had been key to Labor campaign efforts over many elections and had Kevin's confidence. So did Mark Arbib, who had held the powerful position of General Secretary of the New South Wales Branch of the Labor Party. In that capacity and as a leader in the Right faction of the ALP, Mark had been a powerful ally for Kevin in his bid to become leader. Mark had since become a senator and remained a key adviser to Kevin. His predisposition to speak blunt truths to power meant his relationship with Kevin was an ongoing series of bust-ups and awkward rapprochements. Even so, the logic of his inclusion in this group was undeniable. He was a savvy campaigner. Karl Bitar had worked closely with Mark in New South Wales and served as National Secretary of the ALP. As a quiet person in the loud world of politics, Karl was often underestimated. He had never achieved an easy rapport with Kevin, but he had good political insight and a pivotal organisational role, so it was imperative he be in the room.

To me, this team had the right mix of experience and ability and, importantly, was the appropriate size. A small team like this had been the only kind of structure Kevin had been prepared to work with during the 2007 campaign, albeit that even then, many decisions were made solely by him while he was on the road. My hope was that working with a similar team could be the first step in getting Kevin away from day-to-day tactical, media-driven decisions and into a more strategic approach.

While Kevin honoured his commitment to the PSG often in the breach rather than the observance – by moving meetings around and leaving them early – I consoled myself that it was a start to corralling him into some kind of effective dialogue.

On that I was wrong. Winning the formation of this PSG did not put me on a roll to solving other problems with decision-making. All the problems remained, so, patiently and persistently, time after time, I explained to Kevin the need for him to change his way of working and to confront and resolve the major issues before the government. Because I was talking to the Australian Prime Minister, I expressed my views respectfully. I was also ever mindful that I was interacting with a man who did not like to hear criticism. Others who spoke the truth to him ended up frozen out. There was regular banter about who was in the freezer. I was confident that Kevin could never put me in the freezer, because of my status within the government and the leadership team bond between us. Typically he would respond with placatory words, promises to consider what I had said or a half-hearted agreement to some limited change.

Whenever I put to Kevin the need to have cabinet genuinely drive decision-making, rather than it continuing to be confined to a second- or third-rate status behind Kevin and his office and the SPBC, he would counter with his concerns about leaks. In this he had genuine cause for worry. The leaking from Kevin's cabinet was not the methodical leaking of a leadership campaign but the indulgent and foolish tendency of a couple of people to chat with selected journalists to curry favourable personal coverage. Understandably this angered and frustrated Kevin, me and the vast majority of cabinet ministers. But in many ways the worst outcome of certain celebrated leaks was that they provided Kevin with a handy excuse for not having a true cabinet process even though an occasional leak would have been the far lesser problem.

Notwithstanding Kevin's wariness of leaks, I pushed him and pushed him to disband the SPBC and go back to real cabinet processes, with decisions taken at the end of full and proper debate, instead of the ineffectual and disheartening meetings they had become. Sadly, when the SPBC was dissolved, methodical cabinet processes were not instituted in its place. The culture of late, inconsistent decision-making and the paying of lip service to cabinet had become entrenched. I kept raising the need to have strategic discussions with cabinet, allowing people to put a view about both the priorities of government and our political problems. These discussions were always scheduled, but in reality it was only rarely that one occurred with Kevin in the room and genuinely engaged.

I became the fix-it person ministers turned to. I would endeavour to resolve their problems, either by working directly with Kevin's staff or, if that failed, speaking to Kevin. On top of managing my own mammoth workload, I would spend time going to Kevin's office, trying to bolster the spirits of the staff, fishing out documents ministers were screaming for, getting Kevin to sign them or, when Kevin travelled, signing them myself as acting prime minister. As the wear and tear on ministers, staff members and public servants grew, I kept my own counsel and focused on persuading Kevin to adopt more-effective practices. To other ministers, I would defend him and try to jolly along frustrated public servants kept waiting for meetings. But the sense that things were out of control was becoming impossible to contain.

The realisation that so much was wrong and needed to be fixed was not confined to me. Wayne Swan was also alarmed by the scatter-gun approach to decision-making and consequently the lack of actual decisions on big-ticket items. Increasingly we combined efforts in our advocacy of more involvement by our colleagues in decision-making and settling on answers to those policy problems that were just being allowed to drift.

External events added to this accumulating anxiety for the government. To our bitter disappointment, circus-like images of the Copenhagen United Nations (UN) climate change conference damaged public support for pricing carbon. And with Tony Abbott's ascendancy on 1 December to the position of Opposition leader, complete with a hard-hitting negative campaign, another political challenge emerged.

The government's cost-of-living policies had delivered new benefits for Australians but had become mired in the spectacular failures of ill-conceived policies such as Fuel Watch, a website to give information on petrol prices, and Grocery Watch, a website to do the same for supermarket shopping. Courtesy of the GFC there was lingering anxiety about jobs. In this environment, it was easy for the Opposition to roll up carbon pricing, the cost of living and jobs into one big scare campaign.

The government left 2009 with no real planning or preparation work done for the 2010 election campaign and with enormous issues like carbon pricing, tax reform, health reform and the growth in asylum-seeker numbers all unresolved.

By this stage Kevin was completely spooked by the way the politics of carbon pricing had withered from the feel-good factor of signing the major international agreement on climate change, referred to as the Kyoto Protocol because the key meeting that gave birth to it was held in that Japanese city. He had dreamt big dreams for Copenhagen and his role in it. His sense of hurt that the world had not achieved more was palpable. Certainly he did not know what to do next on carbon pricing and appeared to have no appetite for hard campaigning on it.

On health reform and hospitals, he was a dreadful mixture of sharply political and indecisive. He became wedded to the political tactic of a federal hospital takeover plebiscite – though this would have no legal effect. While time was chewed up discussing this kind of game-playing, the real hard grind of devising a policy that would work and could be funded became infected by indecision. What the Australian people wanted was change that would give them a health-care system to meet their needs now and in the future: less waiting time in an emergency department or for a hospital bed, better access to a doctor and other health practitioners in their community. They wanted to know that the health-care system would be affordable over time and that costs would not overwhelm them. They did not want a mock referendum about nothing.

In addition, Kevin seemed determined to ignore the increasing numbers of asylum-seekers arriving by boat and the damage the *Oceanic Viking* incident had done to the government's standing. The *Oceanic Viking* was an Australian ship that Kevin despatched to rescue asylum-seekers at risk at sea. Hoping for a quick-fix to a complex problem, Kevin decided to return these asylum-seekers to Indonesia rather than take them to Christmas Island. Weeks of stand-off resulted, with the asylum-seekers refusing to disembark the vessel. For the Australian people, the sight of asylum-seekers virtually seizing control of an Australian ship reinforced the Opposition's claim that the government had lost control of our borders.

When the all-encompassing tax review Kevin had ordered, conducted by Ken Henry, the head of Treasury, was delivered, Kevin seemed not to know how to respond to it and digest its many politically difficult recommendations. The Australian tax system did need change to more efficiently raise what is needed to fund vital public services. Such a huge public policy agenda required government working at its best. Alas the only thing to come out of Kevin's summertime musings was drift.

In February 2010, Kevin's senior staff talked frankly to me about the problems. Such was the trust established between us, they knew I would listen and try to help. They painted a picture of a leader who was not coping. Kevin would clear his diary of commitments, often at the last minute, but stay in the office and then without warning call in a particular policy staff member and interrogate them on an issue. Individual policy staff lived in fear of being the one he chose to drag into a meeting in those vacant hours. Indeed I will always remember one of his senior male staff weeping uncontrollably in my office, so psychologically taxing was the atmosphere. But Kevin was stressing people to breaking point for no purpose. No strategy emerged for any of the nation's big reform needs or the government's political problems.

In this environment I kept stepping up my efforts to force Kevin into strategic discussions. But where in 2009 I had felt that I could find a way to help Kevin change, in 2010 I was more despairing. Increasingly I was asking myself the question, how can you assist a person who does not want to be helped?

Kevin's demeanour was now unremittingly one of paralysis and misery. He appeared to hate every minute of his day and to be frustrated by every person and every event. Conversations quickly became a stream of complaints about how hard he was working, how little sleep he was getting, how all the pressure was on him. If a document was handed to him, with an eye roll and a sigh he would let the world know how substandard it was. If someone fussed around him with tea or food, his look was often one of irritation.

Yet he found it impossible to delegate, to find ways to reduce the burden on himself. In fact, his answer to not being able to make a decision was to demand more paperwork about the decision, sometimes just the same documents reformatted. It was a horrible political Catch 22. He bemoaned how little people were helping him but would not let anyone help. Rather than dig himself out of the pile of undone work heaped on top of him, he ordered more paper to be piled on top. On it all went and Kevin just could not make any decisions.

The question of what to do next on carbon pricing drifted. Only the looming deadline for printing the budget forced Kevin into taking a decision. His backflip on the key policy to address climate change, which he had described as 'the great moral challenge of our generation'[3] hurt him dreadfully in the community's eyes. The pain was intensified because he was not prepared to get out and explain why he had come to this conclusion and what should be done next.

There was also indecision on whether or not to announce a profits-based tax on mining. Kevin had Wayne and Treasury continue to work on the preparation of the tax, but without making any decision about whether or not to announce it. The more that was done to get it ready, the more it became a fait accompli. But Kevin withheld both active political consent and personal effort in coming to grips with all the policy and political details. Long hours would pass at key budget meetings with Kevin lavishing attention on minor budget measures but refusing to finalise the government's approach to the Resources Super Profits Tax. When the tax was announced it drew forth a furious response from the mining industry, including a highly resourced advertising campaign of devastating political effect. Kevin's answer to this campaign was anger, more paralysis and then an erratic approach to discussions on finding a political fix to the problem.

Asylum-seeker boats kept coming but apart from deciding to suspend the processing of claims of those from Afghanistan and Sri Lanka, Kevin did not meaningfully and continually engage with the problem.

In contrast, Kevin did get moving on the health reform agenda, going day after day to hospitals around the country and securing a landmark agreement with Labor premiers. But despite all the time spent and the great merits of much of the policy, little political dividend was reaped as the very complexity of the package made it hard to sell and other policy problems crowded in.

As the unresolved issues spun around worryingly, I endeavoured to cover as many gaps as possible. I wanted us to govern well for the Australian people, I wanted us to win the election due in 2010. I worked as hard as possible to try and achieve both. With Kevin's agreement, I took to playing a managerial role in his office and to giving his staff some direction. I convened diary and media-planning meetings with key staff. I tried to bring structure to something that had descended to chaos.

Kevin also brought in Bruce Hawker, a long-time Labor identity and political consultant, to review his office. It amazed me that Bruce later became such an ardent Rudd supporter: as he sat in on meetings I convened, he expressed disbelief at how bad the situation had become.

None of this is meant as a criticism of Kevin's staff. They were extraordinarily hardworking individuals, many of them incredibly talented. But their efforts were stymied by Kevin asking several people to do the same thing, insisting on ridiculous deadlines for work he would never use, upending arrangements at the last moment in favour of a new idea.

Working with Karl Bitar, our National Secretary, and others, I was attempting to get consistent and effective messaging into our campaign for the mining tax, even going to the extent of personally editing Kevin's speeches. Once, sitting on a bed in a hotel room in Perth, I finished drafting well after midnight Perth time, well after 2 am in the time zone I had flown from. After I emailed the recast speech, I fell asleep with the laptop open beside me on the bed. I had not had the energy to even shut it, let alone put it away.

Meanwhile, within the ranks of the Labor caucus, resentment towards Kevin was mounting. As the polling tightened and the sense grew that he was directionless, people talked about him leading us to a defeat. Many wanted to talk to me about our political position, the problems with Kevin and their frustrations. When colleagues came to vent their concerns about how much political trouble we were in, I would talk with them. If they ever raised the suggestion that the solution to our political troubles was changing the leadership, I would hold my hands up and say firmly that I was not prepared to have such a discussion. By this stage, I was resolved to work around Kevin in order to keep the government working. I had decided to help whether or not he wanted me to. In our discussions, I continued to pitch to him the need for change but I was not waiting for his answer anymore. To the best of my ability, as the second most powerful actor in government, I just got on with it.

But this kind of throwing my weight around could only happen if those I was dealing with – political staff, senior colleagues, the campaign team – saw me as a trusted proxy for Kevin. What I would have liked, indeed loved, was for Kevin to truly lead. But in the absence of him doing so, at least with him allowing me to get things done, I felt I could hold things together.

As the budget parliamentary session drew to an end, Labor members were fractious and brooding. I did not background journalists negatively about Kevin. I did not contrive to create photo opportunities where I would look good and be contrasted with a struggling prime minister. I did not canvass my colleagues for support. But on Wednesday 23 June 2010 I did ask Kevin for a leadership ballot. That morning I had woken up to a news story written by Peter Hartcher and Phillip Coorey in *The Sydney Morning Herald* which questioned my loyalty.

Peter was known to be very close to Kevin. The piece crystallised for me a nagging fear that I had been pushing to the back of my mind, the fear that Kevin, in his disarray and despair, was becoming wary of me. I could no longer avoid confronting the truth that the only remaining bond holding the government together, the one between Kevin and me, had dissolved. If Kevin did not trust me then there was nothing left.

I asked to see party elder John Faulkner, at that stage Defence Minister. In his earlier capacity as Cabinet Secretary, John had spent much of his time mopping up behind Kevin. The workload in Defence, a highly demanding portfolio in which he excelled, had made it impossible for him to continue to do so. At the meeting with John, I surprised myself by dissolving in tears. I remember pointing at the newspaper and saying over and over that I did not deserve the accusations contained within it. It is the only time in my political career I have shed tears for myself, the kind of tears I was determined never to cry as prime minister. The accusation hurt so much because of all the effort I was putting in for Kevin: managing his diary, editing speeches, driving work on election preparation, cajoling public servants fed up to their back teeth with his management style, smoothing the frayed tempers of ministerial colleagues; in short, doing everything I could to support Kevin and the government.

John Faulkner hugged me as I cried that day. Later that night, he was to become witness to history as he attended a crucial meeting between Kevin and me. In the time in between I spoke to other colleagues about what I should do in these untenable circumstances.

After John, I asked to see Tony Burke, Minister for Agriculture, Fisheries and Forestry, and a member of the NSW Right. In many ways, he and I are unlikely political confidants. However a bond between us had grown during the days of government. I found Tony very insightful and from time to time I sought his views on particular policy or political problems confronting the government. I trusted that he could keep a discussion confidential. On this day, for the first time ever I raised with him the leadership. I tested with him my view that now, facing an environment of suspicion and mistrust, I had only two choices. To challenge for the leadership or to resign as deputy prime minister and go to the backbench. He agreed with this analysis and generously described himself as an 'immovable supporter' of mine. I left that discussion knowing that if I did seek the leadership, Tony would support me. If I resigned and went to the backbench then he would very likely come with me. To feel such loyalty and support helped stiffen my spine.

The parliamentary day rolled on with its own implacable rhythm. My discussions with my colleagues were in sharp contrast to the routine of the parliamentary proceedings.

I reproach myself for two things on this harrowing historic day. Neither of them is asking for a leadership ballot. First, I regret that I entered the House of Representatives chamber late for Question Time. As a result, I did not realise that Kevin, who was on his feet in the chamber, was not delivering an answer to a question but a speech of condolence for three soldiers lost in Afghanistan. When I sat down, instead of listening I struck up a conversation with Anthony Albanese, the Leader of Government Business, known to all as Albo. I will always deeply regret that I did not show the respect required for a loss so grievous. My second regret is that when I met with Kevin at the end of the day, with John Faulkner as witness, the conversation went as long as it did.

Routinely this scene has been portrayed as one of me eagerly wielding a knife. Actually in the moment I was hesitant. I entered the conversation full of conflicting emotions. Despite knowing that Kevin's conduct over many months had effectively destroyed his prime ministership and leadership of the Labor Party, I wished for him, for all of us, that it was different. After so many false promises from Kevin, I knew he was tragically incapable of changing his behaviour, yet I wished he could. Despite knowing – as I did when tears had welled up that morning – that trust was gone, I wished the easy friendship between us that existed in the earlier days of government was still there. But gone were the days of sitting companionably together over tea or coffee or a meal, of silly jokes and laughter, of feeling a sense of joint endeavour. Now the times were so different.

In the conversation, I was dismayed that Kevin was still in denial about the ugliness of the truth. He did not seem to want to acknowledge the depth of the problems that loomed or the animosity he had created. It was like having a conversation with a patient with terminal cancer who is maintaining that it is merely a head cold and they will soon be better. It was hard to find the words to communicate what others had experienced, felt and believed about his leadership.

This experience of Kevin in seeming denial was not new to me. In earlier conversations I had seen him exhibit the same demeanour when I discussed with him the many problems his leadership substance and style were causing. It spoke to me of conflict within: that of a smart man who intellectually can understand the problem but who refuses to let reason overcome the emotional need to deny it.

The lengthy conversation turned to the canvassing of alternatives to a leadership ballot, to giving Kevin more time to change. This was unfair to Kevin because it gave false hope. To allow the conversation to go on and on was even more unfair to the Labor Party. As the discussion continued, Albo came in and delivered a blunt message: that as we talked the Labor Party was dying. This was the first time I realised that outside the quiet of that office, Labor's internal turmoil had become a public spectator sport. A little later my then chief of staff, Amanda Lampe, asked to see me outside. She was being bombarded with messages of support for me from caucus colleagues. Her message was that from television studios to Parliament House offices it was being assumed a leadership contest was already underway.

The power of Albo's words truly struck me. The time for talking was over. I re-entered the room. With the pulse of my blood audible in my ears, I asked Kevin for a ballot. We shook hands.

I returned to my office, which was filling with Labor parliamentarians offering their support. Next I walked to Wayne's office and asked him to be my deputy prime minister. Late into the night, I made phone calls to my colleagues.

The following day, I was elected unopposed by my caucus colleagues as Labor leader and, as a result, became the 27th prime minister of

Australia and the first woman ever to hold that office. Kevin chose not to contest the ballot, having been advised by his remaining supporters that he was likely to only receive 14 votes. Even as Kevin's tears fell in his press conference at noon, it was my strong belief that after some recovery time, his dominant emotion would be relief – he had become so wretched while leader.

The decision of caucus members to overwhelmingly support me has been described since as the result of arm-twisting by factional warlords, the so-called faceless men. This is a convenient caricature for those who want to deny the more complex truth. Factional players have been involved in every leadership decision in modern Labor: Hawke versus Keating, Beazley versus Crean, Latham and Rudd. Nothing was different in 2010. But in no leadership contest are caucus members automatons who exercise no judgement. Labor parliamentarians think. Indeed they agonise.

For so many to move to support me so quickly had the feel of uprising around it. Caucus wanted change, not because factional leaders told them to support it but because they were despairing of Labor's political circumstances, Kevin's leadership ability, its impact on the work of government and the nation, as well as his lack of simple human respect for them.

The closer you were to the centre of the Rudd Labor Government, the more critical you were of Kevin. But the Labor team had done a remarkable job of shielding these chaotic inner workings from public view. Consequently, from the perspective of the Australian people, the change in prime ministership happened without warning and for no reason. It shocked them. It was the hardest of circumstances in which to become prime minister.

I made it harder. Because I wanted to treat Kevin respectfully, I offered no real explanation of why the change had happened. This was a decision I came to regret. I should have better understood and responded to the need of the Australian people to know why.

But while an explanation of the circumstances which made me prime minister was lacking, I knew what I had come to do. Certainly it was to strive to resolve the immediate unresolved policy problems for the nation and the resulting political problems for the government.

Absolutely it was to try and win the election. But neither of those things was my driving sense of purpose. I had come to politics and now to the office of prime minister as a result of my deep, unshakeable beliefs in the power of education to change lives and nations, the benefits and dignity of work and the need for human beings, individually and through the policies of government, to show each other decency and respect.

For three years and three days I was prime minister. Three years and three days of resilience. Three years and three days of changing the nation. Three years and three days to give me a unique perspective of our future. Three years and three days for you to judge.

2

The first days

'Good day for redheads!'

ME TO KERRY O'BRIEN, REDHEADED PRESENTER
OF *THE 7.30 REPORT* (ABC1), ON MY FIRST DAY
AS PRIME MINISTER

JOKING ABOUT RED HAIR became one of the routines of my prime ministership. People would send me 'ranga' T-shirts. At schools, I could always get children to laugh by saying 'great hair' to a redheaded child. I became convinced that welcoming parties at school gates were being deliberately stacked with redheads. Pity those harried principals searching through their classrooms so they could turn out the rangas.

Of course, not all responses to my appearance were as gentle. On my first full day as prime minister, I went to a shopping centre with the media in tow. It was unashamedly a picture opportunity to show me out and about in my new role. Although I was a woman who bought and wore suits, and had little colour in my wardrobe, I did own a trench coat with some muted colours in its design. On that cold Canberra day, I wore it to the shopping centre. The media reaction was so over the top, I took to jokingly referring to it as 'the trench coat that divided a nation'. In the sharpest and most humorous of the criticisms, it was described as being like a cheap motel bedspread.

While the fashion debate raged, I was coming to grips with my new life, with the immense direct and indirect power that comes with being prime minister, and the fact that almost everything had changed overnight for me and those I loved.

The weight of being prime minister usually does not descend onto a person's shoulders in one big hit. Rather it hits piece by piece. Inevitably for every prime minister there is some uncomfortable wriggling around, working out how best to carry it. Becoming prime minister in an unexpected instant, as I had done, had allowed no time to brace for the new weight. There was no choice but to get on with it; that also applied to my family members.

On the morning I became prime minister, I had to make urgent arrangements to get some support over to my parents, John and Moira, who were being besieged by the media. Mum and Dad were living in what is termed a 'lifestyle village', a gated community for people over 55 years old. The gates had not worked to keep the media out. Television stations with outside broadcast vans rolled up at their door. My hospitable father was letting everyone in, making them cups of tea, much of this going live to air. The phone was ringing nonstop with media requests and a young female reporter had helpfully taken to answering it and writing out messages.

The scene was revealed to me by my niece, Jenna, who rang to see how her grandparents were doing and ended up talking to the young reporter. Startled she drove around to find a scene of cameras, cables and journalists crowding into my parents' small lounge room. Thankfully Kate Ellis, an Adelaide-based Labor minister, was able to have staff from her office go around and they imposed some semblance of order.

Meanwhile Tim was flying to Canberra to be at the swearing in. Having dressed early and quickly to catch the flight, he had managed to put on, along with a suit, one black boot and one dark brown one. It just had to do for the rest of the day.

While we did not quite appreciate it at the time, our life together in the form we knew it was coming to an end. Tim and I had met in 2004 in the hairdressing salon in Fitzroy where he worked. Every four or five weeks on a Sunday morning, I used to go in and work my way through the newspapers as my hair was done. Tim and I got talking about politics; initially he thought I was a state member of parliament. We had later run into each other on a tram and had a chat. He then moved back to Shepparton, his home town, for a period and we lost sight of each other. On a couple of occasions, at key points in my political career, he rang my electorate office to wish me well but did not get through to talk to me. He had more luck ringing in 2006. The two of us talked and we made arrangements to have lunch in Carlton during the politically quiet time of the Melbourne Commonwealth Games. The rest is history: we have been together ever since.

Our relationship was forged when I was already senior in politics, working hard and travelling constantly, but we both needed to take another big step up in our ability to deal with public exposure when I became deputy Opposition leader and then deputy prime minister. As deputy prime minister, I did not have much down time. But in the little pockets of time off I had, Tim and I would go to a local coffee shop or bar, catch a movie, go for a walk together.

From the minute I left my office on the night I challenged for the leadership, all that changed dramatically. A personal protection detail of the Australian Federal Police (AFP) was waiting for me. Although I never tracked down who assigned me this team, I assume Tony Negus, the AFP Commissioner, had decided to make sure that whatever happened the next day, he had the security in place.

Of course, in my many stints as acting prime minister, I had grown used to having a team of police officers with me. But it is one thing to have that cocoon surround you for days, quite another to live in it for years. Tim and I started a period of our lives where we always had security. Not only did I have police protection whenever I was out, I was not allowed to drive myself or be driven unless a specially trained commonwealth car driver or police officer was at the wheel. Our days of popping out for a drink or to go to the movies or for a walk on the spur of the moment had come to an end. Instead we spent time and relaxed together in private spaces, inviting family and friends into that space rather than going out to see them. The same applied to family visits. On Boxing Day, it was card games rather than visits to the cinema.

Ripples of change engulfed all my family members and friends. On the first weekend I was prime minister, my sister, Alison, niece, Jenna, and her partner, Damien, came to visit me so we could absorb the change together. After we had spent some time moving in to my new office, I suggested that, along with Tim and his daughter Sherri, we all go to Queen's Terrace Café – the only place open in parliament on a weekend – for coffee and sandwiches. Within minutes, television cameras surrounded us – so much for our casual family bite to eat. Sally, one of my media advisers, who arrived to try and manage the mêlée, shook her head at my naivety: wander off for a lunch? No more.

My family had grown used to a police presence around me; time I spent with them at Christmas tended to coincide with periods when I was acting prime minister. While I was deputy prime minister, they had also become accustomed to seeing me in the media but it was already clear that this was all going to be much more intense and constant.

For my parents, this was a time of pride. The public attention for them at this point was enjoyable and benign.

For Alison, who has the Gillard surname, the connection was obvious and ever-present. For my niece, Jenna, and nephew, Tom, who have the surname Malone, the connection was less obvious but still present. Jenna works as a research scientist and Tom as an electrician. Tom tells an endearing story: at a lunch-time discussion at work, when he volunteered the information that I was his aunt, the news was met with a sceptical 'as if'.

For my staff too, this was a time of immense change. In my office as deputy prime minister, I had 17 staff. The prime minister's office has a staffing complement of around 50. Tabloid newspapers will have fun from time to time pillorying politicians for keeping an army of spin doctors. But the roles played by political staff are far more complex than this lazy characterisation.

A large number of staff are policy specialists who receive the advice coming from the Department of the Prime Minister and Cabinet – this is impartial public service advice – and add their political analysis to it. For large projects, such as completely changing the school funding system, policy advisers and public servants will work closely together, knitting into a coherent whole the public policy and political values driving it. Policy advisers are so trusted, they speak on your behalf to stakeholders and meet people who wanted to see the prime minister but for whom, with the best will in the world, you could not make time.

Policy staff and a dedicated team working on cabinet papers manage the work and paper flow to and from you as prime minister. This comprises all the meeting papers needed for cabinet and committees like the National Security Committee, all the letters to sign, the information to absorb such as meeting briefs, national security information, economic data and policy-decision documents.

As deputy prime minister and then prime minister, my world featured a continuing cycle of paperwork in coloured folders. I would always start work by putting briefs into colour-coded piles. Red briefs were urgent; purple were national security; yellow were for information; green, correspondence to be signed and so on. Keeping up with the paperwork was something I forced myself to do and prided myself on.

Administrative staff are also required in large numbers. From the patient call-takers, who speak to the thousands of people every year who ring and ask to talk to the Prime Minister, to staff who keep the paper flowing and manage the diary, with its complex intersections of travel – domestic and international – and the requests that flood in for time with the Prime Minister.

For media staff, working their way through how the Prime Minister and government overall can best communicate what is being done, the demands are ceaseless. From dealing with a junior reporter at a country radio station who wants to know when the Prime Minister is coming to town to the most seasoned and cynical doyen of the Canberra press gallery, from the 6 am radio news to the late-night television news bulletins, these staff are active and trying to manage the message.

Under the leadership of my chief of staff, Amanda Lampe, we had to quickly weld together a team from my own staff and those who chose to stay on in the prime minister's office. Amanda had started her career as a political staffer working for Labor minister Con Sciacca when he was Minister for Veterans' Affairs in the Keating Government. A former journalist and a talented, forceful woman, she had honed her skills working with Premier Bob Carr. She had come on board as my Communications Director while I was deputy prime minister and became chief of staff when Ben Hubbard left.

Later Ben came back to the position while I was prime minister. A boy from Bendigo, he had worked as John Brumby's administrative and political aide as a very young man. I had been Ben's boss as John's chief of staff. Ben had gone on to a senior role in the Bracks Government and gained management experience in the public sector. He brought to the role of chief of staff sharp management skills and political nous.

As the staff team was assembled, I also built my relationship with the public service. A key figure was Terry Moran, the Secretary of the Department of the Prime Minister and Cabinet, a powerful central agency in government alongside the Department of Finance and Administration and the Treasury. The work of line agencies, such as the departments working on health and transport, is chewed over by these central players. Each advises powerful actors in government: the prime minister, the Treasurer, the finance minister. The work of these agencies and their political masters is critical to shaping the disparate activities of government into a whole meaningful plan. In my first meeting with Terry, we discussed how best to start afresh with the paperwork that had mounted up. He advised me to formally ask him to recall all briefs sent to the prime minister's office under Kevin's leadership.

Politically I did not have the luxury of starting afresh. I had inherited many political headaches, most particularly the three issues on which I had described the government as losing its way: the Resources Super Profits Tax, carbon pricing and asylum-seekers.

Of these the most urgent for resolution was the mining tax. In my first press conference as prime minister, I announced that the government's public advertising on the mining tax would be suspended and I asked industry to do the same. To their credit, they did so quickly. My office and I contacted major industry players to confirm that there was a strong mutual commitment to resolving the differences of view constructively. I agreed that representatives of the sector, through its leading firms, should meet with senior ministers as soon as practicably possible, and a series of meetings was scheduled for the following week in Canberra. The negotiations that flowed were conducted minute to minute by Wayne Swan and Martin Ferguson. The mining companies agreed to open their books on a confidential basis to Treasury so that as the newly named Minerals Resource Rent Tax (MRRT) was designed, there would be no confusion about its impact. Crucially, through this process, Wayne believed he had brokered a clear understanding with the industry about what the government would receive in tax revenues over the four-year budget period.

On the day of the final discussions, I returned to Canberra late in the evening to complete the agreement. I walked into the anteroom outside the cabinet room to find spent but satisfied people. At the conclusion of an incredibly intense eight days, an agreement had been struck.

During this same period, I was working to get us into campaign-ready shape. Here the load fell heavily on Karl Bitar and Mark Arbib. I turned to Jenny Macklin to lead a team to generate campaign announcements for my consideration. Even with the unstinting efforts of Jenny and those around her, our late start on this task meant we were scrambling in the campaign itself. Cabinet was also directly engaged in addressing the government's problems and readying for the campaign.

On the thorny issue of climate change, I commissioned Penny Wong to develop a fresh approach to consulting and implementing a carbon price. It was discussed at cabinet more than once. Cabinet agreed to an approach that kept our commitment in principle, and this commitment included proactively advocating for a carbon price, not shelving it. This reflected my view that one of the biggest problems with carbon pricing was the lack of explanation and engagement with the wider community. My intention, as I outlined to my cabinet colleagues, was to find an approach to reform which took the community with the government, step by step.

I also started to tackle the problem of asylum-seeker arrivals. While Kevin was prime minister, I had prevailed upon him to bring together the relevant ministers to work on policy answers to address the ever-increasing number of asylum-seeker arrivals by boat. The group made good progress until, late in his prime ministership, without warning Kevin scuttled that process. Among the ministers were Stephen Smith, then Minister for Foreign Affairs; Chris Evans, our long-suffering Immigration Minister; my close political friend Brendan O'Connor, who was Minister for Home Affairs; and Simon Crean, who, as former leader, had contacts and authority for back-channel discussions.

They had favoured the idea of a processing centre in Timor-Leste, previously known as East Timor. For Timor-Leste, this would generate jobs and money flow. For Australia, this return to offshore processing in and of itself would not provide the necessary long-term deterrence but it might provide some break in arrivals and give time and space for consideration of other policy measures.

With Kevin's full knowledge and agreement, Simon had been asked to pursue quiet discussions with Steve Bracks, who at that stage was volunteering his time to assist Prime Minister Xanana Gusmão with the growth of effective government and political structures in Timor-Leste. According to the soundings Steve took – contrary to what the official structures of government suggested – the best avenue for further discussions was with President José Ramos-Horta. Although surprised not to be directed towards the Prime Minister for discussions, I followed this advice.

On 6 July 2010, I gave a frank speech about asylum-seeker policy, to give the Australian people the facts, to get away from the hyped rhetoric used by all sides in what has become such an emotionally and politically charged debate. Having spoken to President Ramos-Horta and the United Nations High Commissioner for Refugees (UNHCR), I announced the government's intention to pursue discussions with Timor-Leste about hosting a regional processing centre. In the days that followed, the proposal became hotly divisive within Timor-Leste itself and a cynical reaction to the policy in Australia followed. At least I had spoken the truth about the dimensions of asylum-seeker arrivals and placed some focus on the need for regional arrangements.

As I sought to carefully defuse these leftover political time bombs, I was conscious I needed to call the federal election, and soon. On the day I became prime minister, I pledged that Australians would shortly be able to vote. Instinctively I felt people wanted the chance to endorse or reject a new prime minister and there was a limit to how long they would think it fair to wait. Plus, with the media in a frenzy – one that, in my view, was only going to intensify – constant fevered speculation about when an election would be called was not going to allow even a little bit of extra time or space for governing.

At the start of the campaign we were in front; my becoming prime minister had lifted Labor's electoral standing. Internal Labor Party polling showed my assuming the leadership added six per cent both to Labor's primary vote and its two-party preferred vote. This was achieved against a backdrop of continuing decline in the Labor vote and Kevin's standing as prime minister dating from after the first three months of government – other than upswings during the immediate days of the GFC, during the aftermath of the scandal known as 'Utegate', which fundamentally damaged Malcolm Turnbull because he made demonstrably false claims, or in the midst of Liberal leadership convulsions.

Most Australians thought Labor would win the election. Our Labor Party polling at the start of the campaign showed 68 per cent of Australians expected us to win compared to 17 per cent who believed the Coalition would win. Even at the end of the campaign, 54 per cent of Australians expected us to win compared to 23 per cent who expected the Coalition to win. Guided by a simple appraisal of the polls, the common belief of journalists was that it was impossible for Labor to lose.

This media mindset was reinforced when the first few days of the campaign went well for Labor and badly for the Opposition. Consequently all the media scrutiny was directed at Labor – journalists could not be persuaded of the need to really analyse anything announced by the Opposition. As a result, the media would miss reporting in any meaningful way the $10.6 billion funding hole in the Opposition's costings.

As always, though, polling does not convey the deeper truths. My perception was a totally different one from the public's happy assumption that the ALP would win the election. We were entering the campaign underprepared because no real campaign strategy work had been done prior to me becoming prime minister. Plus the election would take place under the shadow of the leadership change and hard policy issues like carbon pricing, the MRRT and asylum-seekers.

Further the Labor campaign would be shockingly under-resourced because no systematic work had been done to fundraise. No one in politics would say fundraising is their favourite pursuit but with our current system, in which public funding is sufficient to pay some but not all of your campaign expenses, it is a necessary evil. The easiest days of fundraising are when your political fortunes are high and businesses and high-net-worth individuals want to donate. Labor's easiest fundraising days would have been in the first year of government, when almost everyone was beating down the door to see new ministers and spend time with the new government. Yet in October 2008, the Labor Party was still over $14 million in debt. The Labor Party would have been bankrupted if the 2010 campaign was run as anything other than a financially prudent one.

Of necessity, crucial expenditure areas like our advertising budget were of a modest size. For the 2010 election campaign, just over $14 million was spent, compared to nearly $22 million in the 2007 campaign. Indeed, following the 2010 campaign, the Labor Party emerged with its debt down to $7.7 million.

What it boiled down to was this: I was facing a cashed-up opponent who had no pressure on his shoulders – because so few people thought he could win – and the luxury to solely run a protest-vote campaign.

With all these problems surrounding me, on Saturday 17 July 2010, I was driven in C1, the prime minister's commonwealth car, to Government House in Yarralumla. It was my third trip in a little over three weeks: once to be sworn in myself, then to swear in my ministry, and now to call the election for 21 August 2010.

I looked out the window and mused about the electoral contest to come. It was time to give people a vote. Such a precious thing, often taken too lightly. Many a time on polling booths, I had spoken to people in big queues who, while waiting to vote, complained about the inconvenience. My response was always that around the world people fight and die for the right to vote, so ten minutes in a queue was not such a burden.

For me personally, this election would be the toughest challenge of my life. We certainly needed a good campaign and my performance would be critical to whether Labor formed government again. I also knew that during the campaign, some of my energies would be taken up doing things that should have been done already, including fund-raising and policy development work. But even as I coolly analysed the obstacles in my way, I was confident I was up to the challenge. It would be tight but I believed that Labor could overcome the difficulties and win.

As the car glided past the media teams broadcasting live and through the gates of the Governor-General's official residence, a wave of applause went up from among the many individuals who had turned out to watch me drive in.

Inside, once again Quentin Bryce's warmth embraced me. Talking with her was a moment of ease at the start of what would turn into the election campaign from hell.

3

A campaign sabotaged

'There are three men here who are not standing for prime minister – Kevin Rudd, Mark Latham and Laurie Oakes – and each of them think that the election campaign is about them. Now, would this have happened if this competition were between two men? I'm not sure. I think we have to unpack this and see what we are actually seeing with our own eyes, which is a lot of blokes trying to monster up a woman.'

GEORGE MEGALOGENIS, *INSIDERS* (ABC1),
SUNDAY 8 AUGUST 2010

GEORGE MEGALOGENIS IS A POLITICAL COMMENTATOR and author. His is the not unusual but always heartwarming Australian story of a migrant kid made good. A self-effacing character, George's reaction to being cast as the White Knight in a dark and moody political tale would be hearty laughter. But in the 2010 campaign, George was my White Knight.

By the end of week three, the election campaign had become the political equivalent of one of those horror movies in which, right when you think things are as bad as they can possibly be, there is another shocking burst of guts and gore. What had not been factored in to my political calculations about our ability to win the election was ongoing internal sabotage of the campaign.

Certainly I understood Kevin Rudd would be in emotional turmoil. I know more now than I did then about the emotions that course through you when you are deposed by your own party from the leadership and prime ministership. The dimensions of the feelings of hurt, of anger; the pain of the leave-taking from those who have been so much a part of your life; how hard the exhaustion hits when you come to a sudden stop. But I also know that intermingled with all of that is some sense of relief. The hardest thing you will ever do in your life has come to an end and stress ebbs away.

In 2010, I truly did believe that for Kevin what would emerge most strongly from the emotional vortex would be the feeling of relief. After all, he had been so unhappy during 2010 when serving as prime minister that many around him were concerned about his psychological state. I was wrong. His dominant emotion was a need for revenge.

In election campaigns, even piercing emotions are usually set aside. Historically Labor's campaign culture is so strong that bitter enemies campaign side by side without complaint. Internal hostilities are suspended and any settling of scores is postponed until beyond election day. In 2010, Labor's cultural norms were shattered.

The first warning that this was to be an election campaign like no other came at the National Press Club on Thursday 15 July. In that address I threw a spotlight on the themes that were to define my prime ministership saying:

> I believe a strong economy is the foundation of everything else that I as prime minister want for Australia. It's the foundation because I believe lives are given shape and purpose by the benefits and dignity of work . . . A high-participation economy will sustain stronger growth, stronger public finances, and will better support the pressures on services caused by an ageing population. A high-participation economy will sustain hope and purpose in individual Australians and give security and choice to their families. I will make education central to my economic agenda because of the role it plays in developing the skills that lead to rewarding and satisfying work – and that can build a high-productivity, high-participation economy. It is difficult to think of any investment that will generate returns as enduring as our investment in a child's education.

The importance of this speech cannot be overstated. It was a crucial scene-setter for the weekend on which I would call the election. I had been prime minister for such a short time and, despite my prominence as deputy prime minister, for the vast bulk of Australians, who only tune into politics intermittently, I was still an unknown quantity. I wanted to lay my values before the nation ahead of the start of the election campaign, to give an insight into my understanding of the economy, now and in the future, because I believed that capacity for economic management should be central to the voting decisions Australians made. The speech deliberately contained key contrasts between my approach and that of the Leader of the Opposition.

Twenty-four-hour news channels have changed life for senior journalists: they no longer need to attend significant political speeches or even campaign events. They can watch from their offices and start work on the analysis immediately. Laurie Oakes, Channel 9's political veteran, almost always does his work this way. He is most definitely not inclined to sit at a function where a speech is given or, heaven forbid, stand at a press conference.

From my seat on stage, where I waited for the cue to start speaking, I surveyed the scene before me. It was of an audience in various stages of eating their lunch. Some journalists were bent over copies of the speech provided to them. Then I saw Laurie Oakes in the audience. Something unusual was going on. When question time came, he put to me a version of what had happened in the room on the fateful June night that Kevin Rudd, John Faulkner and I had met. He alleged I had agreed with Kevin that he could have more time as prime minister and then had reneged on the deal.

From day one, I had made it plain that I would not speak of that conversation. Even under this pressure from Laurie Oakes, with the Canberra press gallery watching mesmerised, I stuck to that policy of silence. To start detailing the conversation word by word would have inevitably led to a need to describe the chaos of Kevin's leadership. Out of respect for Kevin, I was determined to stick rigidly to the formulation that a good government had lost its way. Further, given that the election campaign would be underway in a few short days' time, it would not bode well for Labor's re-election fight if the lead-in to the campaign was a painstaking examination of the internal failings of the government Kevin had led.

Undeniably I had been guilty of letting the crucial leadership conversation with Kevin meander in a way that fed false hopes but the blunt version conveyed to Laurie Oakes was deliberately skewed to be as damaging to me as possible.

Feeding this material to a journalist constituted a significant and malicious act. It was not only a deliberate tactic to seek to overshadow my speech on the eve of an election campaign, it was designed to raise doubts about my character, precisely when most Australians were making up their minds about me.

John Faulkner is not the kind of man to disclose such a conversation. His reputation for being the keeper of internal secrets is well deserved. I had not detailed the conversation to anyone. It was therefore crystal clear that Kevin was the original source of the material used by Laurie Oakes.

Over a number of years, Kevin had done the smart thing and courted Laurie, seeking to establish a good relationship. He was by no means alone. It is common practice on both sides of politics to seek to inveigle one's way into Laurie's good books. I had not done so. Frequent wining and dining with the media was never my style. In addition, from Laurie, while I had not felt animosity, I had never felt any rapport.

So confronted with the worst bastardry at the outset of an election campaign that Labor has ever known, my only physical reaction was to blink as I limited my response to joking about Laurie Oakes attending the press club.

As bad as this first act of sabotage was, it pales into insignificance compared to what happened on 27 July 2010, ten days into the election campaign. Laurie Oakes, on that evening's news, delivered an exclusive and blistering report that I had opposed in cabinet both Labor's paid parental leave scheme and its pension increases. When I arrived in Adelaide from Coolangatta at almost eight o'clock at night to this news, I concluded that at this point Labor's campaign could spiral out of control and we would lose the election and lose badly.

The next day, I did the only thing I could do, calling a full news conference where I took question after question to deal with these destructive allegations. I explained how, following the GFC – as the government managed a huge fiscal stimulus program and faced the daunting task of getting the budget back into surplus after spending to save the nation from recession – it was appropriate to strongly scrutinise the roll-out of new measures. Of course I supported a paid parental leave scheme and more money for pensioners but I made no apology for holding these policies up to the light and ensuring full debate. My performance at the news conference was praised as strong and effective, but both my standing and Labor's had been damaged.

We were using polling to track voters' responses every day of the campaign, as did the Liberal Party. Towards the end of week one of the campaign, we hit some normal campaign-style problems when our climate-change event was the subject of a protest and footage of the ensuing scuffles with police were flashed all over the nation's television screens. Climate-change policy continued to be problematic for us. While I won the only debate with Tony Abbott on the Sunday night, he had exceeded the very low expectations voters had of him. Our track polling showed us down by two to three per cent compared to our starting position in the campaign of a 52 per cent two-party preferred vote. This was not an unusual campaign fluctuation and was recoverable. After the Laurie Oakes report, however, our vote tumbled by six per cent overall. It was the difference between having a primary in the forties, a position from which you can win, to having a primary at 37 per cent, a position from which you cannot win.

Oakes's story had been devastating in its electoral impact. It had played to questions voters were already thinking about in relation to me: if I was unmarried, childless, could I really understand the pressures and concerns of families? Obviously the contents of the report led some voters to conclude that I did not understand the need for help for families when children came along or Mum or Dad struggled with the bills in retirement. Consequently Labor was now careering towards a loss. Labor's culture of solidarity during election campaigns was in tatters.

What I had not disclosed was that in questioning those policies, as much as anything I had wanted to impress on Kevin that we could not afford more new announcements, more new measures. The immediate issue was whether we could afford either or both new expenditures at this time. I canvassed the best possible sequencing and potentially a delay of a year of the paid parental leave scheme. A legitimate debate had followed. The measures proceeded with no delay. But the point I was really making was that we already had a huge amount to digest, to manage, to sell. I never succeeded in breaking Kevin's addiction to another policy announcement to get another headline and to try and boost the next poll.

Those strategic conversations about the cost, timing and political merits of the policies had taken place in meetings attended by four politicians – Kevin Rudd, Wayne Swan, Lindsay Tanner and me. The account of my arguments had been skewed and fed out in an endeavour to cripple the re-election chances of the Labor Party and me.

It has been suggested by some that – to deflect attention from Kevin's culpability – Laurie could have been briefed by a public servant in the room. This is an explanation that does not pass the laugh test. If the senior public servants who attend such meetings were in the habit of leaking, they could have filled edition after edition of newspapers with tales of Kevin's poor and eccentric conduct towards them. Instead they had bitten their lips and got on with the job.

No one in their right mind would accuse Wayne Swan of being the leak, given he was working night and day to support his and my chances of re-election.

Lindsay Tanner had no motive for the leak. He had determined for personal reasons to leave politics at the 2010 election campaign and would have done so whether or not Kevin had stayed on as prime minister. While he stayed personally loyal to Kevin, the bond between them had been tested during the days of government. I remember the sick feeling in the pit of my stomach when Kevin pulled Lindsay, Wayne and me out of an SPBC meeting about the set-up of the Health and Hospitals Fund and the Building Australia Fund to scream at Lindsay for disagreeing with him in the meeting. Lindsay was no fan of mine and had always viewed me as a political rival. We had contested against each other for preselection for the electorate of Melbourne when Gerry Hand retired from politics in 1993. But other than a general antipathy towards me, he lacked any reason for such an egregious act.

It is also implausible that this information could have been planted by one of Kevin's staff without Kevin's consent. These are the same staff who would sweat for days trying to work out the best way to break bad news to Kevin, such was their fear of his temper. None of these individuals, who had taken so much punishment, would have risked Kevin's wrath by, without his consent, doing something which for all time would shape public perceptions of him.

The only rational explanation was that Kevin, having been the ultimate source of the first Laurie Oakes story, also created the second story, either directly or through the agency of a loyal staff member. Kevin not only had the generalised motive of wanting to pay me back, he had a specific motive. I knew exactly what Kevin wanted. He had communicated it to me with clarity.

Instead of doing the decent thing and retiring at the 2010 election, accepting the judgement of his colleagues, he decided to run again and to demand an appointment as Foreign Minister in a re-elected Labor government.

It is not easy to lose a leadership contest and take yourself immediately out of politics. Having done precisely that, I know. But it is absolutely the right thing to do if you want your political party to prosper; you spare them from dealing with any distractions from the cause of re-election. I left the political scene, stayed silent and lived my life like a fugitive, going to great lengths to avoid being caught anywhere by the media in the 2013 campaign. Consequently not once was I in the top five most talked-about issues as measured by the media monitoring that tabulates each week what is discussed on radio, television, the internet and in newspapers.

Kevin could not have avoided all publicity in the 2010 campaign, given that he suffered a bout of ill health and was hospitalised. When this happened I felt natural sympathy for him. Had he been trying to avoid all media, my sympathy would have been heightened, given how hard it is to maintain privacy when you want to do so in such circumstances. But Kevin never took my attention-avoiding approach. Instead he became the most talked-about issue for the first three weeks of the campaign. He consistently ran on the front pages of newspapers. The attempt to smear me as callous and uncaring about helping families with children and older Australians dominated six days of the media coverage in the campaign. No, Kevin had not put Labor first.

I had publicly confirmed that Kevin Rudd would serve as a senior member of my cabinet in a re-elected Labor government. I was reluctant to give him the position of Foreign Minister, knowing he would try to refuse instruction from me and endeavour to run his own race. In addition, for the nation's sake, as a re-elected prime minister I knew I had work to do with China to rebuild that relationship after their adverse reactions to Kevin's presumption of a special bond with them and his expletive-laden insults following the Copenhagen climate change summit. No one takes well to being accused of ratfucking. The Chinese most certainly did not. Consequently I had in mind a domestic portfolio, perhaps a singular focus on Indigenous Affairs, given the huge status Kevin had gained with Indigenous Australians following the delivery of the apology to the Stolen Generations.

From the moment I was first told of the Laurie Oakes report about paid parental leave and the pension increase, the campaign of blackmail was plain to me. Either Kevin would get what he wanted or he would see Labor defeated.

On Saturday 7 August, as week three of the campaign was turning into week four, I met Kevin for a photo opportunity. John Faulkner had brokered the agreement between us for the meeting. In my eyes, it was an attempt to stem the damage done by Kevin's sabotage of the campaign and the ongoing political hangover from the leadership change. His price for the photo had been a guarantee he would be Foreign Minister if the government was re-elected and I had accepted his demand. I had little choice: I had to stop what I considered to be the acts of treachery on his part.

Kevin made no real effort to make the meeting work, refusing to look at me and pouting instead of passionately supporting Labor. But from then, there were no more political grenades lobbed into the campaign. This fact alone shows that the argument that a political actor other than Kevin was the source of these damaging stories does not withstand scrutiny.

If I thought things could not get harder or worse, I was wrong. Following the excruciating experience of the photo opportunity with Kevin, I then went to announce a policy for older Australians with Jenny Macklin. Unbelievably former Labor leader Mark Latham was pacing at the back of the press conference pack. Channel 9 had engaged him to cover the campaign. Across the campaign we had to contend with media bias, with particularly the *Daily Telegraph* determined to promote the election of Tony Abbott. But Channel 9's conduct broke all norms and was even repudiated by Laurie Oakes,[1] one of their own.

The event Mark Latham appeared at was held at a senior citizens' home in Queensland. Endearingly a few of the residents gave Mark a piece of their mind. But the reaction of the journalists in the press conference pack was febrile. Unsurprisingly the questions focused on Labor division, with the following question forming a pithy summary of the problem I faced: 'Prime Minister, there's another former Labor leader just standing over there, in Mark Latham. Why should Australians vote for you when you have one leader who has just been dumped, who won't say you're a great option for PM, and another former leader wandering around, criticising you and your key policies?'[2]

Jenny Macklin later congratulated me on keeping going through this weird, wild press conference.

I got back in my car thinking this was as low as this campaign could go. But no, the horror show had one more scene to play. Later that day, Tim joined me in a walk-around at the Queensland Show, known as the Ekka. As people thronged, looking to get a photo with me, Mark Latham materialised in front of us and blocked our path. The television pictures flashed into homes that night were ugly ones, of me physically having to find a way to get around a confrontational former Labor leader. Labor looked, and was, out of control.

Who knows what was motivating Mark at this time! When he was Labor leader, I was one of his most loyal supporters. When his leadership ended in a mess, with him bitterly launching into print with a deluge of unpleasant observations about politics and his colleagues, I did my best to urge some generosity towards him. Although I had not seen or spoken to him in years, during the 2010 election campaign it appeared that he was still feeling antagonistic towards the political party he had led and all within it, even former supporters. Mark ended up urging that people protest by deliberately lodging an informal vote on election day.

Enter the White Knight. On the *Insiders* that Sunday 8 August, George Megalogenis delivered his withering critique, which sparked a general discussion on the show about how increasingly pathetic the press pack's approach was to media conferences on the campaign trail. The words obviously hit home. Later that morning, at a press conference in Darwin, I was asked respectful question after respectful question about the structure and merits of the policies being released – about sport and education.

Nevertheless, while the sabotage was finally behind me, the wreckage of Labor's campaign effort lay all around. A Labor loss seemed inevitable.

Already I had tried to press a reset button for Labor's campaign with a pledge to adopt a campaign style more natural for me. On the weekend after Laurie Oakes's report had torpedoed Labor's campaign, I went to the footy and watched my team, the Western Bulldogs, record a win. Against the advice of the AFP and some of my staff, in the closing minutes of the match I walked up the players' race to the edge of the ground. Very visible to the crowd in the stands on each side, I was greeted with applause and shouts of 'Good on you, love'. The fears of my advisers and the police – that some idiot, a little the worse for wear at the end of the match, might spit at or tip a drink on me – were not realised, fortunately, and the feeling was all good.

Next I was embraced by big bad Barry Hall, the hard man and legendary player with a soft heart, as he ran off the ground. I then revelled in the unusual privilege of joining in the players' circle to belt out the team song. Despite being unscripted and slightly risky, this generated some of the best television news pictures of the campaign.

On the same weekend, I was interviewed by Phil Hudson, a veteran Canberra journalist who hailed from Melbourne's west. The *Herald Sun* ran the interview on the front page on Monday 2 August with the headline, 'I'm taking control: It's time to unleash the real Julia'. In this interview I had deliberately canvassed with Phil a move to a less stage-managed campaign style, one in which I was more authentic. I felt I had shown what could be achieved by going with a freer approach but, above all, I was weighed down by how Labor's campaign had become subject to two contradictory narratives from the media.

The first was that it was too stage-managed, too spin driven, too controlled. The pulse behind these criticisms was that somehow the feisty funny woman who had been deputy prime minister was not around anymore and she had been replaced by a new, contrived politician.

The media's second narrative for the campaign, in complete contradiction to the first, was that it was full of wild leaks and wanton acts of political violence.

As a result of Labor's planned campaign, I was being parodied as a campaign strategists' puppet, even though our campaign was much less scripted and controlled than the Opposition campaign, which ruthlessly confined Tony Abbott to doing little other than spouting three-word slogans.

As a result of the out-of-control elements of the campaign, I was being painted as a heartless and dishonest shrew who was out of touch with family needs.

It was all bad. Behind the scenes, all of us involved in the campaign felt the burden of these contradictions. In our lighter moments, we would joke that we would love it all to be as planned as the media was alleging. If only this actually was a 'by the campaign manual' job. I felt hemmed in and believed I had to find a way of asking Australians to look at and assess me again.

In what became called, in shorthand, being 'the real Julia', I had found a clumsy way to grab new attention. Although, mercifully, on the Monday Phil Hudson's piece was published, for once in a doorstop interview I was not asked about Kevin, the whole thing was a mistake. Inherent in the 'real Julia' approach was a concession that I had been less than true to myself. I had made the common but silly error of talking up a tactic rather than simply getting out and doing things differently and allowing the media to join the dots. Still unused to the deafening volume of the megaphone I held in my hand as prime minister, I had underestimated how loud and long the Hudson interview would reverberate.

My more successful strategy was forcing the campaign, deliberately and strategically, back onto my key policy themes. Even as I did my best to manage a day-to-day campaign that oozed with treachery, I demanded and worked on this policy fightback. I had said the campaign was going to be about my values, my priorities: work and education. Behind the scenes, as the Labor freak show played itself out, I worked to make sure it was.

At my insistence, the ALP paid for Alan Milburn, the former British Labour Party member of parliament, to come to Australia and work with us. A savvy strategist, Alan had been an integral part of the 2007 campaign; in fact he had helped create 'Kevin 07'. I had always found Alan full of no-holds-barred insights, a person who could ask the right questions, who could provoke and steer a truly strategic discussion.

Alan and I had become friends, and it was in a discussion with him just before the 2007 election that I had decided to ask for both Workplace Relations and Education as portfolios if we were elected. Politically it gave me the benefit of not feeling trapped in what would be perceived as yesterday's debate if a defeated Coalition engaged in the pretence of politically abandoning Work Choices. It was a way of combining my key passions of work and creating opportunity through education. For me, a dream come true.

In the darkest days of the 2010 campaign, in conversation with Alan and other key advisers I decided how I would rebuild Labor's campaign based on my passions, the policies I cared about the most. With key staff members, I designed the policies for week four of the campaign. On flights from Newcastle to Cairns on 3 August, from Townsville to Sydney and then Sydney to Melbourne on 5 August, and any other stolen minutes we could find late at night, we laboured.

At this stage, logic suggested that the election would be lost but I was determined to give winning it everything I had and to do this on my terms, with my themes, my policies and in my style, with a focus on interactive events with community members, day after day, outlining my vision for the nation.

On 9 August in Perth, I announced a suite of new policies for education. On the topic of Australia's future, I said:

> If we look at the great economic reforms of our age, the things that have driven wealth and prosperity in this country – making sure that the dollar was floated; making sure interest rates were set independently; bringing down tariff barriers and making sure we were competing with the world – these great Labor economic reforms have brought the prosperity that we enjoy today. Now is the time for the next major round of reforms, and education is the linchpin for the reforms we need for the future. It is about fairness and giving every child a great education. It's about our future economic prosperity.

The announcements were both fresh and controversial. Among them was a plan for rewarding schools that were improving the most, building on the transparency and accountability established through the My School website. There was also a plan to better reward the best teachers, another area always sure to spark a discussion.

We had already announced plans for a National Trade Cadetship. I signalled my intention to introduce a new high-status academic qualification at school level, the Australian Baccalaureate, modelled on one of the most prized qualifications in the world. Rather than shy away from debate about having national tests for children, 'teaching to the test' and putting every school's results online, I announced a plan for tests to be available easily so parents could work with their children at home and see their achievement levels.

The next day, at my old school, Unley High School, I announced the creation of Teach Next, a way of encouraging people who wanted to change career direction midlife to go into teaching. I had already created Teach For Australia, a plan to attract high-performing graduates into teaching. I had met accountancy graduates with first-class honours who could have taken an incredibly well-paid job but preferred to teach maths in a disadvantaged school. I wanted to see the same enthusiasm for making a difference in the life of kids from professionals undergoing mid-career change.

Across the days that followed, the policy discussions I kicked off ricocheted around the country. The media rewarded us with a newspaper banner that read, 'Labor's Policy Push'.

During week four of the campaign, education policy and then economic policy were the two most talked-about issues on radio, television, the internet and in the newspapers. Kevin Rudd had been pushed into third place, with Mark Latham coming in fourth. Our track polling showed the electorate was rewarding us too. I had dragged the two-party preferred vote back up to 50 per cent and the primary vote up to 39 per cent.

In the way of modern politics, where so-called campaign launches occur late in the campaign, I launched Labor's campaign in Brisbane on the Sunday before election day. The centrepiece was outlining how new technology, including Labor's National Broadband Network (NBN), would deliver health services differently. It was a deliberate and visible embrace of the future, the kind of future only Labor could create.

Although I had collaborated with our policy team on the announcement, the speech drafts somehow felt underdone and did not gel with me. Breaking with the tradition of the launch speech workshopped by speechwriters, I decided to largely write it myself, commit it to memory and then deliver it off dot-point, memory-jogging notes. As the anchor to bring me back to where I needed to be to deliver the rallying call-to-arms conclusion, I would write out the final paragraphs in full.

Late into the night and on the morning of the launch, I worked on the speech. Physically and emotionally, for me this was the hardest period in the campaign. I felt worn down. Tim and my family were with me but it was a case of so close but so far: it was an important speech and the demands of getting it right made me feel like I was being imprisoned.

Getting ready that morning was a stress and a shambles. Nothing seemed to go right, from trying to find Tim's tie, to locating a working blow-dryer, to being told that for some reason we needed to get to the venue earlier than planned. My usual style is to not sweat the small stuff and to joke my way through any day-to-day problems. On this occasion though, having had little sleep and while still desperately trying to get the speech into my head, it all seemed too much. I felt overwhelmed, close to tears. The small things going wrong somehow triggered a response in me to all the big problems that pressed on me. Aided by a hug from Tim and a young staff member, Alexandra Williamson, who meant the world to me, I drew on my resolve and managed to steady myself.

Meanwhile yet another headache was brewing. The briefing to the media had inadvertently overplayed how I was going to deliver the speech. The media was told no notes would be used. A photograph of my notes on the lectern flew around, fuelling a kind of 'she wasn't honest' backlash. The fact that I delivered the speech straight to the audience, clearly not reading it, was overlooked by some in the media. As was the contrast with the Opposition leader, who read word by word off an autocue at his launch.

Even with all that byplay, we campaigned hard in the final week on policy – and also on fear about what the three-word-slogan-fuelled Opposition would actually do if it formed a government. But it was not enough. Our primary vote drifted down by a percentage point over the final week. Beyond doubt, prior to the electronic blackout period, the Liberal Party's advertising blizzard was doing its intended work.

On the last night of the campaign, I had dinner in Penrith with David Bradbury, our Labor Member for the ultra-marginal seat of Lindsay, and his family. David is a thoughtful, decent man. We made the best of our meal although unspoken between us was the view that he would not be re-elected the following day and there was a fair chance the government might not be either.

I had done my last-minute live television crosses from David's electorate and I started my day there the next morning, making a final pitch to the voters. Then I flew back to Melbourne to cast my own vote with Nicola Roxon, Labor's Health Minister. Both lawyers, we entered parliament at the same time in adjacent electorates. Despite those similarities, there is much in our background that is different. Nicola's grandparents on her father's side were Polish Jews who found refuge in Australia before the outbreak of the Second World War. Tragically losing her father when she was ten years old, Nicola and her sisters were raised by their strong, proud mother. A true friendship grew between us over our years in parliament together. We were accompanied to the polling booth by Nicola's young daughter, Rebecca, who found the intensity of the media pack a bit scary.

After that last taste of campaign crush, there was stillness. As a party leader there is an eeriness about election day. Unlike on-the-ground candidates, who spend the day frantically touring voting booths, you get to a stage where there is nothing else you can do. A mix of exhausted and frantically restless, you simply have to wait until the polls close, the votes are counted, the results come in.

In the hotel that is part of the Melbourne Convention Centre, I greeted my family, who had come from interstate to be with me and Tim. Then I waited.

4

Minority government

'The world is run by those who turn up.'
TONY WINDSOR VALEDICTORY SPEECH,
HOUSE OF REPRESENTATIVES, 26 JUNE 2013

Election night was the bleakest of nights. Tim and I sat in
one hotel room watching the results come in. In the adjacent room,
my family mixed with friends who had gathered for what everyone
hoped might be a celebration at the end of the night. Robyn McLeod
had organised the shindig. It did not turn out as she had so desperately wanted. Steve Bracks sat with my father, talking him through the
meaning of the results.

Periodically I went through and said hello to everyone but I did not
spend much time in the room. I needed to absorb what was happening. I needed to be ready. As the results came in, the mood became
darker and darker. The call came through for me to go from the hotel
room to a back room at the Convention Centre. I was walked through
basement tunnels to avoid being caught by the media.

John Faulkner and others were waiting for me in a room full of
computer screens and phones. Coffee cups and scraps of uneaten food
lay all around. John broke to me news I already had guessed at, that the
most likely result of the 2010 election was a hung parliament.

Though I felt the ugly power of those words, above all I felt numb.
Looking back, I cannot say whether that was a result of the news being
so overwhelming, the weird anaesthetic that comes from exhaustion or

a psychological protection mechanism so that I could keep up and keep moving.

In the hall beyond our electoral statisticians' haven, a sombre crowd was milling. These were the Labor supporters who, after a day handing out how-to-vote cards or doing other duties for the campaign, had gathered for the celebration. Now it was more drinking together for comfort than partying with pleasure.

To the cheers of this sad but dutiful crowd, I walked out on stage and gave a speech neither of victory nor defeat. While lamenting the loss of good colleagues, I did have the presence of mind to show respect for those whose decisions would create a minority government by saying:

> Obviously this is too close to call. There are many seats where the result is undecided and where it will take a number of days of counting to determine the result. Friends, as we know in our great democracy, every vote is important, every vote must be counted and we will see that happen in the few days ahead of us. And what we know from tonight's result is that there will be a number of independents in the House of Representatives playing a role as the next government of Australia is formed.
>
> I acknowledge the election of these independents and a member of the Greens to the House of Representatives. I have had a good track record in the federal parliament working positively and productively with the independents in the House of Representatives and working with the Greens in the Senate. I believe in respecting the role of every representative in the House of Representatives, including the independents.

I returned backstage and went to a room where my family, the friends who had gathered in the hotel room, more key supporters and staff now mingled. Many in the crowd were simply shell-shocked. No one quite knew what to do next. What do you do when there is no victory to celebrate and no defeat to grieve?

Fortunately someone rustled up some drinks. After sipping a glass of red wine, I took my leave.

What followed was a night of little sleep. On getting up, I could feel that the numbness was gone; the misery was real. One of the strengths of being surrounded by family is the need it brings to engage with the small things and each other. Somehow, making sure everyone had breakfast and consoling them, particularly my very anxious father, was restorative. Not letting people down has always figured large in my life. If there is something I should do, my impulse is to do it, not shirk it. Not only do I do better by others, but I feel better about myself. Even in these extraordinary circumstances, getting moving and doing things for my family helped. Duty was calling me. I had a job to do. My resolve was to keep moving. I had to for the Labor Party and for my own sense of self.

On Sunday, I engaged in the obligatory photo shoot and some interviews. I had my first meeting with the Greens, with Bob Brown and Adam Bandt. It was too soon for undertakings to be made but it gave us all an opportunity to acknowledge, face to face, the very real prospect that we would end up in discussions about whether Labor could form a minority government.

I also started the process of ringing every Labor member and every marginal-seat candidate who had lost. These are gut-wrenching conversations, with people who have worked incredibly hard and put themselves out there – right on the line in their communities. Now they had to deal with the emotional and practical consequences of being repudiated.

On the Monday, I headed back to Canberra. Because on becoming prime minister I had vowed not to live at The Lodge until elected by the Australian people, Tim and I were still living in our Wentworth Avenue apartment. Occasionally, when Tim was not with me, for security reasons I stayed at the AFP Commissioner's apartment at the Police Training College. From the moment I set foot back in Canberra, my intention was to leave no stone unturned until I had formed or failed to form a minority government.

While others could help, most particularly Wayne Swan, whether this could be pulled off would come down to me. Would the individuals whose support I needed in that moment look at me and see someone they had enough trust and confidence in to say yes? I could only be that person if I was in complete command of myself and the negotiation process. I could only be that person if I could put aside the physical and psychological exhaustion of the campaign and result. I could only be that person if I was, and appeared to be, unbreakable. So I promised myself I would be unbreakable. I would not let the pressure show. I would be the one who rallied my panicking colleagues and harried staff along. I would sleep well, eat well.

During the 17 days between the election and forming government, I attended two military funerals. While the political world was in turmoil about the prospect of the first minority government serving nationally since the 1940s, the tragic consequences of our engagement in Afghanistan were once again before the nation's eyes. Appropriately Tony Abbott also attended the funerals of Trooper Jason Brown and Private Grant Kirby.

Following the election, apart from a Friday and Saturday night in Melbourne I stayed put in Canberra. My focus was hands-on negotiation in the space people most expect to see a prime minister: in Parliament House, in the nation's capital.

But before negotiations really had any meaning, there was the teeth-on-edge wait for the final results in a number of close marginal-seat contests. Would Labor even be in a position to form a minority government or were we facing an outright loss? All depended on these results and I made regular phone calls to those who could give me the best information about what was happening. Hope and despair circled day by day as votes cast by post or in far-distant polling booths were received and carefully counted and then recounted.

The electoral result across the country came to be described as ALP success in those states that love Aussie Rules and defeat in those passionate about rugby league. While there was some truth to this generalised analysis, it missed much of the complexity. It also missed the haunting 'what ifs', as the results came in.

What if the swing to us in Tasmania, where Labor recorded over 60 per cent of the two-party preferred vote, had given us all five seats and that one was not taken by independent Andrew Wilkie?

What if the swing to us in South Australia, where the hometown girl effect favouring me was strong, had also given us Boothby, one more Labor seat? The result was so close that we briefly contemplated taking a claim for a new election to court because of an irregularity with some votes.

What if Labor member Jon Sullivan had not become involved in a last-minute scandal about allegedly insulting the parents of a child with disabilities and we had held the Queensland seat of Longman?

And the most evocative of all: what if we had enjoyed the luxury of a campaign free of sabotage?

The 'what if' game was not just about how we could have done better. There was also the cold fear about how the results could have been worse.

What if my leadership had not been as warmly received in Victoria and we had not held Corangamite in a nail-biting finish, on top of winning both La Trobe and McEwen?

What if I had not done that last mad dash to Perth and restricted our losses there to one seat, that of Sharryn Jackson, a high-quality person and great campaigner, who sadly lost the seat of Hasluck?

What if great campaigning had not contained our losses to a net one in New South Wales? Here, we had feared major losses. The state Labor government was incredibly on the nose and the electorate would throw it out comprehensively, even gleefully, the following March. Given the federal election came first, New South Wales voters could have seized this opportunity to give Labor a kicking. Our fears were magnified because of the ugly and biased nature of the media in Sydney – the anti-Labor diatribes on radio stations like 2GB and the viciousness of the tabloid newspaper the *Daily Telegraph*.

Trying to counter the media negativity, I had a conversation with the editor of the *Telegraph*, Garry Linnell, in the dying days of the campaign. He had given Tony Abbott dream coverage for a next-to-nothing announcement in his final address at the National Press Club on the Tuesday before election day. I rang to urge as good a run for the solid announcement of paid parental leave for fathers that I made in mine on the Thursday. I also canvassed with him who he would edit-orialise for, even though I fully expected it would be for the Liberals. Garry did not have the guts to tell me that in Friday's edition of the

Daily Telegraph, the day before the election, he would run a banner headline 'Yes He Can', with huge and rapturous praise for Tony Abbott.

Despite it all, effective campaigning meant David Bradbury held on to the seat of Lindsay, a result I found heartwarming. On the Central Coast of New South Wales, in difficult circumstances, Deb O'Neill took the seat of Robertson for Labor, replacing the Labor member Belinda Neal, who had been dumped as a candidate following a fracas arising from her conduct at a local restaurant. Michelle Rowland also campaigned her way to victory in the former Liberal seat of Greenway, which had become a potential Labor seat following redistribution of the electoral boundaries since the 2007 election. The incumbent Liberal member for Greenway, Louise Markus, had moved to the seat of Macquarie, which the same redistribution had made a notional Liberal seat. Effectively there had been a one-for-one trade.

The other loss, that of Bennelong, had no compensating gain. Bennelong had been John Howard's seat and was won by Labor's Maxine McKew in 2007 in an incredibly high-profile and energetic campaign. The redistribution had cut Labor's margin. Maxine had found it hard to adjust from the adrenaline of the 2007 national-spotlight campaign to the day-to-day slog of being a marginal-seat member. As far back as October 2009, Labor polling had shown Bennelong would be lost, and it was.

What if New South Wales had been the bloodbath for Labor many had predicted?

What if we had lost both seats in the Northern Territory, if Warren Snowdon had not managed to hold the outback seat of Lingiari, despite huge swings against us in predominantly Aboriginal areas? The Northern Territory intervention of the Howard Government had been unpopular with many local Indigenous communities and its continuation by Labor was seen as a betrayal.

Every one of these 'what if' moments sent shivers down the spine, yet Labor's real Achilles heel was Queensland, where seven seats were lost. Although it was portrayed as being all about Kevin Rudd not being leader, was that the whole story? Not when you consider that Kevin himself had a nine per cent swing against him on first preferences. Of course, it mattered that Labor was no longer being led by a

Queenslander, but the mining tax had also hurt us. In mining communities, resources companies had pushed hard the message that Labor's tax was a threat to jobs. Some of the old mining towns showed their usual cynicism about pleading messages from profitable employers and still voted Labor. But many who were newly building their lives in communities that had just turned to mining and started to see its prosperity were susceptible to this attempt to generate fear.

In addition, the Liberal Party campaigned strongly on the association between the federal Labor government and the desperately unpopular Queensland Labor government. Indeed, the Liberals spent a lot of energy in the campaign punching through the message that Premier Anna Bligh would be my boss if I was prime minister because she had become President of the Labor Party.

While the close results were counted, I had little time to play the 'what if' game. But at the end of each day, when I would wind down before bed with a bath, sometimes with a glass of wine in hand, the sadness of seeing so many good friends and Labor members lose was strongly with me. In every other waking moment, the grieving needed to be shelved so all my focus could be on creating a government. I felt I did not have a moment to spare.

The history of my forming a government tends now to be told as though it was inevitable. It never felt like that and it never was like that. This was a tight game of personality, politics and policy.

In dealing with the Australian Greens, I knew raw politics would dictate that they could not enter an alliance with Tony Abbott and the Liberals. Their voters are an amalgam of progressives who clearly identify themselves to the political left of Labor and individuals alienated from the major parties – people sick of politics as we know it. Their left-leaning constituency would never forgive them for making Tony Abbott prime minister.

For the Greens, the election had been a good one. Having succeeded in taking the seat of Melbourne off Labor, they would have Adam Bandt in the House of Representatives. Plus they were heading for a record number of senators. The Greens were likely to flex their muscle and make demands. Their addiction to symbolic politics deeply worried me. While Kevin was prime minister, their determination to be seen as 'pure' and different to Labor had led them to voting with the Liberals to destroy Labor's Carbon Pollution Reduction Scheme (CPRS); they had stopped effective action on climate change. Could the Australian Greens overcome their protest culture and give sufficient assurance to me, the parliament and the Australian community that they could hold to a responsible arrangement for three years? This seemed a particularly open question.

At least the Greens were a known quantity. I had never met Andrew Wilkie. Off the back of an incredibly low primary vote – less than 22 per cent – Andrew had won in a contest against a new Labor candidate selected to replace the urbane Duncan Kerr, an intelligent campaigner who had long held the seat and decided to retire from politics. The event in Wilkie's life that had sparked his political career was his concern, as an intelligence analyst, that the Howard Government was distorting the intelligence picture to justify involvement in the Iraq war. Consequently he had no love for the Liberals. Yet in order to win he had campaigned strongly against Labor and had been the beneficiary of Liberal preferences.

In the 2004 and 2007 elections, he had run for parliament as a member of the Greens and then split from them in acrimonious circumstances. Trying to corral him and the Greens into being supporters of a Labor government might bring those strains to the surface and drive him to the Liberals. Furthermore he was being advised by Senator Nick Xenophon, a canny maverick independent senator for South Australia who had started his political life in the Liberal Party.

The simple politics, however, was that Andrew had won what had been a Labor seat; he would lose it at the next election if he helped create a Liberal government. In order to have any chance of re-election, he needed to come with us. That raised the question, was he such a maverick he did not care about prospects for re-election or, having fought so many times for a political career, did he care desperately?

There were three other independents: Tony Windsor and Rob Oakeshott had quickly tied themselves into a negotiating threesome with Bob Katter. Of these, I knew Bob best. When I was deputy prime minister, he had taken to occasionally following me out of Question

Time and back into my office, expressing his concerns about particulates in the air and the effect these were having on human health. He wanted me to fund a major research program on this topic. While I was always polite in these conversations, sometimes I had to be a little short with him in order to get him out of my office so I could start my afternoon's work. Bob's convoluted pattern of speaking devours time, but I was not lulled into underestimating him by his eccentricities. He is much smarter than he sometimes liked to let on.

Tony and Rob were independent representatives of country electorates. Both had taken conservative seats off the National Party. My only dealings with them had been as deputy prime minister, over a student income support package that I was trying to get through the parliament.

In designing a new system which would better target the students who needed assistance the most, I had made an error. The transition to the new student income support approach was a fast one and students who had deferred their university studies in order to work and qualify for a status independent of their parents, and consequently for student income payments, found the change of rules difficult. The uproar was deafening, particularly from country students, who disproportionately took this approach. Even though when in power the Coalition had sat back as the participation of country students in university declined, they opportunistically joined hands with the Greens to block the legislation in the Senate.

In resolving this problem and managing a change of position, I sought the advice of Tony Windsor and Rob Oakeshott. While they had channelled the anger of their constituents, both had understood the policy issues and what I was trying to achieve. At least I went into the intense days of trying to form a government having had some contact.

As the 17 days started, I felt like I was looking down a kaleidoscope. All these very different people needed to land in the right place in the right sequence. What was that sequence? How could I get them in the right place? What I wanted was to do a crash course in understanding these individuals who now bore the huge responsibility of creating a government. I reached out to them quickly, fully and openly, first by phone, then face to face. The best way to get to know someone is to listen to them. I did a great deal of that. To try and understand their policy views and predispositions I also researched their public statements.

In most cases, there were back channels: Wayne Swan had a wonderful rapport with Bob Katter. Bruce Hawker had a connection to the Windsor family. Andrew Wilkie's wife had worked for Duncan Kerr, so Duncan and some Labor staff members knew her well and through her had met Andrew.

Bit by bit, through a flurry of phone calls and meetings, as well as hours spent absorbing briefings on past policy positions, I gathered the information necessary to see the world through their eyes, to glean an insight to their thinking, to what was likely to motivate them to join hands with me and Labor. A great deal rested on the quality of my analysis about what would move these people.

Early on in the 17 days, to myself I laid down two political bets. Bet number one was that this was a game of momentum: if you looked like a winner, you would become a winner. Bet number two was that in their heart of hearts, policy-wise Tony and Rob wanted to come with Labor. Their connections to our policies were strong. Both were huge advocates of the NBN, understanding its power to trans-form the economies of, and service delivery to, regional Australia. The NBN could turn the tyranny of distance on its head. Regional Australia could represent a great lifestyle choice, offering instanta-neous access to the best of the world without the crush of big-city life. The 2010 campaign proved that the NBN was understood and desired by a large section of mainstream Australia, particularly in the regions. Indeed Tony Abbott's confusion about broadband during an interview on *The 7.30 Report* in the campaign, his apparent belief the benefits were limited to downloading movies faster – rather than the unbridled power to access world markets, the best educators and leading health specialists – had made him look ill at ease with the future. Both Tony and Rob understood climate change and its impact on the land, on farming. Rob had voted for the CPRS legislation and Tony only voted against it because he thought the carbon pollution reduction target lacked ambition.

Winning my private political bet came down to how brave these men could be. For all the policy ties, going with Labor would probably be committing political harikari. It would be met with fury from many in their conservative electorates. Rob and Tony faced the hardest decisions. No one – politicians, business leaders, civil society leaders – finds it easy or natural to take a decision which is more likely than not to be career ending.

Only they could look inside themselves and find the courage. What I could do was provide political space for them to move in, to make a difficult decision easier by enabling them to point to clear reasons why they had gone with Labor.

I hit upon the idea of suggesting to them that they formally ask me to give them access to the public service, specifically in order to have Treasury and the Department of Finance do new costings of the promises of both sides of politics. This I did with absolute confidence that Labor's costings would receive a big tick and the Opposition's costings would be exposed as flaky when subjected to independent scrutiny. Their costings had been released on 18 August, with only two days to go in the campaign. They had not been checked by the departments of Treasury and Finance as required by the Charter of Budget Honesty, which hailed from Peter Costello's days as Treasurer in the Howard Government. Instead, a private accounting firm had reviewed them somewhat superficially.

Despite how obviously flimsy these costings were, the media – with the notable exception of *The Age* – while engaging in some adverse comment, did not give them front-page treatment. It had been impossible to make them the kind of campaign issue they should have been. I knew that if we could unearth the dirty secrets hidden in those numbers, it would reinforce the view that the Coalition was not ready to govern and Labor was: Labor's costings were right, and we had met all of our expenditure promises during the campaign, with savings. It would show Rob and Tony that Labor was the responsible choice.

But more than a 'shock horror' exposé of the Opposition's dodgy maths would be needed. Rob and Tony would also need promises of real policy and campaign value so they could demonstrate what the benefits were for their constituents and the nation from the choice they had made. These became our promises to equalise the wholesale cost of broadband for the city and the bush, to ensure regional Australia received a fair share of expenditure on health and education, and to dedicate new, specific resources to the regions.

The obstacles to getting Bob Katter to make a political decision for Labor were not like the ones for Tony or Rob. Bob's seat was more Labor-leaning; he enjoyed the active support of the trade union movement. Then again, his constituents would object long and loud to him supporting an unmarried atheist woman – the woman who had supplanted a Queenslander. It was impossible to fix any of those things and I could never agree to his policy predisposition for a return to tariff walls and the economic approach of the 1950s. But given Rob, Tony and Bob had said they would negotiate as a bloc, then the strategy I was embarking on about costings, momentum and policy might also pull Bob to us as well.

Inevitably all of this was going to take time, and it did. The public service was timid about being drawn into this unique process. I had to work with them to create clear boundaries about what they would do. The process did grind into gear. Amid the tension there were hysterically funny moments. Hour after hour, Tony, Rob and Bob sat in the cabinet room talking to key public servants. On one occasion, when I walked in to check how it was going, I witnessed an exchange between Bob Katter and the suave, professional head of Treasury, Ken Henry. Bob was expounding his lack of belief in free trade, an open economy or any of the tenets of modern economics. For Ken, this was his life-blood; he worked hard to suppress any look of distaste as Bob, like a spinning firework, showered him with his ideas. Ken would try to answer, but always after a world-weary sigh.

In parallel, a process that would lead to another unusual moment was underway. Rob Oakeshott was committed to using the opportunity of a hung parliament to negotiate new parliamentary rules, including a better Question Time and more time for individual members, rather than government, to bring proposals to the parliament. Tony Abbott and I both agreed to a process whereby Labor's Bruce Hawker and Simon Banks and the Liberal's Graeme Morris and Arthur Sinodinos would provide advice about new rules.

Anthony Albanese did a fantastic job in negotiating a package, which was announced on 6 September 2010 in a press conference at which Rob, Tony, Albo and the Liberals' Christopher Pyne engaged in a group hug. Strange days indeed, though this bipartisanship was to be short-lived.

I spoke regularly to all of the independents, but most frequently to Rob. Whether with Tony or Rob or Bob, each discussion was a curious mix of matesy chat and more serious matters and was vibrant with tension. At the start of our first formal meeting, which was held in front of television cameras, I presented to each of them a folder containing a summary of what Labor's promises meant for their electorates. The media reported I had made a 'serious mistake' presenting the folders, labelling it as 'an unsubtle gesture described by one who is close to the three men as offensive'.[1] I beat myself up about that. I had hoped the folders I prepared with some of my personal staff would be well received as showing diligence. The off-hand, off-the-record comment underscored the tension. For those 17 days, in dozens and dozens of conversations, formal and informal, I walked on eggshells, not wanting to put a foot wrong while negotiating a deal with such high stakes.

My whole strategy was predicated on Tony, Rob and Bob being the last over the line, after Labor was already on the move towards government. I thought that gave them the most political space. That meant I could not afford any stagnation in momentum. To be and be seen to be on the move, I spoke at the National Press Club on 31 August, outlining my vision for a better parliament and the need for political continuity for key programs.

As the key marginal-seat contests were finalised, the newspapers were consistently reporting that Labor was behind the Opposition in the vital race to achieve 76 votes – a majority in the 150-seat House of Representatives. By the time the close contests were called, it was being reported that the Coalition was in front with 73 votes, Labor had 72, the Greens had one and there were four independents: Tony, Rob, Andrew and Bob.

I set out to alter that dynamic, to get another vote onto Labor's count and to take one off Tony Abbott's. If Tony Abbott secured the first deal and was perceived to be at 74, then all the momentum would be with him. I could not let the impression linger that Tony Abbott was a step closer to government than Labor.

This thinking informed the timing of the agreement with the Australian Greens. Hindsight-driven media commentators later argued that I did not need to give the Greens any concessions to support Labor, and I definitely should not have agreed to carbon pricing. Such commentary misunderstands the crudest of politics and the call of history. Crude politics meant I needed to add a vote to Labor's count. History demanded that in a political system where compromise in the Senate, most likely with the Greens, would always be needed to price carbon, this was an opportunity for real cooperation that should not be missed.

Even while the count of seats was closing out, with my sanction, discussions had commenced in earnest between staff on what an agreement with the Greens could potentially look like. I was determined to ensure the Greens had no executive authority within government. Through this process and then directly from Bob Brown, I fielded a number of ambitious asks and said no. But I did set in motion a process that led to Labor legislating an emissions trading scheme (ETS). It would prove to be a fateful step.

On 30 August, I dined with Bob Brown. We knew that the next day we would sign an agreement. As we ate, I assessed him; I thought we could make this work.

There was a jaunty awkwardness as we gathered in the prime minister's office, my office, on 1 September before the public signing of the agreement. Neither Wayne nor I had ever pictured ourselves in such a situation. With two men, Bob Brown and Wayne Swan, signing with two women, Christine Milne and me, it was always going to be compared to a bizarre marriage. And yes, the sprigs of wattle we were wearing for National Wattle Day did not help.

Nevertheless one had been added to Labor's count. Now it was 73 to 73.

At the same time as the agreement with the Greens was being finalised, work was being done to tear a vote out of the Opposition's column.

The newspapers were putting into Tony Abbott's seat total the newly elected Member for O'Connor, Tony Crook, who had ousted the long-time and highly eccentric Liberal member Wilson Tuckey. From my own experience with the West Australian Nationals in their state parliament, I knew them to be a different and more independent breed than the wimpy federal National Party and had a hunch Tony Crook might not be a straight-out Coalition number.

Following up this guess, I consulted with Gary Gray, one of our West Australian members of parliament. Gary had been a Labor Party National Secretary before entering parliament. He had worked in the mining industry, knew the West Australian political scene well and had made it his business to understand the maverick nature of the National Party over there. Gary believed in cultivating good relations across the political spectrum. When I was deputy prime minister, he had prevailed upon me to go to the Ord Valley Muster and particularly the Kimberley Moon concert, an event held just outside Kununurra. Dutifully Tim and I had turned up, sharing a river cruise with the state Nationals leader Brendon Grylls and his wife and new baby. In a forthright manner, Brendon had explained to me – during this boat ride on a warm night through the startling red and green landscape of that part of our nation's far north-west, over waters home to many crocodiles – that he had gone into a government with Liberal Premier Colin Barnett because his demands for mining royalties to be spent on regions had been met. Brendon was about getting things done and had not ruled out dealing with the Labor Party.

Gary took some soundings and assessed Tony Crook to be similar – a far cry from the compliant Nationals always in coalition with the Liberals, the norm in federal politics.

As early as 23 August, *The Australian Financial Review* had reported that Crook wanted to be seen as independent but he had sent out mixed signals, including attending the first meeting of the National Party after the election. When I spoke directly with Tony Crook, I confirmed that at this stage of his federal political career, he was in an independent frame of mind. My media team worked hard, priming the press gallery, backgrounding journalists to get them to ask Tony how he viewed himself. His answers to them were the same as the ones he had given to me. He moved to publicly playing out his own demands for money for the regions. On the day Wayne and I signed the agreement with the Greens, the *Herald Sun* was reporting Tony Crook wanted to be seen as an independent. The count was now 73 Labor, 72 Coalition, five independents.

If we could now reach an agreement with Andrew Wilkie, then the maths would become 74 Labor, 72 Coalition, four still unaligned independents. This would be an attractive position to be in: if Rob, Tony and Bob stuck together, then by supporting Labor they could create a government, whereas by supporting the Coalition they would take them to a position of being one short and needing Tony Crook. Had this happened, Tony Crook would no doubt have done a deal to create an Abbott Government. But the fact that Labor was closer provided Rob, Tony and Bob more political space, more ability to publicly explain within their electorates and to the nation why they supported Labor.

Of course, I was pushing too the argument that Labor had secured more of the two-party preferred vote; that is, more Australians preferred to see a Labor government. However it is the seats in parliament on which government is formed, so working to that number, 76, was all-important.

This numbers tally was important for Andrew Wilkie too. With Labor at 73, if Rob, Tony and Bob moved first, he would no longer be pivotal to the political calculation about whether or not government would be formed. He was enjoying the attention and publicity too much to want that result.

Andrew Wilkie was always hard to read. Over the life of the government, he became increasingly transactional and disingenuous, but at that stage he presented strongly as wanting to do the honourable thing. He accepted, in exchange for his agreement to support the government, a carefully negotiated commitment on poker-machine reform and a fiscally responsible promise on rebuilding the Hobart Hospital. As with the Greens, I held him back from stronger claims. He had started out demanding $1 bet limits on poker machines, a policy I knew would cause a riot in the clubs of New South Wales. While the policy I agreed with him became tremendously controversial, it was far less than he asked.

On 2 September, Andrew Wilkie announced he had entered an agreement with Labor to form government. We had reached 74.

*

For Tony and Rob, deciding which party to back was centrally about policy. They cared deeply about creating a good government. As the days went by, I came to know and respect them more and more. They knew this was the biggest political risk of a lifetime and potentially offered the biggest rewards of a lifetime, not for them as individuals, but to deliver the policies they believed in.

Already their different but compatible characters were becoming clear to me.

Tony was the tremendously decent but wily, experienced player. He had been here before, because he had been pivotal to creating the minority Greiner Liberal New South Wales Government. He had an internal balance that was not going to be thrown off. Rob was more engaging, outgoing, excitable. He felt the pressure more but was enjoying imagining all sorts of big things that could be done in a new and different way of governing. He spoke to me frequently, often late into the night. Tony was more inclined to keep his own counsel. But I could feel with both of them that trust was growing.

Labor was in front in the seat count. The Coalition's costings had been blown out of the water. I thought my efforts to make political space for Rob and Tony were paying dividends. As I worked through rigorous and important policy commitments with them, key things that should be delivered for regional Australia – like a uniform wholesale price for the NBN – I allowed myself to let hope grow.

As the days went by I sensed more and more impatience from the community for an answer. I injected that sense of urgency into my conversations with Rob and Tony. I was clear with them that the nation was now over the waiting. It was never going to get any easier. It was time to act. A detailed written agreement, with many rounds of amendment, had been worked through. Now was the time to sign it.

On the final weekend, 4 and 5 September, I stayed in Canberra. Ready and available. Tony Abbott went home. I turned up. Much of my time that weekend was taken up with Bob Katter. He was stressed, sleeping poorly and unwell. I had one very difficult discussion with him where we did not seem to communicate at any level. Soon after, we had a much better exchange. But I worried more about where he was at.

Throughout the whole 17 days, for all the assistance that third parties could provide, I had to stand at the centre of these negotiations. Many issues were cross-cutting – a promise to one then affected promises to all. I was rigorous in ensuring the negotiating process did not fray, that everything went through me and was carefully calibrated.

Wayne Swan was my most constant adviser. Cabinet met at one point, as did the leadership team of me, Wayne and Labor's Senate leader and deputy leader, Chris Evans and Stephen Conroy. My policy director, Ian Davidoff, provided excellent support in this work, with both policy and tactical advice. It was not proper for the public service during the 17 days to help me with the policy content of the agreements. Instead I relied on a few staff in my office, most especially Ian. Indeed he became an actor in the negotiations, able to talk directly to key players on policy positions; he earnt their respect for his intellect.

Overwhelmingly my anxious colleagues were on the sidelines waiting to see if I could form a government, feeling helpless. I felt this powerfully when I rang Penny Wong and discovered that at ten in the morning she was roasting spices. She had decided to make a complex dinner from scratch to release her energies and fill in the time. Of course, like me, ministers had some business to do in caretaker mode, but for them, used to a 24/7 workload, the change of pace while they waited was dislocating.

As we moved into the final weekend of the 17 days, Kevin Rudd made contact to say he would have dinner with Bob Katter to assist. At this stage, I did not fear a spoiling role. After all, I knew how much Kevin wanted to be Foreign Minister. But I did fear a prima donna role, which I could ill afford during so many delicate and interconnected negotiations. I was firm and clear with him about not making any promises or generating any publicity. Kevin was resentful and angry in response. In any case, his dinner did not make any real difference to Bob's eventual position but it was worth a shot.

Tuesday 7 September, the end of the 17 days, finally dawned but this political play had one more act to go. In a bizarre press conference in his office, Bob Katter announced he was breaking off his joint negotiating approach with Rob and Tony. He would not be signing an agreement with anyone. Were we being flung back in time? Would more days be needed? Fortunately Rob and Tony held firm to their commitment that Tuesday was the day for a decision. I watched the press conference in which Rob Oakeshott and Tony Windsor announced their support for Labor. I believed I knew what Rob and Tony were going to say. Even so, the tension was electric; some of the staff were so stressed they cried throughout it.

The roar that accompanied Rob's final words was enormous, equal to the flood of relief I felt.

Both came by my office to shake hands and kiss cheeks in a moment of celebration before dashing to catch planes back home. I had the agreements for them to sign. Such was the degree of trust already, they did not doubt that I had made the finishing-touch amendments as agreed. They signed them without a further read and ran out the door.

Once again, I went to see Quentin Bryce. I have never been more delighted to see anyone in my life.

It was not a night of wild jubilation. Rather, upon return to the flat, I experienced a mixed moment of happiness and relief. This was the start of the journey, not its end.

Fortunately, as the government got underway, Bob Katter let Wayne Swan know he would give him at least two budgets. The extra reassurance was welcome.

Minority government delivered the nation effective and stable government. This was the most productive parliament, able to deal with the hardest of issues. During the term of my government, members of parliament sat for more than 1555 hours and 566 pieces of legislation were passed. This is more legislation than was passed in the last term of the Howard Government, notwithstanding their complete command of the parliament with a majority in both the House of Representatives and the Senate.

The number of bills passed while I was prime minister leading a minority government tells part of the story, but the quality of the legislation is vital too. Among the tally of 566 are huge reforms that changed our nation for the better, making it stronger and fairer. Despite this stability and effectiveness, in a relentlessly negative way

Tony Abbott constantly questioned the legitimacy of the government. This political tactic is now viewed as smart, given the political benefits it brought him and the Coalition. But it broke the mould on how Australian politics had worked. It has embedded in our political culture a take-no-prisoners approach that I believe the nation will come to regret.

The media loved the drama of not knowing automatically how votes were going to go in the House of Representatives. There was plenty of hyperventilation, even though the political norm in Australia in contemporary times has been that a government always needs to negotiate to get its political program through the parliament because it does not have the numbers in the Senate. Minority government actually meant negotiations at an earlier stage and, with those negotiations concluded, passage through the Senate on Labor and Green votes was automatic.

None of that stopped the media from continually reporting the government as being in political crisis, fuelling expectations that it was always about to fall. The reality was there was never a moment I seriously worried that the government would go less than a full term, that we would be unable to manage government.

With the quick and continuous developments in new media platforms, journalists are forced to look for more and more content and pump it out quicker and quicker. Puffing up every move of a minority government into a 'shock, horror, government may fall' format was for them a godsend.

The combined effect of the Opposition and the media's approach was to turbo-charge politics and to pound it out to an increasingly drama-weary public. More than that, it enabled the Opposition to weave around me a political critique that anything I did was not because I believed in it, or because it benefited the nation, but rather to save my own political skin and remain in government.

Behind this wall of political sound, I simply got on with the job of being prime minister, focusing on the issues that I believed in the most, creating jobs with decent working conditions, getting our economy ready for the future, improving education. The approach I took to leading a minority government was the same one I have taken to team-building my whole life. I do not do anything artificial. I am myself with people; I try to treat them well, try to see problems through their eyes. In the political world, where every glance or hand gesture is read and read again to try and diagnose the political calculation behind it, in some respects this is an odd way of being. But it is, and was, my way of being. Across my life – whether it has been with friends at school; the circle of political confidants who supported me in student politics; the believers who stuck with me in my battle to get into parliament; my parliamentary supporters as a Shadow minister, then deputy prime minister, then prime minister; my staff members – this approach has never failed me. Being myself, reacting genuinely to people, has always brought me the loyalty and respect of those who work most closely with me.

I am not naive. I have thrived in an environment where you sink or swim based on whether you can garner support. In reaching out to others, I have been conscious of the potential benefits. But I have always felt the hair rise on the back of my neck when I have heard people talk about 'networking strategies' or 'finding a mentor'. In my experience, relationships work if they are built on human interaction, not political or managerial calculation. For example, with my caucus colleagues, as a new member of parliament I got to know people and organised social events so we could spend time together. Bonds grew. Friendships were formed. That is what being human is all about. I have been gratified, indeed often overwhelmed, by how much loyalty has grown from simple interactions like these.

In minority government, my natural approach to bond-building worked well with Tony Windsor and Rob Oakeshott. We became friends. It is so fitting that Tim's and my last dinner at The Lodge with invited guests was with Tony and Rob, a relaxed evening of easy conversation with plenty of laughter. It worked somewhat with Bob Brown and Christine Milne too. I always expected that their first loyalty would be to their political party, not to me, and so it was. But even within that constraint, there were times when purely out of a sense of personal bond, they cut me the bit of slack that I needed. I more than reciprocated by granting them greater forgiveness than I should have for some of their naked seeking of political advantage.

However, my approach and style did not work with Andrew Wilkie. Unlike Tony and Rob, who with practised political eyes looked for benefits for their electorates, but who always were prepared to put the national interest first, Andrew was bluntly all about deals. I found him an odd character but an intriguing one. Time after time, I watched with dismay as he generated breathless headlines by saying he would bring the government down if we did not pass his poker machine reform bill. The absurdity of this, of hurting a government prepared to work on poker machine reform and thus benefiting the Opposition, which was totally opposed to it, never ceased to amaze me.

In January 2012, I went to Tasmania and spent time with him. It was summertime and we both worked and also relaxed. Tim came with me and we dined with Andrew, his wife and their lovely girls at his home.

He admitted to me that he regretted painting himself into a polit- ical corner. We talked and talked about poker machines and our agreed plan to legislate to try and reduce the harm done by them. I put before him my analysis that even with every Labor member voting for his poker machine reform proposals, there were just not the numbers locked in to pass the legislation in the House of Repre- sentatives. While Adam Bandt, the Australian Green, would vote for it, Bob Katter and Tony Windsor would not. Rob Oakeshott was unlikely to. Tony Crook had been polite to Andrew Wilkie during his lobbying efforts but had never given a commitment to vote for his legislation. As a government, we had not been prepared to bring legis- lation to the parliament and see it defeated. I was not prepared to do so on his gambling reform proposal, knowing a lost vote would inev- itably trigger a debate about the government's survival. However the government would introduce new laws that could muster majority support.

Andrew agreed with me that because his preferred laws would not be passed, he would hold to his word and end his agreement with the government, but he would still support us effectively on confidence and supply. He vowed not to publicly deal with all this in terms of my honesty or my preparedness to keep promises. He was more optimistic than me about the prospects of getting the votes for his plan but recognised that I was motivated by my clear analysis of how it lacked support.

All those undertakings to me by Andrew were breached. Following our intense discussions and pleasant social time, he publicly announced the end of his agreement with the government, slamming into me on the grounds of honesty and character. Nick Xenophon, a long-time anti-poker machine campaigner, followed suit. With these actions, Andrew Wilkie became a harmonious chorus to Tony Abbott's siren song that I was a liar, a backstabber: not a legitimate prime minister.

While after the passage of some time I resumed dealing with Andrew because I had to, I remain to this day disgusted by his performance. Ironically but completely unsurprisingly, the man Andrew politically benefited, Tony Abbott, has dismantled the gambling reforms we enacted and Andrew supported.

Minority government imposed huge political costs on me and my ability to win the trust and respect of the Australian people. This is part of the real story of minority government, not the false story of chaos and dysfunction which became the Opposition and media critique. I proceeded with method and purpose. Things I believed in passionately got done.

Yet the real story has three more parts – three more burdens.

First, there were the additional pressures on me and the Labor team, not only because of the bruising political critique popularised against us, but the extra time needed to deal with minority government stacked on top of everything else. To the already overflowing job of being prime minister were added thousands of hours of extra work. To give just one graphic insight, as prime minister I had to have the division bells connected in my office so I knew when votes were on in the House of Representatives and when it was time to run there. Other prime ministers had not needed the bells to ring because there was no expectation that they would have to attend every vote.

Second, there was the need to do the only arrangement I ever felt truly uncomfortable about. For all the public heat and fury, I never regretted coming to agreements with Tony and Rob. Quite the reverse. I was glad to have them on my side. While there were plenty of grit-your-teeth moments with the Australian Greens, I never doubted the need for equalising the parliamentary numbers and the forward momentum that gave us during the 17 days. For all the pain associated with it, I never regretted seizing the opportunity to tackle climate change and create an ETS. As painful as dealing with Andrew Wilkie was, I never regretted coming to the necessary agreement with him either.

I did come to regret the decision to make Peter Slipper the Speaker, though not for the reasons most would imagine. With Andrew Wilkie constantly threatening to bring the government down, I needed to create more political certainty. When Anthony Albanese came to me with the suggestion of Peter Slipper replacing Labor's Harry Jenkins as Speaker, I could immediately see its merits – Peter's vote would be taken away from the Opposition's count and Harry's added to the government's – and its downsides.

Throughout the life of the government, Albo worked hard and did a terrific job keeping the parliament working and the government in power. I have known Albo all my adult life, since he was a teenager in young Labor and I was up and coming in student politics in my early 20s. At one level, we have always had a bantering friendship. At another, throughout my political career, he has always opposed me. The national Left, of which we were both members, had two sides. Though I thought much of it was nonsense, I was in one and Albo was in the other. Consequently Albo never supported me in my climb through politics. Neither did he support me against Kevin. However, in the days of minority government, we forged a solid working relation-ship and grew fonder of each other.

In this complex relationship in the parliament, I knew Albo had my back. As with all his suggestions, I immediately took the one about Peter Slipper and the speakership seriously. My impression of Peter Slipper was that he was an unusual person, not especially nice. Once I saw him berate a woman, a Qantas employee, in a flight lounge because he had missed his plane. I have always thought that you can best judge people by how they treat those in positions of less status and power than them. In the case of Kevin Rudd, I had ignored that good instinct. On this occasion, I ignored it again.

But I thought he would be a competent Speaker. As Deputy Speaker, he had bravely suspended the Member for Indi, Sophie Mirabella, on 11 October 2011. Mirabella's rudeness was legendary, a fact that eventually her electorate registered, to her cost. It was a brave decision because at the time Peter made it, he could not have known whether the House would support him, and without the support of the House he would have had to resign.

So I accepted Albo's idea. I put it to the wonderful Harry Jenkins, the sitting Speaker, that in the interests of the Labor Party, he would need to step aside. On the last sitting day of 2011, I sat in the parliament for its opening ritual of acknowledging the traditional owners of the land and reciting The Lord's Prayer. Harry stood in the position of Speaker one last time. With a catch in his voice he announced his resignation. Harry is his own man and made his own decision to give our Labor government more breathing space. He asked for nothing in return. Harry in this conduct showed himself to be a truly great Labor man.

After the switch to Peter Slipper was made so dramatically, for a period his speakership worked well. He was decisive and effective in the Chair. But the move to appoint him blew up in my face when on 21 April 2012 the *Daily Telegraph* reported that Peter Slipper was the subject of explosive allegations relating to the sexual harassment of a staff member, James Ashby, and the misuse of Cabcharge vouchers.

This story was another special from News Corp Australia's Steve Lewis, the journalist who was duped by Godwin Grech into making false claims about Kevin Rudd and a ute. Steve Lewis paid no price for being the writer of those falsehoods. This time around, when the Ashby matter was heard in court, the judge made adverse comments about Steve Lewis's explanation for text messages between him and James Ashby, which appeared to show conniving, not objective reporting. It looked as though the Liberal Party was involved with James Ashby and his allegations; in my view, the full truth has yet to be revealed about how deeply.

The story set in train a series of events for Peter Slipper, including the loss of his position as Speaker and the bringing of criminal charges about misused parliamentary entitlements; I came to fear that either he or his wife or both of them would take their own lives. There are many things more important than the cut and thrust of daily politics, and the potential human cost of this scandal was one of them. The political and human damage the matter caused, but more importantly the human damage, was the second real cost of minority government.

The third real cost was the inability to discipline misbehaving Labor members. In a majority government situation, I could have acted differently in relation to Craig Thomson, who was later found guilty of misusing union funds – to pay for prostitutes, among other things. There still would have been complex questions of appropriate burdens of proof to consider, given Craig's look-you-in-the-eye unequivocal denials of all wrongdoing. But the pressure that came from needing his vote for government would have been off my shoulders.

Apart from strengthening my hand with any individual wrong-doer, majority government would have empowered me to immediately and decisively deal with the insurgency and destabilisation of Kevin Rudd and his group of agitators who called themselves 'the cardinals'. I could have done what should have been done to those who showed so much disloyalty to the Labor Party. Of all the prices paid as a result of minority government, this was by far the greatest.

5

The enemy within

'Kevin Rudd will become the leader, not because he's made a compelling case but because Julia Gillard cannot hold the confidence of her caucus.'

PETER HARTCHER, THE SYDNEY MORNING HERALD,
18 FEBRUARY 2012

'As he returns, in all likelihood, to the prime ministership in the weeks ahead, this is the most important lesson for Rudd to remember. The good opinion of the Australian people is his best asset. His most serious liability will not be his enemies but potential lapses of his judgment.'

PETER HARTCHER, THE SYDNEY MORNING HERALD,
20 FEBRUARY 2012

'Gillard is destined to win the ballot but that will not break the impasse . . . As the next election day approaches and Labor's unelectability is confirmed, rising panic in the caucus ranks could fuel a second Rudd strike in the year ahead.'

PETER HARTCHER, THE SYDNEY MORNING HERALD,
27 FEBRUARY 2012

'Julia Gillard has triumphed over Kevin Rudd 71 votes to 31 in a battle for the Labor Party leadership.'

THE SYDNEY MORNING HERALD ONLINE, 27 FEBRUARY 2012

I WAS ELECTED BY THE LABOR PARTY AS ITS LEADER in June 2010, unopposed, after Kevin Rudd decided not to contest the ballot. I was re-elected as leader, unopposed, after the 2010 election, at Labor's first caucus meeting, held on 27 September 2010. Then, in February 2012, I won a ballot against Kevin Rudd by a margin greater than Rudd's defeat of Beazley or Keating's defeat of Hawke and certainly far greater than the margin by which Tony Abbott defeated Malcolm Turnbull, which was just one vote, in disputed circumstances. A year later, in March 2013, I opened the leadership for a vote and was elected unopposed. In June 2013, I was finally and quite narrowly defeated for the leadership by Kevin.

Between my re-election as Labor leader after the 2010 election and my eventual defeat in June 2013, I faced 150 publicly reported claims that my prime ministership would be brought to an end very soon or by a specific date or event. Despite repeatedly running these leadership deadlines peddled by unnamed Rudd backers, rarely did a news story include the detail that a revised deadline was being set out of necessity as others had uneventfully slipped by. No journalist ever seemed to say to these unnamed sources, *I won't print or report what you are telling me because this is the third, fourth, fifth time you have peddled a deadline to me and you have always been wrong. You are not a person worthy of belief and credible enough to be viewed as a source for news.*

No journalist apologised to his or her readers when dramatically reported deadlines passed in silence, nor publicly discussed how they themselves were systematically used and misled in order to puff up claims about the number of Labor members who wanted to vote for Kevin Rudd. A few, like Peter Hartcher, became combatants in Kevin's leadership war. But even those who had not picked Kevin's side allowed themselves to be used again and again and again. Why did this happen and keep happening?

It can only be explained by analysing the steps in the bizarre dance between journalists, some Labor Party parliamentarians, the Opposition and Kevin Rudd during the years of my prime ministership. For the politicians and the Opposition, the motivations for taking to the dance floor are obvious. These politicians wanted career advancement. The Opposition wanted to gain a political advantage. The motivations of the journalists are more opaque, rooted in part in the desperation that comes from being in a rapidly changing – many would say dying – industry with relentless work demands.

No longer does a print journalist have seven or eight hours to write their news report for tomorrow's paper or a number of commitment-free days to contemplate their column. Instead key journalists in the Canberra press gallery will receive early-morning calls demanding an immediate comment piece on the events of the day, despite the fact the day is only just starting. Each hour will then be spent frantically tweeting, blogging, appearing on 24-hour news channels, then writing and pushing out another comment piece. Never has the old adage 'Never mind the quality, feel the width' been more applicable.

Good government does not work at the same speed as the media. No journalist is ever going to be happy with a day in which the Prime Minister quietly and methodically reads, has meetings, thinks deeply and makes decisions.

Across the developed democratic world, governments are still trying to find the right rhythm in this new warp-speed media environment. Modern democracies are likely to wear through politicians more quickly than ever before, with cyclical storms of criticism that they are doing nothing, because they are choosing not to engage constantly in the rapid media cycle, or are wasting their time on trivial appearances because they are.

I attempted to slow down our response to the cycle but in a minority-government situation, with a bitterly negative Opposition, leaving the news cycle untended merely left oceans of space for critics to fill. We experimented with various ways to address this, particularly trying to make more use of the team. But whatever approach was taken, too much of the space was always filled with leadership speculation.

With today's frantic media pace, leadership stories can play a role akin to Christmas-stocking fillers – you can always pop in another one with little expense or effort. Consider the time equation yourself: spending hours analysing and getting reactions to a complex new government policy in an endeavour to produce a worthy news article versus one call to a politician prepared to give biting off-the-record quotes and, hey presto, another leadership story is done.

Additionally, in a world perpetually in search of quick content, the seductive power of polls has never been so great. Of course, politics has consistently had the rhythm of fortnightly Newspolls in *The Australian* and regular Fairfax-Nielsen polling in *The Age* and *The Sydney Morning Herald*. These polls have always sparked discussion on how governments and leaders are faring. But today there are more polls because the advent of online and 'robo' call polling has pulled down the cost. Instead of paying people to make telephone calls to conduct a poll, now long-suffering voters answer their phone to an automated message inviting them to record their opinions by pressing numbers on their telephone keypad. Even more cheaply, a media outlet can invite people to 'vote' online. Right when the demand for content has gone up, at minimal cost, close to instantaneous polling can be conducted on almost anything. In one political week, weekend newspapers might blast a leadership story based on a Galaxy poll, with Fairfax newspapers following suit from a Nielsen survey, News Corp Australia papers doing likewise off Newspoll and then television stations adding to the frenzy with their own exclusive polling.

Quick and easy leadership stories can be combined with quick and cheap polls. During my prime ministership, this practice was amped up to an unprecedented degree because of the way in which I became prime minister.

The Canberra press gallery is an insular world and, given the foment in the media industry, a curiously unchanging one at the leadership level. Many of the key personalities who reported politics 20, 30, 40 years ago are still there, albeit more jaded, more cynical – and more annoyed if their assumed mastery of political reporting is in any way challenged. The common assumption across the press gallery was that they had somehow missed the story of the 2010 leadership change. It was impossible for them to believe that, really, there was nothing to see and report until there was everything to see and report. In their estimation, they somehow missed the signs and they were determined that would not happen again. Consequently any leadership straw in the wind was beaten up into a major political story. The rest of the media followed their lead. In any political party at any time there are malcontents who do not like the leader or feel overlooked for promotion. No allowance was ever made during my leadership for this ordinary phenomenon. Any criticism by anyone, on or off the record, was written about as of immense significance for my leadership.

Then beyond anything rationally required of them – even by the changing dynamics of the media industry or the sense of having missed it in 2010 – a number of journalists, and this was not confined to the press gallery, became Kevin's enthusiastic partners in this *danse macabre*.

I understand the burning need for quick content and the way it drives leadership stories. I even understand the hypersensitivity to leadership stories after 2010. But I will never understand the inherent dishonesty in many pieces written by journalists on the leadership. Journalists who were briefed by Kevin himself on his plans to regain the leadership or who knew a journalist who had been – in other words, individuals who possessed direct knowledge that Kevin was duchessing newspaper editors and caucus members – wrote stories asserting Kevin was not doing anything to try and take the leadership. It misled readers and was written to mislead them. It was unethical.

Unsurprisingly a number of media barrackers for the Liberal Party jumped on board and used Kevin as a pawn in their tactical game to make Tony Abbott the prime minister. The combined numbers of the time-poor journalists, many piqued by their assumption they had missed the 2010 leadership yarn, and those motivated by an active desire to support Kevin or to use Kevin to help Tony Abbott, created a snarling, howling media pack running in one direction. Many on the sidelines decided to run with it. The momentum generated by the many helped foster an environment in which it became unremarkable to treat me with less respect than is usually accorded a prime minister.

But there could have been no destabilisation dance without Kevin and other Labor identities taking the media into an embrace and leading off with the first steps. In the days of minority government, when Labor needed to be at its most focused and most united, Kevin Rudd played out his campaign of revenge.

The first visible moves were around the one-year mark of my prime ministership. Kevin started sending the message that he had changed, a whispered appeal to caucus members that if they were ever to make him leader again, he would treat them better. As he stalked me, Kevin found ways to keep himself in the news: soft photo opportunities, tweets, spinning events in his portfolio to make himself look good and me look bad. Much of this was timed for the weekend's Newspoll and other key polls, particularly when head-to-head comparisons of him and me were being conducted. Kevin has always been a firm believer that what happens to be running in the media cycle when polls are being taken affects the results.

There was always a denial of this – one with a veneer of plausibility, a reason he could cite to justify each individual occurrence – but the pattern was obvious.

Kevin did not dance alone. A number of Labor identities joined in because they put ambitions for themselves above the Labor Party. Some of them were former friends of mine.

Losing friends is an emotional business. The loss that mattered the most, both to me personally and to the course of events during my prime ministership, was my friendship with Simon Crean. Over my years in parliament, I formed a bond with Simon and his family; we had holidayed together on more than one occasion. While Simon was Labor leader, I was passionately loyal to him. When I entered parliament, I was close to Martin Ferguson but our friendship faltered as a result of Martin's part in the delegation that tapped Simon on the shoulder and forced him to stand down. That rift worsened when I supported Kevin for leader in 2006; Martin was dismayed – he loathed Kevin. Later, in a move which I believe was fuelled by a deep resentment of my advancement in politics to a status above his own, Martin embraced for leadership this man he had long despised.

In Opposition, Simon was no friend of Kevin. He viewed him with a highly critical eye and his only attachment to Kevin's leadership was through me. Kevin viewed Simon warily in return. He and his press office were anxious about Simon's maverick style in media performances, which could easily throw the government well off the message it wanted to deliver to the public.

Simon's relationship with Kevin grew no warmer after the election victory of 2007. He was one of the most vocal and persistent critics internally of Kevin's flouting of proper cabinet processes. On a number of occasions he voiced such criticisms to me. As deputy prime minister, I viewed my role as absorbing such complaints, defending Kevin in the conversation and then trying to convey to Kevin the need for change. When Kevin failed to change, Simon's frustration grew.

For all of that, Simon was not an instant supporter when I returned from Kevin's office in June 2010 and started canvassing colleagues for support. As bad as he thought Kevin was as prime minister, in his view my becoming leader at that time and in those circumstances was neither good for me nor the government. Nevertheless, after a one-on-one conversation, he vowed his support and worked well with me in those crucial weeks in the lead-up to calling the 2010 election campaign, taking on all of my old portfolios.

Very unfortunately, Simon had a tendency to raise the hackles of many of his most senior colleagues. After I became leader, although I was still absolutely in the mode of defending Simon, I heard – and understood – the complaints. It is almost impossible for someone who has been the leader of a political party to accept and thrive in any other role. Alexander Downer deserves credit for being an exception to that rule. In contrast, Simon never fully recovered from the loss of the leadership. His underlying anger and disappointment often erupted in discussions if he was not getting his own way. Adding to the exasperation colleagues felt was the sense that Simon had got stuck in a series of policy loops and went back to them in almost any discussion. For example, a debate about budget savings would likely end with him bristling that no one had properly investigated his idea for the government to sell the accumulated loan debts of university students. He would not accept people did not agree with the idea and did not see it as an answer. This all created a bad spiral. He was deeply irritated his ideas did not get accepted. He argued for them again, his demeanour belligerent and then plain rude. His colleagues rolled their eyes and dismissed his ideas. Around the cycle went again.

For all of those cabinet problems, Simon remained on good terms with many in caucus. The strong personal connections he had with Tony Windsor and Rob Oakeshott not only helped during the formation of the minority government but dictated he was the right choice for the crucial Regional Australia portfolio. He was not satisfied with that and had also sought to be Finance Minister. I refused, conscious that he did not command the respect among his most senior colleagues necessary to do that portfolio. I also allocated him the Arts portfolio, an area close to his heart.

The essence of working in the Regional Australia portfolio was collaborating with colleagues to ensure government services and the financing of projects were going fairly to regional communities. The aim was to deliver a fair share plus economic development. Sadly Simon found it hard to strike ways of working with colleagues to get things done. Periodically I sat with him to work problems through. Often when he voiced complaints at the cabinet table, I offered one-on-one talks. I feared a freewheeling discussion by colleagues would quickly degenerate into criticisms of Simon.

I gave him immense support for policy areas he cared about, particularly his cultural policy. To get that through, I sought authority from cabinet for me to finalise the policy with Simon. Had I not done so, and left the decision to cabinet, the policy would never have been adopted.

Yet frustration continued to burn within Simon. In the end it drove him to try and secure the deputy prime ministership in an arrangement with Kevin. Indeed Simon was the pivotal actor in both the February 2012 leadership vote and the March 2013 leadership fiasco.

On the morning of Sunday 19 February 2012, the *Sun Herald* contained a screaming headline, 'PM Terminal', based on a quote from the Labor member for the marginal seat of Corangamite in Victoria, Darren Cheeseman. He openly declared that Kevin Rudd should return as leader and said this was the view of a number of people in caucus. This was an incendiary open assault from a man who would not have been re-elected without the swing to us in Victoria my leadership had brought. Kevin and his tacticians had kept the issue of leadership simmering but this was a step into a more open war.

Kevin would have denied having any knowledge that Darren Cheeseman was going to make such a statement and got away scot free, except on the same day Kevin's cloak of invisibility was shredded. The ABC's Barrie Cassidy reported that despite Kevin's public denials about briefing journalists, Cassidy knew the names of journalists who had spoken to Rudd in his office and were told by Rudd he was planning two challenges, a first vote he knew he would lose, followed by a period on the backbench, and then the causing of a second leadership vote.[1] Cassidy added the revelation that Kevin had laughed about the prospect of me stumbling politically.

What was surprising about this report was not the fact that Kevin was briefing journalists about his comeback strategy – that was an open secret in Canberra – but that anyone reported it. Also on that Sunday, Andrew Wilkie disclosed that Kevin had talked to him about the possibility of coming back as prime minister in November 2011. Bizarrely, that same weekend, an expletive-laden video of Kevin was uploaded to YouTube. It showed him foul-mouthed and vicious while attempting to record a message in Mandarin as prime minister. To this day, I have no idea who released this video and I had no knowledge of it until its release. As Kevin left the country for Washington, he was scrambling to explain away his demeanour in the video. But he ensured that he poured fuel on the fire by saying that 'for now' there was no leadership challenge. As all this swirled, I was preparing to release the expert panel report into school funding, to take another step forward in changing the life chances of our children for the better. Once again, the government's positive agenda was being obscured by leadership chatter.

On 20 February 2012, Simon made a stingingly critical public statement about Kevin and his lack of loyalty. My office had encouraged him to speak publicly about Kevin's destructive behaviour but everyone was a little taken aback at how hard Simon went. This precipitated the leadership challenge on 27 February that I won so resoundingly.

Not only did I win the ballot well, for the first time ever I was able to reveal to the Australian public the Rudd chaos behind my 2010 decision. Our subsequent polling showed that Australians still did not like the way Kevin had been removed but finally they appreciated there was a reason for it.

Tragically Simon was also the pivotal actor in the non-challenge 13 months later on 21 March 2013. In that parliamentary sitting fortnight, Simon had been grumbling more actively around Parliament

House than usual. I invited him to my office. In the early evening of 20 March, he arrived with a list of complaints about the operation of the government and we went through them one by one. I am not a person who shouts or raises their voice but I was firm, indeed sharp, with Simon at moments during this discussion. Many of his criticisms were unfair, took no real account of the circumstances of constant destabilisation in which I worked and lacked awareness of how his colleagues actually viewed him.

Our long discussion had to end because I was starting to run hideously late for a prior commitment. As Simon was walking out the door, he mentioned, for the first time, that he was contemplating calling for a leadership spill. Shocked, I asked him not to do anything until we talked again. I explained that the next morning I would be delivering a national apology to those who had been the subject of forced adoptions. The accounts I had heard of mothers and their babies being torn from each other were heartbreakingly sad. I stressed how important this commitment was to those involved and to me personally but that I would find time to talk to him again. Despite agreeing to this, the next morning Simon gave a weird on-the-run press conference in which he refused to support me as prime minister.

I gave my full attention to the delivery of the national apology in the Great Hall, and then I sat in the parliament and listened to all the speeches on the apology given there. It was my duty as prime minister. My emotional engagement with the issue was heightened because of my deep friendship with Paul Howes, then a noted trade union leader.

Our bond had grown, despite early coolness between us. Paul was not a supporter of the challenge against Kim Beazley and resented my role in making Kevin leader. After the election in 2007, however, he needed to work closely with me as I went about consulting unions and business on the legislation to replace Work Choices. The distance between us closed and was replaced with mutual respect. In him, I saw a ferocious intelligence combined with knockabout charm. In me, I think he appreciated my openness to people and ideas as well as my ability to get things done.

On the night I challenged Kevin for the leadership in 2010, without forewarning me, Paul went on television and spoke out against Kevin and for me. At this stage, Paul's support was based on his assessment of my merits versus Kevin's flaws. Not only was he was roundly criticised for this, but peculiarly that night on television earnt him the brand of being a 'faceless man'. He was also marked out as one of my closest supporters. Gradually that did come to be the case. Paul's care and support was personal and political. He would regularly make a phone call simply to see if I was all right.

As a child, Paul had been taken from his mother. This apology meant much to him and he had been instrumental in its genesis. As I gave the speech of apology in the Great Hall, I could see him openly weeping as he sat in the first few rows of the audience. Through his eyes, I especially appreciated the significance of the day. Consequently I was resentful about needing to find time for Simon but I did – between the event in the Great Hall and the related speeches in parliament. Simon informed me he was going to call for a spill of all leadership positions; potentially this would clear the way for Kevin to run against me and for Simon to stand for deputy prime minister. Pointedly I asked him when this act of treachery would occur, when he would go public. It happened as I sat listening to the parliamentary contributions.

Simon knew his call for a spill would, in and of itself, create a political crisis. My choices were to tough it out – and wait to see if enough caucus members put their name to a petition calling for a meeting to deal with a spill – or I could bring it on by calling a special meeting to have a ballot. In our hurried discussion, I did not give him the satisfaction of saying I would call a ballot. Once Simon went public and called for a spill, however, I quickly consulted with others, including Paul Howes, and we agreed there was no choice other than to bring it on.

There was also no choice but to sack Simon from the ministry, which I did in a heated phone call just before Question Time. Then I left my office, walked to the parliamentary chamber and defiantly started Question Time with a challenge to Tony Abbott to take his best shot. In reality, he was the least of my problems that day.

A harried few hours were then spent ringing caucus members canvassing for their support. I was confident I would win the ballot by a respectable margin, albeit less than the amount by which I had won the earlier ballot. For colleagues, staff and my family this was a time of stress, of fearing the worst. Preparing for every contingency as good staff do, one of my speechwriters, Michael Cooney, without even asking me, started working on a defeat speech.

Late that afternoon, in the most ridiculous comedy of errors, minutes before the caucus meeting in which the leadership would be decided, Kevin declared he would not stand. I was re-elected unopposed alongside Wayne Swan as Deputy and returned to my office to the cheers and applause of my staff.

Now my dominant emotion was one of embarrassment, but not for myself. Simon had ensured that his political career, which was a long and meritorious one, would always be remembered for an attempt to become deputy prime minister that degenerated into a shambolic farce. It was awful for him and the Labor Party had been embarrassed by him.

Much political reporting has speculated that views hardened against Labor when in late January 2013 at the National Press Club I announced my intention to have the election in mid-September. I had done so to prevent the year being consumed by election-date speculation and the Opposition's carry-on that the government was going to fall any minute. I was trying to put the focus on vision, purpose, policy. Contrary to the views of commentators, voters' attitudes truly hardened as a result of this phantom leadership challenge fiasco. The Labor government was seen as a slapstick comedy show.

Simon came out of this shambles incredibly badly but, amazingly, kept talking and talking in the media, making himself look worse with every word. When Kevin returned to the leadership, Simon stood for deputy leader and was soundly defeated. His colleagues had rendered their judgement on him.

Simon failed while Kevin, who had been at the centre of all the destabilisation, collecting the malcontents, the people who were not motivated by their view of who was the best leader or what was best for Labor but rather by their own positions, succeeded.

Kevin's campaign of destabilisation also boosted the Opposition as he and his lieutenants became a supportive Greek chorus to Tony Abbott's hard-hitting negative campaign against me. 'She's a liar,'

Abbott would proclaim. *She's lying about how she got the leadership*, the chorus would chime in. 'She cannot be trusted,' Abbott would bellow. *Kevin trusted her and she knifed him*, the chorus would mutter. 'She's only doing this to stay in power, not because she believes it,' Abbott would accuse about carbon pricing. *She does not believe in it, she stopped Kevin pursuing the Carbon Pollution Reduction Scheme*, the chorus would intone. And on and on it would go.

Only a fool would try to write the history of Labor in these years as being that of a loyal and quiet Kevin Rudd waiting to be asked by a desperate political party to lead it again. The truth is one of remorseless pursuit of a return to the leadership, even if a Labor government was destroyed in the process.

Kevin was a highly disorganised prime minister. But I have seen up close how he can be a ruthlessly organised political plotter. Kevin leaves nothing to chance. He works out the couple of hundred people he needs to most influence – politicians, business leaders, journalists – and plans contact with them. From catching up for coffee to calling on family birthdays, Kevin woos. He constantly communicates with newspaper editors by text. Indeed, I have had editors complain to me about the volume of his texts, the frequency of his dinner invitations. He is a master of the off-the-record briefing and of day-to-day media management, including social media.

To attract support, he tailors his political positioning. In the days of Opposition, I was told by one of Kevin's closest confidants that Kevin had authored his admiring essay about Dietrich Bonhoeffer, a man of faith executed by the Nazis, to impress parliamentary members from the Left of the party: he wanted them to support his leadership bid.

His family, to their credit, takes a Team Rudd approach and supports Kevin absolutely and publicly, including through social media.

Kevin applied all his formidable skills to bringing me down and seizing the leadership. Across the life of my prime ministership these tactics rolled out. In the face of the onslaught, I had to endure and I did. It took, day by pressured day, a continuing display of personal resilience.

In my final weeks as prime minister, I drew heavily on that resilience. As we entered the final two parliamentary sitting weeks before the 2013 election, I concluded that, far more likely than not, I would not be prime minister by the end of them. David Bradbury, a strong supporter who at one point had humorously said he was prepared to get my name tattooed on his body to prove his loyalty to me, asked to see me. We met in my chief of staff's office. The prime ministerial office has two doors, one from the corridor, through which you welcome guests, the other behind the desk, which leads to a dressing room and separate bathroom. Off the dressing room is a door that takes you through to the chief of staff's office. That second door enables the prime minister and chief of staff to get easy access to each other's office. It also gives you as prime minister the option of seeing someone without others observing them coming into your office. That I met David in that manner is an indication that I sensed something in the air.

Quickly he degenerated into tears in our meeting: he had come to ask me to consider standing down in favour of Kevin Rudd. His prediction was that I was going to get torn down during that fortnight and it would be better for me and my legacy to go voluntarily. Clearly David was putting a view out of genuine concern for me. I thanked him for it.

I concluded that Kevin and the forces mobilising for him were breaking through with a fresh argument. To date, principled members in New South Wales had resisted the pressure to go over to his side. People like Deb O'Neill and Michelle Rowland viewed his conduct in destabilising me to be so despicable that they would not reward it, even at the cost of their own seats. That had always been David's position.

Quiet investigation by supporters uncovered the new argument being put: it was that these good people should move their votes, not to save themselves but to save valued colleagues like Chris Bowen and Jason Clare in safer seats. The pitch was, 'Do it for your mates.' As this line was pursued, the fact that constant internal destabilisation had fed into our political position and the published opinion polls was put to one side.

I was never going to voluntarily submit to the Labor Party being taken over by Kevin and those who had behaved so disgracefully for so long. To do so seemed to me a tacit endorsement that their tactics were acceptable. That modern Labor invites and accepts the ugliest brutality in the pursuit of self-promotion. That putting the party first means nothing today. Even more importantly, to do so would be to signal that Labor was no longer a party of purpose.

In every leadership contest in every political party, the electoral appeal of the combatants is a key factor. What was being contemplated here was a giant step beyond anything that had gone before. Never in ALP history had parliamentarians endorsed as leader someone they knew had no talent for governing, someone they knew could not actually do the job, simply because they thought he might do better at an election.

Allegedly some of Kevin's supporters were whispering in the corridors to colleagues anxious about his proven lack of leadership ability, 'Don't worry, we'll make him leader to get us through the election and then shoot him the day after.'

Kevin himself was offering no sense of purpose. His whole leadership campaign had been about him and his popularity, his weapon of choice contrived photos of himself surrounded by adoring fans. Despite having the time to do so as he sat on the backbench, he never developed one truly new, original policy idea for our nation's future.

I joked with some of my closest supporters that on the logic of the arguments being put in support of Kevin's return to the leadership, Kylie Minogue would be a perfect pick for Labor leader. After all, she is popular, has millions of Twitter followers, and fans gather wherever she goes.

Frankly I could not stomach this rejection of purpose, which, above all else – in politics, in government and in Opposition – matters. Believing in a purpose larger than yourself and your immediate political interests matters. Labor was contemplating abandoning this for what I believed would be a sugar-hit rush in the polls, which would dissipate rapidly. I also anticipated that if Kevin was leader, he would run a shocking and purposeless campaign.

As things sat, it was going to be hard for Labor during the election, but I was going in with a plan to grind down Tony Abbott's lead, built on my sense of purpose versus his of populist protest. Now, as the forces against me gained momentum, it appeared I would not get that opportunity.

Doubts nagged me: was Kevin genuinely trying to trigger a last-minute ballot? With trusted colleagues like Wayne Swan, I discussed our assessment of his intentions. Did Kevin truly want to be leader again? Or did he want the Labor Party to spend its last parliamentary fortnight in turmoil, so that when history was written he could say he had been available to lead Labor to the Promised Land and Labor had spurned him. The status of Messiah was really only available to him as long as his actual electoral appeal was never tested.

In those final days, in addition to Wayne, I spoke to many close colleagues: Stephen Conroy, Greg Combet, Craig Emerson, Stephen Smith, Brendan O'Connor and Don Farrell among others. Paul Howes was a source of constant support. My supporters and I discussed the odds of the destabilisation ending at the conclusion of the parliamentary sittings on Thursday if there was no leadership spill. Most were convinced it would continue right up to election day. Craig Emerson was the optimist among us, putting the chance that Kevin would desist from further undermining at a miserable 30 per cent. Most were convinced too that if there was a spill and I defeated Kevin, even then the bad behaviour would persist until the election. Views about tactical questions varied. Greg advocated putting pressure on Kevin to show his hand; that would be better for Labor than to drift out of the fortnight with nothing resolved.

Whatever was going to happen I thought I needed to generate a Plan B. During the first parliamentary week, I sounded out Greg Combet about him becoming leader. Should the second sitting week bring with it a leadership showdown, however it was triggered, I said if he was prepared to stand, I would not. In a contest against Kevin, I would put my support behind him. This approach would give the federal parliamentary Labor Party the ability to choose a new leader without endorsing the tactics of destabilisation and the vile culture that was killing us.

Greg was eminently capable of the role; if the government were to go into Opposition, he would be the right choice to lead the Labor Party. This would give others like Bill Shorten more time to prepare for the possibility of leadership. If, against the odds, Labor was re-elected,

Greg would make a fine prime minister. He is a person who feels Labor's purpose in his bones.

Wryly Greg remarked he was being asked to go on a suicide mission, given the political terrain Labor faced for the forthcoming election. But he agreed to consider it over the weekend. Realistically the chance of Greg saying yes was slim. He had worked so hard as Climate Change Minister and then as Industry Minister, his health had suffered grievously.

I have never been a hugely fit or sporty person, but my body did not let me down during the rigours of politics. I was rarely ill with anything, I absorbed the stress, I kept up the work rate, I slept well. Greg was not so lucky. In the latter part of the government, as a result of some circulation difficulties, he frequently experienced pain in his legs. Flying was not good for him and he was at greater risk than most of deep vein thrombosis. Speaking at an event, he had fallen off a dangerously constructed stage and suffered broken ribs. He did not complain, though; he just got on with it.

Some time back, he had flagged to me in the strictest confidence his intention to bow out at the next election, given these health issues. As he was on a trajectory to leave politics, I knew asking him to consider the leadership was really pushing against the odds. And so it proved. Early in the second sitting week, Greg came back to me and said he simply could not do it. Physically he was not up to the job. Emotionally he was drawn by the life beyond; even the prospect of the leadership was not enough to draw him back. Politically he doubted a pitch by him for the leadership would solve Labor's problems. Kevin's campaign had created a climate in which he was the only alternative to me. Although disappointed, I understood his decision.

As the hours of the second sitting week went by, it was clear that a number of people who would have supported me had there been a ballot in February would not do so now. When people stop talking to you, they give away their position; you can always tell.

Those loyal to me did everything they could to rally support for me. A core group comprising Craig Emerson, Stephen Conroy, Brendan O'Connor, Don Farrell, Chris Hayes, Warren Snowdon and Gary Gray met at least twice daily and late into the night. Wayne left no stone unturned. Stephen Smith, Nicola Roxon, Kate Ellis, Joe Ludwig, Mark Dreyfus and Michael Danby, among others, did all they could to help. They were all magnificent. Laurie Ferguson, Mike Symon, Rob Mitchell and Andrew Leigh were especially brave in their support.

Once the shadow boxing started about whether or not a petition was in circulation asking for a leadership ballot, I decided to take control of the final act and call the ballot. The only way of giving the Labor Party any hope of a respectable showing at the September election would be if either Kevin or I were to leave parliament. I made this a condition of the leadership spill. Walking into the caucus room with my supporters, we knew I could not win and it would be me who would be leaving.

The curtain came down on my leadership with a vote of 57 to 43, a relatively narrow margin given all the pressure heaped on people's shoulders.

Of course, I could have followed the path Kevin had marked three years earlier: I could have spoken publicly about the caucus members who cast their vote in or near tears – not because they were voting for me and I was going to lose, but rather it was hurting them to vote for Kevin. I could have invited conclusions about factional intimidation. I could have claimed the vote was not truly the judgement of my colleagues, but it was all the work of factional faceless men. I could have distracted the media, shaped the contest differently and run for parliament again, demanding a ministry.

No, I was never going to do that. It is not the way to show loyalty to the Labor Party. It would not have shown respect to my colleagues, who are not simpletons told what to think by others. It shows no true sense of purpose. It simply is not right.

Instead, in my final speech as prime minister, as I confirmed my exit from parliament, I said:

> I understand that at the caucus meeting today, the pressure finally got too great for many of my colleagues. I respect that. And I respect the decision that they have made.
>
> But I do say to my caucus colleagues: don't lack the guts, don't lack the fortitude, don't lack the resilience to go out there with our Labor agenda and to win this election. I know that it can be done. And I also say to my caucus colleagues that that will best be done

by us putting the divisions of the past behind us and uniting as a political party, making sure we put our best face forward at the forthcoming election campaign, and in the years beyond.[2]

On that last day, my life came full circle and I was back with the Governor-General. Quentin had worn a huge smile and a sunny yellow outfit when she first swore me in as prime minister. Now dressed in funeral black, she offered her condolences. I appreciated her genuine care and concern for me.

After all the formalities were done, I joined loyal supporters and staff members and drank and partied at The Lodge until around 2 am. Wayne Swan and I spoke to the crowd about the need to fight on in support of the Labor Party. There was laughter as well as sadness.

My final parliamentary day was an emotional one. Good colleagues saying their parliamentary farewells. Rob Oakeshott saying in his valedictory speech that my father would be proud of me. Even on that final day, I remember the laughs too.

Wayne and I walked together into the House of Representatives chamber for what would be my final Question Time. Peter Garrett, Greg Combet and Craig Emerson had announced their resignations from the ministry and parliament and we had all been allocated new seats – for one day – on the backbench. As we approached the door to the chamber, a couple of minutes before Question Time, I asked Wayne, 'Where are we sitting now?'

He said, 'It's all fine. Near Dick Adams; we just need to look for him.'

Dick is a very large man; ordinarily he would be easily spotted. Wayne and I swept into the chamber. Photographers started snapping their pictures. Wayne and I looked and did not see Dick. He had not arrived in the chamber yet.

I laughed and said to Wayne, 'What do we do now?'

Fortunately, in the time since, we have both found answers to that question.

6

The curious question
of gender

'Weekly Bauer Media rag *Woman's Day* was the first media
outlet to seriously tread on a yet taboo territory: John Howard
and Janette Howard's relationship. The cover of its latest issue
screams "Torn Apart" . . . Which begs the question, why the
hell haven't any other media organisations chased this huge
story? Surely the immediate break-down after losing office of
the former prime minister's relationship is news of national
significance? . . . Indeed regular images of Janette grinning
dumbly and waving from the steps of the prime ministerial
jet as she flitted off overseas on another state junket riled
plenty of journos (and voters).'

THESE WORDS ABOUT JOHN AND JANETTE HOWARD are shocking.
But of course they were not written about John and Janette
Howard. It is unthinkable that a piece oozing such calculated disrespect
for Janette and the relationship between the Howards would have been
published. These words were written about Tim and me and appeared
in *The Australian Financial Review*, the newspaper that markets itself as
the paper of choice for Australia's business elite.[1]

Why would the Howards be treated differently to Tim and me?
Veracity – or lack of it – does not explain the difference because both
relationships – John and Janette's, mine and Tim's – are strong and
ongoing. Is it the fact John Howard was a Liberal prime minister and
I was a Labor one? Reread the paragraph substituting the names Kevin

and Thérèse. No, it would not have been written about them either. Can it be that de facto relationships of long standing can be dismissed lightly whereas marriages cannot? In today's Australia, that seems unlikely.

Or is the real explanation gender? Is that why less respect flows – because the gender roles just do not seem quite right? Accordingly a man performing the standard ritual of waving from the steps of the plane so the media can get the photo is parodied as dumb, whereas a First Lady doing the same thing would not be. She would be viewed as appropriately supportive.

In contemporary Australia, despite so much progress being made, both women and men continue to be trapped in gender prisons. As Australia's first female prime minister, I came to see the outlines of the bars of mine. But of all the experiences I had as prime minister, gender is the hardest to explain, to catch, to quantify.

If you point to specific examples, they sound trivial. There's the television footage taken from behind of me getting into a car, the lens trained on my bottom, not something done to male prime ministers. Even before Germaine Greer's attention-seeking outburst about my body shape and clothing,[2] apparently my arse was newsworthy. The front-page image, followed by a full-page frame-by-frame spread of me tripping over in India.[3] No prime ministerial stumble, even John Howard's physical stumble[4] at a time he was politically stumbling, warranted a frame-by-frame front-page spread in the *Daily Telegraph*. Howard's stumble was reported on page 5. A television network commissioning and airing a full comedy series about my prime ministership.[5] Something never done before and with no signs of it being done again now we have a male prime minister.

If instead of going to specific examples you talk more broadly, every general conclusion drawn can be countered by one example that points in the opposite direction. It is because the issue of gender is so hard to wrestle with that I said in my final address as prime minister that gender 'doesn't explain everything' about my prime ministership, 'it doesn't explain nothing; it explains some things. And it is for the nation to think in a sophisticated way about these shades of grey.'

In all these shades of grey are there any facts to cling to? One is that our brains recognise gender in 200 milliseconds. In fact, research has shown the first characteristics we compute about people we meet are gender and race. If you feel like you notice people's height or weight or clothing first, you are wrong. In this split second, our brain does not impose on us any stereotyping of what gender means. Our culture and experiences do that.

Sheryl Sandberg, in her 2013 *New York Times* bestseller *Lean In: Women, Work, and the Will to Lead*, has popularised the results of a Harvard Business School case study where the story of achievement by a businessperson was given to students to read. Half the students read a version where the businessperson was a woman, half read exactly the same story except that the businessperson was a man. A poll was then conducted on how likeable the businessperson was and whether the student would want to work with them or for them. The students found the man likeable and the woman selfish and not likeable. Disturbingly both the male and female students came to these conclusions. As Sandberg points out, success and likeability are positively correlated for a man but not for a woman. The results of this study and the many others like it are driven by cultural stereotypes that live so deep in our brain we are not really conscious of them. Distilled crudely and simply, these are that men think, women feel; that men are to be judged on their actions, women on their appearance; that men lead while women nurture. These stereotypes whisper to us that a woman leader cannot be likeable because she must have given up on the nurturing and feeling.

Of course, these stereotypes are not immutable. The fact that today's Australia is a vastly different and better place for women than yesterday's shows us that change is achievable. This means that it is possible for the generations to come to take a better, more balanced approach to gender questions than we have reached to date.

But learning for tomorrow requires us to work patiently and carefully through these complex shades of grey. With regard to that work I have a special perspective, having been at the centre of the gendered reactions to my prime ministership. I am conscious too of my own subjectivity: having had much heat directed at me, having myself become heated on the topic, my perspective may well be too close to be as dispassionately analytical as one should be when dealing with these complex problems. What I can do is try to describe how I lived it and felt it.

Sometimes it felt lonely, I was so visibly the oddity. As prime minister, day after day, time after time, I would find myself in a room, often a business boardroom, where I was the only woman, apart perhaps from a woman serving coffee or food.

The face of corporate Australia is still overwhelmingly a male one. That does not necessarily mean the face is unfriendly. Some of our most senior male corporate leaders are personally committed to seeing change and making sure that in the years to come their boardroom events are filled with as many women as men. But some just did not know how to treat me.

The lack of women in these rooms is telling us that merit is being denied. If you believe, as I do, that merit is equally distributed between the sexes, then women of merit are missing out and the few women who make it into those rooms will look – and may feel – like interlopers.

Corporate boardrooms were not the only predominantly male place I encountered. Many institutions in Australian society are disproportionately male, including federal parliament itself. I am glad that Labor has made such a difference to the number of women in parliament, that I had good female colleagues in the ministry, that we drove appointments to government boards so that they now contain 40 per cent women.

But whatever we did as a government, most likely the news would have reached you through the eyes or under the leadership of a man. The media in Australia is a bastion for males. It seems close to impossible to be a woman and an editor of a newspaper, or a CEO of a media company or a news director for a television station. No daily newspaper in Australia today is edited by a woman. Across our nation's history there have only been a few times when women have edited newspapers. Both Fairfax and News Corp Australia have male CEOs. Neither has ever had a female CEO. All the news directors of our television stations are men and there has very rarely been a woman news director. The news reports out of Canberra are overwhelmingly brought to you by men. While there are female journalists of quality and stature, such as

Laura Tingle, and new media is enabling women's voices to be heard through sites like Mamamia, there is no excuse for our media industry not recognising the barriers it must be putting in the way of talented women.

What difference did this male dominance of the media make to the reporting of the work of the government I led and specific reporting about me? Honestly I do not know. What I do know is that I was not a graduate of the boys' drinking circles involving male editors, male reporters and male politicians. I do know that when I exhibited anger in a telephone call to an editor about a false and damaging newspaper article that the obligations of 'off the record' were breached in relation to me and I was described as 'hysterical', the word men facing anger from a woman so often choose.

I did deal with male journalists who seemed unable to refer to me as prime minister. I did have a male journalist yell at me while I was conducting a press conference in the Blue Room and looking down the barrel of the camera which was above the seated heads of the journalists, 'What are you looking there for, we are down here!'

Because politics at senior levels in our nation has been almost always the pursuit of men, the assumptions of politics have been defined around men's lives not women's lives. It is assumed a man with children brings to politics the perspective of a family man, but it is never suggested that he should be disqualified from the rigours of a political life because he has caring responsibilities. This definitely does not work the same way for women. Even before becoming prime minister, I had observed that if you are a woman politician, it is impossible to win on the question of family. If you do not have children then you are characterised as out of touch with 'mainstream lives'. If you do have children then, heavens, who is looking after them?

I had already been chided by Liberal Senator Bill Heffernan for being 'deliberately barren' and then had to stomach reading follow-up pieces like the one entitled 'Barren Behaviour' in *The Australian*, which stated:

At the Junee abattoir, manager Heath Newton knows what happens in the bush to a barren cow. 'It's just a case where if they're infertile they get sent to the vet to get checked and then killed as hamburger mince,' he says . . . In the Kimberley region, near Broome, where Heffernan issued his public apology for his remarks on Wednesday night, the barren cows even have a name: killers. It's the ultimate fate of an animal that can't breed.[6]

In early 2005 there had been the ridiculous carry-on about my bare kitchen and the supposed lack of fruit in the fruit bowl. The fact that a Labor leadership crisis had forced me to urgently return from overseas and there had not been time to shop somehow never worked its way into the story. For the record, the bowl is not a fruit bowl, it is a decorative piece that looks best if you can see the bottom of it.

Before becoming prime minister, I had also worked out that what you are wearing will draw disproportionate attention. It did when I became deputy leader of the Opposition. Pleading, 'I like to wear suits' or 'I have been on the road for days' simply did not cut it. Undoubtedly a male leader who does not meet a certain standard will be marked down. But that standard is such an obvious one: of regular weight, a well-tailored suit, neat hair, television-friendly glasses, trimmed eyebrows. Being the first female prime minister, I had to navigate what that standard was for a woman. If I had appeared day after day in a business suit, with a white camisole and blue scarf, the reaction would have been frenzied – and, I suspect, vicious. Of course, other female politicians have had to work through these issues too, but none with the spotlight as white hot as it was on me.

It is galling to me that when I first met NATO's leader, predominantly to discuss our strategy for the war in Afghanistan, where our troops were fighting and dying, it was reported in the following terms: 'The Prime Minister, Julia Gillard, has made her first appearance on the international stage, meeting the head of NATO, Anders Rasmussen, in Brussels. Dressed in a white, short jacket and dark trousers she arrived at the security organisation's headquarters just after 9 am European time and was ushered in by Mr Rasmussen, the former Danish Prime Minister and NATO Secretary General.'[7]

This article was written by a female journalist. It apparently went without saying that Mr Rasmussen was wearing a suit.

*

The issues with appearance went beyond a question of whether I made good or bad clothing choices. While the old saying is that 'Clothes maketh the man', during the days of my prime ministership I came to realise that the issue of appearance for a woman was not simply a judgement on her clothes, but that it morphed into a judgement of who she was as a person.

The flashpoint of this was when I went to Queensland in 2011 during the summer of devastating floods and the cyclone. I had been criticised for not being emotional enough at a press conference in front of a lounging, bored Canberra press gallery at which I offered my condolences on the loss of life in flash flooding in Toowoomba. The level of interest from the room was indicated by the nature of the first question: I was asked about health reform. The criticism of me was about to get much worse.

It does not surprise me that in comparison to Anna Bligh in those critical days, I came off second best. I do not resent that one bit. The reality is that Anna put in such a magnificent performance as Queensland Premier during those floods that any other political leader would have paled alongside her. She had the right tone of emotion and inspiration, every detail at her fingertips. At the following state election, she did not reap any political dividend from this performance. But I know from spending hours with Anna in the depths of the crisis that it was not political advantage she was looking for. She wanted to keep people safe, guide them through and help them rebuild.

On 11 January 2011, I watched Anna's press conference and spoke to her directly. I had already visited Queensland during the early days of the disaster and met with local communities hit by floodwaters. It was now clear that the floodwaters were going to bring their destructive power to Brisbane. I decided to go there the next day, to satisfy myself all our coordination mechanisms between state and federal agencies were working as well as possible and to be physically present to assist in any way I could.

It was not a time to obsess about clothing. In the press conference I watched, Anna was wearing a black suit. I flew to Queensland wearing a suit. On that day, Anna wore a white shirt, casual pants and boots.

At our joint media conference, she took the lead, which was appropriate given how much more practical news she had to share with Queenslanders hungry to know what would happen next. Time pressures disrupted Anna's intention to leave the Disaster Control Centre and tour evacuation centres; however, I was able to. I visited a number of sites in Brisbane, where I received and gave plenty of hugs, plenty of kisses, got to laugh with some and comfort others who were openly weeping. One human being to another, I did what I could to reassure.

This day was portrayed in the media in terms like these:

Yesterday as the floodwaters threatened her state capital, Bligh fronted the media in a utilitarian white shirt, hair looking like she had been working all night . . . Beside her, Ms Gillard stood perfectly coiffed in a dark suit, nodding. For women politicians, it is always a fine balance between showing emotion and being perceived as too emotional. Gillard has perhaps erred towards being too cool. Professor Ross Fitzgerald, a Queensland historian and emeritus professor of history and politics at Griffith University [said]: 'In contrast [to Anna Bligh], Prime Minister Gillard has seemed wooden and not caring. I am not saying that she doesn't care; it's just she doesn't appear to care.'[8]

Silly me, I thought actually caring mattered. Holding people's hands. Listening to children tell you in their singsong voices the story of the horror they had endured. Making sure relief was being delivered where it was needed, resources were available when requested. Connecting with people so intensely in a moment of crisis that you remain in contact with them years later.

Some but by no means all of my interactions with people during these days were captured by television. On 11 January, the media could have shown footage of me being mobbed by friendly crowds in evacuation centres. It was not shown. The damage was done. My clothes on one day sparked a thread of commentary that ran for six weeks. It became so nasty that a good friend of mine remarked to me that it was making her cry; it was like when one chicken in the coop gets pecked so hard she bleeds and then all the others turn to peck her to death.

What of this is gender? Certainly a male prime minister standing next to Anna Bligh would have rightly seen Anna's performance praised and his likely to be contrasted adversely. But I doubt wearing a suit would, in and of itself, have become an issue, and been equated with his not caring.

Beyond the question of clothing, in all of this there is another question – about how the reactions of male and female leaders during a crisis are judged. For a man in a time of crisis, I think it will be received as enough if he appears to be across the situation and authorising the necessary responses. He is not automatically looked to for a channelling of the emotion of the moment. John Howard's press conference following 9/11 was not judged on its emotional resonance. Tony Abbott is on the record as saying emoting is simply not his job. A female leader performing the same way is likely to be marked down for failing to capture the emotion. It is women who are supposed to feel. If a woman can both be in command and capture the emotion – as Anna did during the Queensland summer of disasters – it is a truly remarkable combination and will receive a hugely warm public response.

But gender stereotypes do not work in only one direction. Had Anna Bligh been a man and said, 'This weather might be breaking our hearts at the moment, but it will not break our will' with a quaver in his voice, would he have received the same public embrace as Anna or would questions have been asked about whether or not he was coping?

That does not mean men cannot show emotion or be viewed well for it. Kevin Rudd's genuine tears when surveying the horror caused by Victoria's Black Saturday fires were viewed well by the community. But they were not shed during a moment of command.

This gender stereotyping, in the context of that terrible Queensland summer, was at the more benign end compared to much of what I faced: 'Ditch the witch' on placards. The ugly ravings of 'Women are destroying the joint' from Alan Jones. The pornographic cartoons by Larry Pickering. The vile words on social media. Hate, misogyny.

It would have been one thing if it had been confined to society's margins, but it was mainstreamed by the Opposition, business identities and the media. That Liberal fundraising menu, repeating words that have been used in the United States against Hillary Clinton: 'small breasts, huge thighs and a big red box'.[9]

Tony Abbott's channelling of words that have been used against women for years, such as: 'Are you suggesting to me that when it comes from Julia, no doesn't mean no?'[10] Or 'I think if the Prime Minister wants to make, politically speaking, an honest woman of herself, she needs to seek a mandate for a carbon tax.'[11]

These words entered our lexicon in the context of denying rape, of criticising unmarried, sexually active women. These words are in our lexicon alongside the words women have always shuddered to hear – 'She asked for it', 'slut'. Even if you are the single most powerful person in your country, if you are a woman, the images that are shadowed around you are of sex and rape.

And that's not to forget the images of death, some of which were not explicitly tied to gender, like Alan Jones asserting that I, with Bob Brown, should be put in a chaff bag and thrown out to sea or the *Herald Sun* publishing a mocked-up image of me lying in a grave.

Gender and death were explicitly tied together by David Farley, CEO of the Australian Agricultural Company, in his 'joke'.

'So the old cows that become non-productive, instead of making a decision to either let her die in the paddock or put her in the truck, this gives us a chance to take non-productive animals off and put them through the processing system . . . So it's designed for non-productive old cows. Julia Gillard's got to watch out.'[12]

Words were used to spin an image of me that fitted with our culture's worst caricatures about women. Christopher Pyne was one of the worst perpetrators – in a single speech to parliament, he managed to compare me to two female villains in one sentence: 'What we are seeing at the moment in Australia is a Prime Minister who has gone from being the hunter to the hunted. She started as Lady Macbeth three years ago, and this week we see her in the role of Madame Defarge, who thought she was going to an execution and it turned out to be her own.'[13]

As early as 1975, in her book *Damned Whores and God's Police*, feminist and author Anne Summers explained that during our nation's history, women were always categorised in one of these two roles. It felt to me as prime minister that the binary stereotypes were still there, that the only two choices available were good woman or bad woman. As a woman wielding power, with all the complexities of modern politics, I was never going to be portrayed as a good woman. So I must be the bad woman, a scheming shrew, a heartless harridan or a lying bitch.

Hard things happen in politics. As Paul Keating put it when he called to console me on the day after I lost the prime ministership, 'We all get taken out in a box, love.' But the portrayal of those hard things in relation to me was different. Surveying media coverage from various sources makes the case. Certainly I felt it keenly.

Almost every leader in modern politics has got there by challenging another leader and winning. Rudd against Beazley. Rudd against me. Abbott against Turnbull. Keating against Hawke. Yet the word 'backstabber' or the dramatic image of having knifed a colleague have not been as routinely employed against them as they were against me.

On questions of honesty, the same kind of analysis can be made. Paul Keating promised tax cuts at the 1993 election. So confident was he that they would be delivered he described them as 'L. A. W. Law'. Certainly Paul paid for reneging on those tax cuts but his name was not twisted into 'Pauliar' and the media coverage about his honesty was not as vicious and frequent as that which surrounded me.

Is this merely a new harshness in modern politics or gender at work? Undoubtedly politics and the media accompanying it are more brutal. But on gender, consider this. Kevin said to the Australian people in March 2013 that he wished to make it '100 per cent clear to all members of the parliamentary Labor Party',[14] including his own supporters, that there were no circumstances under which he would return to the Labor Party leadership in the future. In the week after he defeated me in a ballot, having broken this promise, there were hardly any references in *The Australian* to him being a liar. Interestingly the attention given to his appearance or clothing was effectively zero.

On the use of the word 'liar', of course it can be contended there are other explanations. My challenge to Kevin was a shock. Despite his unqualified words about never being leader again, his challenge to me, coming at the end of years of destabilisation, was not unexpected.

After I left the prime ministership, I did not seek to influence the reporting of Kevin's challenge to me in any way. Kevin took a completely different approach. But with all that, these variations in media reporting are calling to us to think about gender, to think about the shades of grey.

This binary world of good women and bad women, the one-dimensional portrayal, meant it was impossible to be received as a full human being, with all the normal complexity that comes with being neither perfect, nor evil. Living in the middle of all this name-calling and double standards, I had to harden my heart.

As a younger person involved in politics, I had watched the trials and tribulations of women in politics like Carmen Lawrence and Cheryl Kernot. I saw that being viewed as the golden girl, the one on the pedestal, was a dangerous business. There was such a long way to fall. When they finally did fall, the imagery was harsh: for Carmen, liar and even murderess; for Cheryl, precious followed by adulterer. I learnt never to allow people to position you as the one, the woman who is going to make it, to be the first. They may as well have been painting a target on my forehead.

In addition, for much of my career I never imagined I would be the first female prime minister. At the start of 2010, I remarked to Paul Kelly, the longstanding journalist and author, that the reason Peter Costello was viewed as a political failure was that he had flirted so long with being prime minister and never got there. He had denied himself a place in popular memory as a successful long-term Treasurer and was stuck with being known as the one who had failed. I told Paul that if what my career brought me was many years as a senior minister doing portfolios I loved, I would not conduct myself in a way which would allow that to be viewed as a failure because I was never prime minister. Getting to be prime minister was not the test I was setting for myself; I would not allow others to set it for me.

From watching the experiences of other women, and from politics in general, I also realised the folly of feeling good about yourself on a day of good headlines and badly on a day of shocking ones. On both days, you would be the same person. You needed a sense of self that was not reliant on media positioning. I joined this learning to my natural sense of who I am. I have never defined myself through approval in the eyes of others. Everyone likes to be liked. I am no different. But I have always had an inner reserve, a sense of purpose that drove me on even when I did not feel liked. During my prime ministership this grew stronger. It had to.

I toughed it out. I refused to let any negativity get to me. I could watch or be briefed about the worst of things and respond relatively dispassionately. It is not that the sense of anger and hurt was not there. I just did not let it rule me. I congratulated myself on how well I was coping. But looking back on it, I see that if you swallow hard, bite your tongue, check your emotions too often for too long, some time, somewhere, those emotions will burst through. For me, that moment was my famed misogyny speech.

Peter Slipper, hounded by the Liberal Party, against which he had turned, was revealed to have sent crude text messages about women's genitalia to a male staff member. A wave of disapproval was crashing all around and was likely to destroy his speakership. I knew he would have to go but was intent on giving him the time and space to reach this inevitable conclusion himself.

The irony of my situation did not escape me. Here I was, Australia's first woman prime minister, and proudly so, badly let down by Craig Thomson and Peter Slipper, two men who had behaved in a way women would not. Would a male prime minister in my position have had two women cause him the same problems?

I knew Question Time, in which I always took most of the questions from the Opposition, was likely to be devoted to this issue. To prepare for it, I always followed a ritual. In the run-up to a parliamentary week, my staff, working with my department, would prepare a folder with notes on any and all questions on policy issues liable to come up. I would study it on the weekend.

Each parliamentary day, after assessing what was in the media, my staff would update the folder. For example, if one of the newspapers was running with a rubbishy, hysterical, smash-up story on how pricing carbon was going to destroy the world, my folder would contain the facts and some suggested lines for the answer to the almost inevitable Opposition questions.

Question Time started at 2 pm, and from noon onwards, I would work my way through this folder, normally in a pretty adrenaline-fuelled rush. During this period, staff would brief me on where the media was up to that day and any intelligence they had gleaned on likely questions.

On this day, my staff and I knew not to expect questions about any policy. It was plain the Opposition would try and skewer me as a hypocrite for supporting Peter Slipper. My office had prepared a few pages of Tony Abbott's most sexist quotes.

On this day, getting ready, I was fired up. I do not normally think in swearwords but my mind was shouting, *For fuck's sake, after all the shit I have put up with, now I have to listen to Abbott lecturing me on sexism. For fuck's sake!*

You can feel it inside yourself, when you walk to the chamber for Question Time, whether you are in the right 'zone' for the contest to come. As I made my way across the shiny parquetry flooring, along the glassed-in corridor that leads to the chamber door, into the belly of the chamber's sea of green, I felt settled, loose-limbed.

When I took my seat in the House of Representatives, instead of facing a barrage of questions on hypocrisy as I had expected, Tony Abbott immediately moved a motion to remove Peter Slipper as Speaker. While he spoke, I gathered my thoughts for my response, listing keywords in the order I wanted to put my arguments. Because my handwriting is almost completely illegible, sometimes even to me, when I looked at the notes, I decided the writing was too scrappy and that I had a few more thoughts. I rewrote the list, adding to it.

Then it was my turn to speak. I let the Opposition have it with both barrels.

As a parliamentarian, you can tell how a speech is landing in the chamber. You can particularly tell as prime minister because you are the person seated closest to the Opposition. You can see the Opposition leader and their front bench clearly: their eyes, the smallest tremor in a hand, a stress-induced pulse above the eyebrow. It was evident, as I spoke, that this speech was hitting hard. I did not feel heated or angry. I felt powerful, forceful.

Initially the Opposition yelled at me, interjecting to put me off. Then they went quiet. They dropped their heads, started looking at their notes, their phones. Tony Abbott looked at his watch – I incorporated that gesture into my speech.

A clock runs down time as you speak so you know how many more minutes and seconds you are allowed. I timed the last words perfectly to fit in the last few seconds allotted to me. I sat down. I felt cool and calm.

The second Opposition speaker in favour of Tony Abbott's motion started to speak. I spun my chair around to Wayne and said, 'Now I will be trapped here listening to them. I should get some correspondence to sign run in.'

Wayne looked at me oddly and then leant forward and whispered, 'You cannot give the *j'accuse* speech and then settle down to doing your correspondence.'

I swung my chair back around to the front and considered Wayne's words. It was my first inkling that the reaction to this speech would not be the norm.

The second inkling was when Anthony Albanese, the government's hard man, the one whose role it was to do all the most aggressive stuff in parliament, said to me, 'Gee, I felt sorry for Abbott when he looked at his watch.'

Back in my office, it seemed the world had gone crazy. The phones were already ringing madly with congratulations. Social media was on fire. It was the first wave of reaction to the speech, which became a global sensation with now more than 2.5 million hits on YouTube.

For me those waves still continue. For many people I meet around the world, it is really the only thing they know about me. For many in Australia, even with everything else in my prime ministership, it is the only thing they want to talk about.

The speech has been raised with me by world leaders. By mothers who said they watched with their daughters and cried and then watched it again. By women who say they have watched it hundreds of times, that it cheers and rallies them. By a woman in India – one of the police detailed to look after my security – whose first words to me, other than her name, were 'Great speech'. By men who say things like, 'My wife made me watch it and I am glad I did.' By corporate leaders who have told me that it started a huge conversation about gender in their workplace. By union leaders who have told me the same thing about discussions on the shop floor.

That speech brought me the reputation of being the one who was brave enough to name sexism and misogyny. And it brought with it all the baggage that stops women naming sexism and misogyny when they see it: I was accused of playing the gender card, of playing the victim. Dumb, trite arguments that entirely miss the point. Someone who acts in a sexist manner, who imposes sexist stereotypes, is playing the gender card. It is that person who is misusing gender to dismiss, to confine, to humiliate: not the woman who calls it for what it is. Calling the sexism out is not playing the victim. I have done it and I know how it made me feel. Strong. I am nobody's victim. It is the only strategy that will enable change. What is the alternative? Staying silent? So the sexism is never named, never addressed, nothing ever changes?

The paucity of the arguments is easily shown by drawing the comparison with race. If the first Indigenous prime minister of our nation objected to being called one of the many ugly racist terms that circulate, he or she would not be told to stop playing the race card, playing the victim. Rather our nation would join in condemning the racism, as we have done so well when its ugly face has been shown in elite sport.

There was more baggage. Following the speech I faced weeks of questioning in parliament on my relationship with Bruce Wilson and matters associated with the Australian Workers Union which occurred nearly two decades earlier. As has been made publicly clear, these old allegations were rehashed by the Opposition as payback. Despite the fact I did nothing improper, the Opposition made a conscious choice to mainstream this attack on me by picking it up and running with it.

None of that kind of blunt brutality made me regret the speech. Pretending there is no problem or vilifying anyone who raises it will never take us anywhere. It definitely will not take us to being a nation where at every level and in every way, women and men participate in our society and are judged by the same, not different, standards.

During days of living through so much gendered claptrap as prime minister, I have to confess that I frequently felt let down. Early on, there was no visible, loud campaigning by women's organisations and groups to shine a light on all of this. When I became prime minister, I decided I would not campaign on being the first woman. It was so obvious that it did not need constant reference. Having made that decision, I made a second decision – to tolerate all the sexist and gendered references and stereotyping, on the basis it was likely to swirl around for a while and then peter out. I was wrong. It actually worsened. As it degenerated, some noted women, such as Anne Summers, entered the field to point it out. Over time their voices grew. But by then, it seemed like sexism had been normalised. It was just the way things were for me as prime minister. By then too, there was so much other noise around me and the government as a result of internal and external political difficulties, it was increasingly hard to shine a spotlight on the sexism. One of my own efforts, the speech about Australia being at risk of being governed by men whom I jokingly referred to as all wearing blue ties like Tony Abbott, was ill timed and not savvily packaged for media, but the content has stood the test of time.

Should I have been clearer about it all earlier? Started press conferences by taking to task particularly stupid sexism in reporting? Would it have made a difference or only started allegations of playing the gender wars earlier? Honestly I do not know.

One thing that genuinely would have helped would have been for men beyond the world of politics to name the sexism. Men who were not political partisans could have said that they agreed with me on some things and disagreed with me on others but thought the sexist tones in the debate were plain wrong.

At least by the end of my prime ministership, political commentators were recognising that I had faced more abuse than other prime ministers because I was the first woman.

The Canberra press gallery had entirely missed the dimensions of the misogyny speech, the way it spoke to people. Their vision telescoped to the politics of the day; all the wider context about women, leadership, equality and rights was lost on them. This was a flaw evident well beyond this one day. Finally, however, there was recognition from a few of them that I had faced sexist abuse. To me, that seemed a step forward. Unfortunately, though, the analysis then ran that while

I had faced this gendered abuse, it made no difference to my political fortunes. This is truly absurd.

Common sense would tell you that if schoolchildren filed into a classroom every day and instead of saying, 'Good morning, Ms Smith' to the teacher, said, 'Good morning, fat, ugly, dumb bitch' that it would impact on their levels of respect for the woman in the front of the class. Somehow that common sense fled the scene while I was prime minister.

In my final speech as prime minister, I said, 'I am absolutely confident . . . it will be easier for the next woman and the woman after that and the woman after that. And I'm proud of that.'

I remain confident and proudly so.

But should women and men in Australia sit back, assuming it will be so? No. We have an obligation to be working through the shades of grey so that for the next woman prime minister, business leader, union leader, military leader, factory manager, office manager, it will be easier than it has been before. That requires us to restore the common sense. It requires women and men in all sections of Australian life to, day by day, point out sexism when they see it and change it. Persistence, constancy in this purpose, will result in us being a stronger and fairer nation.

How do I feel about it all now? Not bitter. Energised. Eager to see the change that must come.

7

Resilience

'Resilience is the presence, at any given moment, of emotional maturity or emotional intelligence, characterised by self-esteem and self-confidence, the capacity to create and maintain friendships with peers . . . a well-founded sense of trust; a sense of purpose; a set of values and beliefs that guide responses to the world; and a feeling of having some internal locus of control.'

MOIRA RAYNOR AND MARY MONTAGUE, 'RESILIENT CHILDREN AND YOUNG PEOPLE', A DISCUSSION PAPER PUBLISHED BY DEAKIN UNIVERSITY

I AM NOT GIVEN TO SELF-ANALYSIS, to trying inner voyages of discovery. I am not like Elizabeth Gilbert, the author of *Eat, Pray, Love*, questing for self-discovery in Italy, India and Indonesia. Indeed my only real connection with that book or the subsequent movie was hearing some of the administrative staff working with me jokingly referring to our trip to some of the same countries as the 'Sweat, Sweat, Print' tour. Life on the road is often not easy. Despite my natural inclination being to look outward, not inward, I have spent time since I was prime minister trying to truly answer the question, 'How did you do it?'

My first and best answer is that a sense of purpose sustained me. I only went into politics because, depending on the twists and turns of electoral politics and party politics, I believed it would give me the opportunity to do the most in pursuit of the things I believed in. For all the trials and tribulations, politics most certainly did give me that.

My version of Eat, Pray, Love is Purpose, Perseverance, People. I meet lots of bright-eyed young Labor people contemplating a life in politics. Whenever they ask for tips, I always counter with the question, 'Why do you want to do it – to change what?' Some give the most eloquent answers, some have really not thought about it.

Purpose, I always say to them, purpose is my best advice. Perseverance comes next because achieving big things is hard. And people matter. I have always been sustained by people who believed in me and believed, like me, in making a difference to the world.

Fundamentally I believe resilience is like a muscle. It grows stronger with use. Needing to persevere in pursuit of a goal provides the work-out that muscle needs. It is one of the many reasons that I believe schools should have a high-expectation, high-achievement culture. It will breed resilience.

My resilience was strong when I came into politics because I had needed to fight hard to get there. I almost did not make it, not because I lacked the passion or the skills but because I was constantly repudiated by my party, my much-loved ALP.

For several years, I served in the student movement. By the time I left, I was ambitious for a federal parliamentary career. My passion was education. As a student leader, I had worked on improving education at the federal level. I believed that was where you could make the most changes, so it was to federal parliament I wanted to go.

In the early 1980s, I came out of student politics with a wonderful circle of mates and political allies. People like Michael O'Connor, Gerry Kitchener, Julie Ligeti, Tom Pagonis, Jo Taylor, Jane Hollingshead and Dave Kirner, many of whom have made a contribution in the trade union movement or by working for the Labor Party. In the student movement, we had been pragmatic progressives and we wanted to take the same stance within Labor. At this stage, the Left of the Victorian ALP was still fighting a longstanding war. At one point the Victorian ALP had been in the clutches of the extreme Left, the main face of which was a formidable political warrior called Bill Hartley. His hatred of mainstream views condemned the party to

Opposition; his embrace of tactics that excluded people from participation in the party kept him in control.

A political movement called The Participants developed in response. John Cain, who would later be state Premier, was one of the leading lights. Their campaigning culminated in the national ALP intervening to sort out the Victorian branch.

While this addressed many problems and paved the way for John Cain's political victory in 1982, it was not a complete solution. Bill Hartley and his supporters continued to be involved in the ALP and particularly its Left faction. Known as the Old Guard, they nursed old hatreds and maintained the faith in extreme politics.

In a war with them for control of the Left was the New Guard, led by people like Bob Hogg, who would go on to be an impressive National Secretary of the ALP, Peter Batchelor, who became a very successful Victorian Government minister, and Gerry Hand, whose talents took him to the heights of becoming a senior Hawke Government minister.

Intellectually my friends and I were drawn to the New Guard, but our embrace of their policies did not extend to an embrace of their tactics. We believed they needed to democratise the processes of the Left, not simply replace one exclusive leadership group with another. We thought others beyond the inner circle should be included in decision-making, including us.

After leaving student politics, I sought to join the Left, which required a formal process of acceptance. My application for membership was effectively rejected. According to the Old Guard, my record in student politics was 'right wing', and I was not the kind of person who should be in the Left.

Slowly but surely, I managed to organise enough people to support me to get into the Left. When my joining became such a struggle, I should have realised that everything else within the Left was going to be as well. But I persevered. Working with my friends from student politics, we set out to change the Left.

Our efforts were largely unsuccessful and resented by almost everyone. Looking back on it now, I can see how brash and pushy we must have seemed to many of the seasoned leaders of the New Guard.

As a group – and myself individually – we did gather ardent support-ers during this process. But we also made some enemies within the New Guard and, of course, we were the enemy of the Old Guard. We had intended to be. Views of us as a group and as individuals grew more adverse when we joined an organisation called Socialist Forum. I am well aware of how startling that name can seem in contemporary Australia. But the name and everything else about the Forum was a product of its times.

From 1920, Australia had been home to a Communist Party which survived Prime Minister Robert Menzies' attempt to ban it in the early 1950s. It had seen many schisms and splits during its life. Those who maintained their support of the Soviet Union after the revelations about the human rights horrors and other abuses within it split to form a separate organisation. Those who believed in Chairman Mao formed another. What remained included a group of individuals committed to democracy, empowerment and progressive change. They had either never believed in, or long ago had given up on, revolutionary politics. Finally many of them rightly gave up on being a political party at all and tried to bring the party to an end.

In the student movement in the late 1970s and early '80s, activ-ists associated with the Communist Party had fought the wild leftist tendencies in student politics as hard as we did as Labor Party members. We were in common cause against the people who thought that the Australian Union of Students (AUS) should be devoted to international causes. In contrast, we believed it should focus on the things students cared about: education and student services.

The internal push to end the Communist Party at first did not succeed. There was division on even this. But those who thought the party was dead in 1984 left it and decided to establish a progressive think tank and debating group. This was Socialist Forum. Its aim was to bring together progressives, people from the centre of politics and its left, both within the Labor Party and beyond it, to debate and develop ideas.

I was attracted and stimulated by this prospect, a world beyond the contest of factional politics, where people could stop and think. On its formation, I went to work for the Forum part-time, taking an organising role that meant attending to the logistics of bringing people together. In the days before email, that involved plenty of typing, printing, folding, envelope-stuffing and stamp-licking.

At this stage, I was studying to complete my Law and Arts degrees at the University of Melbourne, so it was the best kind of part-time job, certainly more interesting for me than waitressing. It also gave me wonderful access to a world of deep thinkers and big personalities. Among these was Mark Taft, who worked full-time at Socialist Forum. A man steeped in political history and intellectual debate, he studied law as an adult and became a County Court judge. Mark was the son of noted Australian communist Bernie Taft, with whom I also spent time. I met blue-collar workers who had become entranced by political debates and policies. Trade union officials and public servants who thought deeply about their role and contribution to the nation's future. Artists, businesspeople, the young and the old, the wealthy and the poor.

In the fevered world of Victorian factional politics, it seemed incomprehensible to the many combatants that anyone would want to do anything as quaintly naive as sit around discussing ideas. From the start, Socialist Forum was viewed by the entirety of the Old Guard, and many in the New Guard, as an attempt to create a new subfaction within the Left.

Much later, in the also fevered world of federal parliamentary politics, it was impossible for many conservative conspiracy theorists in the media and beyond to believe I could have this history and never have been a member of the Communist Party. I was not. I was a Labor person, interested in policy and debate, nothing more.

My association with the Forum meant I now faced a formidable array of enemies in trying to get support for preselection and entry into federal politics. In fact I struggled for years.

I lived in the federal electorate of Melbourne, in the inner city. Gerry Hand held the seat and I thought that when he eventually retired, I would put my hand up to replace him. Gerry decided to call it quits earlier than most people had been expecting, me included. In 1993, I contested the preselection against Lindsay Tanner. Lindsay and I were close in votes until the bloc of Greek votes controlled by Dimitri Dollis, who was a Victorian state parliamentarian, came in solidly behind Lindsay.

In subsequent years, I contested within the Left for preselection for the number two spot on the Senate ticket and lost. Once again, within the Left I went for preselection for the number three spot on the Senate ticket at the 1996 election and lost again, this time to Jennie George, then at the Australian Council of Trade Unions (ACTU). Indeed she had been approached to run as a tactic to block me. Jenny later repudiated the position and I was selected, only for Labor to lose that spot in the election. The result was close; it took six weeks to finalise the count. In all of these preselection contests, I was strenuously opposed by Kim Carr and Lindsay Tanner.

I did not do what I think was expected and give up. Finally I was preselected in 1997 to contest the safe seat of Lalor for Labor in the 1998 election, beating off strong competition from a union official supported by Lindsay and Kim. Despite my opponent being a long-time local resident, I won over the support of the Lalor ALP branch members. Martin Ferguson and Michael O'Connor organised for our small sliver of the Left to break away and join the Right in voting for me and other candidates in the central component of the preselection process.

In essence, I entered federal parliament as a member of the national Left faction who had been preselected against the wishes of most of the Left and with the support of the Right. Not an easy way to start. By now, I well and truly considered factional politics to be nonsense. What had initially enshrined differences on policy ideas had degenerated into competing power and patronage machines. While I needed to win these factional games, I did not believe in them.

It was my absence of belief in factions that led me to give a speech at the Sydney Institute on 7 March 2006 denouncing the lot and calling for the Labor leader to pick the front bench. At that stage the factional game-playing had degenerated so much that candidates would be selected for marginal seats, not on the basis of who was best to win it for Labor, but on the basis of which subfaction they would put their vote with when it came time to elect the Shadow ministry. A truly dreadful thing.

When I entered federal parliament, I had long experienced the need to be sustained by purpose. Had I not truly wanted to make a big difference on the causes I believed in, I would never have made it through this period. I would have given up. My resilience muscle had received a thorough workout.

I had also gained experience in not viewing myself through the eyes of others, but having a sense of self that was not hostage to the outcome of battles or perceptions of popularity. Mark Latham used to say that 'politics is Hollywood for ugly people'. Like most great sayings, it was borrowed from others. But in this succinct phrase he named one of the things that attracts people to politics. There are some who come to politics because they crave the public exposure, the celebrity, the applause of the crowd. Most come to politics with a sense of purpose and then develop one of two attitudes to the celebrity aspects. Either they come to love it, even become a bit addicted to it, or they merely view it as part of the job. The latter camp was where I always belonged, perhaps an unusual thing to confess given how absolutely publicly exposed I have been.

When I was first starting to make appearances on television, I would remark to friends that if there was a way of doing politics without the public exposure, then that is what I would have chosen. Of course, there is no non-publicly exposed way of doing politics, particularly not at senior levels. You need to explain what is happening in our nation to its people. You need to popularise causes and your proposed policies as part of campaigning for change. At times you need to find the words to grieve, to reassure, to celebrate. I always understood that. I did not go into politics and then suddenly discover the celebrity side of it, but I was not entranced by it either.

I think this character trait, combined with my sense of purpose and my experience with persevering, gave me a great deal of padding and protection when the going got tough. Because I was never motivated by the applause, it hurt me less when I was not receiving it.

Then there was the sense of comfort I found in those around me. My family have never treated me any differently because of my position. The woman in her 20s who was immersed in student politics. The professional in her 30s working in the law. The politician in her 40s, the prime minister in her early 50s. At whatever stage, I have received the same non-questioning embrace.

Other than Dad, no family member ever spent hours talking to me about politics. In part, the relief in their company has always been the ability to switch off, chat, eat together, play cards, watch the most trashy of action movies, do things where nothing is demanded of me. There is also the joy of the great family events, like my niece Jenna's marriage to Damien in 2011, and the incidental catch-ups, like seeing my nephew, Tom, in New York when he was on a world trip with his girlfriend, Laura.

On the flip side for them lay a world of extra burdens: extra scrutiny, extra pressure observing what was happening to me. In the last years of his life, my father worried a good deal about my physical safety. Some ugliness washed up directly at their door. On one occasion awful things in the mail. On another, a mentally ill man threatening my sister at the hospital where she worked, solely because she was my sister. I had to ring my sister, asking her to prepare my elderly mother because she would inevitably hear that Alan Jones, for the amusement of laughing Liberal Party members, had said my father died of shame.

Then there were the practical ramifications. The demands of my work created barriers to my availability – I could help so little with my parents' ageing and my father's illness. My sister went to live with Mum after Dad's death. When I spoke about this with Greg Combet, memorably he remarked about how much our families give us so that we can do these jobs. That too is part of the wonderful benefit of family.

I found comfort in my relationship with Tim. He watched the media constantly, in some ways obsessively. He felt the pain of adverse coverage more deeply than I did. On some occasions, I ended up consoling him about the impact of something horrible that had been said about me. Still, the fact he was feeling the hurt and I could jump into the role of dismissing it actually helped me. It was a kind of shielding.

Kindness and support were forthcoming too from my closest friends. The people you have known so long that even if you do not see them for months, the conversation resumes easily, as if only minutes have passed. Jacqueline Potton, my sometime Liberal-voting mate, and her partner, Jeff Salt, are certainly in that category. After my time as prime minister, someone asked me, 'Have you worked out who your real friends are?', meaning the ones still with me at the end of the journey.

The question bemused me. I was never in the slightest of doubt about who my real friends were.

The sense of family I developed with those constantly around me helped too. It is an odd thing to live at The Lodge or Kirribilli House, in a world with staff who come and go. It is a curious mixture of home and workplace. The staff who work within those walls are limited in number and rise flexibly to all sorts of demands. One day, they might be preparing and catering for a function for hundreds. The next day might be one on which the only food they needed to prepare was a bowl of soup for when I got back after a long day. There is a necessary intimacy to these relationships: these are people who clean where you live, prepare food for you, help with packing for your trips.

I suppose there are a number of ways of reacting to this kind of living arrangement. To resent the loss of privacy. To start conducting yourself like a bad parody of *Upstairs, Downstairs* or *Downton Abbey*. Or to do what Tim and I did, which is view everyone as part of an extended family. That family included the police officers who were with me, first from time to time as deputy prime minister and then every time I left the premises of The Lodge, Kirribilli House or my hotel room as prime minister. Most but not all of them are men. They came with me as I went about my work and were also required to escort me to every aspect of my daily life – to beauty salons, to the hairdresser. A favourite story is of the assumption they made on my first escorted trip to the hairdresser that it would only take around half an hour! They shared Christmas with me in Adelaide, got to know my family. I felt both well protected and cared for with real warmth.

That degree of care and concern was needed on Australia Day 2012. In the wake of the many natural disasters our nation faced, I conceived the idea of striking medals for emergency service personnel, with the first to be presented on Australia Day in a bipartisan ceremony involving me and the Leader of the Opposition.

Earlier in the day, Tony Abbott had made a public statement about the ongoing Aboriginal protest in Canberra known as the tent embassy. On this Australia Day, the tent embassy was celebrating its fortieth anniversary. Abbott mused about its contemporary relevance in the following words:

Look, I can understand why the tent embassy was established all those years ago. I think a lot has changed for the better since then. We had the historic apology just a few years ago, one of the genuine achievements of Kevin Rudd as prime minister. We had the proposal which is currently for national consideration to recognise Indigenous people in the Constitution. I think the Indigenous people of Australia can be very proud of the respect in which they are held by every Australian, and yes, I think a lot has changed since then and I think it probably is time to move on from that.[1]

This was reported as Abbott suggesting the tent embassy should be closed down. Unbeknown to me, the fact Abbott had made a statement and the way in which it was being reported was conveyed by the press secretary accompanying me to the event to a person at the tent embassy. His aim was to ensure that someone with the other view was reported that evening juxtaposed against Abbott. He did not want the Leader of the Opposition getting a free run on a matter of some importance about which many Australians would disagree.

Such conduct may seem alien to those outside of politics but it is commonplace. There is no doubt that the Liberal Party network was circulating my location during my campaigning for carbon pricing – so protesters could confront me wherever I turned up.

Unfortunately the message that my press secretary had tried to send was misconstrued. The upshot was that an angry mob marched from the tent embassy to the function centre where the event was being held. Named The Lobby, it is constructed of glass from floor to ceiling. The crowd banged on it and as their numbers grew, it was realistic to worry that the glass would smash.

The AFP officers with me made the judgement call that we should get out and I insisted Tony Abbott come with us. It was his statement the crowd was protesting, so he was the one most at risk. The police formed up around both of us and shielded us as we ran from the door, down some steps and to the car. It became dramatic: a number of police officers were punched on the back, one of my shoes flew off as we went down the steps, and I fell. The Federal Police officer shielding me, Lucas Atkins, picked me up, literally hurled me into the back of the waiting commonwealth car and then threw himself on top of me to protect me, lest a protester try to force their way into the car. While covering me like this, he swivelled around and grabbed Tony Abbott, dragging him into the car too.

As C1, my commonwealth car, sped off, we righted ourselves. Somewhat uncomfortably, I found myself seated on one side of the car, nursing one shoeless bleeding foot; Tony Abbott was on the other side and Lucas was in the middle.

I was driven to The Lodge. I invited Tony in. He declined and Gordon, the highly professional driver of C1, dropped him back to his office.

What had been scary in the moment became a source of ongoing banter between me and the police officers. Lucas entertained us with the story of going to his favourite coffee shop the next day and then uncomfortably realising his image was on the front of every news-paper – with me in his arms. He endured in good spirits the public comparisons of us to Kevin Costner and Whitney Houston.

Bonds also grew when, for my 50th birthday, Tim presented me with a dog. Reuben, a cavoodle, a cavalier King Charles spaniel crossed with a poodle, joined our household in October 2011. It proved to be an inspired gesture on Tim's part because for all the adults who came and went from The Lodge, Reuben became a playful, endearing common point of reference. The police officers, while waiting for me to be ready to leave, would find themselves patting him or throwing his ball. The Lodge staff showered him with affection. Reuben bound us together.

I genuinely found comfort and support in the many personal rela-tionships that formed between me and those who work to support the person and office of prime minister, including cleaners, attendants and friendly Comcar drivers around the country, like my long-time friend Diane in Melbourne.

My political staff in my office also provided tremendous compan-ionship and comfort. My two chiefs of staff across the period, Amanda Lampe and Ben Hubbard, remain valued friends. I relied on the counsel of my senior staff, appreciated their formidable loyalty and enjoyed their company in the many long hours we spent together. Of course, like any group of human beings, there were some moments of genius and some errors. But the work done was to support me and for me, so I take responsibility for all of it.

Some who work in these positions have connections within the party and have political aspirations themselves. Yet time after time all my staff put me first, even to their own detriment. For that I am grateful. Some were drawn solely by the opportunity to work on progressive policy. I had the benefit of incredibly smart, indeed visionary, policy staff. Some dedicated themselves to keeping the government alive, working with the independents and the Greens. The fact the government lasted the full term is testament to their efforts.

The media staff led the hardest of lives, trying to wrangle fair media in the hysterical hothouse environment spawned by minority parliament and the destabilisation campaign. I was always grateful for their efforts and admiring of the press secretaries' dedication – at task so early in the morning; still there so late at night. Sean Kelly, who was my senior press secretary for a long time, was an amazing source of guidance and support. Though it saddened me, I understood his decision to take a step back from the physical rigours of the work and the emotional angst of dealing with the Canberra press gallery during my time as prime minister.

Generally staff work silently in the background. Seldom in Australia have political staff been media personalities. With the changing media environment, this tradition may bit by bit become a thing of the past. Unquestionably one of my staff, John McTernan, became a controversial figure, featuring in media reports. A Scot, he had worked for British Labour in government.

The television series *The Thick of It* is much loved by political insiders. It satirises Tony Blair's Labour Government; the leading figure is a foul-mouthed Scottish spin doctor called Malcolm Tucker. When John came to work for me, the rumour swept through Parliament House that the Tucker character was based on him. John claims he was the inspiration for the character who is Tucker's second-in-charge, also a foul-mouthed Scot, but viewed as the nice one compared to his boss.

For me, John played an important role in trying to go around the Canberra press gallery and through other media, including forging connections with women who work online speaking to other women, so-called mummy bloggers. But his tough edge was felt and resented by many. As the pressure grew, so did his frantic efforts to make a difference and the toughness of that edge. Still, when I picture some of the steely Liberal press secretaries who have stalked the corridors of Parliament House, he would not win the award for the hardest bastard.

My enjoyment of my working relationship with staff extended to all of them and contributed immeasurably to my capacity to endure. The work they put in, long day after long day – with good humour, amid unrelenting pressure – and the support they gave me were incredible. From the administrative staff, the ones who most personally supported me, I received plenty of hugs and could bask in their fierce protectiveness of me – it sustained me through good times and bad. I remain in contact with many of the wonderful people I was able to work with. Our discussions used to be of political problems; now it spans new jobs, new babies, new challenges.

In my electorate, from those who worked in my office and in the local community I received unstinting, enveloping support. From the first moments I ever spent in the electorate, coming to it as a stranger seeking preselection, I sensed I could make my way there. The ties I developed are lifetime ones. People who worked with me, particularly Michelle Fitzgerald, who was there the whole time, will always be the closest of friends. Rondah Rietveld, who started work in my electorate office and then joined my office during my journey as deputy prime minister and prime minister, is also a great mate. There are local Labor Party members I will always seek out for a coffee, a drink, a laugh. Local community members, in the council, the football club, the schools, who will always be mates.

With such loyalty, even in the most adverse of circumstances, I felt encircled by support and affection. My circle included trusted colleagues. It extended from the intensity of the relationship with Wayne Swan to the close personal help I received from so many ministers, to relative newcomers like Yvette D'Ath and Amanda Rishworth. I was blessed throughout my time in government to have had the unstinting support of one of my oldest of mates, Brendan O'Connor.

The very fact we had known each other for so long meant his presence was comforting for me and he went to extraordinary lengths to help me. Then there were the many valued friendships forged during my parliamentary days. Numerous women rallied around me, with Nicola Roxon's friendship being especially sustaining. Long-term supporters like Kirsten Livermore, Sharon Grierson, Julie Owens, Kate Lundy and Jan McLucas were also very dear to me. The women who helped included those who had been on the opposing side of Labor leadership events, such as Tanya Plibersek and Jenny Macklin, whom I had replaced as deputy leader. Jenny's capacity to move beyond that, to give me complete loyalty, speaks volumes about her generosity and character. Tanya's bravery in continuing to support me when many of her closest allies would not was spectacular.

This incredible loyalty and generosity was also shown by the Labor Party organisation, Labor colleagues in state parliaments, and the trade union movement. I continue to be grateful to them. Not much that is fair or good is written about people in the trade union movement. I have seen up close some of the best of the movement. The people who selflessly dedicate their lives to the advancement of others. The long-serving and determined, like Dave Oliver, Michael O'Connor and Joe de Bruyn. The young and incredibly talented, like Paul Howes, now moving on to a different life. The women who have made such a difference, like Sharan Burrow, Cath Bowtell and Ged Kearney. They have my respect and I appreciated their support.

Not only did I have the benefit of being at the centre of a world of goodwill and help, in terms of resilience my starting point was an even-tempered disposition. I am not a stress head. I do not sweat the small stuff. I sleep well. Though I can be firm, I am rarely angry.

In my early years in parliament, a colleague disclosed to me that he never slept well except in his own bed. I remember thinking to myself, *Heavens, are you in the wrong job!* Federal parliament, particularly at senior levels, entails ceaseless travel. Luckily I am good at settling and sleeping in new locations. Given true privacy, I refresh quickly. A day without appointments, even if I was doing paperwork, would leave me feeling restored. This capacity to keep at bay feelings of too much stress, too much worry, too much hurt, too much anger, stood me in good stead for political leadership.

South Australian Premier Jay Weatherill once remarked to me, reflecting on his experiences, that you are kidding yourself if you think that negativity does not hit or hurt you in any way. Sometimes you need to stop and let yourself feel it, work through it and then discard it. If you do not, then it shows in other ways.

In truth, apart from my misogyny speech, I never properly allowed myself to stop and feel it. Maybe Jay is right. In what other ways did it show itself? Perhaps I was more defensive in public appearances, less confident than I might have been? Did it show in the tendency to appear more wooden, less open, less engaging than I am in casual situations? Should I have let myself feel more?

I will never know. In the middle of it all, it seemed to me as though if I gave way even an inch, if I let it hit me, then I would be drowning in the emotional reaction before I knew it. Better to keep running in front of the tidal wave and not look back.

Not once has the tidal wave hit me with full force. Since my prime ministership ended, I have felt waves of emotion break when I have had time to reflect and let myself sit back and feel. But I have never felt swept away by it.

From my experiences, what can I impart as tips to others facing hard situations? I am no guru.

The best I can say is, know your purpose. If you are clear on why you are doing something, then that sense of purpose will sustain you.

Nurture your sense of self, who you are in your own eyes, not as seen through the eyes of others.

Make choices about how you will react to events. You do not have to let life buffet you or screw your stress levels up tight. You can choose how you react. It is one of the great blessings of being a mature adult.

Cherish your family and friends. Make friends of those around you. Do not look down on others. There can be as much comfort and stress relief in a bantering conversation with the person who makes coffees for a living as there is in the most focused conversation with someone who does the same work as you. In fact there can be more, because that banter offers the release of a human exchange where little is expected of you, where there is no intensity. Warmth begets warmth.

In the political world, where loyalty can be in short supply, I always felt I enjoyed more of it than I lost. That is a good feeling. So is showing, in tough circumstances, that you can hold yourself together and stay true to your purpose.

SECTION TWO

Why I did it

SNAPSHOT

George Mallory, the mountaineer, is famously reported to have answered the question 'Why do you want to climb Mount Everest?' with the simple three words, 'Because it's there'. He lost his life in the attempt. 'Because it's there' could never be enough of an explanation for entering politics. Certainly not enough of an explanation for drawing upon resilience day after day in the face of harsh and unique pressures.

For me, politics was always about purpose. I had a clear vision of what I wanted to achieve. A driving passion to get it done. I could not have kept going without always being able to sit calmly, put that day's hurly-burly to one side and replay the answer in my mind as to why I was there.

Purpose is not ubiquitous in politics. For some, politics is about power and prestige. Power is transitory, prestige an illusion. Those who enter politics without purpose are those who are most easily buffeted off course when the going gets tough.

Purpose endures. Purpose sustained me. These pages explain my purpose, my achievements in its pursuit and my failures.

8

My purpose

'Over the years I have suggested to many politicians they write a one-page account of what they are about, what their purpose is. You are the only one who ever has.'

ALAN MILBURN, FORMER BRITISH LABOUR
CABINET MINISTER

MORE THAN ANYTHING ELSE, it was my sense of purpose that propelled me into the prime ministership. What enabled me to drive the 2010 election campaign to a position where we could achieve a minority government was displaying to the voting public my sense of purpose. Keeping sight of it enabled me to govern, even in the most difficult of circumstances. On becoming prime minister, despite finding myself in a maelstrom of pressure – being briefed, establishing my office and preparing to fight an election campaign – I made time to sit and write out my purpose. Alan Milburn had suggested I do so. He persuaded me that while that sense of purpose was fused into me, it should be on a sheet of paper – to be a touchstone for me on the toughest of days and a guide to those around me about what we were governing for.

In modern politics and in the media, there is much discussion of a government's narrative. 'What's the narrative?' people would ask in cabinet and in campaign discussions. 'Your government lacks a narrative,' journalists and commentators would thunder. In truth, much of this reaching for a narrative was actually a search for slogans.

The media is well fed by slogans, a fact proven by their reaction to both the Coalition's 2010 and 2013 campaigns. Overwhelmingly the media accepted the Coalition's disciplined repetition of slogans as enough and never asked for details of their purpose.

Slogans have their place in retail politics, in retail everything. The short, catchy statement that stays with you. The best ones occur after a great deal of thinking. After all the decisions have been made about what you stand for, what values drive you, the slogan is the distillation. 'Moving forward', Labor's slogan for the 2010 campaign, attempted to capture the concept that our nation had to keep readying itself for the future; it could not afford to slip back to no NBN, no education reform, no action on climate change.

Even though clever slogans are powerful tools, Alan was advocating something much deeper and more thoughtful than slogan selection. The document I produced read as follows:

As prime minister, I will be driven by the values I have believed in all my life. The importance of hard work, the fulfilling of the obligation that you owe to yourself and to others to earn your keep and do your best. The need to respect and value other people, an obligation that extends from simple courtesy and respect to supporting each other in the good times and the bad. A fair go through a great quality education, which with rigour and discipline enables a child to develop the character and skills they will need for a successful life.

I learnt these values in my family home, from my father and mother, who migrated to this country and worked unbelievably hard to give my sister and me the best of life's chances. Life is given direction and purpose by work. Without work, there is corrosive aimlessness. With the loss of work, there is a loss of dignity. Therefore the key economic goal for the Australia I lead will be maximising jobs and inclusion in the workforce.

However, work, whether it is paid work in our economy or the unpaid labour of running a home and caring for others, best gives dignity to individuals when that work is recognised and appreciated. In the modern Australian economy, fair work laws and the right to be represented by a union are part of ensuring that appropriate recognition and appreciation. As a nation, we can show through our support, our recognition and appreciation of the work of nurturing children and caring for others.

But part of recognising and appreciating the work of others is a culture that values effort more than status. I believe as a nation we should try to keep the great Australian cultural tradition of prizing informality and do more to foster politeness. We should reject the sort of snobbishness and expectations of obsequiousness that infect other societies. By focusing on inclusion in the benefits and simple dignity of work, I believe we can overcome the divisions in our nation that result when some suburbs and towns are ghettos of disadvantage. Many will require a big helping hand to get out of disadvantage and into a meaningful role but, despite the challenges, inclusion in work should be our national aim and expectation. Of course, there are some in our community who, because of illness, disability or age, cannot care for themselves and to them we owe the best of our care and concern. But Australians with a capacity for work and effort should contribute that work and effort for their own good and the good of the nation.

My father and mother were denied the ability to get a great education and felt that loss keenly. They always told my sister and me that we had to listen, read and learn. That education was not just the key to a good job but the foundation stone of a good life. Driven by these values, under my leadership, I am determined that our nation should honour its belief in a fair go by giving the best education to every child and the best chance of personal growth and improvement to every adult. For a child born in today's Australia, their birthright should be the best education our prosperous country can provide. And their birthright should not be denied them, even if their parents do not value or understand the life-changing power of a great education.

And for today's Australian adults, their citizenship should give them a right to continue to learn and improve their skills and life chances. Ultimately we should be able to say that there are no impediments in our nation to those from the poorest of circumstances being able to work their way to the top.

Because I believe in nurturing and harnessing the full potential of every individual, I am a complete optimist about the future of our country. I firmly believe that the best days of our nation are in front of it, not behind it.

I understand that the challenges of today and tomorrow can easily leave us yearning for what we remember as a kinder and simpler past age. But I do not believe in romanticising the past, I do not believe in being afraid of the future. We best combat fear by taking deliberate steps to shape the future together.

We can live sustainably together on this fragile land. We can create new wealth, reward hard work and extend a helping hand to each other. We can harness the best of new technology.

As prime minister, I will start and lead the discussions and debates we have to have to shape our future. I will speak plainly about the challenges, truthfully about the risks, methodically about the steps we need to take. I will respect the views of others and their choices.

In my life, I have made my own choices about how I want to live. I do not seek anyone's endorsement of my choices; they are mine and mine alone. I do not believe that as prime minister it is my job to preach on personal choices. However, it is my job to urge we respect each other's personal choices.

Australia is a wonderful country, the greatest country on earth. We are privileged to live here and we best respect that great privilege by going forward together and shaping a better future.

My focus on work comes from childhood and my own personal experience. My parents, particularly Dad, taught me through word and deed that the world does not owe you a living. That you should expect throughout your life to be required to earn what you intend to spend.

Looking back on it, this was in some ways an unusual message to drum into a girl in the 1960s and '70s. The message was never that my life would be spent full-time at home as a wife and mother; my mother worked. Whatever else life brought you, the expectation was clear: it would bring you work.

More than this, my father spoke frequently of work being its own reward. How, alongside love of family, it gave definition to life. Idleness, having no purpose, drift – all these were seen as evils. Dad was an avid Lotto ticket buyer but always firmly stated that even if he won big, he would go to work the next day. His determination on this was never tested; no big jackpot ever came our way.

All my life, I have worked hard. Mostly I have been able to choose the work I wanted. Consequently, because I cared about my work, being dedicated to it came easily. But even in jobs I needed to do solely for the pay cheque, I felt the need for diligence. I am hard-wired to go at my work hard. In those jobs I also experienced the resentment that comes from being treated unfairly or dismissively. I have felt what spurs workers to unite and organise to be accorded more dignity.

In my family home, unionism was an article of faith. It had been so in Dad's village of Cwmgwrach in South Wales. While in the end coal-mining militancy went too far, the genesis of that militancy in the fight against unsafe working conditions and exploitation had our family's respect and appreciation.

Most of Dad's siblings went mining or married miners. When I first visited Cwmgwrach, to my shock, almost every older man had a ridge of coal dust embedded in the skin of his nose. It was where the dust would gather on top of the mask. At least the protective mask was an advance. In the years before its use became compulsory, black lung had killed many. A related condition, emphysema, killed one of my uncles.

A belief in both work and being treated fairly at work always drove me. It drove me to savour the fight against Work Choices, the Howard Government's hated industrial relations deregulation, and the creation of its replacement, the Fair Work Act. It drove me to add to the Fair Work Act by finding new ways of bringing fairness and dignity to workplaces. It meant that the government always put job creation first and foremost.

When my family migrated to Australia in 1966, we arrived in a bad drought and a slow economy. Those early days left their mark on

Dad. He never forgot banging on doors looking for work or the spirit-crushing rejections. Consequently for me, doing everything possible to help create jobs is not about tabulating statistics and seeking applause for a low unemployment rate. It is about fundamentally altering lives, putting money in wallets and purses, fostering self-respect.

When confronted by the GFC, the Rudd Labor Government had worked to maximise employment. The Labor government I led took that focus into new economic days and pursued it in different ways, including endeavouring to bring the benefits and dignity of work to the long-term unemployed, people with disabilities, teenagers who have children of their own.

I wanted my passion for education to be at the centre of my government because of its life-changing power. Once again, I had imbibed this belief as a child. My mother's ill health as a child had cost her a good education. My father lost out because, even though he passed third highest in South Wales in the examinations administered to all 11-year-olds – called the Eleven Plus – and this achievement qualified him for a scholarship for all of high school, his family needed him to be earning. At 14 years of age, Dad left school and went to work.

Both my parents made successes of their lives but both regretted not having the education that, combined with their keen intelligence, could have given them different life choices and chances. My sister and I had the benefits of education drummed in to us from the time we were infants. Mum prided herself on having taught us to read before we went to school. School report cards were scrutinised. We were constantly urged to do our best. Schooling was zoned when Alison and I were growing up. Basically you had to go to the local state school. The non-government sector was limited to elite and expensive schools our parents could not have afforded or else the Catholic system. Luckily for Alison and me, our local state schools were great schools.

Our parents wanted both of us to receive a university education, a dream brought within reach as a result of Gough Whitlam's Labor Government abolishing fees. In this environment, I thrived. The combination of parental aspiration for me, good schools and access to university equipped me to realise my potential and made the rest of my life possible.

My earliest experiences in public action and advocacy were in protesting against Liberal government-inspired cuts to university education. A fire was ignited in me for seeing the benefits of a high-quality education extended to all.

That fire drove my work to expand access to and improve the quality of early-childhood education, to change everything about our approach to schooling, to invest in apprenticeships and skills, to transform our approach to universities. It drove me through controversies like a threatened teacher strike, a caucus revolt against tying welfare payments to children attending school and the shenanigans of vested interests on all sides in the reform of school funding. It will drive me to the day I die.

My purpose encompassed treating people with respect. Fundamental to the Australian identity is our own brand of egalitarianism, a rejection of class distinction. Of course, we have differences in income, education, inherited wealth, life's opportunities. But we have an admirable and instinctive distrust of any sense of 'to the manor born'.

At its best, this Australian ethos means we do not genuflect to anyone and we do not look down on anyone. Unfortunately in modern Australia, the first tendency is far stronger than the second. The indifference or even rudeness with which people feel free to treat those they view as below them or individuals in low-status jobs is something I cannot abide. Everyone has an off day, a stressed and hurried moment, when they are too abrupt. But for too many, such behaviour is not an occasional lapse of manners but a way of living. In every sense, I wanted to reinforce both arms of this Australian ethos. I wanted to see our nation better include, value and respect Indigenous Australians, those from other cultures, those with disability, all those who have helped build our nation.

When I wrote Alan Milburn's suggested one-page document, I could not see all the ways in which I could translate this into action, but I resolved to look for them.

Much of the work the government ended up doing alongside Australians with disability and Indigenous Australians fulfilled the aspiration I set out but I would be the first to say there is so much more to do. This first draft, the first expression in words, of my sense of purpose, pleased me in some ways and felt hauntingly incomplete in others. It had captured my essence but not everything I wanted to say.

I was determined to keep thinking, keep revising. As a result, I increasingly felt the need to find a way to tell our nation the big story about the times we live in and what we need to do in these times to emerge a stronger and fairer country.

I governed in a world markedly different from the one in which I grew up. In that world, the domino theory of communism pushing its way from China and Vietnam all the way to us was fashionable. Economically Asia was viewed as a region of poverty. Australians looked over it to Europe and America. We followed the politics and cultural trends of the United Kingdom and the United States. The 'smart kids' like me were made to study French and German.

Now the opportunity for our nation flows from our location in the growth region of the world, where the future of the 21st century is being minted. A foreign policy analyst needs to understand Asia's rise, as does a military commander, but so does a businessperson, a parent trying to give their child good advice about their future career and an artist striving to expand and reflect the cultural influences in our world. I sought to explain these changes to the broader community, to galvanise not only government action, but the actions of business leaders, journalists, civic leaders and educators around a shared understanding of the benefits and potential problems we would encounter in this century, which will be defined by Asia's growth.

No one can hold back change. In our modern globalised world, no government can wholly shape the future. But we can bend change, shape it so it serves our purposes and what happens reflects our values, our embrace of fairness. This is what modern Labor governments at their best have sought to do.

While I was prime minister, there was much commentary suggesting the government I led was not in the tradition of Hawke and Keating. I fundamentally reject this analysis. Yes, there were clear differences. Neither Hawke nor Keating had to manage a minority government.

Hawke did not sabotage the 1993 election campaign. Keating did not have Hawke destabilising.

But with all these differences, there are so many similarities. The embrace of consultative structures involving business, unions and civil society. The drive to modernise our economy and our outlook on our region. The focus on jobs, skills, innovation, infrastructure, regulatory reform – all the drivers of productivity. A fresh approach to service provision. An understanding of the power of markets, which led to our careful design of those that provide services like childcare and aged care as well as the embrace of the modern tool of transparency to achieve quality, choice, empowerment. A drive to include all in the life of our nation, to not divide and discriminate, to give a hand up to those who need an opportunity, to expect personal responsibility in return. The bringing of a sophisticated and practical approach to protecting our environment. Responsible management of the budget to achieve jobs, growth and fiscal sustainability.

Yet while these are the golden threads that tie modern Labor governments together, every leader brings a different perspective and emphasis to leadership. I was clear on mine. Whatever problems we faced day to day, I made sure our government had a long-term vision, that we worked to grow and more fairly share wealth and opportunity in our nation.

Work, education, respect. I defined my purpose and it drove me on. I led a government of purpose and it made Australia stronger and fairer.

9

Fighting a war

'We have a card for you.'
THE FAMILY OF PRIVATE NATHANAEL GALAGHER
AT HIS FUNERAL, 13 SEPTEMBER 2012

ON 7 SEPTEMBER 2012 I ARRIVED IN VLADIVOSTOK to attend my third meeting of the Asia-Pacific Economic Community (APEC). The establishment of APEC is an outstanding Labor achievement, delivered by Prime Ministers Hawke and Keating. Like them, I understood that our economic future lay in our region and that our nation needed to be in the best possible economic shape in order to seize the opportunity. When I received the final briefings for this APEC meeting on the plane, I could almost feel them standing behind me.

As prime minister, flying domestically or going to international meetings, you travel on a Boeing 737, one of the VIP aircraft operated by Squadron 34 in the Royal Australian Air Force (RAAF). The plane has a prime ministerial cabin with four seats and its own bathroom, a ten-seat middle executive cabin and then a rear cabin with rows of ordinary seating. Its maximum flying range is around 11 hours. Flying this way had three huge advantages. You can leave when you want to and arrive quicker than you would on a commercial flight. Meetings can be conducted in privacy on the plane. Onboard meetings are the best way of doing the last, intensive briefing for the matters to come.

Then there are the wonderful RAAF staff, who you see so often they become friends.

Tim accompanied me on a number of international trips. When he did come with me to multilateral meetings, he would routinely be the only man attending the spouses' program. Thanks to his background in hairdressing, he was at ease meeting lots of people, particularly women, and getting them chatting. Trip by trip, Tim and I would discuss whether or not he would come; we had decided on this occasion that he would stay home.

After landing in Vladivostok around 10 pm, I was driven to Russky Island, where the meeting was to be held. The whole venue, including the bridge, had been constructed for APEC. All of the buildings were later to be repurposed as a university. My accommodation was in an apartment that would become a lecturer's residence within a student residence. Most of the staff and officials travelling with me were allocated student rooms.

From time to time when travelling internationally, we were advised not to use our normal phones and temporary phones were allocated to us. On this trip we were issued with old Nokia phones and we all struggled. Technology that seemed wonderful not so long ago now felt maddeningly antiquated.

The next day, having attended a run of events and bilateral meetings, I was in a holding room waiting to be told it was time to get into the motorcade and be taken to the main meeting venue for the formal greeting by President Putin. Every multilateral meeting comes with its own special version of motorcade madness, where organisers struggle to get multiple motorcades to arrive with precision timing at the venue.

Ahead of my arrival, a staff member from my office with the curious title of 'advancer', one of the AFP officers who attend to prime ministerial security, and an official from my department's protocol section would work through every detail with the host of the event. This is the normal system for Australian prime ministers and what we do to prepare for such meetings is incredibly simple and lightly resourced compared to leaders of other countries.

Knowing how good a job the team did with setting up arrangements, there was nothing for me to do but sit and wait. It was in this break that I finally worked out on this old phone that I had missed a call from my sister. I rang Alison back and she broke the news to me that Dad had died.

When Felicity, from the protocol section, came in to update me about our leaving time, she found me weeping and gave me a hug. I asked for Trade Minister Craig Emerson, who was travelling with me, and Michelle from my office. Both knew my father. Both are true friends. Along with Richard Maude, my Foreign Affairs adviser, we made arrangements for Craig to attend APEC on my behalf so that I could go to Adelaide to be with my family as quickly as possible.

A somewhat startled President Putin greeted Craig Emerson and then announced to APEC and the world that my father had died. It was how Dad's surviving brother and sister found out that their sibling had passed away.

It was a long afternoon and a horrible night. The unexpected departure time meant the plane needed to be readied so I had no choice but to wait. Then the flight seemed never-ending.

My father was in his 80s and had been unwell, including having to deal with the growth of a cancer behind his knee; his leg had been amputated. This once strong man had moved into residential aged care. Both body and spirit were suffering. But somehow, no matter what age your parents are or the state of their health, when it actually happens, their passing is a shock. There had been nothing to indicate when I left Australia that this would be Dad's time. An infection took hold while I was out of the country and carried him away, even more swiftly than his treating doctor anticipated.

Once in Adelaide, with Dad's death huge news around the country, I grieved with my family.

I returned to Canberra on 12 September so that in the days that followed I could attend the funerals of Private Nathanael Galagher, Lance Corporal Mervyn McDonald and Sapper James Martin, three of five soldiers lost in Afghanistan in two separate incidents within a day: one a helicopter crash, the other an insider attack from a rogue Afghan National Army soldier at Patrol Base. It was the season for mourning.

When I arrived at Private Nate Galagher's funeral in a small town in country New South Wales, his family asked me to join them behind the building, slightly away from the gathering crowd. They did so in order to hand me a sympathy card and to express their condolences on the loss of my father.

That Nate's father, mother, sister and girlfriend, who was expecting Nate's child, having lost their much-loved 23-year-old son, brother, partner, could spare such kindness for me, mourning the loss of an 83-year-old man, was unbelievable and enriching in equal doses. I learnt something about generosity and perspective that day.

I had learnt something about courage at the funeral of Lance Corporal Jared MacKinney on 10 September 2010. At that Brisbane funeral, I watched Jared's heavily pregnant wife, Beckie, wringing her mother's hand. That morning she had gone into labour but was determined to make it to the funeral. By the end of the service, you could see the pain and resolve etched starkly into her face. Stoically she sat at the morning tea afterwards. A family member told Premier Anna Bligh and me that Beckie was determined not to leave before the dignitaries. Anna and I immediately shooed everyone into their cars. As we drove away, an ambulance shot by: it had been on standby and Beckie was in the back. Baby Noah Jared entered the world a short time later.

I learnt another lesson about courage the day I paid a visit to the 2nd Commando Regiment at Holsworthy Barracks in New South Wales to privately meet with soldiers recovering from physical and psychological wounds.

The memory of courage like this, as well as the celebrated courage of our Victoria Cross recipients, stays with me. I will never forget meeting Ben Roberts-Smith, a huge man, in my office with his wife, Emma, and their twin girls. Holding one of these tiny babies in his hands, with the exaggerated carefulness big men bring to the holding of small children, Ben recounted his tale of bravery with a factual, unassuming modesty. The contrast between the gentleness I could see in him and the fighting he had done was surreal. I will also never forget meeting Daniel Keighran with his wife, Kathryn, who knew nothing of his outstanding bravery until Daniel had no option but to tell her because he was being awarded the Victoria Cross. Mark Donaldson, another VC recipient, also impressed in every way on meeting.

Courage and Afghanistan are inextricably linked in my mind. As I write, our fallen number 41. The courage of the families of those lost and of their mates who kept on fighting endures. So does the special kind of courage needed every day by the most grievously hurt of the more than 250 wounded.

I attended 24 funerals. I watched and tried to comfort as people grieved. Shy people, with no experience of public speaking, would go to the pulpit or stage and give the most emotional, witty, heartfelt reflections on their lost loved one.

Defence commanders' speeches revealed a modern take on the ethos that drives our military personnel. Their language is not that of love of Queen and country, though undoubtedly those who serve are great patriots. Rather now the ethos is of being a warrior, the kind of individual whose internal motivation to help others is so strong they are willing to risk all. The sort of person who has no illusions about the risk but chooses to do the job anyway. An individual who understands fear and conquers it.

For these people and their families, belief in the mission is paramount. Our defence personnel choose to believe in the merits of the war on terror. Families left grieving find comfort in the belief that their loved one died in pursuit of a real and honourable purpose. Only once did a relative aggressively ask me if their loss was in vain.

Belief sustained me too as I led the nation during our biggest losses in Afghanistan. Australian lives had been lost on 9/11 in New York and in Bali in 2002 and 2005. In each of these attacks there were links to Afghanistan – a safe haven for training. Our nation went to war to deny terrorists the continuing benefit of that safe haven. We went to war to support our ally the United States, which had been attacked on its own soil. These reasons justified the fight. For the Labor Party, our support was also grounded on the UN mandate for that war.

During my prime ministership, like the countries we fought alongside, Australia faced strategic choices about our presence in Afghanistan. Understanding the obligations this put upon me as prime minister, my first international visit was to Afghanistan. In all, I made three trips there. Each time, I flew to Dubai, got up at around 3 am the next day, drove to the airbase Australian forces operated from, boarded a Hercules aircraft and flew the around four hours into Afghanistan. I would always visit our troops in the Uruzgan Province and go to Kabul to see President Karzai and the all-up commander of the coalition of countries fighting in Afghanistan. On each trip, by the time my contingent and I touched down in Dubai, we had been on the move for more than 20 hours.

Flying over Afghanistan is mostly like flying over a moonscape: desert, seemingly devoid of life. Then jarring against that backdrop is the lushness of green valleys. Our troops not only faced danger but lived and worked in climatic conditions that went from blisteringly hot to freezing cold. Summer is 'fighting season'. Winter is harsh. It is easy to conclude that because of these tough natural conditions Afghanistan is always destined to be poor. But in the 1960s, its wealth was comparable to that of Portugal or Malaysia. The poverty, disease, infant mortality rate and lack of education that are part of the lives of the Afghan people are the result of war and the barbarity of human beings.

There is always an artificiality about a visiting politician, a prime minister, suddenly being amid fighting men and women. I understood not to presume I knew what their lives were like but to genuinely listen. What I saw was grief for fallen mates and the damaged trust between Australians and the Afghans they trained as a spate of insider attacks took lives. The fatigue that came from multiple tours was obvious; some men in Special Forces were on their fifth or sixth tour of duty. There was pride in what had been achieved: stabilising the security conditions, training local forces, helping local people access health care and education. But everywhere, a grinding sense of frustration was apparent – a by-product of dealing with the deeply troubling mix of government incapacity, tribal politics and corruption.

At my first meeting with President Karzai, I experienced that frustration too. When I had dinner with him in the Presidential Palace in Kabul, he was charming. He took the time to show me intricate tapestries, many hundreds of years old, on which the Taliban had strewn paint to hide the faces of the animals and birds. Yet when he asked me, 'How are things in Uruzgan Province?', in the same tone of voice he would have used to ask me, 'How are things in Sydney?', my hackles rose. I offered in return something more diplomatic than the blunt reply, *It is actually your nation and perhaps you should be telling me.*

The meetings with General Petraeus and General Allen – who in turn commanded the International Security Assistance Force (ISAF) – introduced me to another world. For all the economic difficulties of the United States, it is still home to the most sophisticated and capable war-fighting machine the world has ever known. Those who rise to the top are truly impressive. I found both these men so; nothing about the personal-life scandals alleged or revealed since has caused me to revise my view.

On each of these visits, I honed my thinking on our strategy. Shortly after my first one, I presented my conclusions to the parliament. This parliamentary statement and the debate that ensued arose because of an undertaking I gave to the Greens, Tony Windsor, Rob Oakeshott and Andrew Wilkie on the formation of minority government. They wanted the voices of parliamentarians to be heard. I did more than honour my commitment to them for a debate. I reported to parliament each year on our progress in Afghanistan, giving parliamentarians an annual opportunity to have their say.

While this would not have happened if we had been elected as a majority government, I formed the view during the first statement and debate that the process was both appropriate and necessary. I now strongly believe that any time large numbers of Australian combat troops are deployed overseas, fighting and dying, once a year the parliament should devote itself to examining why they are there, what progress is being made, what strategic judgements the government has made about the deployment and whether everything that can be done to support our troops is being done.

On return from my initial visit, I concluded there was a risk that worldwide weariness of war would dictate an earlier exit from Afghanistan and a quicker transition in some areas to security leadership by local forces than was sustainable.

In my first statement to parliament on the war in Afghanistan, I said:

> In some places the transition process will be subject to setbacks.
> We need to be prepared for this. My firm view is that for transi-
> tion to occur in an area, the ability of Afghan forces to take the
> lead in security in that area must be irreversible . . . We must not
> transition out only to transition back in.[1]

I used the same words at my first NATO-ISAF Summit in Lisbon. This
took place on the weekend between the final two sitting weeks of 2010.
It had been a punishing year and my body was crying out for rest but
this meeting was too important to miss. I left parliament at the conclusion of Question Time Thursday, flew to Lisbon, attended the summit
and was back in time for Question Time Monday. It was not the only
trip where I was in transit for longer than I was at the destination.

Big multilateral meetings like this one have their own rhythm. Much
of the work is done in the lead-up through discussions between officials.
Leaders attending give short contributions in an order dictated by negotiation and protocol. Many read word by word a prepared script, never
lifting their gaze from the paper in front of them. In response, the attention paid by other leaders sitting at the table can be scant, with their
attention directed to paperwork they have brought with them. The real
action occurs on the sidelines, where any sticking points are ironed out.

At this and other multilateral meetings, working with officials and
my office I planned what I wanted to say and had dot points before
me as an aide-mémoire. But I spoke looking up, addressing the room,
catching people's eyes. My approach was rewarded: people lifted their
eyes from the documents or iPads they were working on and genuinely
listened to me. General Petraeus sought me out to congratulate me on
what he referred to as the best contribution at the meeting.

Hearing praise is easy. It is much harder to answer the question
of whether – in Lisbon and then at the next NATO-ISAF Summit
I attended, two years later in Chicago, as well as in Canberra at many
National Security Committee and cabinet meetings – we made the
right decisions about the strategy for and Australia's engagement in
the war in Afghanistan.

Did the world at these summits choose the best strategy for the
fight? For war, with lives lost, doubts should always haunt. But my

best judgement is that overwhelmingly the strategy was right. I believe so, even though the decision to make a conditions-based transition to Afghan security leadership increasingly hit up against the limits of international will for continuing the fight. Transition plans for parts of the country became more based on time deadlines and less based on a view of conditions on the ground. War-weary nations were aching for the blessed sense of relief that comes with bringing troops home and increasingly seeing those still deployed performing their duties at their base rather than out on the battlefield. Behind the wire is at least safer, though not safe.

Yet it would be unfair to characterise the ISAF transition strategy as a run for the exit door. Rather it was a march where really no one wanted to be diverted into a longer route. It was also a march-out that increasingly Afghan leaders, and particularly President Karzai, wanted to see happen.

Overall I believe the agreed strategy is enabling sufficient security to be delivered by Afghan local forces to prevent a return of Al Qaeda.

Here at home, many judgements needed to be made about the size of our deployment, its duration and the best way of protecting our forces in theatre. These are inevitably calculations about the risks of losing more Australian lives.

As a government we funded the best force protection measures possible. In Afghanistan, we learnt much about how to better protect troops in the field from the destructive power of improvised explosive devices (IEDs). For many years to come, IEDs will be a favourite weapon for those who seek to wreak terror, so this new knowledge is precious.

Were we right as a government to have our nation shoulder more than what could be thought of as our fair load, which Australia did at every stage of the Afghanistan war? Throughout my prime ministership, Australia was for the most part the largest non-NATO contributor of forces generally and of Special Forces personnel.

The government also indicated that we were open to a continuing role for Special Forces after 2014, when transition had been completed, provided Afghanistan agreed to give our combat troops the legal protections necessary. When President Karzai became too grudging and political in negotiations with the USA about such coverage for their fighting forces, it was apparent we would not be able to get an appropriate legal agreement for ours. As a result, we were alleviated of the burden of making the decision to send our elite fighting forces for longer.

Nevertheless Australians will continue to serve in Afghanistan as part of the NATO-led 'train, advise, assist' mission beyond 2014. On 17 April 2012, I made that clear when I announced to the nation – in my address to the Australian Strategic Policy Institute and Boeing National Security Luncheon in Canberra – that we expected the bulk of our forces to be home at the end of 2013.

From 2015, I agreed to Australia contributing around $100 million each year to the sustainment of the Afghan local forces, around $20 million more than a calculation of our fair share. Australia is also the sixth largest aid donor to Afghanistan, with an enduring partnership agreement I signed with President Karzai in May 2012.

All these decisions, given our status in the world, our capability, our national interest in combating terrorism, our sense of compassion, seemed to me to be correct. Australia should always be very considered, even conservative, about whether to deploy troops, but once it is decided a cause is right to fight for then it is also right to step up strongly.

But whatever long-term judgement you come to about the decisions you took, the anguish of lives lost stays with you. Mostly I would be told about deaths in Afghanistan by Stephen Smith. The tone of his voice when he said hello always signalled that bad news was to follow. We became almost superstitious about not commenting to each other if it had been some time since a fatality. It felt like tempting fate. But as the months rolled on from the loss of Corporal Scott James Smith in October 2012 without further loss of life, Stephen and I, as well as defence leaders, let ourselves start to exhale.

On 22 June 2013 at Yungaburra on the Atherton Tablelands, I attended the opening of the Avenue of Honour, a memorial to Australian losses in Afghanistan. The site was known to me; it was where I had attended the funeral of Ben Chuck, during which a single helicopter flew over the water as a mark of respect to this young man who loved flying choppers. He and fellow soldiers Scott Palmer and Tim Aplin had lost their lives in one. Ben's father, Gordon, had conceived the idea of this beautiful location becoming home to a permanent memorial. I helped to obtain the funding and stayed in contact with Gordon through my private email. I felt we shared much in our exchanges.

The day, attended by so many who had lost so much, had a sense of closure about it. As 'The Last Post' was played, the Chief of the Defence Force, David Hurley, was called by his aide to take an urgent telephone call: a soldier with no vital signs was being brought back from the battlefield. I was pulled away from chatting with families to be told about this latest potential loss. Such information is strictly confidential; the soldier's family members must be the first to find out instead of hearing it on the news.

As we drove back to the plane, our worst fears were confirmed. Our 40th soldier, Corporal Cameron Stewart Baird, had been killed in action. On the flight back to Canberra, David, who is such a good, dignified man, and I shared our grief. Just when we had let ourselves hope that the deaths were behind us, now this. A 32-year-old man, who earlier in his career had won a Medal for Gallantry for conspicuous bravery during heavy fighting, lay dead. He was posthumously awarded the Victoria Cross.

The courage of our deployed defence personnel and police, who have done their work bravely and well, should humble us all. The greatest burden of war always falls on the shoulders of our military personnel and their families. I trust we will show in the years ahead that we are capable of learning how to better care for the bereaved and rehabilitate the wounded, particularly those with mental health needs, who have been too often ignored in the past.

As an international community, we are learning – yet again – how hard it is to grow a liberal democracy. From Papua New Guinea to Fiji, in these days of the so-called Arab Spring, following combat in Iraq and in so many other places in the world, our heads tell us – from often bitter experience – that establishing resilient democracy is error-prone, painstakingly slow work. Yet our hearts seem to stubbornly cling to a belief that the merits of democracy are so self-evident it should more easily flourish.

In Afghanistan, I fear that we are to be disappointed again as democratic progress is stalled, even partially eroded, by poverty, governance incapacity, corruption, tribal politics and the predominance of the Taliban being reasserted in some areas. That does not mean it was wrong to go. Our mission was to deny Al Qaeda a safe haven. But about some of the other things we have prided ourselves on – the creation of a young democracy with rights for women, the improvements in healthcare and education – there is a risk the days ahead will bring hard news.

In my first speech to parliament, I said that building the Afghan nation will be the work of a generation of Afghans. I would now add the words 'at least'. Despite how hard it will be, helping this generation of Afghans and the next generation and the generation after that build their nation will be one of the causes of our time. It will be a way of honouring the lives sacrificed. Of showing that we will remember them.

10

The 1961 kids

'All the best people were born in 1961.'

MY QUIP TO UNITED STATES PRESIDENT BARACK OBAMA
AND PRIME MINISTER JOHN KEY OF NEW ZEALAND

THERE IS A REASON WE GROUP PEOPLE INTO GENERATIONS and give those generations names: the baby boomers, Gen X, Gen Y. It is a shorthand way of saying that for all the differences between individuals in a generation in the Western world, their formative years had common features which shaped their lives. Whether they knew war. The technology in widespread use. The social understanding of women's roles. Whether the global economy and that of their nation was conducive to employment and educational opportunity. The predominant attitudes to premarital sex, alcohol and drug use. Barack Obama, John Key and I, all born in 1961, found the theory behind the shorthand worked. Our shared reference points made for the easy formation of personal friendships.

I first met Barack Obama at the G20 and APEC summits – in Korea and Japan respectively – in November 2010. At the G20 meeting, he advised me not to set my expectations too high, that big summits like this could lack excitement. I wisecracked, 'What happened to the audacity of hope?', a cheeky reference to a book President Obama has written.

By the time of the Lisbon NATO summit later that year, we had established such a rapport that the banter continued. The key photo of us shows me looking like I am telling him off as he laughs. At an otherwise very serious occasion, it catches a quick humorous discussion about our Question Time. When I explained that I had flown out after one Question Time and would fly back into another, President Obama said he envied the opportunity Question Time gave to explain your agenda to the nation. 'Are you mad?' I said, with accompanying dramatic overacting. Once he understood it happened every day and consisted of 20 questions, ten from the Opposition, mostly directed to me as prime minister, he was inclined to agree his statement was a bit mad.

Seasoned diplomats would not advocate kidding around as a textbook way of developing a new relationship between leaders. Yet ours did become a strong relationship and together we strengthened the friendship between our two countries.

The two of us clicked on several levels. Both President Obama and I were unlikely leaders of our nations. Before he burst into the Democratic primary contest against Hillary Clinton with such force, I would have said, if asked, that I would be lucky to live to see the first African-American President of the United States. I would have bet on there being a woman or a Hispanic first. I have pointed to my own apparent disqualifications from office – a childless atheist woman living in a de facto relationship – and joked I would never have made it in America.

We were also from sister political parties, both of us governing in environments of hyper-partisanship, where there was no automatic way to translate ideas into laws.

In President Obama I recognised a sense of deep calm and unflappability, coupled with an easy ability to interact with people and get them chatting. However, for both of us, beneath the public persona lies personal reserve: recharging energies requires time alone or with those closest, not surfing off the energy of the crowd.

But the differences between us are clear too. I do not share Barack's religious faith, for instance. Unlike his, mine was an uncomplicated conventional childhood. I have not had to grapple with the boundaries still imposed by race nor the resulting issues of identity, which he has written about so eloquently.

I definitely envy President Obama's remarkable skills of oratory, his million-watt smile and physical grace. I definitely do not envy all the weight that comes with being the President of the United States of America: from the cares of office to the incredible security machine that surrounds him. The last time we met when I was prime minister, he said to me, 'Julia, I used to say to people, "Gee this office has aged me" and everyone would laugh. Now I say it and no one laughs.' For once, I could not come up with a jocular reply.

All that pressure is a by-product of an incredible opportunity to make a difference to his nation and the world. Certainly, in my dealings with President Obama, I have seen that difference. The difference made to our strategy in Afghanistan. To our world as a result of his and Secretary Clinton's decision to pivot, or rebalance, towards Asia. The difference evident in global economic recovery thanks to President Obama's personal interventions to see more movement in Europe in response to their economic problems.

I saw too the difference Barack is making to the hopes and aspirations of African Americans.

In March 2011, I went to the White House for a formal meeting with President Obama. Having been ushered through security, I waited in the Roosevelt Room while the rest of the delegation was checked through. I had waited in this room before – a few years earlier – when as deputy prime minister I had come to see Vice President Dick Cheney. On that occasion, a somewhat nervous young Republican staff member had mentioned that this was the fireplace President Clinton had stood before when he said, 'I did not have sexual relations with that woman.' I smiled to myself and thought that was unlikely to be a conversation topic recommended by protocol.

On this occasion, I was going to the Oval Office. Curiously, on entering it, you feel a sense of familiarity. It has been the scene of so much action in so many movies. For us, it was the venue for a meeting that went smoothly, with our nations in agreement about so much. With the formalities concluded, I wanted to show you could combine foreign policy with a love of education – and with having some fun. So next, President Obama and I hand-balled an Aussie Rules football back and forth in the Oval Office, fortunately avoiding all damage to price-less artefacts, and then jumped in his car to visit a Washington school.

Of course, jumping in the presidential car entailed a motorcade a mile long, many people in dark suits and sunglasses, vans with funny things on top, helicopters in the sky and boats on the river. Even so, the drive afforded us the chance to talk frankly about where we were both at politically.

Arriving at the school, we emerged from the car into a tent that had been erected so no one with evil on their mind could get a line of sight on the President. We then moved into the school building and passed through an area clearly used to teach automotive mechanics. In a nearby classroom we answered the children's questions and performed a comedy routine about Vegemite, which President Obama had volunteered in an earlier discussion that he hated.

As we headed off, one of President Obama's aides mentioned that the kids who were scheduled to learn mechanics had been told their class was cancelled, without explanation; they had been moved to another room. It was suggested, and President Obama readily agreed, it would be nice to say hi to them.

I accompanied him as he met these students, all African-American boys aged around 15 who had no idea he was coming, and witnessed the ripple effect: stunned, silent, awestruck, then all blurting out to each other, 'It's President Obama!' I watched the emotion wave through the room. Until then, I had intellectually understood what it meant for the USA to have its first African-American president. At that moment, I felt it in my guts. It means Barack Obama is the embodiment of all the better days that people hope can come.

My visit to Washington brought me many other special moments. Addressing Congress, enjoying the standing ovation and Speaker Boehner's appreciative tears for a speech about the dream and capabilities of America. It was the first time I had ever used a teleprompter and thank heavens it worked. As a result of some confusion between my staff and the staff of Congress, the only copy of my speech on the podium was a commemorative bound edition, which would have been too small to read from had the teleprompter failed. Luckily it did not. Senator John McCain showing me through a collection of photographs displaying the 60 years of our alliance with the United States and then his personal collection of Vietnam war memorabilia, including his father's letter requesting that no special favouritism be shown to him as a prisoner of war. Staying at the beautiful and historic Blair House. The trip gave me memories to treasure.

On my return from Washington, we had plans to make. I came back resolved to not only welcome President Obama to Australia but to ensure we were ready, despite nervousness in some quarters, to announce the training of US marines in Northern Australia.

Stephen Smith is a cautious man. It is one of the characteristics that made him such a good Defence Minister. He appropriately brought to the table for consideration some of the concerns in the foreign policy establishment about the regional reaction. He explored whether there was a way of making a start on this new arrangement without agreeing to it as a whole so we could effectively test the responses of others. Within cabinet there was some concern about the likely views at home of another nation's soldiers training on our soil. I understood these concerns but was determined to agree to the whole proposal, which we did.

I came to this view, not because it was going to be easy, indeed managing regional reaction, particularly China's, had a high degree of difficulty. Rather I thought it was the right decision strategically for the future. It would meet an American need. It would facilitate joint training and exercises at a time beyond both our deployments to Afghanistan. It would show our preparedness to modernise the alliance between our nations. It would also send a self-confident message to our region that Australia was not succumbing to a dogma of false choices between valuing our alliance and our relationships in the region in which we live.

I was also absolutely confident that the days of progressive Left protests against an American presence on Australian soil were behind us, and contemporary politics, including an America led by a Democrat, meant this initiative would be well received.

I knew that the end of 2011 would bring an incredible pace of international work. Within the space of a few weeks, I would welcome the Queen to Australia, chair the Commonwealth Heads of Government Meeting (CHOGM) in Perth, travel to France for the G20, to

Afghanistan to visit our troops, to APEC in Hawaii, welcome President Obama to Australia and go to the East Asia Summit (EAS) in Bali.

APEC in Hawaii was one of the multilateral meetings where I was the only woman in attendance. That this could be true of a leaders' meeting representing 40 per cent of the global population and approximately 55 per cent of the world's economy says much about continuing gender discrimination in our world. Fortunately the wearing of funny shirts for the commemorative photos was scrapped. It was the subject of banter between leaders, including about a hula grass skirt and coconut bra having been on the drawing board for me.

More seriously, the meeting made progress, albeit slowly, on better integrating our economies. On the sidelines of the meeting, President Obama spotlighted his intentions for a Trans Pacific Partnership free trade agreement, a visible demonstration of his decision that the United States should pivot towards Asia.

I next saw President Obama in Australia. He and I were able to spend a great deal of time together during his visit, including time one on one discussing politics and leadership.

Our joint announcement of training of marines in Northern Australia was well received domestically. Cheekily *The Courier-Mail* went with the headline, 'US Forces Get the Nod',[1] a line ripped out of a Midnight Oil song that is followed by the words, 'It's a setback for our country.' When I introduced President Obama to all of our cabinet ministers, including Peter Garrett, I explained that Peter had been a rock star, singing these words. Barack was intrigued not by the words but by Peter's career, and ended up ribbing him that politicians wanted to be rock stars; it did not seem right the other way round.

President Obama's speech to the House of Representatives detailed his administration's increasing focus on Asia, including the lyrical but pointed remarks:

As we grow our economies, we will also remember the link between growth and good governance, the rule of law, transparent institutions and the equal administration of justice, because history shows that, over the long run, democracy and economic growth go hand in hand, and prosperity without freedom is just another form of poverty. This brings me to the final area where we are leading: our support for the fundamental rights of every human being. Every nation will chart its own course, yet it is also true that certain rights are universal – among them, freedom of speech, freedom of the press, freedom of assembly, freedom of religion and the freedom of citizens to choose their own leaders. These are not American rights, Australian rights or Western rights; these are human rights. They stir in every soul, as we have seen in the democracies that have succeeded here in Asia. Other models have been tried and they have failed – fascism and communism, rule by one man and rule by a committee. They failed for the same simple reason: they ignored the ultimate source of power and legitimacy – the will of the people.[2]

At the same time as President Obama delivered this speech, Secretary of State Clinton appeared on an aircraft carrier in the Philippines.

Managing the Chinese and regional reaction to the announcement did prove quite a challenge, particularly given these optics, but through comprehensive briefings on the details of the training agreement and by turning the focus to the benefits that could be achieved for disaster management response by having marines available locally, we patiently and successfully worked our way through.

During his visit in Canberra, President Obama and I went to a school, presided at a wonderful formal dinner, paid our respects at the war memorial. Barack was generous with his time and energy, doing things like saying hello to every Parliament House attendant we passed on our walks through the building.

I farewelled President Obama from Darwin. We met those who remembered the Second World War bombing, giving us the opportunity to see that calamitous day through their eyes.

In heat and humidity, we appeared in an aircraft hangar in Darwin to address cheering, foot-stomping Australian troops. On the flight up, Ambassador and former Labor leader Kim Beazley had confided his worry that our troops would not react like American troops to the arrival of the President and that he would find it quiet. I said I thought our troops would be mad with excitement, and fortunately I was right.

Unfortunately the air-conditioning we had installed failed; a secret service agent fainted. As we shook hands and signed items for individual soldiers, President Obama announced to his team, 'It's time to go, now, before Julia's hair gets frizzy', in a good-natured reference to the many complaints he had heard from me about humidity and my hair.

All in all, the visit was a triumph. The American Ambassador to Australia, the wise and warm Jeffrey Bleich, was delighted, as was I. An alliance modernised; shape and content given to the USA's new outlook on our region; a president received with genuine friendship.

In other times we shared together there was less to joke about. I felt President Obama's palpable frustration with the lack of scale and speed in the European response to the Eurozone crisis at the G20 meetings in Cannes, France, and later Los Cabos, Mexico. As the war in Afghanistan cost more lives and President Karzai's conduct caused more difficulties, everyone's demeanour at the NATO-ISAF Summit was one of grim determination. But through all that and watching closely the trials and tribulations of American politics, I have not lost any of my admiration for a leader of and for our times, for President Obama.

In some ways the less likely friendship to emerge was mine with John Key. Where President Obama and I shared the bond of similar values, of being in sister political parties, John Key is a conservative, a National Party leader in New Zealand, a natural ally of the Liberal Party in Australia. But he and I did strike up both a friendship and a way of working together that helped give greater priority to the relationship between our two countries. It was a weird echo of John Howard's apparent respect and affection for New Zealand's Labour Prime Minister Helen Clark.

I inherited a situation where the annual leaders' meeting between Australia and New Zealand had fallen into abeyance. I was committed to getting this back on track, as was Prime Minister Key. So in February 2011, I became the first foreign leader to address the New Zealand Parliament, a very special honour.

Our relationship with New Zealand is unlike any other. I described it as being family. Our Anzac bond is not only one of history, it endures today.

Our economies are among the most integrated in the world. Just as Australia can look anxiously to the United States, to read the entrails of its politics, to try to diagnose the smallest of signs about what is being thought about us, so New Zealand looks to Australia.

We had sent a message of neglect and now strived to send one of renewed friendship.

Throughout this tour of immense goodwill – New Zealanders stopped on the streets and applauded as I drove by – I spent a great deal of time with John Key. On planes, in cars, at schools, around the dinner table. I enjoyed his company, respected many of his policy views, admired his journey – from a battling start in life to the wealth and privilege of banking then into politics – heard stories of his family.

When an earthquake struck in Christchurch, killing 185, including one Australian, and destroying the entire central business district, we responded at once. Australia sent three 72-strong urban search and rescue teams, 16 ambulance officers, 500 police, a 75-bed field hospital and a 24-person medical assistance team. Along with the Leader of the Opposition and the Governor-General, Tim and I attended the memorial service in Christchurch. In view of this disaster, I decided that rather than waiting until the time for the next annual leaders' talks in 2012, I would invite John Key to address our parliament in May 2011. He appreciated the gesture.

We hosted the 2012 leaders' talks in Melbourne and enjoyed wonderful New Zealand hospitality in Queenstown in 2013. Over the course of many meetings, Tim and Bronagh, John's wife, also came to enjoy spending time together.

Our nations celebrated the 30th anniversary of the Closer Economic Relationship between New Zealand and Australia. While I could not accede to every anniversary decision John Key would have liked, including equalising welfare benefits for New Zealanders who are long-time residents in Australia, we took important steps forward during all our work together, including facilitating investment and moving closer towards the goal of passport-free travel. Importantly for New Zealand children growing up in Australia, a number that includes many disadvantaged young people originally from the Pacific Islands, we opened access to our universities.

At many multilateral meetings, John and I would catch up and exchange perspectives on the issues at the meeting. We collaborated closely on our shared goal of seeing democracy return to Fiji.

John ably led a meeting of the Pacific Islands Forum in New Zealand, of which Australia is a member. As the only woman at the meeting, in the leaders-only session, I sought to lead a discussion about women's empowerment. According to the World Bank, of the five countries in the world with no women in their parliaments, three are in the Pacific. When the discussion bogged down into a series of statements from leaders like, 'We have equal opportunity, it's just the women don't want to be in parliament, they are too busy looking after the children', John did his best to get it back on track.

During our time together there was much dumb joking about sporting contests between Australia and New Zealand and silly bets about who would win and who would have to eat an apple from or wear the sporting paraphernalia of the other nation.

There were also some frank discussions about life and politics. I appreciated John's practical approach to politics, an ever-present sense that it would be part but not all of his life. That he had done something important before it and would find things to do after it. That when the time came to leave, he would not live with regret.

That is an outlook this 1961 kid certainly shares.

11

Australia in the
Asian Century

'Predicting the future is fraught with risk, but the greater risk is in failing to plan for our destiny. As a nation, we face a choice: to drift into the future or to actively shape it . . . I want our nation to be a winner as our region changes and I want every Australian to be a winner too. Put simply, as a Labor prime minister, I want the new opportunities that will come in this century to be seized and shared. I want us to take an approach to the looming change that is farsighted and focused on fairness.'

MY 'AUSTRALIA IN THE ASIAN CENTURY' WHITE PAPER

ON MY FIRST INTERNATIONAL VISIT, I SAID, 'If I had a choice, I'd probably be more [comfortable] in a school watching kids learn to read in Australia than here in Brussels at international meetings.'[1] Already some in the media were unable to view any statement by me in any other context than a comparison with Kevin. My simple statement was spun by them into meaning that, unlike Kevin Rudd, the former diplomat, I was not going to cope with foreign policy. The fact that Howard, Keating, Hawke, Fraser, Whitlam, Menzies – and the list goes on – did not come to the prime ministership from a foreign policy background was tossed to one side.

In stark contrast to all this cant, I knew I could master foreign policy engagements. At the end of the day, for all the machinery, doctrine, commentary and academic debate that swirls around foreign policy, in execution it is two or more individuals, leaders of nations, coming together to see if they can find common accord. Everything about my work in politics, indeed the life I had lived, prepared me for that.

As I worked through both foreign policy and economic briefings, what did exercise me increasingly was the need to explain to the Australian community the opportunities and the risks of the age we live in and the times to come. Specifically I wanted to paint the picture of Asia's rise, which will be a defining feature of this, the 21st century, and how we as a government were readying Australia for this future.

Craig Emerson suggested to me a White Paper would be the right vehicle to explain our vision. There was some nervousness among colleagues that this was a diversion from the main tasks before government or even that it would be a net negative with voters who preferred to turn inwards rather than outwards. I took a different view. That telling the bigger story would help people better understand why we were pursuing many of our policies. If the contest was to be between a documented record of our vision and the Opposition's negativity, then I was happy to be in the vision business.

I asked Ken Henry, who by this stage had retired from the post of Treasury Secretary, to lead the drafting of the White Paper. A thorough process of consultation ensued. The drafting and redrafting work was complex and would not have been completed without the work of my office, Craig Emerson and the then head of the Office of National Assessments, Allan Gyngell.

But I was satisfied when we launched the paper that it appropriately distilled what I most valued in the extraordinary governing context of our times. In short, the thesis of the White Paper is that Asia's remarkable rise, which has already lifted hundreds of millions of people out of poverty, will continue and dramatically change the world.

Shortly our region will be home to the biggest middle class the world has ever known, people who will live in cities and aspire to have access to the kinds of goods and services that we do. For Australia, what has long been viewed as the tyranny of distance, our remoteness from Europe in particular is now an advantage of adjacency. We are right where the action is and will continue to be.

The resources boom is the first downpayment for our nation in this century of change. Our iron ore is building the cities of Asia, particularly in China, and our coal and gas powering them. But Asia's rise could create a new tide of prosperity in all sections of our economy. Food, wine, tourism, international education, legal and financial services, high-quality customised manufactured goods.

Becoming the supplier of choice for any or all of these does not happen by chance. We have to be poised, be ready, be the best. Better schooled, better skilled. The better researchers, the better innovators. Our infrastructure has to be world class, with us particularly seizing the advantage that comes from moving information around more quickly with the NBN. We must have better functioning markets and a seamless national economy. We must be in on the trade deals. Vitally we must ready our economy for a lower-carbon future.

The media reaction to the launch of the White Paper was unexpectedly kind. For once, cynicism and short-termism were suspended in favour of a more analytical approach.

Fully conveying a vision to the Australian people takes time. Time I did not have. The White Paper did give us a better ability to join the dots for people. But what was both unexpected and gratifying was the reaction from the countries of our region. Leader after leader remarked how impressed they were with the White Paper, how it said to them that Australia finally understood and was articulating a vision of its future in the region.

Having delivered this work, I wanted us to go further, to deliver alongside our Asian Century plan, which ranged across domestic and foreign policy, our plan for national security. The rise of Asia brings economic growth and strategic change. A truism of life is change brings opportunity and risk. As we needed to modernise our economy, so we needed to modernise our approach to national security. We resolved to produce another Defence White Paper ahead of schedule and the first-ever National Security Strategy.

In part, the early Defence White Paper was deemed necessary because a number of key changes were about to happen. The war in Afghanistan was ending, as was our deployment to Timor-Leste and our defence mission in the Solomon Islands. There was also a pressing need to move beyond the Defence White Paper produced by Kevin Rudd, which had been unrealistic in a number of respects. The over-blown nature of the prose had drawn an adverse reaction from the Chinese and the budget rule laid out in the White Paper for defence expenditure was unrealistic and almost immediately breached.

While I was deputy prime minister, Kevin had asked me to chair a pivotal National Security Committee on his Defence White Paper, the meeting which would decide how much money would be reallocated within defence to invest in the newly identified priorities, along with other financing questions. When the meeting had to break into a series of side conversations in the corners of the cabinet room, it was obvious that the process was unravelling and the final product would suffer as a result.

As government tax revenues fell against Treasury's expectations, it was left to the government under my leadership to manage reductions in the defence budget. It was a painful process, which Stephen Smith led remarkably well. The White Paper produced under Stephen's oversight set more modest and realistic ambitions. It largely stayed with the force structure of the 2009 White Paper but it clarified our procurement decisions, including 12 new submarines and three air warfare destroyers.

Defence has historically faced massive cost, time and capability problems when undertaking major procurements. Our government did not find the complete solutions. But the methodical and careful approach we took to commencing the work on procurement of the next generation of submarines will stand the nation in good stead and should support manufacturing in South Australia.

The same can be said of the National Security Strategy, which I launched. It identified and responded to the main challenges and threats facing our national security – some age-old, some emerging, such as cyber-security. The strategy outlined that the national security challenges of our age are not ones that can be responded to by government in isolation but require deep partnerships with business and the community.

I am pleased to have developed through the Australia in the Asian Century White Paper, the Defence White Paper and the National Security Strategy such an integrated and explicit plan for our nation's future and to have improved the image of our nation in the eyes of leaders in our region.

At the same time as all this work was occurring, a future for defence had to be planned that addressed the glaring long-running problems with attitudes to women and to new recruits. As distressing as the Skype scandal was, involving a young female Australian Defence Force Academy cadet and the broadcast without her consent of images of her having sex, the scandal that spoke of a deeper seated cultural problem centred on the so-called Knights of the Jedi Council. These officers, some of whom had been in the Defence Force for more than ten years, were involved in circulating or receiving sexually explicit images of women alongside demeaning commentary. Six soldiers were stood down, and more than 100 investigated internally.

In addition to this sexism and misogyny, revelations of physical and emotional abuse, particularly of young recruits, led to the unhappy conclusion that in some parts of defence a bullying culture persisted. The response of our government was thorough and uncompromising. It involved multiple inquiries addressing both sexism and bullying. In it we were supported strongly by the defence chiefs. A particular highlight was the video made by the Chief of the Army, David Morrison, with his blunt message that those not up to treating others in a decent and non-discriminatory way should get out.

Even as we faced up to these problems, working with defence gave me the opportunity to meet some of the finest people I will ever have the opportunity to know. Angus Houston, a long-serving Chief of the Defence Force, is a man who always deeply impresses as capable, caring and honourable.

Meeting many of the emerging leaders, as well as large numbers of our fighting men and women, gives me every confidence for the future. The Australian Defence Force will grow even stronger because of them and our preparedness to face up to the need for change. It will be stronger too for the decision we took to have women able to enter combat roles.

There is never a day to waste in government. You cannot hit the pause button as you work on painting a grand vision. Rather the process is iterative. My values and sense of purpose always defined where I wanted to go. As I worked as prime minister, the fuller my knowledge became, the sharper my sense of what we needed to do as a nation, of how it all fitted together. So even as I patiently went about laying out our long-term plan for the nation by developing the interlocking strategic papers on Australia in the Asian Century, on defence and national security, as a government we were taking steps internationally and domestically in pursuit of that ever more sharply emerging vision of the future.

In all this work, I received wonderful support from many of my colleagues, but I was let down by others. After the 2010 election, I never had a Foreign Minister I could rely on.

Kevin used that role as a platform for leadership games. In the run-up to his failed February 2012 tilt against my leadership, he resigned from the ministry. After his comprehensive defeat in caucus, he had asked me if he could be reinstated as Minister for Foreign Affairs; he made it clear he was not asking to be considered for any other ministry role.

It was an impossible request. I knew I could not trust him, that he would continue the campaign of destabilisation and that he would use the status and resources of being a minister to do so. I also knew he would keep leaking from cabinet and I was doing everything in my power to get a cabinet that was secure. Had I acquiesced, good cabinet colleagues, who were sick of Kevin's treachery, would have thrown up their hands in horror.

Was this a misjudgement and would Kevin have laid down the cudgels if I had given him back the Foreign Ministry? Every piece of evidence about his conduct shouts the contrary. On this I made the right decision.

Then I made a wrong one. I decided to bring former New South Wales Premier Bob Carr to Canberra and into my cabinet.

A New South Wales Senate position was vacant because – in a move that shocked me – immediately after the leadership vote Mark Arbib told me he intended to resign both from the ministry and the Senate. Recently I had given Mark new and important responsibilities, including as Assistant Treasurer. He was talented and on his way up in politics.

Kevin had done everything he could to popularise with the media and the public the view that his loss of the leadership was as a result of the conduct of faceless men, shadowy factional leaders who had made caucus do their bidding. Mark was constantly marked as one of these faceless men.

Mark explained that as New South Wales General Secretary, he had often met with state Labor ministers who had become political liabilities. Always, he had thought to himself, *Why can't you just see you're causing a problem and get out?* With tears in his eyes, he told me, 'Now I'm that guy and I'm going to do the right thing.' I argued with him because I thought he had a big contribution to make and his sacrifice would not clear out the spectre of the faceless men. While we disagreed on that, I could not argue with the fact that his frequent absences from his very young family were tearing at his heart.

Although saddened, I resolved to use the unexpected vacancy to strengthen the government's firepower and credibility and offered the vacant Senate spot to Bob Carr. In our telephone discussions, all of which became far too public, it emerged that Bob would only come to Canberra for the Foreign Ministry. I was prepared to appoint him, despite Stephen Smith's understandable disappointment.

Stephen had been a good Foreign Minister and would have been my preference for that position after the 2010 election but during the campaign Kevin had extorted his appointment. With dignity, Stephen accepted being knocked out of the Foreign Ministry for all these wrong reasons and did so again when I decided to appoint Bob.

When I walked Bob into the press conference room to announce his appointment on 2 March 2012, there was an audible gasp of shock from the press gallery. While my consideration of Bob for the position had got out, the journalists had become convinced that Bob was not going to come to Canberra. Presenting him publicly as a new ministerial recruit against these expectations had some wow factor.

Canberra is a small place and Bob is a highly recognisable figure. Getting him to the press conference without him being seen had required a stealthy operation, planned and executed by my chief of staff, Ben Hubbard. It included driving Bob to Canberra and smuggling him in the back door of the Realm Hotel in Canberra, then picking him up in the morning and sneaking him into Parliament House. The operation to get Bob to the press conference unseen worked like a charm, but unfortunately the promise I saw in Bob's appointment never materialised.

Above all, he found the transition from political retirement back into a huge job a hard one. The workload overwhelmed him. He remarked to me that he had not understood quite how retired he had been. As a result, he was beyond fully stretched doing the Foreign Ministry work and never made a broader contribution to the government.

The other negative was Bob's struggle with the focused discipline required for Foreign Ministry work. It is one thing to chat knowledge-ably and engagingly about world affairs at a dinner party. It is quite another to methodically pursue Australia's interests in carefully cali-brated diplomatic exchanges all around the world.

At the time of his appointment as Foreign Minister, Bob was a voluble critic of Kevin.

When I declined to give him the Foreign Ministry, Kevin asked me to structure a role for him so he would be able to continue some work in the area of foreign affairs. As we were in the middle of our campaign to be elected to the UN Security Council, I saw some merit in continu-ity. I thought this could have the benefits of including Kevin without the risks of him using a ministerial role or the resources that came with it in pursuit of a leadership campaign.

I had various discussions with Kevin about a role. He engaged in a typical over-reach and effectively wanted free range across every aspect of foreign affairs. I tried to structure a workable proposition that would give Kevin some status but not have him supplant the minister or demand huge resources from the Department of Foreign Affairs and Trade.

Ironically, given that Bob Carr became a supporter of Kevin, Bob dealt with all of these suggestions in a prickly and obstructive way. The whole thing simply became unworkable.

While these internal matters were vexed, my direct engagement in the world of diplomacy was not. I set some clear goals for myself and pursued them. A fundamental goal was working to improve our key relationships. I particularly wanted to show that you could improve

Australia's relationships with the USA and China at the same time. That this was not a zero sum game. For Australia in the Asian Century, with our huge economic exposure to China, with China's strengthening role in reshaping our region and our world, this seemed to me pivotal. It was the right call.

CHINA

In building a better relationship with China, I was mindful that community attitudes are layered and contradictory. All in the same moment, Australians can be welcoming of China's current contribution to our economic growth, fearful of Chinese investment, anxious about China's future military might and hopeful that a bright economic future for them can mean a bright economic future for us. Plenty of politics can and does get played in the mire of these conflicting thoughts, particularly around foreign investment.

On my first visit to China, in April 2011, I was received with full pomp and ceremony. But even the most ceremonial of welcomes could not disguise the difficult context I was working in. Our relationship with China was not in good repair. It had become coloured by events both beyond and within our nation's control. Mining executive Stern Hu had been sentenced to ten years in jail on 29 March 2010, heightening sensitivities in some parts of the Australian community about the perceived risks of doing business in China. Tension between China and Japan had continued to rise over disputed islands in the East China Sea, and China's conduct in the South China Sea had become a focal point for uncertainty over strategic control and influence in the region.

When China emerged from the GFC without a significant economic downturn, its robust performance triggered a fresh wave of commentary about the decline of America's geopolitical influence. Certainly China was enjoying its newfound power. At the G20 meeting in South Korea, China's President Hu dug his toes in over some text in the communique President Obama needed politically on currency issues. I watched Chancellor Angela Merkel of Germany and Prime Minister David Cameron of the United Kingdom execute a pincer movement, then he conceded.

On Australia's side of the ledger, tensions had risen when our government had eschewed the involvement of the Chinese company Huawei in building the NBN. We also risked Chinese ire by not stopping a fierce critic of China's approach to human rights, a leader of the Uyghur ethnic group, from visiting Australia.

China was also smarting about the price hikes they had experienced in coal and iron ore sourced from Australia. Businesses such as BHP-Billiton had seized the opportunity when demand spiked and new sources of supply had not yet become available. Inevitably the market would correct and supply would expand. While Chinese customers understood this underlying dynamic, there was a sense that Australia's market advantage had been pushed savagely in the short term to the detriment of longer-term relationships.

Then there were some particular problems that had been caused by Kevin. Understandably Kevin was proud of his mastery of Mandarin and his expertise on China. On his ascension to the prime ministership, no doubt many in China's diplomatic and foreign policy community would have expected new warmth to be injected into the relationship. Instead Kevin hit an uneven stride, sometimes over-familiar, sometimes too critical, the most spectacular example of which was his expletive-laden rant post the Copenhagen climate change conference. My aim was to relegate all this to the past.

In my meetings with President Hu and Premier Wen, I was left in no doubt that they had a list of concerns about Australia's conduct. I needed to smooth over the old irritations, stand my ground on important issues and raise hard issues like human rights and Australian consular cases.

My April 2011 visit cleared the air. I also sowed a seed for the future about improving the established meeting pattern between our two countries' leaders so that focusing China's attention on Australia was no longer a question of grace and favour but a standing part of the diplomatic calendar. On this matter, I told the Chinese I would come back with a proposal.

I also judged that the best step forward we could take on our commercial ties was enabling direct trading of our currencies. No more middle step. Australian dollars direct into the Chinese currency and back again.

Returning from China, I faced three considerable hurdles in taking the next steps in the relationship.

The first of these was settling within the government what proposal to put to the Chinese about the structure of the diplomatic architecture. It was vitally important to our nation. Locking in leader-level dialogue and structured foreign, strategic and economic dialogues would guarantee Australia privileged access at a time of intense competition for the attention of Chinese leadership. Regular meetings would provide scope for the development of a coherent work program, focusing the Chinese bureaucracy. They would enable us to manage the periodic inevitable differences.

Any proposal had to include leaders' meetings but also ministerial meetings of significance. Given the trade significance of the relationship with China, ongoing economic dialogue was another key aim.

Kevin had sought to combine economic dialogue with strategic dialogue in one structure. This would have meant him personally being included and viewed as the senior ministerial player. By contrast, Wayne pushed to separate the two into different meetings; this would limit Kevin's role to the strategic dialogue. This was a debate about, but also beyond, the question of personalities. Everyone understood that we were trying to develop a structure that would endure well beyond our time in politics.

There was a policy question to be debated about how to properly position the economic relationship. Australia had never been in a position before where our major trading partner is neither an ally nor a democracy. It posed new challenges and required us to ask new questions. We resolved to seek the two-track structure Wayne advocated.

The second challenge, on my return home, was to ignore the ridiculous crisis of confidence about the relationship with China that was playing itself out in academic circles, the media and the business community. The latter two groups had worked themselves into a self-reinforcing circular dialogue about how bad the relationship with China was. 'It is bad,' a business community leader would say. 'It is bad,' the headlines would blare. 'Do you know how bad it is?' says the next business community leader. 'Just look at today's headlines.' Of course, the Opposition was deriving political profit: some days dog-whistling about Chinese investments in Australia, other days complaining our relationship was not close enough.

All this circular dialogue contained precious little unpacking of the things a mature democracy like ours must do, like make appropriate national security decisions about providers of national broadband infrastructure, or of the subtle but meaningful moves the government and I were making to improve the relationship. Once again, behind the wall of sound, patient work was underway.

My third challenge was to manage the improvement of the relationship with China while at the same time seeking to strengthen our alliance with the USA.

I resolved to time my next China visit for shortly after the election and commencement of the new Chinese leadership. My goals for that trip were to achieve the new architecture and direct currency trading. Day by day, we laboured to bring that about. To ensure that China felt our presence and enthusiasm for closer ties, in the 12 months prior to my visit, 11 ministers went there.[2]

In the meantime, at multilateral meetings, I sought to have personal interactions with President Hu and Premier Wen, to keep Australia and me visible to them. I talked to the Premier about his children. I joked with President Hu about Australian lingo and, to the amazement of other leaders and diplomats who witnessed it, as a joke he produced an Aussie 'G'day'. A number remarked that they had never seen him laugh. Of course, relationships between countries are shaped by so much more than the chemistry or lack of it between leaders. But being warm and seeking to develop a human relationship came easily to me and I believe that in a small way it helped.

After the farce of the aborted leadership challenge against me in March 2013, I travelled immediately to the federal electorate of Richmond, held by Labor's Justine Elliott, in the north of New South Wales. This gave me an opportunity to visit an electorate I had not been to in some time and to personally view two projects funded by the government – a new road and a community centre. It also gave me the opportunity to drop in on a school, unannounced, just for fun.

While in this beautiful region, I also planned to attend the wedding of Wayne Swan's former chief of staff, Jim Chalmers, to my press secretary, Laura Anderson. Although I was looking forward to spending time with friends, after the rollercoaster of the week that had been, I was in a fog of exhaustion. Because the failed conspirators had resigned, I needed to front up to another reshuffle of my ministry.

On Friday 22 March, the evening before the wedding, from my hotel room I spoke to the newly appointed Premier Li of China. My staffer, Caterina, had to dial in and hold the phone for an hour prior to the Premier coming on the line. At the click at the end of the call, tiredness gave way to a sense of achievement: I was on track to announce that Australia was now one of the few nations on Earth with regular meetings with China.

On 5 April, I arrived in China for the prestigious Boao Forum. When I met President Xi at the forum, it was clear that China was deliberately turning a page in the relationship. There was no reference to any earlier concerns. The feel was now fully positive.

My next destination was Shanghai, where I linked up with Gail Kelly from Westpac and Mike Smith from ANZ to announce the commencement of direct trading of the Chinese renminbi (RMB) and the Australian dollar. To make it from Boao, in the southernmost province of China, to Shanghai in time for a business breakfast had meant a brutally shortened sleep for me and everyone travelling with me; Tim had come too. But to commence a market that on its first day traded 250 million RMB, or just under A$40 million, in value was worth it. Australian businesses are now converting around $30 billion a year directly. No double handling, no double fees.

The same day we flew to Beijing for a business dinner. The following day, I visited a school and then took part in the formal dialogue with Premier Li Keqiang, which was characterised by personal warmth from the Premier. I emerged from that meeting with a written agreement for annual leaders' meetings between Australia and China. Such a relationship is enjoyed by only Russia, Germany, Britain and the European Union.

In the face of this achievement, media reaction was enthusiastic. *The Australian* caught the general sentiment, reporting:

Julia Gillard has scored a foreign policy coup, signing a historic pact with China for direct annual meetings with Premier Li Keqiang and pledges for formal cooperation on climate change, international aid and currency trading.

Capping a five-day visit to China by Australia's most senior political delegation, the deal represents one of the most significant breakthroughs in the Australia–China relationship since Gough Whitlam recognised the communist state more than 40 years ago.

The Prime Minister's foreign policy success clinches a key priority of the government's Asian Century agenda.

It means the nation now has strategic relationships with the emerging powerhouse economies of China and India.[3]

We had secured agreement to hold annual foreign and strategic dialogue between foreign ministers and an annual economic dialogue between the Australian Treasurer and Trade Minister and the chair of China's powerful National Development and Reform Commission, as well as the leaders' meetings.

Being clear about my purpose and exercising patience and perseverance had paid off.

INDONESIA

Like so many Australians, I have been to Bali too. In fact, before I became prime minister, my sister and I had been twice; accompanied on the first visit by Alison's daughter Jenna and son Tom and on the second visit by Tom and his mate Bob.

The second time we visited, in 2002, we left Bali on a Thursday night and arrived home Friday morning. It was that Saturday night that the first Bali bombing happened. Given we were travelling with teenage boys, my sister and I would never have been in a nightclub. But still, it was an eerie feeling, knowing you had just been on the very streets that were targeted.

Ten years later, I returned to Bali for a commemoration of all that we lost in that bombing. As a government, we decided to help with travel and associated costs for the bombing's victims, bereaved families and those injured, to make sure they could participate in this event. I extended a personal invitation to former Prime Minister Howard to attend, given his role at the time.

The outdoor ceremony was a moving one but for me the true emotional power of the journey was in the discussions I had with those who had lived through the bombing, the opportunity it gave me to see the horror through their eyes.

A woman told me how just before the bomb went off she had been dancing to the song 'Murder on the Dance Floor' but decided to sit out the next song, which she did not like. That decision moved her out of immediate range of the blast and probably saved her life.

I talked to a man who was carried by local people on a garbage truck to the hospital for treatment. When I went to the hospital, I saw the difference Australian investment in it had made. It was one way we said thank you for the help rendered to our people at the time of the bombing.

Some survivors described to me the sheer guts it takes to recover from a bad burn. How bad the pain is, how slow the healing, the ongoing fragility of the scar tissue.

There was story after story of the kindness and concern of the local Balinese people.

I met the Governor, who had been the lead police investigator at the time, and heard from him and the police travelling with us about the diligence and success of the police response.

It was a visit that not only touched my heart but brought home to me the depths of our relationship with Indonesia and the intricacies of our coexistence. In Australia, these things are little understood and appreciated. Australian media reports about Indonesia focus on people-smuggling or Australians in trouble.

What gets lost is any sense of the miracle of having as our neighbour a country that is both home to the largest Muslim population in the world and a flourishing democracy.

As a new backbencher in parliament, I attended the first free and fair elections in Indonesia as an election monitor on 7 June 1999. I was sent to West Timor and toured villages where everyone came out and sat on the ground at the polling place for the whole day and night. First they waited patiently for their name to be called and then they went and cast their vote by taking their ballot paper and putting a hole through the logo of the political party they wanted to vote for. Second they waited after the ballot closed as every ballot paper was taken individually from the ballot box and shown to them and counted.

Democracy was viewed as a wonder; it is, and needs to be supported. Yet our endeavours to support democratic values by countering tendencies towards Islamic radicalism were met with cynicism. The decision I announced during my first official visit to Indonesia in November 2010 to provide $500 million to expand up to 2000 schools and to support 1500 Islamic schools to become properly accredited was both derided by our shock jocks and earmarked to be cut by the Opposition.

The depth and success of our counter-terrorism cooperation and our growing military cooperation, as evidenced in September 2012 by our entering into an Australia–Indonesia Defence Cooperation Agreement, was obscured by the telescoping down of our domestic political debate to whether or not boats could be turned back.

Similarly the extraordinary development of the Indonesia, Australia, Timor-Leste trilateral discussions, the first of which I attended on 9 November 2012, was woefully under-appreciated. In 1999, the country was engulfed in violence and Australia's relationship with Indonesia became extremely tense. The Timorese people had voted in a referendum for independence from Indonesia, and Australia had deployed thousands of troops to it, leading the international peace-keeping force. At that time it would have seemed impossible that just over ten years later an Indonesian President and the prime ministers of Australia and Timor-Leste would be sitting together for amicable discussions. Yet this is precisely what has been achieved.

Our relationship is mature enough to tolerate difficulties and differences. Friction between our two nations did result when we decided on 7 June 2011 to suspend live animal exports after the revelation of the most egregious acts of cruelty during the slaughter of Australian-sourced cattle in Indonesia. Even though the new system – with the facility to track and trace where animals were slaughtered and verify appropriate standards were being complied with – was announced as quickly as 6 July 2011, this was a hard diplomatic issue to manage. I understood the huge disruption for the industry arising from the suspension and was always prepared to speak directly with industry leaders. As trade resumed, there was a conflation of residual issues from the suspension with the effects of the politics in Indonesia that swirl around the stated but unrealistic goal of self-sufficiency in foodstuffs like meat. However, if as a government we had failed to act, it is inevitable, in my view, that more and more instances of animal cruelty would have occurred and been revealed. The intensity of community outrage generated in Australia would have led to the whole live animal export industry being shut down for good. It was best to act swiftly and put the industry on a sustainable footing.

Even with an issue such as this in play, I was confident the depth and breadth of our relationship with Indonesia, the professionalism of our diplomats like Ambassador Greg Moriarty and my growing personal connection with President Susilo Bambang Yudhoyono would enable us to manage it.

I had met President Yudhoyono when he addressed the Australian Parliament in April 2010. My first bilateral meeting with him as prime minister was in Indonesia in November 2010. The economic relationship between our two countries is much thinner than it should be, considering our proximity and Indonesia's rising wealth. Out of our discussions, negotiations commenced on the proposal for the Indonesia–Australia Comprehensive Economic Partnership agreement. It was also pleasing that during my period of prime ministership, Indonesia became party to the ASEAN–Australia–New Zealand Free Trade Agreement and we engaged in strategic dialogue between our respective foreign affairs and defence ministers.

I saw President Yudhoyono frequently in formal and informal settings. One of the great benefits of multilateral meetings is the time spent in the leaders' lounge, where informal discussions that build a sense of connection can occur.

The relationship between our nations appeared to return to a more positive track when he and I met in Darwin in July 2012 for the annual Australia–Indonesia leaders' meeting. According to a senior person from our foreign affairs department, the two of us had the longest one-on-one discussion ever conducted by an Indonesian president and Australian prime minister. It was a frank, practical discussion; we were wholly mindful of each other's political needs and constraints.

The relationship between our two countries grew and deepened. From experience, I know it is a long journey between agreeing something as leaders and seeing it implemented in Indonesia. Progress with prisoner transfers that may assist Australians incarcerated in Indonesia proved slow.

I would have liked additional practical assistance in dealing with people-smuggling. A quicker reaction on visa-free arrival for Iranians into Indonesia, which facilitated the travel of many who were intent on seeking passage to Australia. A greater preparedness to respond and take responsibility for those rescued in Indonesia's search and rescue zone. It also took time to criminalise people-smuggling in Indonesia. But I realised that what looms as a major issue for us looms less large in a nation still developing, still lifting people out of poverty.

Another thing I came to appreciate was the reach of President Yudhoyono's contribution to regional and global dynamics. President Yudhoyono has a wealth of experience in the affairs of our region. He has been vitally important to the dynamics of our region as the countries of the ASEAN determine their strategic posture as China rises. Whenever I sought his advice, I found him to be both wise and patient.

At his request, I attended his Bali Democracy Forum in early November 2012, though it potentially opened me up to domestic ridicule because of the attendance of President Ahmadinejad of Iran. I supported President Yudhoyono's long-term strategic goal of promoting democratic practice and his dedication in reaching out to the Muslim world to highlight Indonesia's blend of democracy and plurality. President Yudhoyono in turn understood my decision to agree to have US marines train in the Northern Territory. He assisted with managing the regional reaction.

For our nation, in our contemporary political discourse, the popular complacency and narrow view about Indonesia must give way to a perspective that is thoughtful and broad. Our national interest demands it.

JAPAN

Australia's relationship with Japan should be a continuing cause of optimism for us and for the world. It is a model of how old enmity can give way entirely to contemporary friendship. Japan is our second biggest trading partner, a key investor in our country. We are both allies of the United States; in recent years we have engaged in joint and trilateral exercises. Our soldiers and peacekeepers have served together, our aid programs are complementary and we share a strategic outlook on our region and the world. Unsurprisingly, given Japan's history, we have worked together strongly on nuclear nonproliferation.

The only real irritant in the relationship is Japanese whaling, where proceedings appropriately instigated by the Rudd Government in the International Court of Justice won through.

I first visited Japan to attend APEC in November 2010. But the visit that left an imprint on my heart occurred in the aftermath of the earthquake and tsunami that devastated Japan on 11 March 2011. As the shocking news of Japan's earthquake, tsunami and nuclear crisis first came through, I called together our National Security Committee. We needed to understand what we could do to help and whether the many thousands of Australians in Japan were safe. Our embassy was led by a seasoned and talented Ambassador, Murray McLean. He and his team worked through as Tokyo continued to be shaken by aftershocks and a number bravely ventured into the Fukushima region to check Australians were all right.

At Canberra meetings, we frequently patched Murray through by video link so we could hear his direct reports. During one of these link-ups, Murray's image started to shake. Without saying a word, he reached down, picked up a hard hat, put it on and continued the meeting. Even with a major aftershock in progress, he was not leaving.

We also frequently heard from the head of the Australian Radiation Protection and Nuclear Safety Agency, Dr Carl-Magnus Larsson. For the first few days he gave reports aimed at debunking the rising tide of hysteria in the media about the problems at Fukushima. However, on the third or fourth day, in words that chilled, he said that in his view the problem was no longer under control. Like the rest of the world, we watched and worried as the situation was slowly stabilised.

Considering the scale of everything that happened in Japan, it is remarkable no Australians were killed. But thousands of Japanese people were dead, grieving or homeless. We authorised extensive support to Japan, including a 72-person urban search and rescue team; a team of defence operations-response officers; the use of C17 aircraft in relief operations; and a donation of $10 million to the Australian Red Cross Japan and the Pacific Disaster Appeal. Upon their return, members of the search and rescue team told of working in snow and ice, not finding anyone to rescue because everyone was dead.

As the world's media talked up the radiation risks of being in Japan, I had to make a decision about whether or not to proceed with my planned visit, which would start a tour of North Asia that included Korea and China. Would my visit be an unwelcome distraction from relief efforts? Inquiries were made and the message sent was that the Japanese Government would be delighted to receive me. At this stage, while the humanitarian efforts were still intense, the Japanese Government was trying to prove to the world that Japan was safe and still open for business.

So I decided to go. On 20 April, Tim and I arrived in Japan, along with the usual travelling party of officials and members of my staff. I was the first foreign leader to make a substantive visit after the disaster.

The night we arrived, Tokyo was hit by a major aftershock. Our hotel room felt like it was being lifted up and down by an enormous ocean swell. No damage was done but it gave all of us a small taste of the ever-present sense of continuing disaster afflicting the people of Japan.

A goodwill dinner had been arranged in honour of my visit and in order to bring people together to share reflections on what they had lived through. Kylie Minogue was visiting Japan on her worldwide concert tour and agreed to attend and light a candle of remembrance with me. I had not met Kylie before but enjoyed the opportunity to share dinner with her. She explained to me how Japan had been on her tour itinerary and, while conscious of the worldwide publicity about nuclear risks, she decided that the planned concerts should still go ahead.

Kylie gave her staff the option of coming with her or simply missing Japan and going to the next destination. Consequently her Japanese show was scaled down so it was still possible to stage it with the crew available to her.

For someone under no diplomatic obligations, Kylie had taken an impressive approach. It showed both sensitivity to the Japanese people – to not be treated like pariahs in a time of need – and considerable courage.

My visit to Tokyo included my official meeting and dinner with the then Japanese prime minister, Mr Kan. The missing piece in our otherwise close relationship was a free trade agreement granting Australia good market access for our agricultural produce. I pressed for it.

After the formal meeting, we moved to a tea-house in the prime minister's compound. Seated on the ground, we shared a traditional Japanese meal of many courses, with wines whose ages were matched to significant dates in my life, including a red wine from my year of birth, 1961. It was a touching gesture; so much trouble had been taken and at such a difficult time.

Towards the end of the many courses, Prime Minister Kan announced to our small party that all the food served that night had been sourced from the Fukushima area to prove that it was safe. As he spoke, I was holding a morsel of food between my chopsticks, literally in midair. I could feel eyes upon me. I smiled and ate. The other Australians present – diplomats and staff – followed my lead. We were certainly doing our bit for Australia–Japan relations.

But we wanted to truly grasp the scale of the disaster. Consequently we travelled to Minamisanriku, the town that had most felt the destructive force of the tsunami. Our RAAF plane took off amid concerns about fog at our destination. Throughout the flight, the weather updates were quite depressing and the odds of being able to land uncertain. I felt a keen sense of not wanting to let down those who were there to meet us but the decision about the safety of the plane had to be in the hands of the pilots.

In a demonstration of true flying skill, the pilots did get us on the ground. I counted less than five seconds between breaking out of

My parents, John and Moira Gillard.

My sister, Alison, and me, in Wales.

A family portrait taken in our home in Barry, Wales.

In my Unley High School uniform, 1975.

In my student politics days in the early 1980s.

My father, on the morning I became prime minister, receiving and entertaining the media in his Adelaide home. (James Elsby/Newspix)

At the welcome to country ceremony for the opening of the 43rd parliament on 28 September 2010. My parents look on proudly. (Getty images)

My great-nephew Ethan, already on his way to a great education!

Jenna Malone, my niece, at her wedding to Damien Raidis.

My nephew, Tom Malone, and his partner, Laura Teakle.

My sister, Alison Gillard, and her grandson, my beloved great-nephew, Ethan Raidis.

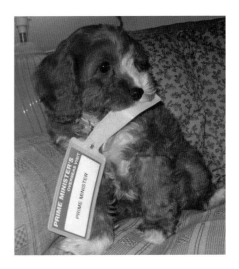

My 50th birthday present, Reuben, looking after my prime ministerial luggage tags.

Tim and me at the wedding of Robyn McLeod to Barry Smith.

Me and Tim at the turning on of the lights in Geelong. (John Tass-Parker)

11 November 1998, my maiden speech as the Member for Lalor, to the House of Representatives. (David Foote – AUSPICS/DPS)

The notorious 'fruit-bowl' photograph, taken at my home in Altona. (Ken Irwin/Fairfax Syndication)

At the Cabinet table after winning government, 29 November 2007. (Kym Smith/Newspix)

The Greens and Labor seal the deal, 1 September 2010. (Ray Strange/Newspix)

Wayne Swan and me meeting Bob Katter, Rob Oakeshott and Tony Windsor, in Canberra, 25 August 2010. (AAP Image/Andrew Taylor)

(L to R) Julie Collins, Kate Ellis, Nicola Roxon, me, Quentin Bryce, Jenny Macklin and Tanya Plibersek after the swearing in at Kirribilli, 14 December 2011. (Howard Moffat – AUSPIC/ DPS)

Laying a wreath in honour of Australian Korean war veterans with Christine Lagarde, Stephen Harper and David Cameron for Remembrance Day at the War Memorial of Korea during the G20, November 2010. (David Foote – AUSPIC/DPS)

Labor caucus, March 2011. (David Foote – AUSPIC/DPS)

Greeting dear friend and honoured Labor man Bob Hawke at the launch of the Labor election campaign, Brisbane, 16 August 2010. (David Foote – AUSPIC/DPS)

With Trade Minister Craig Emerson at APEC in Hawaii, November 2011. (Ray Strange/Newspix)

Inspecting flood damage in Queensland with Wayne Swan. (John Tass-Parker)

At The Lodge with Tony Burke, signing an environmental agreement. (John Tass-Parker)

Being briefed by advisers in my office in Parliament House. (John Tass-Parker)

Talking constitutional recognition with Patrick Dodson, Mark Leibler and Jenny Macklin. (John Tass-Parker)

In Minamisanriku, Japan, surveying the havoc the tsunami had wrought, April 2011. (AFP/ Newspix)

With Kim Beazley, Australian Ambassador to the United States of America, Washington DC, March 2011. (David Foote – AUSPIC/ DPS)

Hand-balling a Sherrin in the Oval Office at the White House with President Obama, March 2011. (David Foote – AUSPICS/DPS)

Visiting a school in Washington DC with President Obama, March 2011. (David Foote – AUSPICS/DPS)

At the State Department with Secretary of State Hillary Clinton. (David Foote – AUSPICS/DPS)

At an event to mark International Women's Day with Secretary of State Hillary Clinton and First Lady Michelle Obama. (David Foote – AUSPICS/DPS)

I was honoured to deliver a speech to a joint session of the US Congress, 10 March 2011. (David Foote – AUSPICS/DPS)

A joint press conference during the visit of New Zealand Prime Minister John Key to Australia, 19 June 2011. (Howard Moffat – AUSPIC/DPS)

In Afghanistan with Australian troops. (Alex Ellinghausen/Fairfax Syndication)

Meeting with the crew of HMAS *Anzac* while berthed at Dubai, United Arab Emirates, 13 October 2012. (David Foote – AUSPICS/DPS)

the dense fog and being wheels down on the tarmac. You know you have made a landing that is right on the edge of what is possible when you walk up to congratulate the pilots and they are still high-fiving each other.

In dank cold, we made our way by bus to what was left of the township of Minamisanriku. The mayor was there to greet us. As rain fell, accompanied by a translator, he took us through the remnants of his town. Everywhere buildings had been smashed to smithereens. One surviving four-storey building had a boat perched on it. Along with some others, the mayor had survived by running to the top of a three-storey building and clinging to the radio antenna as the water struck. It was actually the town's emergency management centre and had a steel frame.

Despite the language barrier, I could feel the depths of this man's distress and visualise the horror that had taken place here. I was chilled, wet and mesmerised. This was strongly evident in the photo taken, which ran in the next day's papers. Unbelievably the reaction it sparked was not one of empathy for the Japanese people but criticism of my appearance from racing identity Gai Waterhouse.

'She desperately needs a make-over. It wasn't the carnage behind that gave me the horrors, but the woman standing in front of it,' Gai expounded.[4]

Horror is in the eye of the beholder, I guess. The horror of almost 10,000 lives lost where I was standing haunts me still.

I will never forget the feeling I had standing there nor the incredible stoicism I saw in the Japanese people when I visited a nearby evacuation centre. As I gave out koala and kangaroo toys to the children, I was rewarded with smiles and joy. That something so small could light up their faces in such grim circumstances gladdened and broke your heart all at the same time.

Leaving Japan, I knew we were doing all we could as a nation to help a dear friend in a time of extreme need but that recovery would be slow and painful. Many wounds, both physical and psychological, would never heal. Memories, including my own, would never fade.

INDIA

My first visit to India was in late August 2009; I was deputy prime minister. For weeks Australia had been reported as a vicious racist country, following a series of ugly incidents involving Indian students. One – a bashing at Werribee train station – had occurred in my own electorate.

I confronted some of the biggest and most aggressive press packs I had ever seen. Their aggression was directed both towards me and each other. Later I discovered many Indian photographers are only paid if their shot is used. In their desperation to get the photo, they knock each other over and out of the way.

The enigmatic Indian prime minister, Dr Singh, was an elderly gentleman, increasingly in poor health, who exuded an air of calm and spirituality rather than political focus. He had done Australia a considerable favour by not seeking to inflame the international students crisis for domestic political advantage.

I was able to assure him that, even prior to the attacks, I had been working through a process of remedying the lack of regulation of international education, which had allowed rogue operators to flourish. I worked with states on student welfare approaches and we have not seen the same kind of violence since.

India is both a fascinating and frustrating country. There are many ties that bind us to it, the world's largest democracy. History, language, culture, cricket all play a part, as does the rapidly growing Indian community in Australia.

But India's challenges are many. A sclerotic public service, an economy desperately in need of reform, an education system that lacks reach and quality, millions still living in poverty and, as too many tragic recent events have shown, some underlying attitudes to women of critical concern.

Kevin Rudd had succeeded in upgrading our diplomatic relationship to that of a strategic partnership in November 2009. Like many initiatives with India, the declaration was one thing, generating momentum to do it was going to be quite another.

On becoming prime minister, I set myself a goal to improve this relationship and that meant clearing away the big stumbling block of our refusal to export uranium to India.

Labor's policy of not exporting uranium had come about for good reasons. As a political party dedicated to nonproliferation, we had a policy position that we would not export uranium to countries that were not signatories to the Treaty on the Non-Proliferation of Nuclear Weapons (NPT). India was not a signatory. The treaty recognises only five nations as nuclear-weapon states: the United States, Russia, the United Kingdom, France and China. While not a member of this named group, India has nuclear weapons. An ever-watchful, wary eye is kept on Pakistan, which has been in the business of testing and stock-piling nuclear weapons since the 1970s.

For a long time, the rest of the world used signatory of the NPT as the lens through which to look at questions of uranium supply. But in 2006 the United States agreed to supply India with civil nuclear technology. Even more decisively, in 2008 the Nuclear Suppliers Group (NSG) smoothed the way for India to receive uranium supplies, despite it not being a signatory to the NPT.

Australia had ended up in the irrational position where we had supported the NSG waiver but we would not supply uranium. In India, Australia's decision was of no immediate practical effect. It could source all the uranium it needed for energy generation elsewhere. Rather it had become a question of status and face. Australia's attitude was received as an insult.

When I first met India's prime minister, Dr Singh, as his full counterpart in October 2010, I assured him I would resolve this problem. It took me from then until the conclusion of the debate at Labor's national conference in late 2012 to do so.

When Kevin was prime minister, Labor's national conference was a Mogadoned affair. No controversial issues like uranium sales to India could be on the agenda. I decided to have a different conference. To view debate as a strength. The debate on India and uranium sales was full of passion. Cabinet ministers took different views. In a development that surprised me, Stephen Conroy gave one of the most heartfelt speeches in opposition to change. He spoke of his family in the United

Kingdom and of a relative who worked in a nuclear reactor who was required to cover up an incident. His views on uranium and its evils had been fixed and immutable since that day. The vote to change Labor's platform and allow uranium sales to India was won 206 to 185.

I personally conveyed the news by telephone to India's Prime Minister. He thanked me for my courage and I knew that a significant step forward had been taken in a strategically important relationship for us.

On my next trip to India I encountered open doors and warm welcomes. Prime Minister Singh applauded my attention to the relationship, saying it had ushered in 'a new chapter in India–Australia relations'.[5] We also agreed to regular leaders' meetings.

KOREA

During my tenure as prime minister, the Republic of Korea was host to vital multilateral meetings, including the G20 and the Nuclear Security Summit. Consequently I visited democratic South Korea on three occasions. Initially my reception by President Lee Myung-Bak was a cool one. He had formed a special bond with Kevin Rudd and resented his absence. Of course, diplomatic politeness prevented that sentiment being put into words but his demeanour said it all. In my efforts to turn things around, I made a point of seeking out President Lee at multilateral meetings and our relationship went from cold to decidedly warm: the President went from avoiding eye contact to holding my hand.

Australia's relationship with Korea is growing warmer too. It is as if we have gradually become conscious of our similarities as middle powers and have been drawn to do more work together.

Our national bond goes back to the Korean war. With Australian veterans, I went to Korea to commemorate the 60th anniversary of the Battle of Kapyong. It is a story of Australian heroism, holding out against the odds, and is insufficiently remembered here in Australia.

Some of the veterans accompanying me had become fascinated by Korea and travelled there many times since the war. Others were making their first visit since marching out of the battlefield. For them to return and see Seoul, one of the great cities of the world, in a nation that was once home to so much blood-soaked ground, was life-affirming.

Our defence partnership has been strengthened in recent years and, like our friends in South Korea, we are alert to the dangers of North Korea's periodic acts of aggression. For Australia, the risk posed by North Korea is one of our most pressing and entrenched security challenges. The opacity of its regime combined with its nuclear weapons program will test us in the years ahead.

Our highly experienced ambassador, Sam Gerovich, told me a story that captures so much about the cruelty and erraticism the people of North Korea must endure. While a guest of North Korea, he visited a state-run home where four sets of triplets lived. These children were not orphaned. Rather, Kim Jong-Il, the father of the current leader, had deemed that triplets were special and should be taken by the state. Sam found the children starving and gently cajoled these most ill-treated and apprehensive kids to take chocolate from him. A rare moment of pleasure in miserable lives.

It is easy to lose a sense of how close North Korea is to Seoul: the demilitarised zone (DMZ) is less than 70 kilometres away. As a visiting dignitary, I was able to enter one of the rooms at the DMZ that sits right on the border. These rooms are used for periodic meetings between the military of the North and South to try and deal with daily tensions and defuse misunderstanding. While I sat there, the guards from North Korea peered in. A photographer captured an image of me staring defiantly at a North Korean soldier who aggressively returns my gaze.

Despite the eventual warmth of my friendship with President Lee, I was not able to conclude our free trade agreement with South Korea. Our agreement was parked behind the US–Korea Free Trade Agreement, which became bogged down in Korean domestic politics, particularly over a clause that enabled foreign companies to have special rights to bring disputes about domestic government policies.

Having been prepared to stare down internal dissent about this Investor State Dispute Settlement clause, President Lee could not agree to a deal with us without such a clause being in our agreement. As a matter of policy, we opposed such clauses, worrying about the implications they could have for challenges to important domestic policies like our drug pricing arrangements through the Pharmaceutical Benefits Scheme or the plain packaging of cigarettes.

When I saw President Lee for the last time, I was not only fondly farewelled by him but by his interpreter, Jonny Kim, as well. I had spent time chatting with Jonny and, at official dinners in Korea and elsewhere, I had caused smiles and laughter by smuggling food off the official table back to the interpreters, who were sitting behind on call.

Perhaps one of the reasons I broke through in this relationship was because I showed respect and goodwill to the President's people, not just the President himself.

In every area of policy, no matter how intellectually hard or easy, it is people that matter.

MALAYSIA

From the moment I met Prime Minister Najib, he received me with an easy cordiality. During my prime ministership he showed a remarkable preparedness to maintain a good relationship with Australia even while Australia appeared to be doing its best to snub Malaysia.

Our Minister for Immigration and Citizenship, Chris Bowen, working with his Malaysian counterpart, Hishammuddin Hussein, conceived the idea of deterring asylum-seekers from making the dangerous journey to Australia by striking a deal where newly arrived asylum-seekers would be transferred to Malaysia and never be able to come to Australia. In return, Australia would resettle refugees who were already within Malaysia.

This idea was innovative, tough but principled. Asylum-seeker numbers were increasing. So too were the numbers drowning at sea. From a humanitarian perspective, it was vital to try to stem the flow of boats, to reduce the risk of more deaths. Also informed by humanitarian values, we wanted to extend more opportunities for refugees to secure a new life in Australia without getting on a boat. Associated with the arrangement that we struck with Malaysia was an increase in the number of refugee resettlement places Australia would make available to some of the poorest and most at risk people on Earth.

The government was in possession of the clearest possible public service advice that putting into operation this arrangement would send a sharp shock to people smugglers; it would be like the one sent up the pipeline when the Howard Government opted for the Pacific Solution. To use a hackneyed phrase, it would stop the boats.

The numbers favoured Malaysia better than four to one; that is 4000 of their asylum-seekers would be settled in Australia in return for accepting 800 asylum-seekers from Australia. The bureaucratic advice to us was that the full 800 places were unlikely to be used because arrivals would plummet, so our focus was not on the numbers aspect of the deal. Besides, whereas Malaysia was agreeing to accept people in an unpredictable pattern, we would be receiving our quota in a stable and measured manner.

Malaysia's motivations in agreeing to the deal were not about the numbers either. It was genuinely an act of friendship to Australia and a way of showing to the world that it was working productively on refugee issues. The arrangement had the added benefit of bringing the UNHCR into structured, formal discussions with the Malaysian Government, something that had not happened before. Protections for the asylum-seekers Australia transferred to Malaysia were negotiated with the deal.

The internal politics for Labor was always going to be difficult and so it proved. But the real problem was external to Labor's caucus. The Malaysia Agreement initially foundered because the High Court stayed the first transfer of asylum-seekers under it and then ruled that effectively all offshore processing of asylum-seekers was not lawful under the Migration Act.

Showing sick-making double standards, the Coalition opposed the necessary amendments to the Migration Act designed to enable the Malaysia Agreement. Thumping their chests, with tears rolling down their cheeks, they proclaimed they would never allow asylum-seekers to be sent to a country not signatory to the Refugee Convention. The fact the Howard Government had done this was ignored in all the hype and hypocrisy. The fact their own policy was to turn boats around to

Indonesia, so asylum-seekers would be forced back to a country not signatory to the Refugee Convention, was ignored too.

In the course of this argy-bargy, the Opposition, the Greens and sections of the media declared open season on Malaysia, each vying with the other to make the most dramatic declaration about the prevalence of ill-treatment and lack of human rights there. All of Malaysia's strengths were overlooked. Every weakness was probed for.

Prime Minister Najib's forbearance throughout this unseemliness was incredible. Despite the insults being hurled at his country, he continued to pursue a good relationship with Australia.

He visited Australia in March 2011 and we agreed to try to conclude a trade deal between our two countries within a year. Minister for Trade Craig Emerson and his counterpart finished it with a day or two to spare. As a result, most tariffs between the two countries are being eliminated.

EAST ASIA SUMMIT

As well as pursuing our bilateral ties within the region and beyond, I had the privilege of attending meetings of the EAS at a turning point. At my first meeting in 2010, the EAS brought together the ASEAN countries with China, Japan, South Korea, Australia and New Zealand. By its next meeting in 2011, the United States and Russia had joined. Kevin Rudd as prime minister had vigorously advocated the need for America to join and can take much of the credit for their involvement.

The strategic implications of having the countries of our region, but especially China and the United States, joining together in an annual leaders' level dialogue, with the capacity to range across all issues, are immense. As our region grows and changes, there are bound to be moments of tension. Anything that brings nations together so trust and cooperation have time to build is valuable. Something with this regional spread is pivotal.

But realising that promise will take time. With ASEAN at its centre, the EAS mirrors that slow style of consensus decision-making.

Frustrations will inevitably arise as a result of both the pace and the tendency to avoid confronting hard issues directly and thoroughly. Hectoring will not work. Perseverance will bring rewards.

The meetings are largely formulaic. Leaders in many languages reading aloud their prepared contributions in a predetermined order. The room is full of aides and advisers. The tables at which you sit can be so grand in size that it is not possible to turn and have a conversation with the leader next to you. They are simply too far away. Luckily leaders are brought together in more intimate and dynamic settings as well.

When I spoke with President Obama in Washington in 2011, I had the opportunity to personally brief him on what he should expect from his first EAS later in the year. It was my turn to warn him not to get his hopes up too much.

At my second meeting of the EAS – and President Obama's first – in Bali later in 2011, the thorny question of a code of conduct in the South China Sea was discussed at a leaders-only session, which facilitated the robust engagement of views. It is in these waters, sailed by the ships that make trade between our nations possible, that the sharper end of the implications of China's newfound power is felt. Small rocky outcrops are contested, not because of the inherent value of that land but because each bit of land brings with it an exclusive economic zone, encompassing resources like gas that lie under the surrounding sea. Disputes over potential sources of wealth always have the ability to spiral out of control.

The South China Sea was also discussed in the leaders' meeting at the 2012 EAS in Phnom Penh, Cambodia, even though Chinese pressure had kept any reference out of the documents emerging from the foreign ministers' meeting. Unfortunately the US debt default crisis prevented President Obama's attendance at the summit in 2013.

While I could not foresee all these events, I could tell even in 2011 that the EAS would test US reservoirs of strategic patience and I counselled the need for it.

It will also test ours. But the maturation of the EAS into a forum for meaningful exchanges on the things that most matter in our region is a prospect worth striving for, and taking all the time necessary.

The need for patience is sharply at odds with the sense of urgency and opportunity felt by many leaders; I felt it too. Your mind races, as you get your time-limited chance to make a contribution.

For me, this sense of wanting to make a big difference was particularly acute because of the way in which our world is being remade by Asia's ascension. Our government fundamentally understood this and had a clear vision for how to manage our nation so new opportunities were seized and shared.

Moment by moment there are always problems and challenges. In a minority government, with internal instability, I saw more than the usual share. But I was determined we should keep our eyes on the long term and govern today in a way that created that better tomorrow. It is what I thought about in the quiet moments, on the plane flights, in the hotels. It is what I worked to achieve with our regional neighbours.

12

Respected in the world

'Australia will host in 2014, Turkey will host in 2015; it is not easy but it is decided.'

PRESIDENT NICOLAS SARKOZY AT THE
G20 MEETING IN CANNES

'Argentina, Australia, and Rwanda are elected members of the security council for a two-year term beginning the 1st of January 2013.'

UN GENERAL ASSEMBLY, 18 OCTOBER 2012

THROUGHOUT AUSTRALIA'S HISTORY there have been too many moments of turning inwards, of under-appreciating our capacity to influence change in our world. There have also been moments of over-reach and of misunderstanding our limitations. It is not easy to steer the middle course, mindful of your limitations but determined to use what might you have to achieve regional and global goals.

At our best, under great Labor governments like those of Bob Hawke and Paul Keating, we have understood and achieved the difficult balance that needs to be struck to have impact as a middle power.

In our Labor government, I sought to do this again.

THE G20

One of Kevin Rudd's resounding successes as prime minister, for which he is owed many accolades, was making the G20 the prime international forum for responding to the GFC.

Kevin's efforts not only got Australia in the room, he also influenced the decisions made inside it. In the depths of the GFC, leaders committed to coordinating action on stimulating their economies. As those present represented 80 per cent of global output, the economy of the whole world would feel the impact.

The first of the three G20 summits I attended took place in Seoul. The fact of South Korea hosting was itself significant. Previous meetings of the G20 had been in London, Washington, Pittsburgh and Toronto, so it was the first meeting to be held outside a G8 country. Australia is not a member of that exclusive club, which embraces Europe and North America plus Japan. In its own way, South Korea's hosting was recognition of the Asian Century analysis that was driving our government.

This honour for South Korea reinforced in me the desire to see our nation take the world stage and host a G20. Hosting a meeting of this importance is prestigious but it also has practical benefits. It brings to your nation the world's leaders. It also brings the world's business leaders, who attend a companion event called the B20. That exposure can mean investment, trade and jobs.

With the heat of the GFC beginning to moderate, at the Seoul meeting the G20 shifted gears from acute crisis management to dealing with what caused the crisis in the first place. United States officials, with strong backing from Canada, which had hosted the previous G20 meeting, latched on to the 'global imbalances' theory. It held that economies like China, which have huge amounts of money to invest overseas because their exports are vastly more than their imports, through that flood of investment pushed down global interest rates. That in turn was seen to have fuelled excessive risk-taking in advanced economies, where imports exceed exports and there is a need to suck in foreign investment. It was this cheaper, plentiful money that drove the creation of the sub-prime housing bubble, the giving of housing loans to people who were at high risk of not being able to repay a loan on a property for which they may well have paid far too much. When the bubble burst, thanks to globalisation, failure in one part of the financial sector quickly became the contagion that was the GFC.

It was in this context that the politics around the 'currency war' between China and the USA played out. The American and indeed global complaint was that China was obtaining an ongoing economic advantage by keeping its currency low and this was fuelling its surplus of money to invest.

The solution advocated was multi-pronged. More realistic – essentially floating – exchange rates and, for economies like China, deliberately lifting domestic demand by investing in social safety nets such as old-age pensions and health care. People would then spend more of their money and save less, safe in the knowledge government would provide a helping hand when needed. Added together, the increased demand in combination with the higher value to their currency would reduce the country's large surplus, the imbalance.

Of course, China and others were always going to argue that countries like the United States preferred finger-pointing to owning up to lax financial regulation and an inability to manage their own budgets.

I needed to steer a path through this conflict. Wayne Swan was viewed as a global leader by his G20 counterparts. Australia stood tall. We recognised and had contributed to the intellectual underpinnings of the imbalances theory. But we also recognised that the United States had contributed to its own misery through regulatory failures and the political gridlock that had prevented proper budgeting. My contribution focused on the rising risk of nations trying to ameliorate unemployment and their nation's economic slump by closing the door to trade and the world, rather than working together.

In the end, commitments were made at the G20 to resist protectionist measures and turning away from trade. The imbalances theory did inform the decisions and there was agreement about moving towards more market-determined exchange rates. As I write, the Chinese currency has appreciated in value significantly since 2010.

Moves were also made to even up the playing field. Emerging economies, led by China, forced advanced economies, including the United States, to commit to avoiding excessive volatility in their currency movements. Moves like America getting more of its dollars into circulation helped its economy by lowering its dollar and making its exports cheaper, but hit the competitiveness of emerging economies and made capital flows in and out more unpredictable.

New banking regulations were endorsed. The GFC had taught the world that such new, tighter rules were required.

Any discussion of the global economy is necessarily a complex one. Inevitably journalists find the going tough. I was not at all surprised when many chose to put more time into reporting that the statues of leaders the Koreans had erected for the G20 had me in an Austrian outfit.

My next G20 summit took place in 2011 in the world-renowned French city of Cannes. The lead-up to the meeting was dominated by a rapid escalation of the sovereign debt crisis in Europe. Basically markets were concluding that some countries were so indebted that you could not trust them to repay.

Greece had already entered into a second bailout package, and speculation was rife about the potential break-up of the Eurozone, which has a common currency but encompasses economies of many different strengths. Would strong economies continue to bail out weaker economies or force them out of the Eurozone? At this point, both solutions seemed possible. What had to be avoided at all costs was allowing these weaker economies to fail in a way that would spark runs on banks, banking collapses and a meltdown of the interlinked financial system of the strong and the weak.

As I boarded the plane to Cannes, I had two goals. I knew Europe would dominate the meeting and I wanted to mobilise support to increase the resources of the International Monetary Fund (IMF). With bolstered resources the IMF could build a financial firewall around Europe and give financial markets confidence that the global financial system was adequately resourced to lend money to countries in crisis.

My second goal was to secure the 2014 hosting of the G20 for Australia. To do so, I had to see off a strong challenge from Turkey.

As it turned out, the crisis escalated dramatically in the 12 hours it took for the plane to fly to the United Arab Emirates, our refuelling stop en route to France. The Greek prime minister, George Papandreou, announced his country would hold a referendum on whether to accept the terms of its most recent bailout package. After months of trying to convince markets that, under the terms of the package, Greece would eventually regain financial viability, Papandreou's surprise announcement flagged the possibility of a Greek exit, and thereby increased the risks of the Eurozone breaking up.

Understandably President Nicolas Sarkozy of France and Chancellor Angela Merkel of Germany, who had worked so hard to stabilise the situation, were furious. They summoned the Greek prime minister to Cannes the evening before the official meetings were to begin.

All we knew was that somewhere in the beautiful seaside town of Cannes, Angela Merkel and Nicolas Sarkozy were dressing down the Greek prime minister. The next morning, Papandreou capitulated and called off the referendum. He resigned his post two days later. Greece and the world waited nervously for an interim Greek government to be formed, with elections to be held the following year.

As the G20 meeting swung into action, Chancellor Merkel, one of the few women in attendance, was centre stage. Besides us, there were only three other women at the meeting: Brazil's President Dilma Rousseff, Argentina's President Cristina Fernández de Kirchner and the extremely impressive IMF head, Christine Lagarde. I had initially met Angela at the Asia-Europe meeting in Brussels, my first international multilateral outing. She lived up to her reputation as a blunt, no-nonsense woman, saying to me, 'What happened to Kevin?' She wasn't annoyed, just curious. At this meeting, in many ways the weight of the world was on her shoulders alone. If the Eurozone spiralled out of control, so would the global economy. It was imperative that she work seamlessly with the flamboyant Nicolas Sarkozy. You could not find two more opposite personalities but, largely through her efforts, they formed an effective alliance that stood Europe and the world in good stead in the days of this crisis.

I found Chancellor Merkel's frankness admirable. When I met with her at this G20 meeting, with deep cynicism she described how for photos Germans no longer said 'cheese'. Instead they would grit their teeth and say 'Greeeece'.

Although Sarkozy tried to refocus the G20 meeting on the formal agenda, the European crisis continued to loom large. Before the bombshell of Papandreou's announcement, all eyes had been on Italy. The interest rates Italy was being forced to offer financiers in order to induce them to buy Italian sovereign debt were unsustainably high, threatening the solvency of the Italian state – Europe's third largest economy – and with it, the Eurozone.

Organisers of these events often arrange seating in alphabetical order, other than placing the largest nations next to the chairperson. But at the G20 in Seoul, I had been seated next to Silvio Berlusconi, Italy's prime minister. I did wonder whether that placement was a trick being played on the newbie. During our few short conversations, I had noticed that he was wearing thick orange make-up.

At a meeting in Cannes with Chancellor Merkel and President Sarkozy, also attended by President Obama and Madame Lagarde, Berlusconi was told in strident terms he had to accept much tighter oversight of his planned economic and public financial reforms, not just from the European Commission but the IMF too. This marked the beginning of the end of Berlusconi's tenure as prime minister.

The meeting did resolve to ramp up the IMF's war chest and I made a pledge on Australia's behalf. Despite the severity of the European and global challenges and Australia's clear interest in the fortunes of the global economy, this decision was criticised by the Opposition, though appropriately welcomed by business.

In a step forward in the 'currency wars', it was agreed to move more rapidly towards market-determined exchange-rate systems. On this subject, China was named in the final communiqué – a first.

In another first, the G20 'Action Plan For Jobs and Growth' was laid out, but much more needed to be done to give it real content.

When the communiqué hit the table, while there was general agreement, there was an elephant in the room – namely the outcome of all the side discussions on the Eurozone. Taking it upon myself to end the silence, I asked President Sarkozy to summarise the situation for the Eurozone after all the sideline conversations, and what should be said about it publicly. He referred the question to President Obama, who outlined the position. As the meeting broke up I was roundly thanked for having the guts to name the elephant.

On the matter of hosting the 2014 summit, Prime Minister Tayyip

Erdogan of Turkey desperately wanted the G20 for Turkey in 2014, an election year. In our meeting, he came forcefully at me four times trying to pressure me to agree to Australia hosting in 2015. While our relations with Turkey are excellent and the way they facilitate our Gallipoli commemorations is incredible, I did not relent. At the end of the leaders' dinner, when President Sarkozy announced Australia would host in 2014 and Turkey in 2015, I was delighted.

My final G20, in Los Cabos, Mexico, took place only eight months after the November meeting in Cannes. In the interim, the crisis in Europe had remained hot. While the Greek elections earlier in the year effectively gave sanction to the terms of the European–IMF bailout package, the Eurozone economy continued to shrink and unemployment levels reached new highs. In the weeks leading up to the Los Cabos summit, there was intense concern about the status of Spanish banks, and the impact that their insolvency might have on Spain's sovereign debt should the government need to bail the banks out.

Two major debates were swirling around the Eurozone crisis at this time. The first debate was how much austerity is too much. Wayne Swan and the United States were putting the argument that the rate at which debt-laden European economies were cutting back spending was too severe and choking off growth. The second debate was about whether 'there should be more Europe, not less', to use the words of Angela Merkel. By this she meant that there needed to be a greater integration of banking, to put a common backstop to banks at risk of failing. Without it, the risk was that a large bailout could drive a weak and indebted sovereign nation over the brink. This deal had to come with budget rules to which all Eurozone nations would adhere; otherwise a nation could go on a spending spree confident that if one of its banks failed others would prop it up. That took the circle back to austerity: how tough should the rules be?

The difficulty at Los Cabos was that a few days later, the Europeans were to have their own meeting and they did not want to be told what to do. The rest of the delegates had no patience for European resistance to scrutiny and debate, not when our fortunes were all inextricably linked.

Wayne Swan had long been saying that the problem with European responses was that they only did enough to stay 'one camp fire in front of the posse'.

While I lent my voice to the chorus of world leaders urging Europe to act decisively, I also used the formal and informal meeting opportunities provided by the G20 to try to procure assistance for an Australian national, Melinda Taylor, who was being held in Libya by a local militia. Along with a Spanish national and a Russian national – fellow members of an International Criminal Court team – she had been imprisoned.

When I approached the new Italian prime minister, Mario Monti, the 'technocrat' who had been sworn in to clean up the Berlusconi mess, I found him impressive. He later paid me the great compliment of saying he felt more confident when I was around. Prime Minister Monti's immediate intervention proved vital. Indeed when our Australian was freed and flown out of Libya with her companions, it was on an Italian-provided plane.

Because a Russian national was involved, I had also approached President Vladimir Putin. I had an extraordinary conversation with him in which he described Libya as 'Barack's', displaying a simple chessboard view of the world.

On the economic issues, at my opening press conference and at the B20 I spoke about lessons Europe could learn from Australia's management of the GFC, specifically when it came to balancing short-term stimulus and medium-term budget repair. This was a direct intervention in the debate about austerity and growth.

The Australian press displayed a curious cultural cringe in their reaction to this. Notwithstanding Australia's undisputed achievements, apparently it was wrong to speak about them on the world stage. Dennis Shanahan of *The Australian* went so far as to suggest a statement made by the head of the European Commission, Manuel Barroso, as part of the general chorus of views from Europe arguing it should do its own decision-making, was aimed at me.[1] This was nonsense and President Barroso himself approached me and told me so. *The Australian*'s article had turned up in his press clippings and he could not believe his remarks had been interpreted that way. He then recalled the impression formed on his visit to Australia that the paper was owned by our conservative party. Coming from a region in which it was common for political parties to operate newspapers, a couple of quick reads of *The Australian* had obviously driven him to this conclusion.

Even after it was made clear to journalists travelling with me that President Barroso himself denied his remarks were a response to mine, Simon Benson of the *Daily Telegraph* produced a piece referring to me as a 'European Bloc Head'[2] and restating the same criticisms.

What reporters missed in all of this silly carry-on was that Australia's national interest lay not in silently acceding to European demands to be left alone but being vocal on behalf of our interests and our people.

While the formal business of the G20 focused on the global economy, the tragic situation in Syria dominated the sideline discussions at the summit. Efforts were made to stop Russia supplying weapons to the regime of President Assad, who was turning those weapons on the Syrian people. When I raised this personally with President Putin, with a flick of the hand he suggested that hundreds of millions of dollars of weapons was somehow not very much.

Among the key outcomes of the summit was a commitment from Eurozone members to safeguard the Eurozone's integrity and stability. In essence they agreed to pursue policies that promote growth and austerity, not growth or austerity. This statement marked the beginning of recognition that austerity needed to be scaled back.

There were also undertakings to step up integration of the European banking system – some of those initiatives came to fruition in 2013 – and for more fiscal integration, meaning budget rules.

The resources of the IMF were increased again and a commitment to no further anti-trade measures was extended to 2014, Australia's year of hosting.

Globalisation has brought extensive benefits and new risk. The G20 at its best can be the forum that helps heighten those benefits and mitigate the risk. After the burning-platform desperation of the early days of the GFC, the pace and reach of G20 decision-making has diminished.

To some extent that is natural. As crisis abates, more normal decision patterns will take hold. Also it is obviously easier for leaders to come together and agree to spend money to stimulate economies than to broker agreements on painful reforms to address deep-seated problems. But drift cannot be allowed to take hold. The G20 will cease to command the personal attendance and efforts of leaders unless it is seen to be delivering.

More generally, Western governments may point to the softening of emerging markets like Indonesia, India, Brazil, Turkey and South Africa as resulting from their failure to address fundamental structural weaknesses in their economies. Successfully mediating these tensions will be key.

Australia will go a long way to restoring the credibility of the G20 if the November 2014 meeting hosted by us makes headway on three things that the G20 has had on its agenda for a few years now. These are progress on the multilateral trade agenda, getting countries to actually commit in specific terms to growth-orientated structural reforms in their economies, and tackling the climate-change challenge, which threatens the world and requires change in the way economies work. I hope, having brought the meeting to our shores, that it is a success.

THE UNITED NATIONS SECURITY COUNCIL

Despite being a late convert to our campaign, I was also pleased to see our nation's status in the world added to by our election to the UN Security Council, the decision-making body that deals with the hardest and most urgent of issues. In government, as deputy prime minister, I watched it start but played no particular role in it. I harboured a low-level concern that this was simply more on the government's already overcrowded plate and that we were coming to this campaign too late. One of our major competitors, Finland, had been actively touting for votes since 2002. But with so much else happening, I did not advocate internally for a changed course of action.

On becoming prime minister, I had no immediate contact with our Security Council quest. I had an election to fight. Desperate for savings to redirect to campaign commitments, I considered calling off the Security Council bid to access the money budgeted for it. However, while the dollars were tempting, I had no wish to make Australia look foolishly indecisive to other nations.

Once the minority government was formed and I started to travel representing our nation, I was fully briefed on the campaign. While the late start had not been ideal, there was a chance we could win. I set about doing what I could to achieve just that. My personal efforts were an add-on to the work being done at every level by the Department of Foreign Affairs and Trade and by our well-respected, incredibly able ambassador to the UN, Gary Quinlan. Tapping into the prestige associated with the nation's leader doing things personally, I lobbied, made calls and spoke to other nations' ambassadors to the UN when the opportunity arose. I also took part in the final vote-getting frenzy that occurred during the UN annual week for leaders in September 2012.

While he was Foreign Minister, Kevin worked hard on the campaign. So did his successor, Bob Carr. Quentin Bryce also travelled widely and did much to convince nations to vote for us. I was prepared to intensely pursue a Security Council seat and push through the carping of the Opposition, but I was not prepared to change our nation's long-held position on Israel to get there.

I had first been exposed to the complex and heartbreaking questions of peace and security in the Middle East when I was in the student movement in the early 1980s. In those days, the legacy of the anti-Vietnam war movement was still shaping, indeed distorting, the work of the AUS. Gough Whitlam ended conscription in the early 1970s and the Vietnam war ended in 1975. After it was all over, hard-left activists within the student movement became restless for a new cause and a return to the days of big protests and high energy. The cause they settled upon was fighting for a Palestinian state. Throughout the late 1970s, the AUS was a vocal advocate for the Palestinian people and a strident critic of Israel.

This stance generated bitter opposition from supporters of Israel. But the bigger cost for the AUS of this foreign policy preoccupation was the way it alienated the vast mass of students, who were studying to get their qualifications, often while holding down part-time jobs. The anti-Vietnam war movement had galvanised students because it touched them and their lives directly through the risk of being drafted. The questions of Palestine, Israel and peace in the Middle East simply did not interest students in the same way and many resented the AUS using student money in pursuit of something so remote from their lives.

Overwhelmingly Labor members of the student movement wanted the union to get on with doing the things students really cared about, representing them in the big debates about education funding and quality, providing them with the services they needed. To break the cycle, we decided that the AUS should ostentatiously have no policy on the Middle East, stay silent, quit the field.

To ensure that the official 'no policy' position held for the future, AUS decided at its national conference to ask students directly through campus debates and votes to endorse 'no policy'. As AUS president, I was the national returning officer and was scrupulous in making sure the process was fair.

Personally I subscribed strongly to a two-state solution. Growing up, I had little understanding of the Middle East but as a university student had read and thought about it. As a young idealist, I innocently concluded that everyone living in peace and harmony in two nations, Palestine and Israel, side by side, would be far easier to achieve than it truly is in the world we live in. Not that I have given up.

After my years in student politics, I had no immediate involvement in Middle Eastern issues until I became a parliamentarian. I gratefully accepted an invitation to lead a delegation of Labor members to Israel on a trip supported by the Australian Jewish community. I had always wanted to visit.

In my formative years, church figured strongly in my life. My parents were churchgoers, Mum more so than Dad, though I now realise that this was less an expression of religious devotion and more a way to meet people in a new land after we emigrated. I was a regular attender at the Baptist Sunday School and then a keen participant in its youth group. I showed a particular flair for remembering slabs of biblical text and would win prizes for reciting every word correctly.

Our house was two doors down from the Baptist manse, where our Reverend, Mr Porter, lived with his family. His youngest daughter,

Helen, was a close friend and I spent a great deal of time with the Porter family.

Belief in God was an unquestioned part of my world until my late teens. There was no cataclysmic moment of revelation but as I moved into my 20s, doubts grew and then overwhelmed. I asked all the questions that beset so many people with and without faith: how can you rationalise so much suffering in our world with the existence of a benevolent God? How can you embrace faith in the one true God and plurality, ancient beliefs and modernity?

I suspect there was nothing original about my journey but it led me to a quiet but firm belief that this mortal world is it and our measure as human beings is entirely defined by what we do within it.

Beyond doubt, I am grateful for the hours spent in Bible studies. They reinforced the value system that I was learning in my family home, about treating others as you would want to be treated yourself. And because so much of our cultural heritage is built on the foundation of Judaeo-Christianity, I passionately believe that such study provides the key to truly understanding it.

As a consequence, in Israel I delighted in the opportunity to set foot in places I had read about so often, such as Jerusalem's historic old city and on the shores of the Sea of Galilee. The visit furnished me with greater insight into all the complexities of the politics and security questions in the region. Our delegation met with Israeli and Palestinian leaders. Having talked and reflected at length, I returned home strongly reinforced in my view that a two-state solution is the way to a lasting peace. Any naivety about the complexities of achieving it was long gone.

Throughout my parliamentary career, I had many opportunities for immersion in the debate. The desire for peace from many on both sides, Israeli and Palestinian, is powerful but the path to get there is littered with obstacles.

I came to know and respect Israel's long-term ambassador to Australia, Yuval Rotem, a charming man with an encyclopaedic knowledge of politics in both countries. I came to know too the key personalities within the Jewish community of both Melbourne and Sydney. A number of them are strongly aligned with Labor and interested in all aspects of Australian politics. As Education Minister, I worked with both the Jewish community and representatives of the Muslim community on security concerns about their schools. Unfortunately even in Australia such schools have to worry about attacks by bigots. As a local member of parliament, I spent time with the thriving Muslim community in and around Werribee. Leading members became strong supporters and good friends.

When called upon to make public statements on events in the Middle East, I stayed true to my beliefs, including believing in Israel's right to defend itself against attack. Inevitably some of these statements were publicly controversial, but I was undeterred. On becoming prime minister and being briefed on the Security Council campaign it was apparent that one of the challenges in us succeeding was Australia's long record of supporting Israel in votes at the UN General Assembly. Canada had sought election to the Security Council in an earlier round and failed. Its prime minister, Stephen Harper, was convinced that a key reason was Canada's inability to secure votes from the Muslim world because of its support for Israel.

I decided that if the only way to become a member of the Security Council was to sell out our nation's support for Israel, then we should accept defeat rather than compromise.

I became concerned that this was not Kevin's view. His approach was more 'the end justifies the means'. He believed that it was so much in Israel's interests to have a nation of the calibre and values system of Australia serving on the Security Council that we could reach an understanding with both Israel and the Australian Jewish community on tactically distancing ourselves from Israel to garner votes.

We disagreed but it was a legitimate debate. When Kevin was briefing cabinet on the progress of the Security Council campaign, I asked him point blank how our pitch for votes related to Labor's long-standing support for Israel. When he did not put his end justifies the means view but replied that we should not deviate from our traditional views for the campaign, I viewed the matter as now decided.

Resolutions on all manner of issues in our world are put to a vote on the floor of the UN General Assembly. The decision about how to vote on these resolutions is made at different levels, depending on their level of importance. The most routine are subject to a judgement call by our Ambassador to the UN. Many are the subject of decisions by our Foreign Minister. On significant and sensitive questions, like the Middle East, the decision is made by the prime minister. Each year a tranche of resolutions about Israel and complaints about its behaviour come up for a vote. From year to year, the resolutions are unchanged or little changed. Year by year Australia exercises its vote.

Despite his answer to my question before colleagues, Kevin as Foreign Minister pressured me to modify Australia's voting stance on these resolutions, not because anything had significantly changed but because it would look better for our Security Council campaign. I resisted this pressure. It seemed to me simply dishonest to assert to colleagues and members of the Jewish community that Australia would not change its stance on Israel as part of touting for votes and then do precisely that. If there was some real reason to alter our vote – say, the wording of the resolution had changed or the factual backdrop had altered in the intervening 12 months – then I was open to a policy debate.

This pressure over resolution votes ramped up when Bob Carr became Foreign Minister. We also differed over how to respond to a letter we received from the Arab League shortly before the Security Council vote was to be held. Bob formed what I regarded as a somewhat hysterical view that if we did not respond immediately – and in nuanced terms that could be read as a slight move away from Israel – we could not win. I disagreed and refused to respond before the vote was taken.

We were victorious in the vote. It was a moment to relish and I celebrated it with the staff of the Department of Foreign Affairs and Trade who had worked so hard and diligently on securing this stunning win for Australia. It was impossible to know then how much being on the Security Council would mean for our nation when so many Australian lives were lost in the downing of Malaysia Airlines flight MH17.

Against this backdrop, I was surprised and dismayed by the debate within Labor that flared over how Australia should vote on a resolution before the UN granting Palestine recognition within its system that would be represented as the achievement of Palestinian statehood. I had directed we vote against such a resolution when it was put at the United Nations Education Scientific and Cultural Organization

(UNESCO). To me it was self-evident this was not the path to peace. A million resolutions, billions of pieces of paper would never create a Palestinian state – only fruitful negotiations would.

Further, however Australia voted, it was apparent the resolution would get carried at UNESCO. Then, as dictated by legislation passed by Congress, the United States would have to stop funding UNESCO. I was not going to put Australia's name to a move that would result in fewer resources flowing to an organisation that works on education.

As the vote for Palestinian recognition approached at the UN General Assembly, I made a call to vote against it. My reasoning was unchanged from the time of the UNESCO resolution. A few licks of flame then combined to make this an incendiary decision.

First, Gareth Evans, a long-time and well-respected former Labor Foreign Minister, went on a lobbying campaign to urge a yes vote. He raised the issue with me at an event associated with the Australian National University, of which he was Chancellor. He never came to me for a specific discussion about it. Gareth believed that the call of history was for the world to take a visible step forward on statehood, and that for long-term supporters of Israel this was the best way of sending a message that the Israelis needed to show more openness to negotiations. His lobbying was effective. A resolution to have Australia vote yes was placed on the notice paper of the Labor caucus meeting. Adoption by caucus would bind the government to directing a yes vote.

The lick of flame started by Gareth was joined by another one sparked by a number of NSW Right members, particularly Sam Dastyari. Historically the NSW Right has justified its power within Labor on the basis of its embrace of centrist policies. Among them has been support for Israel. This tradition was being upended on the basis that some electorates in New South Wales were now home to sizeable Muslim communities and voting yes would be a good move in their eyes.

More heat came from Kevin's supporters within caucus. Many of them would have had no real view about the Palestinian recognition resolution at the UN. They just saw an issue developing where

Kevin had one view and I had another and they decided to use it for maximum damage.

The final lick of flame was Bob Carr's attitude. Bob read into my contrary view that in my eyes he and his advice had a lesser status than the advice provided by my office, which was somehow dictated by the Melbourne Jewish community. He actually screamed at Bruce Wolpe, a staff member in my office, in the reception area of the office. I heard it from my desk. He assumed Bruce was at the centre of the forces ranged against him. Bob's view was incorrect. I was no one's captive. I simply did not agree with him.

At the caucus meeting, as the debate progressed, I realised I might not have the numbers to back my position of a no vote. Even if I won, it would have been because a number of colleagues, including cabinet members, who had said they did not agree with me, voted with me simply out of loyalty.

To drop down the temperature, I sought a compromise – abstaining on the resolution. There was no choice. My colleagues, some for legitimate reasons, some for game-playing ones, had formed a different view from me. In the time since, I have queried myself. Did I call this issue wrong? Even now, I do not believe so.

My next visit to Israel – in April 2014 – coincided with a further breakdown in peace talks. Once again, I met with Israeli and Palestinian leaders. There was the same desire for peace but, despite it, the same lack of progress.

In the too-familiar cycle of recriminations about why talks broke down, the newest weapon of reprisal was the Palestinian president signing applications to join UN bodies and conventions. Before my very eyes, UN processes were being used as a tactic in a mutual process of chest-beating and obfuscation.

In the months since, the outlook has become so much darker. Children have died; violence has been answered with violence. This is not the way to peace.

In its simplest form, peace depends on two leaders, one Israeli, one Palestinian, having the courage to lead two peoples to the compromises necessary so that both can live safely in two lands. That courage, so elusive, is desperately required.

TRADE

As the government tied itself in knots over how to vote at the UN, I felt a faint echo of my student movement days. Just as I used to sense the gaze of students looking at the AUS, wondering why it spent so much time on the Middle East, I pictured Australians looking at the reports of our caucus debate on recognition of a Palestinian state and thinking, 'What about my job, my family, my life? What are you doing for me?'

A big part of the answer to that question lay in how we worked internationally on trade, which translates into jobs for Australians.

Given its global and domestic economic significance, trade understandably looms large on the agenda of leaders when they meet. Everyone at such meetings talks the language of free trade and open markets. Everyone says they are not afraid of robust competition. But back at home, freer trade is unlikely to be politically popular. Many voters are instinctively suspicious of the power of the outside world to hit and hurt their lives. These suspicions have been heightened by the GFC.

For governments of nations with large unemployment problems courtesy of the GFC and budgets that need to be returned to surplus through unpopular cutbacks, preaching free trade is viewed as political poison. The burdens of tariff reductions or eliminating quotas for imported goods tend to be easy to see and protest against. The benefits of more open markets tend to be more diffuse, far harder to get people to actively campaign for.

While our nation emerged strong from the GFC, our domestic politics is not immune from these trends. In government, despite the pressures, we stayed true to the Labor tradition of being economic modernisers and in favour of opening our markets. Our trade approach was to participate in any smart initiative going, in order to maximise chances of success. By the same token, in weighing what is achieved on trade, it is tempting simply to tally the number of agreements entered into. But you can always get a deal. What counts is not the signatures on the bottom line but what the bottom line represents. Whether the burdens for your nation are equal to or less than the benefits.

When I appointed Craig Emerson as Trade Minister following the 2010 election, colleagues in Australia and abroad told him the decade-long global negotiations known as the Doha Round were dead. Routinely leaders would gather at multilateral meetings and call for the completion of the Doha Round. Then nothing would happen.

This complex problem did not daunt Craig. Recognising that going back through the same old loops would not achieve the desired liberalisation of trade, he developed what he called 'new pathways' to completing these seemingly never-ending talks. His approach involved breaking negotiations into smaller parts and completing them as they were ready, rather than waiting for what he called a 'grand bargain' to mystically descend from the sky.

I advocated this new pathways approach in international forums including the G20 and APEC while Craig pushed it with key countries and groupings such as the United States, China, the European Union and the grouping of Least Developed Countries. The World Trade Organization (WTO) formally adopted the new pathways approach in December 2011 and two years later agreed on a set of reforms to facilitate trade by easing customs blockages at ports, plus some early reforms in agriculture. The package, agreed at a meeting in Bali, was the first such deal since 1995 and holds the promise of generating billions of dollars for the global economy. It was a credit to Craig's patient and strategic work that this agreement was made.

Increasingly it is not goods that get traded internationally but services. Having recognised that some major emerging countries would not agree to open up trade in services in the foreseeable future, Craig and the Americans formed a grouping of 44 countries to negotiate an agreement under the auspices of the Geneva-based WTO. Australia co-chairs these negotiations with the United States and they are shaping up as the most likely forum for reaching an agreement on trade in services. China has indicated its desire to join the group.

Freer trade also has climate-change implications. For instance, countries need access to the very goods that enable economies to be cleaner and greener, like solar cells and wind turbines. For two years, the United States had been pushing for a tariff on such goods of five per cent maximum. At APEC in Vladivostok, negotiation to achieve this goal broke down. Working through the night, Craig quickly developed a list of environmental goods and brokered a deal with China, the United States and Russia. Consequently APEC reached agreement on 54 environmental goods, the first large-scale agreement to reduce tariffs in almost 20 years.

To facilitate poverty alleviation through economic development, Craig also led our nation to drop tariffs for goods coming from the least developed countries. Once we had locked ourselves into this with a binding commitment, Craig had the moral authority to advocate the same course of action to other nations.

In a tough environment for both bilateral and multilateral trade initiatives, Craig Emerson as Trade Minister achieved global status as one of the true innovators. This intricate work also garnered Australia considerable respect in the world.

13

Our Queen, my birthplace, who we are today

'Should have no trouble in settling'
FROM THE NOTES OF THE IMMIGRATION OFFICER
WHO INTERVIEWED MY PARENTS, 1966

THE ONLY REALITY I HAVE EVER KNOWN OR EVER WANTED is that of being Australian. Of course, I was not born here. My parents are part of the wave of 'ten pound Poms', British migrants whose travel costs were subsidised because Australia deemed them to be good migrants as it followed the doctrine of populate or perish.

My earliest memories are of being in the Pennington Migrant Hostel, not a happy time in the life of our family. Living in Nissen huts. Refusing to eat because I was overwhelmed by the dining room with its crush of people and noise. For years afterwards, Dad told the story of being allocated a plug to take to the communal bathrooms which you had to return at the end of your stay in the hostel. Apparently too many plugs were stolen when they were left in the bathroom.

My parents quickly moved to a rented apartment and started looking for work and a home to buy. Dad also recalled the heartbreak of leaving me in a childcare centre while my sister was at school so he and Mum could do their job- and house-hunting. He maintained I would stand by the window as he left and still be standing there when he returned.

I have no memory of this. Neither did I really experience the sense of dislocation that comes from being moved to a new environment.

My sister, who is three years older, remembers both Wales and having to start school immediately, ripe for teasing with her thick Welsh accent. She did it much harder than me.

Stories of Wales and the fact of my parents having migrated halfway around the world to seek a better life for us formed the backdrop to what, in day-to-day living, was a very Australian childhood. Good friends, long summer holidays spent swimming, Sunday drives into the Adelaide Hills, playing catch in the backyard with Dad or playing a ball game on the road in front of our house with the kids who lived in the street. And then there was reading. The weekly trips to the public library, coming back with five or six books all to be devoured in a week. We were very Australian before we formally became Australians. My parents made a conscious decision to take out citizenship for our family when Gough Whitlam was in power. Even so, on our only international trip as a family, the much-saved-for visit to Wales, which happened at the end of my high school years, we travelled on British passports. Later I surrendered my British passport when I renounced my citizenship of the United Kingdom in order to be eligible to run for parliament. I had kept it merely for the pragmatic reason that it eased travel in Europe.

The British monarchy figured in our lives but not in a way that truly commanded attention or tugged at the heart. It was more that mine was a generation that sang 'God Save the Queen' at school. In our outdoor assemblies, standing rigid in straight lines, we would salute the flag and recite: 'I am an Australian. I love my country. I salute her flag. I honour her Queen. I promise to obey her laws.' On hot days, the number of children fainting was truly terrifying.

In our family home the only time the monarchy had an impact was on Christmas Day. Mum would try and shush us to make us listen to the Queen's Christmas address. My more irreverent father would then start parodying her extremely upper-class accent.

The advent of Lady Di, another 1961 kid, brought the monarchy into a sharper, different focus. Her story was part of the backdrop of my life from when I was 19 until I was 35 years old. I did not particularly seek out news about her. It was everywhere. It was unavoidable. When she died, I did feel a sense of loss.

My parents, as they made their lives in Australia, became republicans. They had enough belief in their new country for them to also believe it should have its own head of state. I do not remember exactly when I decided to become a republican. For me, it was instinctual. However I am and always have been a proponent of a minimalist model of change. Electing a president would inevitably distort our system of government in a fundamental way. The potential for clashes between the president and the prime minister is too big a risk.

I did not play any role in the Australian Republican Movement. But even though I was certain it would fail, I was an enthusiastic supporter of the 1999 referendum for the republic. Despite the best efforts of many individuals fervently organising for the republican cause, the case for change had simply not been made among the general Australian community.

Like the majority of Australians, including those who are politically active, I have felt the pull of the republican cause lessen in urgency over the years since. Certainly other issues have come to the fore, but I attribute the slip in focus to our growing sense of maturity as a nation.

In 1999, becoming a republic felt like a bold statement of Australian identity. I think we are now so confident in our identity, becoming a republic feels more like a necessary bit of tidying up, one that we will get around to, but with no real sense of a need to rush. The moment of change may well be forced on us. When the current queen dies, which, given the longevity of her mother, may be many years away, and change is upon us anyway, then I think Australians will revisit the question of the republic. In the meantime, Australians are self-assured enough to be able to warmly welcome the Queen and to watch with fascination the lives of the young royals without any obsequiousness.

When the Queen visited, the reaction of the Australian people was not one of deference to 'our Queen' so much as an interest in her as a person. Her appearance of constancy in a changing world, viewed as a liability when it prevented her responding emotionally to the death of Diana, Princess of Wales, is now viewed as an asset. We are intrigued.

*

I saw the irony when I, a republican, attended the 2011 royal wedding between Prince William and Catherine Middleton, partnered by Tim, another republican, to whom I am not married. Yet in many ways, that represented the kind of mixture that is Australia today. A place where people can say, yes I think we should have our own head of state but I am still going to have friends over to party in celebration of Will and Kate's wedding.

The royal wedding came at the end of a long trip that had taken us to Japan, Korea and China. My outfit for the wedding had been carefully carried the whole way, and the degree of media interest in it was somewhere between laugh-out-loud funny and excruciating. Although I passed the commentators' test, at a quick media appearance before the wedding, someone asked the name of the designer and my mind went blank. Fortunately Sally, one of my press secretaries, was on hand to prompt me: 'Aurelio Costarella'.

We went from the hotel to Lancaster House to meet the other 'realm prime ministers', the realm being those countries where the Queen still serves as head of state. All of us travelled together by bus to the wedding. The atmosphere on the bus was light-hearted. When Tim adjusted my fascinator, which had been knocked slightly askew, by rearranging the hairpins holding it on my head, John Key's wife, Bronagh, jokingly asked John why he could never do anything useful like that.

The Prime Minister of Saint Vincent and the Grenadines, Ralph E. Gonsalves, amused the group by suggesting that as we would all be together again at the CHOGM in Perth later in the year, we could have another wedding then – Tim's and mine. I assured him that would not be happening. Tim and I are fine as we are. Much good-natured teasing ensued.

At Buckingham Palace after the 11 am service, we had the opportunity to congratulate the newlyweds in person and then stood in a room next to the one from which the couple went onto the balcony, waved to the onlookers and shared the much-anticipated kiss. From our vantage point, we could see the immense throng which the police had allowed to surge forward in anticipation of the appearance on the balcony. It was a crowd of absolute good humour, no pushing or shoving. Everyone was enjoying themselves, including the police.

Minutes later, I was summoned for my first private audience with the Queen. I found her generous with her time, a lively conversationalist, well informed on global affairs. She has a unique perspective on world events over the last 60 years. Although I knew of Her Majesty's reputation for frugality, the presence of a small radiator in the middle of an ornate marble fireplace in her private apartments still surprised me.

Tim and I then gathered with around 650 others for the reception, part of a full day of celebrations culminating in a disco for Kate and Will and their friends. There is a certain look to the British aristocracy. It is peaches-and-cream skin, an affection on the part of the women for shift dresses with matching coats, an ease that comes with assumed status in the world. Many of the men were in dress uniforms with a leather belt around the waist and over the shoulder, a medallion on the leather in the middle of the back. At one point, a woman we were talking to started squealing and reaching out to us. It turned out her woollen suit had become entangled with the medallion on a young soldier's back and, without realising it, he was carrying her away.

A little later, to our amazement the Queen suddenly appeared and starting wandering through the gathered throng. No trumpets, no announcement, no minder. No one was chatting to her so Tim stepped in and they talked about how she had been to view the lights in the disco and how they made your eyes roll round. The day was an enjoyable cross between world event and family wedding.

I next spent time with the Queen when she arrived in Australia on 19 October 2011 for a tour and attendance at CHOGM. We saw each other at a number of formal events, including the cocktail party Tim and I hosted for the royal couple at Parliament House. Prince Philip was at his roguish best, full of extraordinary one-liners as he circulated with Tim. As I moved with the Queen through the crush, I noted both her practised handling of the situation and the smooth operation of the entourage that supports her. It was easy to see how Paul Keating committed the faux pas of putting his arm around her. In a crowd that size, you had to fight the natural urge to shield her with an enclosing arm.

Of the global multilateral events I attended, CHOGM was the most unusual. It was long – held over three days, including a leaders-only session that lasted for an extraordinary day and a half – but it used to be even longer. A gathering of more than 50 nations, at its best CHOGM has played a role in fighting apartheid and furthering the spread of democracy. At its worst, it has drifted. As host, we were aiming to make the meeting matter by proposing a new charter and presenting recommendations for change developed by an Eminent Persons Group.

British Prime Minister David Cameron also used the meeting to announce he would be seeking to amend the rules for the line of succession for the Crown so the bias against women would be eradicated. Many were already debating what would happen if William and Kate's first child was a daughter. Could it really be possible that in the decades to come she would be passed over as monarch in favour of a later-born son? David had decided to fix this for all time, so the eldest child, irrespective of gender, would succeed to the throne.

Notwithstanding the quirkiness of debating equal opportunity within the context of a hereditary monarchy without debating the anachronism of inherited title itself, I appreciated David's intentions. When we met to discuss his proposal, I joked with him about equal rights for 'sheilas'. Later, mimicking my very Australian accent, he used this for a comedy routine in a speech in the UK. When I next saw him, I assured him no offence had been taken. I always found David easy to deal with and personable, despite being from the other side of politics.

CHOGM saw some of the best of Kevin Rudd. The recommendations put before the meeting proved controversial. In the leaders' meeting, discussion bogged down. To break the impasse, foreign ministers were asked to meet overnight. Kevin ably chaired this pivotal meeting. Along with the charter, around 30 recommendations of the Eminent Persons Group were adopted. Importantly too, the role of the Ministerial Action Group, which gets involved when a Commonwealth nation is engaged in breaches of democratic norms, was strengthened.

The last time I saw the Queen was at the formal CHOGM dinner. The Queen brings with her gold goblets, one engraved for each country, from which the formal toast is drunk. Inevitably there is much banter about popping a goblet in your pocket. As the dinner came to an end,

I walked the Queen to her car to farewell her. She looked back towards the gathering and her eyes moistened. I wondered if the emotion stemmed from her belief this might be her last tour of Australia. Later I discovered another possibility.

In early 2013, I was advised that Sir Christopher Geidt, the Queen's private secretary, wanted half an hour of my time in my capacity as Chair of the Commonwealth, an office the host holds until the next meeting. He would fly to Australia to anywhere I was in order to get it. The upshot of our meeting, which took place in Adelaide on 21 February 2013, was a clearly worded statement for the public record about how succession works for the role of the Head of Commonwealth. In the parliament on 20 March, I duly gave the statement and sent it to all commonwealth countries. The purpose of the statement was a mystery, however, until Prince Charles attended the next CHOGM in Sri Lanka in the Queen's place.

In the 2014 British New Year's Honours List, Sir Christopher was named a Knight Commander of the Order of the Bath. A snippet of the citation caught my eye: 'preparation for the transition to a change of reign and relations with the commonwealth'.

The last days of my time as prime minister will be remembered for an intersection with royalty but of an entirely different kind. Shortly after becoming prime minister, I had appeared on the cover of *The Australian Women's Weekly*. Much later, I discovered that the Liberal Party complained long and loudly about this. The appropriateness of a magazine called the 'Women's Weekly' taking some pride in the advent of Australia's first female prime minister obviously passed them by.

After the non-challenge to my leadership in March 2013, the *Women's Weekly* approached my office about me appearing again in their magazine. What emerged out of those discussions was a story with a benign human-interest angle about me knitting a toy kangaroo for the baby the British royals William and Kate were expecting. Our dog, Reuben, was also going to be in the pictures.

During the life of the government I had rediscovered the joy of knitting. I had knitted as a teenager and in my 20s. Mum was an incredibly good, fast knitter. She taught both Alison and me to knit.

As deputy prime minister, in 2010, on a commercial flight, I got chatting with one of my staff members, Leanne Budd, and discovered she was a keen knitter. One thing led to another and the idea of knitting a campaign blanket was born. Basically anyone who was interested would knit squares for a blanket during the long hours of travel. I found the rhythm helped me make the transition between working flat out and needing to sleep. Even though I only produced a few squares, the blanket was assembled and auctioned as part of the charitable fundraising endeavours of the Canberra Press Gallery's annual midwinter ball.

After that, I kept knitting and made a number of baby clothing items for friends; you can relatively quickly achieve a finished product. Aware we would start getting asked what present Australia was sending for the royal baby, knitting a toy kangaroo struck me as a good project. It was something personal, rather than coldly official.

Quite a few people came with me to the photo shoot and interview, not because I demanded they be there but because a number of them wanted to see the 'glamour' of a full-scale fashion production. It was a day of a lot of fun. The journalist writing the piece spent a lot of time hugging Reuben, joking that Labor's slogan for the election should be 'Vote Labor or the Dog Gets It'. She was so taken with Reuben she thought this would guarantee us victory in a landslide.

Once the pictures for the magazine were done, I asked if some shots could be taken of the people with me, just for us. It was crystal clear I was requesting this so we could have a private memento of the day.

After a day of such apparent goodwill, I was disgusted when the piece was brought forward by a month and was all about the discussions between my office and the magazine about the nature of the article. Such negotiations happen all the time between people appearing in magazines and the editorial and production teams. For obvious reasons, the discussions are viewed by all sides as confidential. But on this occasion, in order to produce the worst possible article at the worst possible time for me, the usual conventions were thrown out the window.

I am not someone prone to complaining directly about my portrayal in the media. Only rarely have I done so, and only in circumstances where a publication was defamatory or outrageously wrong. Some politicians are famous for their frequent abuse-laden phone calls of complaint to journalists and editors. That has not been my style. This time I did, however, complain to the editor, Helen McCabe, in a stiffly worded letter. What drove me to this point was particularly the use in the magazine of the photos that had been taken privately for me. This was such an egregious breach of trust. I wrote that she had treated me 'disrespectfully as a prime minister and shabbily as a human being'. While Helen did apologise, her response made it clear to me that she seemed strongly motivated by the desire to avoid disapproval from the Liberal Party.

Of course, errors were made by me and my team in setting this interview up. I freely admit I did not take as much interest in the discussions about the nature of the article as I should have. My media team made an error in going for such a cutesy angle. Even so, no amount of sophisticated media management can overcome blatant bias and breaching of undertakings.

Post the end of my prime ministership, I felt honour-bound to ensure the completed kangaroo was delivered. Our then High Commissioner, Mike Rann, a former Labor Premier of South Australia, made the necessary arrangements and reported back to me that the toy had both been well received and dribbled on by baby George. Whoever you knit for, it is always good to hear your work is being used.

Out of all of these experiences, I emerge not only with memories to treasure but an abidingly optimistic view about Australia's sense of identity as a nation. We will become a republic one day but our current status as a realm nation is not distorting our self-confident outlook on the world. We are able to command the world's respect, as evidenced by our election to the UN Security Council, our selection to host the G20, our work in trade.

The international relationships of most importance to us are stronger than ever. Our understanding of our place in this region and the future that can lie before us has been thought through and documented. Our economy has been among the strongest and most resilient in the world during the most difficult of times. Our best days are certainly ahead of us if we are wise and active enough to shape the future we want.

14

Our first Australians

'We will reject the "soft bigotry of low expectations". We will set high expectations for the achievement of Indigenous children.'

ME SPEAKING AS DEPUTY PRIME MINISTER AT THE
OPENING OF THE STRONGER, SMARTER SUMMIT
IN BRISBANE, 28 SEPTEMBER 2009

A REFERENCE TO RICHARD NIXON GOING TO CHINA has become political shorthand for the concept that there are some radical things that it takes a conservative to do. It is believed a conservative can bring their constituency to accept change, whereas the same action undertaken by a progressive would have conservatives in open revolt.

In Australia this shorthand makes little sense. After all, it was Gough Whitlam who went to China first – even before Nixon – and our conservatives, the Liberal and National parties, heaped scorn on him for doing so. Gough also poured dirt into Vincent Lingiari's hand to signal our nation's new understanding of the connection of our first peoples to their land.

It was Bob Hawke who legally protected Indigenous heritage. Bob was the one brave enough to launch the royal commission on Aboriginal deaths in custody, which also cast new light on the issue of the Stolen Generations. It was also Bob who asked our parliament to pass a resolution acknowledging the prior occupation of land by Aboriginal and Torres Strait Islander people, their dispossession and the denial of their citizenship rights.

It was Paul Keating who responded to the Mabo and Wik High Court decisions to create our system for recognising native title to land. It was Paul who gave the historic Redfern Speech, recognising past wrongs.

It was Kevin Rudd who said 'Sorry', while the Liberal and National parties feuded internally on whether or not that word should be uttered. Kevin also brought our nation to a new determination to close the gap between Indigenous and non-Indigenous Australians in infant mortality, education, jobs and life expectancy.

There have been some fine bipartisan moments, such as the 1991 passage of a bill establishing the Council for Aboriginal Reconciliation and setting in motion a formal ten-year 'process of reconciliation'. But there have been far more moments when it has been Labor, in the teeth of Liberal and National Party negative campaigning, that has had to make the big changes. I hope in the future that moments of bipartisanship far outnumber moments of conflict.

With Kevin as prime minister, the cabinet met in Yirrkala in Arnhem Land. It was there I first truly felt the power and beauty of Indigenous culture. Previously I had been exposed to many a welcome to country, to singing and to dancing. But at the lead-in to the school assembly, while the children and old women danced, feet stamping, hips swaying, the spiritual and collectively binding power that this age-old ritual unleashed swept through me. Many times since, I have thought back to this experience, which goes beyond words.

In Opposition I served briefly as Shadow Minister for Indigenous Affairs. It was added to my responsibilities for population and immigration. When I moved to the health portfolio, these responsibilities went to other ministers. During that brief time, I travelled and was able to see Indigenous disadvantage in an up-close and personal way. The elderly women living outside on filthy mattresses. The children struggling to learn because they could not hear, the result of curable ear conditions. The grog and the violence. The despair of the emergency department workers who treated knife wound after knife wound. Medical staff came from around the world to study emergency responses to knife wounds at the Alice Springs hospital. So much practice had made the staff experts.

I was exposed to all the debates. The straw-man debate of spiritual versus practical reconciliation. The stereotyping of progressives as somehow only believing in symbols and not being prepared to offer practical help on jobs, health and education. The failure of some conservatives to grasp that for human beings, our sense of self-worth matters to how well we are, how well we function in the world. That things of the spirit can matter in the most practical of ways. The difficulties with ensuring Indigenous Australians get a fair share of the mainstream normal programs that government runs, as well as the benefit of specifically designed programs.

Australians are often alarmed by the big sums spent on programs for Indigenous people. I doubt they recognise that many mainstream programs do not work for Indigenous Australians, that, compared with other Australians, their use of those programs is pitifully low. Consequently, even with additional specific programs, our effort as a nation can be far smaller than it seems.

I had observed the caring of well-meaning white Australians who inadvertently infantilised Indigenous adults, treating them as if they were incapable of doing anything for themselves. I had seen the beautiful smiles of Indigenous children and met the teachers who prized those smiles yet were actually preparing these children for a lifetime of disadvantage. Basically, in the face of overwhelming need, the teachers felt giving children a happy experience each day was enough. Pushing them to succeed was seen as too hard.

For all of Labor's proud successes, I had seen the consequences of one of its big failures: the Aboriginal and Torres Strait Islander Commission (ATSIC). Set up in 1990 by the Hawke Government, ATSIC was a body elected by Indigenous Australians and charged with oversight of government programs that affected them. It became mired in corruption allegations and under the leadership of the controversial Geoff Clark started to stagger towards its demise. As Shadow minister I had quickly come to the view that it needed to go.

The inherent tensions between talk – detailed consultation with communities – and action – addressing urgent need – also struck me forcefully. An Indigenous woman in Darwin telling me about a new plan for health care memorably said, 'It has been the subject of consultation for well over a year now and no one has so much as put a Panadol down a blackfella's throat yet.'

I had seen how good Indigenous leaders in communities could change life for the better for their people. I had also felt the despair of so many concerned non-Indigenous Australians, who were giving up hope that change was possible.

These experiences were my grounding before setting out as Education Minister to do two things. First, to make sure that everything we did in education better responded to need. A system that truly met need, rather than being prepared to leave some children behind, would always better serve Indigenous children. Second, to preach a culture of high expectations, that we should not expect less of Indigenous children than we do of other children.

In speaking publicly about expectations for the achievement of Indigenous children I deliberately used George W Bush's words about the 'soft bigotry of low expectations'.[1] High expectations should not be a partisan issue and quoting his words was my way of demonstrating that. Indigenous children, children from the poorest of homes, can succeed to the highest of standards if we, the adults, are prepared to do everything necessary to get them a great education.

The power of high expectations was brought home to me when I visited a Washington school attended by very disadvantaged children. Washington is one of those places where turning one street corner can take you from wealth and grandeur to poverty and blighted lives. That same turn of the corner is likely to take you from overwhelmingly white neighbourhoods to overwhelmingly African-American neighbourhoods. At this high school, every child I saw except one was African-American. The principal, also an African-American, had led a huge turnaround in outcomes. As he showed me around, he would stop every student we passed and ask, 'What is our expectation?' Each student replied, 'Excellence is our expectation.' The motto caught the changed reality he had brought about.

The same determination was evident in Chris Sarra, an Indigenous Australian who as principal had led a turnaround process at Cherbourg

State School in Queensland. I ensured we backed his 'stronger, smarter' high-expectations philosophy with new resources and that it could be shared in many schools.

On becoming prime minister, I inherited work that needed to be continued and new challenges for Indigenous Australians.

Kevin Rudd, working with Jenny Macklin, had responded in Opposition and in government to the Howard Government's Northern Territory Emergency Response (NTER) following the release of the 'Little Children are Sacred' report, which exposed some shocking truths about the degree of child sexual abuse and neglect of Indigenous children. Labor determined when the NTER was announced by John Howard and Mal Brough, the then Indigenous Affairs Minister, to provide it with bipartisan support.

Many good things were done in the NTER and important new investments were made. But there were many problems too.

Fundamentally problems like sexual abuse cannot be resolved by a defence force-style mobilisation effort. In addition, it is one thing to say abuse and neglect rates are shockingly high, but it is another thing entirely to operate on the assumption that every child is abused and neglected, that every Indigenous man is a suspect.

By the time we were elected to government, the strengths and the weaknesses of the NTER were on display. The first review of it found:

> There is intense hurt and anger at being isolated on the basis of race and subjected to collective measures that would never be applied to other Australians. The Intervention was received with a sense of betrayal and disbelief. Resistance to its imposition undercut the potential effectiveness of its substantive measures. The crisis that prompted the NTER in June 2007 is real. It should remain a national priority for sustained attention and investment by the Australian Government. But the way forward must be based on a fresh relationship.[2]

Under Kevin's leadership our laws were changed to respect the fundamental principle that our nation should not negatively discriminate on the grounds of race and that our Racial Discrimination Act should apply. The NTER had been exempted from this principle.

Kevin brought his very clear views about measurement and accountability to structuring the 'Closing the Gap' response to nation-wide Indigenous disadvantage. He rightly required measurable targets, a coordinator general responsible for the entirety of the government's work and an annual report to the parliament on progress.

To give Indigenous Australians a louder voice in the affairs of the nation, given the demise of ATSIC, Kevin and Jenny worked together to create in 2009 the National Congress of Australia's First Peoples, a central mechanism for the government, corporate and community sectors to engage and partner with Indigenous Australians on reform initiatives.

Kevin attended one meeting of the regular conferences, grandly called consiliums, of the conservative Centre for Independent Studies and immediately adopted an approach to Indigenous job creation conceived by mining magnate and philanthropist Andrew Forrest. Asking me and my office to whip up supporting policy and paper-work, Kevin launched a new government approach within 48 hours. Too hastily conceived, it did not realise its full promise. However the commitment of Andrew Forrest and other major corporate leaders to providing jobs to Indigenous Australians is passionate and real.

I was hoping for the best when I attended on 8 June 2011 at Gove the celebration to mark the signing of a 42-year agreement between the Yolngu people and Rio Tinto. It heralded the promise of sharing long-term opportunities for jobs and education as Rio worked its bauxite mine and alumina refinery. These businesses had operated for over 40 years with no agreement with traditional owners. But bitter disap-pointment was to follow when Rio announced its intention to close the refinery, which in government we worked to save.

Early in my prime ministership, a pressing issue was what to replace the NTER with when the legislation authorising it came to its expiry date.

In the first of three progress reports I delivered to the parliament on Closing the Gap, I said:

I do believe that Australians want our Indigenous people to have a better life. I also understand that many Australians wonder if our country can ever make that happen.

I feel the force of these two Australian emotions – our deep dream of a better life for all, and our deep fear that we can never truly achieve it – as I speak to the parliament today.

I know our people think of the past, of the great policy movements and the passionate debates, of the money spent and the stubborn persistence of disadvantage, and I know they sometimes wonder . . . can we really make a difference?

I am an activist and an optimist. For me, the answer can only be yes.[3]

It was with that activism and optimism for change that my government tackled fresh ways of working in the Northern Territory.

Jenny Macklin as Indigenous Affairs Minister personally guided a process of consultation and policy development. To this task and all others within the portfolio, Jenny took a tough-love approach. She wanted change but sought the right mix of increased opportunity and responsibility. She knew a high priority was to fight the lawlessness and the grog. She understood that in so many Indigenous communities, women were the agents of change.

In the consultation I attended with her, tears were shed by those who spoke about the effects of alcohol and violence in their lives and the lives of their children. There was also residual hurt from the way the NTER had happened around them, not in partnership with them.

Our response to the tears and the needs was the Stronger Futures policy, which put a sharp focus on tackling alcohol abuse, increasing community safety and protecting children while getting on with the business of creating jobs, getting children to regularly attend improved schools, working to make sure everyone was better fed and housed and had decent health care. Our new plan came into effect in July 2012 and included a 10-year funding commitment of $3.4 billion. As I write, it is continuing to make a real difference to the lives of Indigenous Australians in the Northern Territory.

Federal Labor's consistent view of the harm being caused by alcohol came to be shared by the Northern Territory Labor Government led by Paul Henderson. Jenny's persistence in pushing for reform paid off. In 2011, Paul courageously introduced the well named 'Enough is Enough Alcohol Reform Package'. At its centre was the creation of a register of people who had been banned from drinking. It was the toughest of policies, meaning anyone buying alcohol had to identify themselves and a list was kept of people who could not legally make a purchase because they had been constantly in trouble for alcohol-related offences.

Incredibly, just four days after he was elected in August 2012, the new conservative Chief Minister of the Northern Territory, Terry Mills, did away with the banned-drinkers register, arguing that the measure had failed. Yet after its first year of operation, alcohol-related assaults had dropped and there were 10,000 fewer antisocial instances reported. Partisanship, once again, had negatively impacted progress.

Activism, optimism and pragmatism were all required to commence the process that I trust will lead to the recognition of our first peoples in our constitution. Australia's constitution is both a living document and a product of its times. It is living in the sense that our High Court has found new ways of interpreting it over the years. It is a product of its times for the prejudices and predispositions it contains.

Before the unifying moment of the 1967 referendum, our constitution did not count Indigenous people as Australians. That referendum also gave the federal government the power to make laws for the benefit of Indigenous people.

In 1999, John Howard took to the Australian people a proposal to insert a preamble in our constitution, part of which explicitly recognised our first peoples. For a referendum to succeed, a majority of Australians need to vote for change but so do Australians in a majority of states. It can be a difficult combination to pull off. Furthermore Australians are wary of constitutional change. Even a referendum proposal as self-evidently meritorious as specifying that one vote should have one value has been defeated. Australians rejected all proposals put to them in 1999, which included Howard's preamble and becoming a republic.

John Howard in 2007 committed himself to a referendum proposal specifically on Indigenous recognition. Labor under Kevin Rudd backed this proposal for change. This commitment has been Liberal and Labor Party policy ever since but no timetable for change was set.

In the discussions to form minority government, Rob Oakeshott in particular sought a commitment to a timetable for change. I agreed it was time for progress and we set out to try to bring a referendum to the people by the 2013 election.

The first and vital step was precisely defining the wording of the changes sought. While the recognition proposal was not aimed at changing substantive rights, every word of the changes would be important to how well Indigenous Australians thought the work of recognition was done and how likely it was that Australians in their millions would vote yes in the referendum.

Very early in the life of the government, Jenny Macklin and I set up an expert panel to advise on the wording. One of the co-chairs was the man frequently described as the father of reconciliation, Indigenous Australian Professor Patrick Dodson. The other was Mark Leibler, an eminent lawyer who is both well known and respected. Rob was appointed to the expert panel as was Janelle Saffin, representing Labor, and Rachel Siewert, representing the Greens. Importantly Ken Wyatt, the first Indigenous Australian to serve in the House of Representatives, was nominated by the Opposition for membership of the expert panel.

On 19 January 2012, I released the results of the work of this group. Their consultations had been wide-ranging and their recommendations were sensible and smart. They consisted of two deletions from the constitution – the removal of redundant and repugnant sections which enabled states to ban people from voting based on their race, and for laws to be made which discriminated on racial grounds – and the addition of three new clauses. First, a statement of recognition of Aboriginal and Torres Strait Islander peoples and their unique history, culture and connection to this land. Second, a ban on racial discrimination by government, while preserving the ability of the federal parliament to pass laws for the special benefit of racially identified groups, a way of enabling special positive action but preventing negative racial moves. Third, recognition that Aboriginal and Torres Strait Islander languages were this country's first tongues, while confirming that English is Australia's national language.

In making these recommendations the expert panel had steered a middle course through some complex tensions in our community. For instance, some people think anything less than a treaty, a formal agreement between our first peoples and those who came to their lands, is an insult. Other people fear the slightest wording change to the constitution will open a Pandora's box of unwanted legal action and unintended consequences.

There was a collective intake of breath when even before the delivery of the report, the Liberal Shadow Attorney-General, George Brandis, expressed reservations about anything other than a minor change. For the referendum to have any chance of success, we would need enthusiastic bipartisanship of not only the concept but the specific wording of the proposed amendments. On top of that, my colleagues and I were alive to the reality that for a referendum proposal on matters involving Indigenous Australians, politicians could only do so much. A movement to vote yes needed to come alive and grow. More Australians would need to become energised and active than those who are members of political parties. The case for change needed a range of community voices, not just political voices. There would be the need to inform and reassure Australians right around the nation about what the change meant.

Another risk was that those peddling the most ugly prejudice could come to the fore, thanks to the anonymity afforded by certain forms of social media. Even with politicians, community leaders and mainstream media campaigning for a yes vote, it was possible a clever campaign, spreading fear with false claims about the repercussions of the change, could take hold.

Before we proceeded, we needed to diagnose what the prospects of success were for the referendum. Jenny and I knew that the very worst thing we could do was put the referendum proposal forward only to see it fail. What would the day after look and feel like if Australians had failed to recognise our Indigenous peoples, had failed to endorse a non-discrimination proposal? It was too ghastly to contemplate. For a number of members of the expert panel, this was their greatest fear too.

Our thinking matched what was found through Jenny's sounding out of Indigenous leaders. It became clearer and clearer that the case for change could not be effectively mounted in time for a referendum before or even at the 2013 election. Rob Oakeshott was deeply unhappy with this decision and would have preferred full steam ahead.

However, it was the right decision to delay the referendum. But then, to maintain the momentum for change, we brought to the parliament a recognition law. It contained a commitment of $10 million to build community awareness for constitutional change. It had a sunset clause of two years, with a review to be carried out 12 months after the new law was passed to examine levels of community support. This new law would make sure the issue could not fall off anyone's agenda.

Even for this proposal, bipartisanship eluded us. On 21 September 2012 Tony Abbott said he was opposed because the bill was just a measure to lock the next parliament into a referendum. George Brandis announced that the Coalition would not support it. Fortunately Mark Leibler and others, who worked tirelessly with the Coalition to gain their support, won through. Bipartisanship was achieved and the Act of Recognition passed unanimously through the House of Representatives on 13 February 2013 and through the Senate the day after.

I am confident our nation is going to reach this milestone in the journey towards reconciliation and do it quite soon. It will require concerted effort by many Australians, from many walks of life and differing political persuasions. But get there we will.

I am also confident that we will close the gap and enable Indigenous Australians to have lives that are as long, healthy and prosperous as Australians generally. It will take time, demand the best of us and require a broader approach than work directly in the portfolio called Indigenous Affairs. In government, we always understood that Jenny's direct work in that portfolio had to be accompanied by change in education, health, welfare and disability policy. Having our major policies and big agencies of government directed towards helping those in the most need will inevitably mean more and higher quality assistance goes to Indigenous Australians.

Change is hard, but it is possible.

*

While we worked as a government on these transformational reforms, I worked personally to change my own political party, to make sure we succeeded in supporting the first Indigenous Australian into parliament as a Labor member.

It had been a source of continuing shame to me and others in the ALP that no Indigenous Australian had ever sat among our ranks. In 1971 Neville Bonner, an Indigenous Australian from Queensland, had been preselected for the Senate by the Liberal Party. He served in the Senate for many years. Aden Ridgeway, an Indigenous Australian from New South Wales, served as an Australian Democrats senator for six years from 1999. The 2010 election saw the election of Ken Wyatt, an Indigenous Australian, as the Liberal Member for Hasluck, a seat in Western Australia.

My role was not to meddle in preselection decisions. The Labor Party is not the prime minister's personal fiefdom and the party needs to properly attend to preselection matters. If I had a strong view, then of course I would put it, but generally the party just got on with things. I saw my role as endeavouring to energise the party and the parliamentary team around a sense of purpose.

The issue of the preselection for the Northern Territory Senate spot was first raised with me by South Australian Mark Butler. Mark came to the federal parliament having served as an official of the Miscellaneous Workers Union, the union to which my father belonged and performed unpaid roles for, like being on the State Council. Mark was a major figure in the National Left faction and his factional colleague, Trish Crossin, held the Northern Territory Senate spot. Territory Senate spots only have three-year terms so Trish faced preselection each time. She had been a canny survivor of various attempts to replace her. Those who thought Trish might call it a day after serving in the Senate for 15 years were proved wrong when Trish made it clear to all she wanted to run again in the 2013 election.

This was the context when Mark suggested that, despite Trish's intentions, the opportunity should be used to support an Indigenous Australian into parliament. For this, Mark wanted more than my support. It would take my authority to achieve the result.

Not backing a colleague in your parliamentary team who wishes to continue goes against the grain. My inclination has always been to support the continuation of colleagues' service. On the other hand, a healthy political party needs to renew and broaden itself. Trish had enjoyed a long career as a backbencher. It was clear she would not rise further in the federal parliamentary ranks. In respect of income, she would have the benefit of the older, more generous parliamentary superannuation scheme. On balance, I thought it was fair to ask her to make way because it was in Labor's interests and the nation's interests to see an Indigenous Australian enter parliament representing the Northern Territory, the place where so much work was being done to create a better future. I nurtured a hope Trish might come to accept the wisdom of this decision.

Once I made up my mind to do everything possible to achieve this result I asked Mark, with George Wright, the Labor Party's National Secretary, to sound out potential candidates, including Nova Peris.

Nova sent back a loud and clear message that she was interested. Nova was originally from the Territory and her stellar sporting career had yielded Olympic Gold. She had gone back to the Territory and was using her profile to do further important work for Indigenous Australians, including the operation of her own academy to get Indigenous girls to finish school.

Obviously there was immense appeal to preselecting a woman but I insisted on the most careful work being done with Nova to see how she would cope with intense and inevitably hostile scrutiny. Nova would be the first Indigenous woman to enter the federal parliament. From my own experience, I knew it was not easy to be the first. She would be a big target, potentially, for the Opposition, the media and disgruntled supporters of Trish. Ultimately Nova demonstrated to Mark, George, Ben Hubbard and members of my media team that she could handle the heat.

Unfortunately this process took longer than I would have liked and Trish's expectations that she would be preselected again grew. Indeed, needing more time, I had the process of preselection put on hold for a period. I am proud of my decision to back Nova. My regret is the long set-up time, which made it harder for Trish.

Confronting Trish with the unpleasant truth was the next step. There was no scope for her to take time to consider her position. That would certainly have meant it all leaking to the media. I asked Trish to see me at The Lodge in the late afternoon of Monday 21 January 2013. We sat in a small sitting room and I explained my decision.

Trish was angry and upset. She cried. I could absolutely understand all those reactions. I explained that I would endorse Nova publicly the next day. That meant Nova would be preselected by the National Executive of the Labor Party. I told Trish she had an opportunity, as hard as it was for her, to embrace my plan and be seen as the person who had graciously made possible the entry of the first Indigenous woman into the federal parliament by stepping aside for her.

Trish said that her intention had been to be preselected, re-elected and serve for only 12 months, then to hand over to an Indigenous Australian. She had been mentoring some potential candidates to take over her spot. At the end of a long discussion, Trish was not 100 per cent decided about how she would react but she was heading towards taking the dignified and generous path of endorsing Nova. She was even starting to rehearse the kind of things she could say about why she was going.

I made an undertaking to share with Trish the draft media release announcing Nova plus my notes for the press conference, and that these would include some text about Trish and her attitude to Nova running. We agreed to speak again very early the next morning before Trish was due to take a flight to Sydney to attend a Senate committee hearing. This would give Trish an opportunity to provide me with feedback on the draft documents. I asked her not to speak to anyone other than family overnight and she agreed to do so.

It was obvious from the calls I received that night that immediately on leaving The Lodge, Trish had started ringing around people in the Labor Party. She had certainly spoken to Kim Carr. When we spoke the next morning, Trish was no longer prepared to graciously exit. She said she had been informed I did not have the numbers on the National Executive, that she would fight me and win. I tried to explain she had been woefully misinformed. She did not listen.

That day, I stood alongside Nova and endorsed her as my 'captain's pick'. Nova was nervous but performed well. The more time I spent with her and her family in a pressured situation, the more confident I was that she was going to be tough enough to deal with everything that comes with being 'the first' in politics. I was convinced she would make a fine senator.

A week later Nova was preselected by the National Executive by a margin of 19 votes to two. Trish had been used and misled. Although I knew I had dealt Trish a tough blow, I had done it for a purpose and offered her a way through with dignity. Those, like Kim Carr, who assured her she had the numbers, used her for no real purpose other than having a short-term go at me.

Nova succeeded at the 2013 election and said in her first speech to the parliament, 'I also particularly thank the former prime minister, Julia Gillard, from the bottom of my heart, for her faith in me and for giving me the chance to become involved. My duty now is to work hard and make a real difference.'[14]

In the cause of reconciliation, recognition and closing the gap, that is the duty of all of us.

15

Our children

'In coming to this House, I bring with me a passionately held view that it is fundamental to Labor's vision, to our compact with this and the next generation, that Australia not only offers the opportunities I enjoyed but offers the opportunity to train, to retrain, to excel, throughout life.

'The students from my electorate are not any less intelligent than those from Higgins or Kooyong but their educational opportunities are not the same. Certainly this massive discrepancy would be lessened if we as a nation were prepared to seriously tackle the inequality of opportunity that exists in our education system and create a high-class state school system. My predecessor, Barry Jones, used to say that unfortunately postcodes are probably the strongest factor in determining a person's expectations of success in life. It will be one of my priorities in politics to ensure that in the Australia of the future the famous quizmaster is, for once, wrong.'

MY FIRST SPEECH TO PARLIAMENT, 11 NOVEMBER 1998

I ENJOYED SCHOOL AND WAS GOOD AT IT. Growing up in the shadow of my father's sense of loss at not being able to complete his education, I felt going to school was a privilege. Although I did not like all my teachers, I respected them. I aspired to be like them, particularly Mr Crowe, the deputy principal of my primary school, who taught me English. He seemed to effortlessly inspire us to love learning, especially literature. I now know enough about teaching techniques to realise there is nothing effortless about it.

Even if I couldn't name it, as a child I noticed education and income inequality. The girl from a home and family that seemed odd – the word dysfunctional would not have been on my lips – who failed a grade in primary school. The newly arrived Greek children who started to come in numbers to my high school and who found the going tough. The children who had swimming pools at home or the ultimate status symbol, the boxed set of 72 Derwent coloured pencils.

Out of this, I formed the view that education changes lives and the only fair thing is for every child to get a great one. To personally help achieve this, I decided I wanted to be a teacher. I was never the girl who cooed over someone's baby, demanding a cuddle. My motivations were about helping shape and sharpen a child's mind, rather than an emotional desire to hold a child's hand.

Late in my schooling career, I discovered a love of debating. I was great mates with twin girls Kathy and Lyn Pilowsky and their mother, Marlene, suggested that law might suit me. Her words hit home and I changed my plans. Via an unexpected route, my life has rolled out in accordance with my original teenage intention to make a difference to children.

I remember the mix of exhilaration and terror as I took my first steps at Adelaide University's North Terrace campus, there to study law and arts. Marlene's words had prompted me to pursue law but I took out a bit of insurance. In case law was not to my taste, I added an arts degree which combined two things I loved: economics and English.

After the first year of finding my feet, I found student politics in my second year. Perhaps more accurately, it found me. Mandy Cornwall, the daughter of a South Australian Labor minister, on the hunt for Labor recruits, invited me into the circle formed by the Labor Club and progressive student activists.

Then came a cause to get involved in: a fightback against Fraser Government-inspired cuts to university funding. That fight ushered in new experiences: organising meetings; making leaflets; generating copy for the university student newspaper *On Dit*; speaking at my first rally, with Mum and Dad on the fringe of the crowd; having the honour of speaking at a graduation ceremony as an undergraduate, this time with Mum and Dad in some of the best seats.

From then, I focused more and more on student politics and campaigning for better education on campus, statewide, nationally. There was always the next thing to do, the next challenge. I moved to Melbourne to serve as the AUS Education Vice President and then its President.

Now I look back with a sense of awe at my embrace of change and my naivety. At the ripe old age of 20, I thought nothing of putting my pitifully small set of belongings on a trailer and driving off to live in a city I had barely visited. What eased my way was that youthful sense that nothing bad could really happen.

At the AUS I learnt skills that would stay with me for life: working to deadlines, galvanising a team to collaborate with you and share your vision, developing policies, working the media, employing staff and keeping to a budget. It was intoxicating and mind-expanding. You travelled around the country visiting campuses, liaising with local student organisations; you went to Canberra lobbying. Prior to then, I had hardly ever been on a plane or packed a bag. To start living this life of new places and new faces was thrilling.

It was during this period that people started telling me I should go into politics. That I would be good at it. That it was the way to truly change things. After meetings with people like the federal Shadow Education Minister, John Dawkins, I would muse about what it would be like to be on his side of the desk. Slowly the concept that politics could be for me took root in my brain. If the idea had been suggested to me in high school, I would have dismissed it as absurd. Politics was not for the likes of me, I would have said. I would have thought that there was a special breed of super-smart people who went into politics.

During my student politics experience, I came to understand there was no crowd of superhumans from which politicians were drawn. Instead politicians were just motivated people trying to do their best. That meant I could be one.

Post-student politics, I completed my degrees at Melbourne University. The idea of becoming a politician transformed from an inkling to a thought bubble to a burning ambition, and my long fight to get into parliament began. It tested my motivation and resilience but in 1998 I finally got there.

Full of nervous anticipation, I prepared to give my first speech to parliament. I finished the final draft the night before. My drafting and redrafting had started to border on the obsessive. I faxed it to John Brumby and asked for his critique. When I worked for him as his chief of staff, I had been the author of some of his speeches. One day, as he was about to go onstage, I had teased him: 'It's a great speech,' I said, 'but it's all in the delivery.' On the eve of my maiden speech, he returned the teasing by making those words his final ones to me.

The next morning I awoke in my cheap motel, one that was a favourite among politicians, and washed my Ginger Spice-like red and blonde hair. That morning of all mornings, my hair dryer developed a fault. Quite dramatically, it blew up in my hand and a flame shot out of the back of it. Wet-haired but at least not burnt, I dashed around to the better hotel I had organised for my mother and used her hair dryer. It would not be the last time my hair threatened to overshadow all else.

Everything about those opening days in parliament was heady. My sense of direction is bad and I was perpetually getting lost. There were so many new colleagues to meet. So many new things to learn. But for me it was a dream come true. I joined the House of Representatives Education, Employment and Workplace Relations Committee and the Caucus Education Committee.

My first taste of reaching a goal and savouring a moment of pure elation preceded politics. It was as a young person, when I walked away after my final university examination, confident I had passed. The days of going to the dingy Western Annex of the Royal Exhibition Building in Melbourne for up to three and a half hours of adrenaline-fuelled testing were over. I had done it.

That same emotion, that joy, was there as I finished my first speech and looked up at the parliamentary gallery with my mother sitting there and so many friends. On election night in 2007, I experienced another such moment. Finally I had the opportunity to do what I had been wanting to do all my life: to make a difference for children. I was not going to miss the chance.

*

I spent election night in the Canberra Tally Room, a place where the media and the public could gather to watch results being put on a board. Modernity has overtaken it and it is no more. But in 2007 it was throbbing with Labor supporters expecting a victory. I was commentating for the ABC, sitting in a set with the veteran political reporter Kerry O'Brien and the Liberal Party's Nick Minchin, also a seasoned professional.

As the results came in, a Labor victory became more certain. I had to quell my growing sense of excitement. After all, I was not there to party on television but to keep calling and commentating on the results. Nick had to deal with the realisation of the defeat he had expected. He looked so morose that at one point I leant over and patted his hand.

Spontaneously, after John Howard's concession speech, I said he would be remembered 'with respect and . . . some affection as well', something which has come to pass.

As the coverage came to a close, it was time to enjoy the win. I had not figured on the crush that surrounded me as I tried to leave the venue. An enormous media pack. Labor supporters wild with delight. With Tim's arm around me for protection and some help from local police, we finally got through.

A number of friends had come to Canberra to share the moment. We had all hired serviced apartments at the same place. It was champagne all round. The next morning we gathered for breakfast in a garden area at the apartments. Prudently I had gone to bed before many of the others. Someone had brought to the breakfast some beer stubbies. No one wanted them but I think people were keen to keep the feel of a party happening. Unfortunately one was dropped and glass shards and beer went everywhere.

Imagine the scene, the reek of alcohol fumes, the sight of people – some of them looking the worse for wear – scouring the ground picking up all the glass. Into this chaos walked a senior public servant making a special delivery to me.

During an election campaign, the public service prepares comprehensive incoming government briefs for both sides of politics. It is the first advice to you on how to go about implementing your election policies and the likely hurdles you will face as a government. Called the Red Books, for the first period of government these are your bible.

The public servant didn't blanch but handed me my Red Books and left. It would be a long while before the feeling of mild chaos left me.

Transitioning to government is a strange mix of the elevated – like being sworn in by the Governor-General – and the pedestrian – like working out where to put your stuff in your new office. As deputy prime minister, I had the second biggest office in the ministerial wing. Prior to then, I had hardly ever been to that part of the parliament building. In Opposition, the only reason to go there was the unusual occasion when a Liberal or National Party minister condescended to see you in their office about a matter of importance to your electorate. I had never set foot in the prime minister's office, the prime minister's courtyard, the deputy prime minister's office I now occupied or the cabinet room. Apart from the rare leaked cabinet documents that had caused a headache for the Howard Government, I had never seen cabinet papers.

The learning curve is steep. I did my very best to run up it as quickly as possible. I was desperate to start making decisions, bringing change, giving every child the quality education they deserved.

SCHOOLS

Coupled with my enthusiasm for education as the way to create a fairer society was my understanding of some fundamental truths about our economy and the politics of education. Long gone were the days when, for an individual, a second-class education was a ticket to a secure, full-time menial job. In the 21st-century economy, with its new technology, many of those jobs had been destroyed. That second-class education was more likely to precede a marginalised life with no continuing work.

Long gone too were the days of being able to assume that our economy would be a high-wage, high-skill one. The countries of our region, our competitors, were improving their education systems too quickly for that delusion to hold.

To their credit the Hawke and Keating governments had kept increasing funding to schools, and for life after school had created our national skills training system. They had radically changed universities and thrown open the doors to more students than ever. But during the Howard era this progress was supplanted by political game-playing.

For much of the 20th century, social democratic parties, like the Labor Party, and conservative parties, like the Liberal Party, were defined by their belief in the role of government. Labor would say public provision is always better. The Liberals would reply private is always better. Labor would aim for bigger government, the Liberals for smaller.

Under the Hawke and Keating governments, Labor moved on. Assets were privatised. A tight approach was taken to managing the size of government.

In its later years, the Howard Government moved on too, in that it embraced a bigger government approach, collecting record amounts of revenue and paying it out to families and senior citizens in new benefits. But it never lost the prejudice that private is always better. It enabled rapid growth in the number of private childcare providers and private schools, without doing anything effective to ensure the services provided were good quality or putting in the hands of families the information they needed to make informed, sensible choices about which childcare centre or school was right for their child.

Rather than policy development, there was ruthless politics. Government and non-government schools were goaded into dogfights with each other over funding. There were appeals to traditional values through devices like requiring schools to have a flagpole. But what was happening in the classrooms the flag was flying over? Questions of educational quality, whether some kids were being left behind, were largely ignored.

As the newly minted Education Minister, I pored over all the briefing papers. I had not come this far to tinker. I was determined to address the quality issues, to make sure no child was left behind.

In my early interactions with the newly created Department of Education, Employment and Workplace Relations, one thing stood out: our nation did not know much about its schools. Comprehensive information held by state departments of education was jealously guarded. Even if you somehow wrested it from them, the data would not give you a national picture and it would not tell you anything about independent or Catholic schools.

In a sea of politically inspired sludge and general neglect, the one thing the Howard Government had got right in education was brokering with the states and non-government schools agreement to national testing, so that on the same day around the country children would sit down to the same literacy and numeracy tests. However, while the results would generate report cards for individual children and state-by-state results in aggregate, nothing further would be made available. A rich treasure-trove of information about how our schools were performing would disappear into state government public-service vaults.

From my meetings with stakeholders I had gleaned that the current discussion about education was based on shibboleths. Public-education advocates would claim that all disadvantage was in the public sector and the problem was underfunding. In fact, there were a number of very low-fee non-government schools serving deeply disadvantaged communities. Advocates of non-government schools insisted that their focus was excellence, with the implication that their schools could be relied on for great quality. Intuitively I knew many government schools were doing better than they were being given credit for and I suspected there were some non-government schools whose reputation was at odds with their results. While it was assumed by many that disadvantage for children was a life sentence, I was aware, even from my own electorate, that there were schools full of disadvantaged children who ended up succeeding – not as measured by some concessional standard but measured by the same standards as children generally.

Unless accurate information could be put on the table, the school systems conditioned by the Howard Government to savage each other would go on doing so forever. It was time to break through all the noise and deliver the facts, school by school, for every school in the nation. The more I thought about it, the more convinced I was that transparency was the vital starting point. What I wanted was to get and make freely available comprehensive information for every school, firm in the belief this would transform the whole national conversation about education beyond the simple divide of public versus private.

Year after year, government money went into education, with no reliable national measures of what was being achieved. Year after year, advocates sought more money for education, their argument no more sophisticated than saying someone else has more so we should have more too. There was no data to indicate the right amount of money required to educate children to an appropriate standard. No measure of how much extra was needed to give a disadvantaged child a great education. Year after year, sages agreed that teacher quality is the single most important driver of the quality of a child's education. But the years slipped by with no nationally available way of showing what teachers were achieving.

I wanted to discover what we could learn by comparing the results of schools teaching similar children. Nothing would be learnt by a big-league table list which inevitably would have elite non-government schools teaching the most advantaged children at the top and remote Indigenous schools at the bottom. Such a list would only reinforce everyone's prejudices. Rather I wanted us to truly understand the quality of the job being done by schools teaching similar children. Who was taking the disadvantaged children and getting better results? What could be learnt from their ways of working? Similarly who was taking advantaged children and failing to get them to the standards attained by others? What could they learn from those doing it better?

Already I could see that if we had this information out there publicly, and then added to it with information about the funding resources available to every school, we would transform the debate about school funding. Instead of our nation's gaze being on brawling school sectors, it would be truly on the needs of individual schools.

By March 2008, I had developed a plan to put transparency at the centre of my agenda and use it as a lever for further change. I was determined to create My School so everyone in our nation could bring up a website, click and have information about the performance of schools.

I knew I was starting a war and I intended to win it. It would take two years. I had less than a year to win the first stage. New legislation and a new agreement were needed by the end of 2008 so funds could continue to flow from the federal government to non-government schools and to states for government schools. I wanted to make the flow of these funds contingent on agreement to transparency and to the creation and implementation of a national curriculum.

It was easier to make the case for a national curriculum. Having 37 separate organisations and agencies around the country that contributed to curriculum development in Australian schools was ridiculous. Children who moved interstate not only had to find their way around a new school and make new friends, they were also likely to feel unfamiliar with what was being taught. The tricky part was developing the new curriculum. The process involved questions about which state had the best curriculum. At every step along the way, while the states argued the toss the Opposition and conservative commentators played their own politics about what should be in the curriculum.

My publicly stated desire was to see a rigorous curriculum and expressly for grammar to be included. When I was working as a lawyer at Slater & Gordon, I was constantly amazed by the basic errors in the correspondence that was presented for my signature by young solicitors, paralegals and articled clerks. Often I drew a cat with a hat at the bottom of a letter to indicate an apostrophe was in the wrong place; semi-jokingly I would have everyone chanting, 'One cat's hat, two cats' hats. Where does the apostrophe go?'

Even so, I was adamant that the curriculum needed to be written by the experts. There was absolutely no political interference in the content. Anyone calling it 'partisan' now is really calling the curriculum experts involved political partisans.

In schools education, the real battleground was transparency. It is a natural human instinct not to want the possibility of failure widely exposed. Unsurprisingly school principals and schoolteachers were not keen for national exposure of their efforts and state ministers were not welcoming of the political liability it could cause.

In addition, I was pressing on scar tissue. On 8 January 1997 the *Daily Telegraph* splashed with a headline saying, 'The Class We Failed', about students at Mount Druitt High School in Sydney. The story included the claim that the best student had scored a Higher School Certificate mark of 44.4 out of 100. In the end, as a result of the negative publicity the article generated, the school received more resources and it improved. But there were devastating consequences for the students with Mount Druitt on their resumé as they sought jobs. No one wanted to interview, let alone employ, these 'failures'.

Teachers, principals and parents feared this scenario would be repeated time and time again with the kind of data that would be available on My School. All sorts of arguments against My School were put up. At a ministerial council, I was told by a state minister that you could measure the height of a child every day but whether or not they grew depended on whether you fed the child. Well exactly. That was why I wanted to use the data to generate a public debate which would end up in more funding, higher quality, higher outcomes.

I was told that tests cannot measure everything. Schools can be doing a great job in many other areas that will not be caught by literacy and numeracy tests. Once again, absolutely. But however well a school is doing in personal development, sport or drama, there is no excuse for not teaching all the children to read, write and do maths.

I was told that all of school education would be distorted to teaching to the test. Given our national assessments are world leading, teaching to the test actually meant teaching improved literacy and numeracy.

I was asked what the point was of identifying failure if nothing was done about it. My response was to list our bona fides on more resources: in 2008, alongside the agreement for more transparency, I brokered agreements to invest a new $1.5 billion in lifting standards in disadvantaged schools and more than $500 million for literacy and numeracy development.

I was told nothing matters other than teacher quality. To which I would reply, how can we identify quality if we cannot measure it, and, once again, my bona fides could be judged by the negotiation in 2008 of an agreement to allocate half a billion dollars to improving teaching quality.

The debate raged. Bronwyn Pike, Victoria's Education Minister, and Peter Dawkins, the secretary of her department, were outstanding in their support at the ministerial council meetings and associated discussions between public service officials. Patiently, with their help, I led state ministers into accepting that school funding would be tied to transparency and the teaching of national curriculum. Despite a bitter and negative Opposition campaign to stop the legislation to fund schools going through the parliament, by the end of 2008, my deal with state ministers was mirrored in law. Every school, public and private, now had no alternative but to be on My School and to teach the new content.

The next year, 2009, began with a substantial to do list. I had won a generalised tick for transparency and the creation of an expert agency to deliver My School; the concept of developing a new curriculum had also been agreed. Under the world-class leadership of a softly spoken but determined expert, Barry McGaw, the Australian Curriculum, Assessment and Reporting Authority commenced its work.

To nervous state education ministers – at this point all Labor except Western Australia – I kept saying we needed to deliver long-term change to the way the nation thought about education. Forget accepting that, over time, non-government schools, funded mainly by the federal government, would be better and better off while public schools, funded overwhelmingly by the states, lagged further behind. We had to change the terms of the debate. As state ministers, they had a responsibility for the education of all the children in their state. As the national Education Minister, I had a responsibility for the education of all the children in the nation. It was about schools not sectors.

I invited them to harness the power generated by giving the public access to sophisticated measurements of disadvantage, results and funding at the school level. People could then gauge for themselves the difference money was making. If in two schools, teachers of similar quality were teaching similar students but getting wildly different results and receiving wildly different amounts of funding, then I believed the public would clamour for the poorly performing underfunded school to get more.

To the representatives of independent and Catholic schools, I explained that I believed every child had a citizenship entitlement to some public funding for their education.

To those passionate about educating our Indigenous children, I explained my wholehearted belief that judging any child by a concessional standard because of their race, while it may be the product of benign intentions, is both racist and will ensure race-based disadvantage persists. I wanted a funding system that did not view Indigenous education as an add-on. Instead, right at the core of the system, the extra resources needed to educate Indigenous children would be built in.

Everyone in the education community was nervous. However, slowly but surely, trust was growing. As our government fulfilled our election commitments, people could see that I was prepared to not only talk about reform but resource it. The fact that these benefits were being delivered to all schools, government and non-government, helped Australians to realise that I truly was focused on the education of every child in every school.

Despite great care being taken, the delivery of our election commitments was not without problems. While state Labor premiers had bitten their tongues about the burdens being imposed on them by our election commitments during the campaign, understandably they were not prepared to do so afterwards.

I had to manage a messy negotiation about meeting and sharing the on costs of our computers-in-schools policy, a policy that had been costed solely on the basis of providing the hardware. The emblem of this policy in the media's eyes was Kevin Rudd holding aloft a laptop and declaring it the learning tool of the 21st century. Kevin had actually made this statement while announcing our policy to allow people to get a tax rebate for expenditure on things their children needed for school.

But with this picture firmly implanted in their heads, it was easy for the media to swallow Opposition beat-ups of a broken promise when not every child ended up with a laptop. Some schools chose to deliver the policy not through laptops or even personally assigned computers, but in different ways. The policy achieved its objective of a one-to-one ratio of computers to students in years 9 to 12, but shouts of 'broken promise' persisted nevertheless.

Even more absurdly, shouts from the Opposition of 'broken promise' were given credence by the media in relation to our Trade Training Centres policy. In this policy we had promised a grant of between $500,000 to $1.5 million to schools for refurbishment or construction of trade training centres. Many schools exercised the option of working together and receiving funds for $3 million or $4 million or $5 million facilities. Despite this being their choice and the facilities being first class, the Opposition cited this as a broken promise because there was not a new or refurbished centre on the grounds of every school.

For me, at this stage, the media and the Opposition's periodic carry-on was no more than a minor irritant. I was going to schools where I could see our policies making a difference.

I was determined to reach beyond the usual education stakeholders to explain the importance of transparency and the breadth of the reform agenda I wanted to drive.

Businesspeople talk constantly about the challenges of securing the skilled workforce they need. In debates about education reform they have skin in the game. I wanted to mobilise them as a constituency. To make sure they were saying to each other, to the media, to the Opposition, that my reforms were worthwhile.

Consequently I did boardroom lunch after boardroom lunch explaining that, as revealed by international testing, by the standards of the world we had a good education system but we were starting to slip behind, including particularly behind the standards of the education systems of rapidly developing countries in our region. Our economy could not hold its competitive position if our education system did not.

Businesspeople understand markets. They immediately got it that in the 'market' for school education, with public and private providers, I was aiming for better market design, with the key tool of transparency driving change. I was buoyed by having powerful allies in my corner.

Another supporter in my cause was Joel Klein, chancellor of schools in New York. Joel had grown up in public housing and gone to a tough school. One special teacher had inspired him to learn, to achieve. He had completed law school and undertaken many high-status, high-paying legal jobs. He had worked in Bill Clinton's White House. This position as chancellor was his way of giving back. Joel was pursuing a rigorous change agenda that included testing and transparency, closing underperforming schools. By the time I met Joel, in August 2008, I was already totally committed to My School, but it was tremendously bolstering to talk to someone who thought along the same lines.

Convinced that Joel could be a powerful advocate in Australia, in November 2008 I brought him to Australia. I joked that he was my pin-up boy. In many ways Joel's visit proved the merits of the saying 'Never be a prophet in your own land.' While in substance he was saying nothing different to me, his utterances were received as words of wisdom from afar.

My final meeting with Joel during his visit to Australia had been for breakfast with him and his wife, Nicole, in Sydney. Straight afterwards, I flew to Canberra to be available at the Council of Australian Governments (COAG) meeting that would finally sign off the agreement for My School. Nothing went wrong and I experienced a moment of elation when the agreement was finalised. With it, My School could go live in 2010.

I launched My School at Tempe High School in Sydney on 28 January 2010. When the site went down briefly at the start of the day, my heart sank. After the launch I rang Wayne Swan to ask him how he thought it was going. I was too in-the-middle-of-it to be a good judge. He said not to worry about the interruption of the site. Everywhere he looked, My School was dominating the nation's thoughts in a good way.

This impression was reaffirmed when one of the media advisers in Canberra went for a walk through the press gallery to find almost every journalist on My School. Even those not required to write articles were on the site checking out their child's school or their old school. On that first day, 9 million hits were registered.

Previously I had briefed newspaper editors about what to expect from My School. For them it would be a bonanza, likely to boost the number of people who would buy the paper to get the analysis of what was happening in their child's school. I asked for responsible conduct, for no repeat of the Mount Druitt-style reporting, and received it.

Despite a positive first day, the My School war was not over, it was just hotting up. Even though the website showed some high-fee-charging private schools were not doing as well as state schools teaching comparable students, creating pressure on those private schools to explain themselves, many public education advocates, particularly the Australian Education Union (AEU), reacted with extreme hostility to it. The New South Wales Teachers Federation decided to boycott the next round of national testing, due in May. It seemed that the way through would be to bus children from schools to local halls and have their testing overseen by people outside teaching – the way high school and university examinations are conducted. Images of frightened children on buses being pushed through picket lines lodged permanently in my thoughts.

To her tremendous credit, the New South Wales Education Minister, Verity Firth, stood firm. Other state education ministers and my own Labor caucus colleagues were rattled. The Opposition saw a political opening and stepped up its campaign of knocking everything. I did not blink.

Sharan Burrow, then a leader at the ACTU and a former teacher, contacted me to see if the impasse could be broken. We know each other well and I respect Sharan. She understood my intentions and my reform agenda. She also realised I was not going to compromise on my plans for change. Engaging in shuttle telephone diplomacy between the AEU and me, Sharan brokered an agreement. The strike and boycott were averted in exchange for a commitment from me to include the AEU in consultations about what would be added to My School. To me, this was an easy thing to give away; I was always happy to involve people in talks. But I was not going to be stopped.

The deal was sealed in a telephone call with Angelo Gavrielatos, the union's national president. He was emotional during the conversation.

While the process had cost all of us a great deal of stress, I was happy that from that moment, instead of fearing what would happen next, My School was secure for the future. That it would grow and develop over time as more information was added about school finances and the kind of valued-added metrics you can only do when children have been tested across their schooling career. But it would never be taken away.

At the same time as the My School fight was being waged with intensity, I became responsible for the single biggest element of Labor's economic stimulus package. Called Building the Education Revolution (BER), it was a plan that in the long run delivered $16.2 billion for new school buildings and school repairs. The aim was to deliver stimulus in a distributed, soon to be 'shovel ready' way, right around the nation to a construction industry about to be hit hard by the economic flowthrough of the GFC. Its other benefit was addressing a huge capital works backlog, particularly in primary schools.

Overwhelmingly it was a program well received by local communities and delivered quality buildings on time and on budget. Indeed the evaluation undertaken at my request, led by businessman Brad Orgill, received only 332 complaints from over 23,000 projects. Notwithstanding this, I ended up fighting a political war in defence of the BER.

Initially the anti-BER campaign was led by *The Australian*, which decided it would find a new story every day and run it under a Schools Watch logo. Even when a piece was simply a rehash, demonstrably untrue or represented the views of a minority group at a school, it was run prominently. The anti-BER campaign started to get a run on television. Often commentators from *The Australian* who also appear on television would take it there; sometimes it popped up on television because when one outlet pounds a story long enough, other outlets start to worry they are missing a yarn. *The Australian* is also not shy of criticising media outlets who are not running its stories.

The bias and absurdity of much of this came home to me graphically when I toured a school in Perth. The local *Australian* journalist, a young one, was along for the ride. We met the building company that had worked on the school. The boss told me that he had sent out redundancy notices to his workers. Then this BER project came through, enabling him to keep his workers on. The principal enthused about the new library. He told me that the school librarian had been due for retirement but was so excited to get the opportunity to work in this brand-new facility that she had deferred her retirement a year.

When I commented to the young journalist that this was a great story, he blurted out, 'I will never get that in the paper; it's positive about BER.' I laughed.

Refusing to let the matter drop, in the car later I phoned Dennis Shanahan, one of *The Australian*'s senior journalists. He also laughed and said it was a good story, that he could see the headline now: 'Old woman forced to work an extra year by cruel Rudd Labor Government'.

Dennis did ensure a brief positive piece ran in the newspaper the next day. Fortunately it did not have that headline. But behind

Dennis's wit and humour lay a darker truth. The kind of constant barrage the BER received ignored the central fact that when rolling out a multibillion-dollar urgent stimulus program, a complaint rate of three per cent is not unacceptably high.

Reflecting back on my time as Education Minister, what stands out is not the jousting with media or state ministers or the teachers' union. What comes to mind most vividly are my visits to schools. You could feel, touch, see the way our reforms were giving children a better chance in life. Thanks to the BER, Bellaire Primary School in Geelong, long neglected, was now able to teach children in a light-filled, vibrant, large, flexible space. At John Forrest High School in Perth, teenage boys learning motor mechanics in a new trade training centre told me bluntly they would not have stayed in school if they had not had this opportunity to work on cars. There was Goodna State School, serving underprivileged children in Brisbane, which was transformed by new funding made available to enhance teacher quality in schools in disadvantaged communities. The school now had a dedicated response for the children who had special learning difficulties and were likely to become disruptive in class. They could upgrade their literacy and numeracy work. Better results flowed.

While I could see my work making a difference, there was more to do, especially in the area of school funding. A Labor commitment made during the 2007 election campaign meant that the Howard Government's model of school funding would endure until the end of calendar year 2012. For non-government schools, the principle of the Howard Government funding system was fine. It was supposed to measure the socioeconomic status (SES) of children within non-government schools and the needier the children, the more government funding would rise. In practice, though, the funding arrangements had become polluted by political deal-making. By 2011, a decade after the introduction of the Howard Government's SES funding system, 40 per cent of non-government schools were not funded according to their SES score.

A more profound problem was that under the Howard Government approach, assessment of need was limited to non-government schools. The federal government made a fixed amount per student available to government schools, whatever their needs. In other words, even though the majority of Australian children were taught in government schools, there was no study made of their needs.

On 14 April 2010, I announced a review of this funding system, to help us find an approach that answered the needs of all schools, not just some. Whereas usually these processes are undertaken by expert committees, in view of the adversarial politics of school sectors – continually fighting each other for funds – I decided to look beyond the usual education advocates' community. Rather than looking for the compliant, I sought big personalities who could speak loudly to different constituencies and bring intellectual rigour to the task.

Leading the panel was David Gonski, a well-known businessman. Adept at serving on and chairing boards, I knew he would bring the best possible skills to leading the review team to a conclusion and managing the anxious education community stakeholders. His fellow panellists were Kathryn Greiner, a Liberal identity with non-government school connections and expertise in Indigenous and disability issues; Peter Tannock, a Catholic who had long experience with Catholic education; Ken Boston, a senior public servant and education expert; and Carmen Lawrence, a Labor identity who could speak with authority to the public school lobby. Bill Scales, a noted economist who had looked at many issues for the nation through the prism of what would make us more productive, joined the panel later.

On hearing these names, the education community gasped and then commenced to hold its breath. It was a long time before they would fully exhale.

At the outset, I sought to neutralise potential hit-list-style politics by giving a funding guarantee for all schools, meaning no one would get less in the future. This left unanswered what indexation rates would be available, if any, to well-resourced schools likely to be receiving more than any model would generate as their fair allocation. This was accepted by non-government schools, including the Catholic sector, as the show of good faith it was intended to be.

Becoming prime minister gave me more not less power to push hard to improve school quality and funding. In fact I had rebuilt Labor's 2010 election campaign around education reform. Our fourth-week policy push had included new policies to better empower school principals, to reward the best teachers and to encourage a drive for excellence.

But the campaign brought a step back on education funding. Suddenly negotiation with some figures in Catholic education proved inexplicably difficult.

Such was the level of agitation that in the second week of the election campaign, I met with a delegation of senior Catholic education figures in Melbourne, including Cardinal Pell. In this mood they were not going to accept blanket reassurances of any nature. Change was becoming equivalent in their minds to loss of funding despite the clear commitment that no school would lose a dollar. After careful consideration, to relieve their anxiety I decided to extend the current funding agreement period so that it ran to the end of 2013. This would provide sufficient certainty for the time being and give them a clear moment of political fightback if they wanted it because another election would fall before the implementation of the new model.

It hurt me to make this concession. I felt like I was ducking a big debate, an education reform central to treating all of our children fairly. But the politics of living to fight another day descended on me. We were at risk of losing the 2010 campaign. I could not afford to be fighting with the powerful Catholic education lobby. For now I promised myself I would salvage the reform drive and set a timetable which meant we would get this done no matter how hard it was in the doing. For the 2013 election I was prepared to stake our political lives on school-funding reform. Pragmatism now would give me three years to prepare for the fight.

Understandably the decision to delay provoked considerable anger from state school advocates, particularly the AEU. From their point of view, public schools had been getting a raw deal for far too long and another year was unreasonable. Having an extra election in the process introduced the risk that a new system of funding would never be implemented.

I rode through that bumpy period and after forming the minority government, it was time to get back to work on school funding.

To assist me in this work I chose Peter Garrett. I can vividly remember his face when I asked him to consider becoming Minister for School Education. It was the last thing he expected. Peter had come out of his period as Environment Minister politically and personally scarred by the tragic consequences which flowed from the Home Insulation Program. As part of economic stimulus, this program enabled people to insulate their homes for free. Their energy use would reduce, lowering their power costs and increasing the nation's energy efficiency. But shonky businesses, with no interest in proper health and safety for workers, were set up to make a quick buck. Four young people tragically died while doing the installation. It was unutterably sad. A number of houses also caught fire because of flaws in how the installation was done.

This was a totally different role and I felt that Peter needed to refresh himself by working in a new policy area. He threw himself into the challenge and did a remarkable job. Peter oversaw the implementation of the Australian curriculum and his time as Education Minister saw the nationwide adoption of professional standards for teachers. Linking teacher practice to evidence of effectiveness, it makes possible recognising and rewarding the best teachers as they progress in their careers. A hugely powerful change. Peter wore well my interventionist approach to the school-funding work. I think he knew on accepting the ministry that I would not be letting go of work I loved and cared about so much.

The funding review process led by David Gonski was consultative and rigorous. It developed a statistical and financial model which could generate school-by-school results. The final report was delivered in November 2011 and it was a good one. The model recommended that every school, government and non-government, should have available to it financial resources at the level of a school-resource standard. Built into the standard were loadings that kicked in if the children in the school needed a more resource-intensive approach in order to deliver them a great education. For example, there was a loading recommendation if students came from poorer backgrounds or were Indigenous. For non-government schools, the key difference compared to government schools would be the use of a capacity-to-pay assessment. Essentially the more financially well off the parents of the students were, the less government funding the school would receive. But loadings, such as for disadvantage, would always be 100 per cent government-funded. In accordance with my philosophy of a citizenship entitlement, every child would get some public funds devoted to their education. The model was recommended to all governments, federal and state, and to achieve it all governments would need to do more.

On 20 February 2012, I released the review publicly with a general endorsement. By then I had made a number of decisions about how to move from the final report to putting in place a new school-funding system.

Above all, new funding would be tied to an improvement agenda. To me, funding was an instrument to achieve change, not an end in itself. All my life I had wanted to improve education for children, not see them still fail but in more-moneyed schools. I knew some of the changes I sought were liable to be fiercely contested, like schools functioning more autonomously, with principals more empowered to make decisions about their schools; a strong focus on teacher quality; better ways of engaging parents in their child's school; individualising learning so the best and brightest child, as well as the child falling behind, had their own learning plan to maximise their potential.

Our focus on transparency continued. Indeed every school would generate a plan to improve and transparently report against it.

Another decision was that states would need to put in more resources; they would be forced to resist the temptation to take money out as more federal money went in. There would be no free money or free rides. Every school, public and private, would end up consistently funded and constantly improving.

Throughout 2012, there was much to do, including work on the model itself. The review team had worked hard using the statistical information available to it but that information was now out of date and the new figures needed to be plugged in. The loadings initially recommended had sharp drop-off points so that if a school population changed a little, suddenly it was not entitled to any of the loading. Every contemplated change had to be analysed and analysed again. Eventually the reshaped loadings tapered up or down as school populations changed. Loadings were settled on for schools teaching disadvantaged children, Indigenous children, those from a non-English-speaking background and children with disabilities. Extra funds were built in for schools in regional or remote Australia, or for small schools, in recognition that the fixed costs of running a school in those circumstances were shared across fewer children.

It was exacting work. My deputy chief of staff, Tom Bentley, along with other political staff from my office and Peter's, collaborated with public servants across government. Hundreds of hours were put in. Peter was in full public-advocacy mode. Travelling and spruiking. My high workload meant that much weight fell on Tom's shoulders; he was instrumental in bringing to fruition the school-funding work.

Overwhelmingly the education community was holding its nerve and staying in the process. A modelling and consultation process ran from February to June 2012. States remained wary, not hostile.

Internally, however, there was turmoil over where the money would come from to pay for all this. Over a decade, this reform was going to cost the federal government around $75 billion in increased schools spending. The government was in full fiscal-consolidation mode. Government revenues were plummeting against Treasury's predictions. The aftermath of the GFC and the strong Australian dollar put our nation into new economic terrain and the consequences for the budget were both large and unpredictable.

For ministers caught up in round after wearying round of identifying savings, the extra money needed for schools – and with more outlay ahead to fund the National Disability Insurance Scheme (NDIS) – felt like it equalled more pain in their portfolios. To make budget space, we also needed to agree on controversial and difficult measures, such as limiting eligibility for family payments for upper-income families, abolishing the government bonus paid to families at the time of the birth of a baby, reducing the rate of growth in university funding and closing corporate tax loopholes. It was all painful but responsible.

Ministers knew I was literally betting Labor's political future on the public seeing the merits of school-funding reform and the NDIS and accepting all the associated savings and revenue-raising measures. They wanted to be assured and reassured I was making the right bet.

Even as prime minister, I had to fight it out. I genuinely believe that without the combination of my position and this being my passion, a reform agenda of this size with this long-term cost would not have succeeded.

In July 2012, I secured cabinet approval for the financial negotiations. In September 2012, I spoke at the Canberra Press Club, outlining a broad response, linking school funding to the goals of school improvement, setting a target for our nation to be among the top five schooling systems in the world by 2025 and starting up the full, detailed negotiating process. After this speech, formal negotiations between federal government officials and negotiators from state governments and those representing Catholic and independent schools began.

The whole process would never have got this far without the transparency and new national information that My School had delivered. Even so, states and non-government schools still had bigger information sets than the federal government. As part of the negotiations, a modelling tool was made available so that states and non-government advocates could see the effect of changed settings in the model play-out school by school.

At this moment of greatest risk, I lived haunted by echoes of the 2004 election campaign. With the meagre resources of Opposition, Labor took the risk of designing a new school-funding system whereby 67 schools would lose funding and 111 would see their funding frozen, while over 9000 would see their funding increase. The Howard Government, adept at divide-and-rule politics in education, successfully characterised this as a hit list and accused Labor of starting a class war.

It was always open to someone to use the modelling tool, not to generate feedback in the negotiations but to try to generate hit-list claims. With more than 9000 schools around the country and with the fine settings of the new funding system still being worked through and agreed, it was easy to generate 'loser' lists or perverse results.

At this stage the federal Opposition was in outright hostility mode. The Shadow Education Minister, Christopher Pyne, referred to the reforms as 'Conski'. At an independent schools gathering in Canberra, Tony Abbott reinvigorated the educational-sector warfare encouraged in the Howard years by suggesting government schools were overfunded.

In response, I brought forward the announcement of the next necessary commitment for the process of transition. From saying no school would lose a dollar, I moved to a commitment that all schools would continue to see their funding rise.

In the run-up to the December COAG meeting, state governments were agitating for a financial offer from the commonwealth. Several had still not confirmed basic information about their own funding commitments. I held them back, preferring not to make an offer and risk them politically game-playing all over summer with it.

By the dawn of 2013 and with the new funding model needing to be legislated by the end of the year so funding would flow in 2014, tempers were starting to shorten. At Senate hearings about the legislation, independent schools insisted that their current modelling implied funding reductions for schools and that they would have to make details of the cuts available to each independent school within weeks. This was a tactic to get more leverage in the negotiations with us.

Meanwhile the fight for reform was being sustained publicly by a campaign waged by the AEU. Using the slogan 'I give a Gonski', it involved community campaigning and television advertising. It was ironic that my most vehement opponents on My School had become allies. The AEU pulled out all the stops in this hard fight.

The criticism of the 'I give a Gonski' campaign was that you needed to know who or what Gonski was to work out the message. That was a fair point. While the AEU managed to run the campaign intensively in state schools and build understanding of Gonski school-funding reforms there, in the population more generally, Gonski meant hardly anything. As a government we knew this and called our program for change 'Better Schools'. I chuckled when Kevin Rudd resumed the prime ministership and theatrically 'changed' the name of the government's work to 'Better Schools'. Uncritically reported, you could not get a clearer example of the media's love of spin over substance.

In the midst of all this public buffeting – the emerging hit-list claims, the demands for details now, the AEU's campaign fightback – I held firm. I would not be pressured into revealing all of the federal government's hand while negotiations with the states were unresolved.

Serious negotiations commenced with New South Wales. Liberal Premier Barry O'Farrell originally tied himself in COAG to a joint negotiation approach with Ted Baillieu, the Liberal Premier of Victoria. Fundamentally Barry was too different a character from Ted for them to easily work together and that approach broke down. Barry had his eyes firmly on the big picture and the harvesting of political opportunities. Ted had his eyes so focused on the fine details the bigger picture was obscured.

Barry had staged a political coup when he became the first premier to sign on in full to the NDIS. In early 2013, he was quietly positioning to do the same on schools and to reap the political leadership benefits of moving first. Unfortunately the productive negotiations between the federal and New South Wales governments hit a massive bump in the form of the historic indexation arrangement for federal government money flowing for schools known as the Australian Government Schools Recurrent Cost (AGSRC) index. Essentially money flowing from the federal government to schools was increased each year by an amount equal to the average of the indexation rates being used by state governments for money flowing to state schools. One consequence of AGSRC was that if a state government put a lot more money into state schools, it had an automatic beneficial consequence for non-government schools. If you were trying to close the gap in funding between state schools and moneyed private schools, your efforts were always undermined by the AGSRC.

The modelling for our new funding system assumed that states would continue with indexation at around five per cent, the average AGSRC level for the past ten years. But following the GFC, New South Wales had built nothing like a five per cent indexation rate into its own budgets. This was not a quick artificial manipulation to get the federal government to put in more. It was a genuine consequence of their budget challenge.

The gap between money available and the money needed to reach the School Resource Standard suddenly looked almost unbridgeable. After all this time, effort, work and passion, the rug had been snatched out from under us.

A round of Treasury and Finance pushing to retreat from the whole process ensued, even though the flawed higher indexation rate had been used at their insistence. Once again, determination and the status of being prime minister helped me win through. It took intense problem-solving within the federal government between ministerial offices and officials to work out how the different sources of funding could be combined to achieve a fair, growing distribution of funds to schools in all sectors. Once again, much of the weight fell on Tom Bentley. The model was recalculated using more realistic indexation rates of 4.7 per cent for federal funding and three per cent for state funding.

These were better than the low to which indexation was heading if the current system was just continued. Not only would state government indexation rates have tumbled but this would have flown through to federal government indexation rates as a result of the magic of the AGSRC.

With the benefits of this modification, it was back to hard negotiating with New South Wales, which then put in a counteroffer at a much lower level than the parameters of our model allowed. We were on a countdown to COAG on 19 April 2013. Could I get a deal at or before that COAG meeting with New South Wales? If I could, the dynamics of the debate would shift. I would have much-needed momentum.

While my whole reform drive had focused the nation's eyes on what was happening in individual schools, inter-sector politics was not dead. Inevitably the Catholic and independent school representatives were spending plenty of time looking over the fence to see what each other was getting and what state schools were getting.

As the discussions wore on, I knew I would have to cash in my chips, the credibility I had so painstakingly built up with the Catholic and independent school representatives, to get the new system agreed. It would take my personal time to persuade them that the deal was a good and fair one for them and for all.

It was at this delicate stage in negotiations that the Queensland Government swung into destruction mode. It started making up numbers and issued a ban on Peter Garrett visiting schools. Queensland Liberal Premier Campbell Newman was coming to COAG looking for a fight.

A pugnacious individual, at his first COAG meeting Campbell had regaled the other premiers and chief ministers with declarations of his determination to cut regulations. At his local kebab shop, he told everyone, he was appalled to hear how many regulations there were for the handling of the meat, including – to his horror – one about the temperature the meat needed to be at on the spit! He was going to abolish all this red tape. The studiously polite Katie Gallagher, the Chief Minister of the Australian Capital Territory, commented that that would all be fine until the first salmonella outbreak. Although she did not mean the remark unkindly, it produced guffaws all round, including from Liberal premiers.

In need of a breakthrough, I spoke by phone directly to Premier O'Farrell. I never doubted his goodwill or commitment. I also never doubted the political pressure he was under. It was obvious that the federal Opposition was exerting brutal pressure to prevent any state signing on and giving me a win. The fact the winners were really our children did not seem to factor into their political equations. I also gathered that Barry's Treasurer, Mike Baird, was baulking at the size of the financial commitment. Our conversation ended on a dispiriting note: Barry could not come to the COAG meeting ready to do the deal. He was too close to his political limits with his cabinet and the financial limits of his budget. He needed more time to cajole colleagues and find savings.

COAG came and went with some shadow-boxing but no deal was struck with any state. Many commentators concluded I had failed. But beyond the COAG meeting room and the ears of the media, piece by piece we were inching to a deal with New South Wales. Finally, on 23 April, I was able to announce with Barry O'Farrell that New South Wales had signed on to our school-funding reforms.

I was delighted and admiring of Barry's political courage. He had a choice between helping his federal Liberal colleagues or helping the children of his state and he chose the children.

The school-funding legislation passed on my last day as prime minister. I have never been prouder. For a school like Punchbowl Boys High it meant approximately $5 million in funding could flow over the next six years because the school teaches disadvantaged children who are predominantly from non-English-speaking backgrounds. Barry's decision created the momentum needed to ensure agreements would be reached with every state, territory and school sector other than Queensland and Western Australia before the 2013 election.

Without his decision, I would still have waged a war for change, school by school, across the country.

After I lost the prime ministership, I watched as Kevin Rudd announced his ministry. Bill Shorten was given the education port-folio. Bill had turned away from me and towards Kevin in our final leadership contest. I was still emotionally processing my sense of hurt. But some things are more important than who has what position in politics. I picked up the phone and rang Bill. I said I did not want to talk about anything other than school-funding reform but I wanted him to understand in detail where the negotiations were up to and how the remaining agreements could be quickly settled. He listened and worked to get that done.

Had I been prime minister at the 2013 election, fighting to fully secure this reform would have been the backbone of the campaign. I would have contested every day the mealy-mouthed assurances given during the campaign by the Leader of the Opposition, Tony Abbott, and his Shadow Education Minister, Christopher Pyne.

How mealy-mouthed it really was became crystal clear after the election. I would have made it a question of character. It is impossible to describe something as Conski for years and fight it every step of the way and then be believed when you say, 'It is safe in our hands.' This was not a reasoned reconsideration; it was a political sidestep.

The two men were asking for a mandate to implement something they did not believe in. The hollowness of their assurances showed in their eyes on the day and in their conduct since.

But I did take one message of hope from their political conduct. The work Labor did on school-funding reform has so successfully grown political roots that the nation is never going back. Never going back to an earlier funding system. Never going back to ignoring need. Never going back to institutionalising unfairness between schools in different sectors.

It will take the next Labor government to deliver the full model. Indeed the Labor Opposition will have a wonderful issue to campaign for in the next election, the full and proper delivery of the funding agreed for schools in years 2017 and 2018.

It will take a Labor government to ensure that the silliness implemented by the Abbott Government is brushed aside. Silliness which means money no longer comes with an obligation to improve quality. Silliness that means state schools in New South Wales and Queensland that teach similar students will receive different amounts of money to do so. The New South Wales school will be better off because New South Wales will deliver new money, as it said it would under the agreement I signed with Premier O'Farrell. The Queensland school will suffer because Premier Newman is refusing to do the same thing. For all that, a permanent change has been made for the betterment of our children.

On the day Tony Abbott and Christopher Pyne pledged their commitment to my school-funding reforms, my phone beeped. I looked down to see a text message from Premier O'Farrell congratulating me. It was generous of him but what should really be celebrated is a better education for our children and a stronger, fairer future for our nation.

EARLY-CHILDHOOD DEVELOPMENT

Just as schools change lives, so does what happens before school. My mother says she talked and talked to my sister and me as babies. She thought that, even from our earliest days, the words would swirl in our brains. She always prided herself on having taught us to read and count before we went to school.

I am grateful for all of these efforts and for the educational endeavour she pushed us through in our teens. With the words 'A girl can always get a job if she can type', Mum bought an Olivetti Manual typewriter and forced Alison and me to learn. As our world has computerised, the ability to touch-type at speed has been extraordinarily useful for reasons Mum could never have foreseen.

Apparently Mum's proactive parenting style was controversial. She was told that talking to a baby was too much for a tiny brain, that she would damage our minds. Fortunately she stuck to her approach, and in doing so was well before the times.

What has become clearer in the last quarter century is that the early years of life and learning, before formal schooling starts, are perhaps the most influential in shaping life's chances. If a child falls behind then and comes to school lagging in their cognitive and social development, then that disadvantage, without specific intervention and help, will persist throughout schooling and life.

Not all parents have absorbed these findings or do what my mother did. Hillary Clinton, who among so many other achievements is a longstanding advocate of early-childhood development, remarked at an event I attended in 2013 that she routinely says on meeting a mother with a baby, 'You must be having so much fun talking to your baby' and is disturbed by the number of times the answer is, 'Why would I talk to my baby who can't talk back?'

One of Labor's 2007 election policies committed us to measuring how our children are doing in their early years. In an initiative inspired by an outstanding Australian – child development expert and advocate Fiona Stanley – in 2009, children in their first year of school were checked for physical health and wellbeing, social competence, emotional maturity, language and cognitive skills, communication and general knowledge. The data gathered in this exercise, the roll-out of the world-leading Australian Early Development Index, made it plain that large proportions of children living in the most socioeconomically disadvantaged and very remote areas of Australia were considered developmentally vulnerable. It revealed the uncomfortable truth that our approach to nurturing and educating our children was replicating current patterns of status, income and achievement. Today's disadvantage becoming tomorrow's disadvantage in front of our eyes. Children knowingly being left behind.

I cannot say that the government I led or the total period of the Labor government did enough to change this life sentence facing too many of our children. But we can pride ourselves on making a difference and modernising our nation's approach to early education.

Mum's brand of early-childhood education was not exclusively for my sister and me. When we arrived in Australia, her first job was caring for three or four other children during the day, an early example of family daycare. I vaguely remember it as being a mix of good fun because you had other children to play with and horrible because it felt like a home invasion.

Of course, the way our nation provides childcare now is a world away from my mother's small enterprise. Under the Howard Government, there had been explosive growth in for-profit childcare. In 1991, there were 4100 childcare services and most of those were community not-for-profits. By 2007 that had ballooned to 10,700. The number of children in care skyrocketed from around 250,000 to more than 800,000 in 2009. More women were going to work and more places were needed.

Just like with schools, a diversity of new providers had not been met with a focus on quality or appropriate market design and regulation, even though there is nothing more precious than our children.

The Howard Government had provided a 30 per cent subsidy of childcare costs to families, with a cap on government support per child of slightly over $4000 a year. But fees for care were still imposing a high cost burden on families. While workforce participation by women was rising, many mothers complained that by the time they did the equation between childcare costs and wages, it was simply not worth their while to work.

Inevitably there is an ugly tension between cost and quality. Having children cared for by fewer, less qualified, lower paid staff is obviously cheaper. Labor in Opposition rightly identified that cut-price childcare was not the future we wanted for our nation's children and that pivotal to the early education of our children is the quality of childcare.

Consequently Labor came to government with new policies on both cost and quality. In implementing these policies I was assisted by Maxine McKew, who served as Parliamentary Secretary for Early Childhood Education and Child Care. While neither of us had children, we both shared a passion for changing children's life chances. Maxine had read widely and developed a sophisticated understanding of the neuroscience of children's development. Armed with this knowledge, she sought to persuade and cajole others on better meeting the developmental needs of our children.

On cost, as early as October 2008 we implemented our policy to subsidise half of the out-of-pocket costs parents paid for childcare up to $7500 per child per year.

On quality, to implement our promised changes we needed the cooperation of state governments, which historically have delivered funding to kindergartens and regulated staff ratios in childcare centres. We reached one key agreement with them quite quickly and easily. As a result of this deal, each child in their year before school would be able to access a preschool program delivered by a four-year-qualified early-childhood teacher for 15 hours a week and 40 weeks a year. Whether a child was in childcare or enrolled in a stand-alone kindergarten, this investment in their development would be made. It was an achievement to be proud of, with the Rudd Government prepared to put on the table the best part of a billion dollars over five years to get everyone to see the merits of change.

Reaching the next key agreement, whereby more staff, with higher qualifications, would attend to the care and development of children, was much tougher. State governments regulated this area and resented federal government intrusion. Different states were coming off different starting points, making agreement on the right ratios more difficult. Most telling of all, everyone was anxious about the politics of the debate because more and better qualified staff inevitably meant higher costs and fees.

I left the negotiations to Maxine, who reported periodically on her assessment of the likelihood of state ministers responsible for early-childhood education signing on. When her reports were more glowing and favourable than those of the federal public-service negotiators who were dealing with their counterparts, I became concerned. A flashpoint took place at a ministerial council meeting I chaired in May 2009.

Ministerial councils are necessary but unwieldy beasts. Ranged around the room are the federal minister and ministers from every state, assisted by senior public servants and usually with a political adviser and media adviser each. There are a lot of people in attendance. Ministerial councils are most effective when solid work has been done by the public servants in the lead-up, ministers are well briefed on that work, sticking points have been identified and talked through by political advisers and, one-to-one, by ministers. There is always decision-making to do at the meeting, and you need to make an effort to carry the room. That did not daunt me. Often I have been able to use debate and negotiation to nudge ministers towards agreements they did not initially want to accept.

Going into this meeting, Maxine told me that a number of states would agree to her proposal for national quality standards for childcare workers and staff-to-child ratios and this would force the hand of the others. Once in the room, no one agreed. From hurried side conversations with ministers, it appeared that Maxine had misread generalised support for change as specific support for a particular change. Never had I worked harder off the back foot than I did that day to secure agreement, even to the point of sitting at a computer and typing out the communiqué myself. Thank heavens for Mum's typing training!

While all this work was being done to improve life's chances for our young children, the Opposition, in alliance with private childcare providers, was running scare campaigns on the cost consequences for parents. It was a wholly political gambit that would garner attention. Television producers were forever telling my media team that the ratings of their shows always shot up when they screened a childcare story.

This fear campaign did bite among voters, even though the change to staff ratios was to be introduced gradually and the cost rises for families were projected to be modest. But cost always presses people's buttons. In hindsight, it would have been better to phase in the new cost relief alongside the new quality standards so over time families experienced both increasing quality and reduced costs.

Whatever the political backlash of these changes, we were keeping our 2007 election promises and positioning our nation to overcome disadvantage.

Universal access to preschool and high-quality childcare brings a quiet revolution to many poorer communities. It introduces the joy of learning to children who otherwise might enter school having never seen a book or held a pen. Flexible provision models – literally travelling kindergartens – can bring the same revolution to isolated communities, especially remote Indigenous ones.

We added to this attack on disadvantage by increasing resources for the Home Interaction Program for Parents and Youngsters, which helps parents play their crucial role in maximising their children's potential. A study found a return on investment to society of $2.53 for every dollar spent on this program, and when compared to the Australian norm, parents participating in the program were three times more likely to be actively involved in their child's learning and development.[1]

Sadly not everything worked as well. The quality of the early-childhood policies of the 2007 campaign was the usual uneven mix that tends to result when policies are designed in Opposition. With the greatest policy diligence in the world, an Opposition bereft of public-service advice, the ability to pay experts or reach out for wide-spread consultations will make errors.

Labor's policy to develop 260 new childcare centres had started as a slogan, to 'end the double drop-off', a reference to the gauntlet many harried mums and dads run before work to get older kids to school and younger ones to childcare. The catchy slogan and appealing concept of having a childcare centre on the same site as your child's school ran headlong into the real-world difficulties of finding schools with the land and the inclination to facilitate such a development, as well as the maze of potential objections on planning grounds and from established local childcare providers unhappy to see the emergence of a new competitor. The policy, to which full funding had never been assigned, floundered and was messily shelved.

In government you face a mix of the most carefully orchestrated and the most unpredictable of days. Unmistakably 6 November 2008 was one of those wildcard days. With it came the news that ABC Learning, Australia's largest provider of childcare – with a 20 per cent market share, providing care to over 100,000 children and employing approximately 16,000 staff – was going belly up and shutting its doors.

Every generation seems to bring Australia a new flamboyant risk-all entrepreneur. Think Alan Bond and Christopher Skase. In the 1990s and the decade beyond it was Eddie Groves, who with his then wife, Le Neve, created ABC Learning. Their goal to dominate the childcare sector was not confined to Australia – they were taking their model overseas.

Their lavish lifestyle was often reported in magazines. Behind the glitz lay a less seductive story. A story of failed market regulation.

When in 1997 the Howard Government removed all operational subsidies for not-for-profit centres, it opened the way for private centres to compete on equal terms; all centres could obtain the government subsidies for childcare. No thought was given to how this flow of government funds to for-profit centres would change the face of Australian childcare. There was no attempt to design the emerging new childcare market so it incorporated transparency, quality and proper conduct by operators. ABC Learning listed on the stock exchange in 2001. Then it grew and grew through tough tactics, including introducing loss-making childcare centres into suburbs to force the competition to close.

The story is also one of political influence. From the start, the Liberal Party and ABC Learning were entwined. The Howard Government Minister for Children and Youth Affairs, Larry Anthony, who in government introduced the new subsidy policies, post-politics became a director of and consultant to the firm. Sallyanne Atkinson, who as a Liberal had been Lord Mayor of Brisbane, chaired the board. A childcare venture developed by Liberal identities Michael Kroger and Andrew Peacock was absorbed by ABC Learning. It had been a great and well-connected gravy train but now it had crashed. The story became one of the destructive power of greed and poor management.

Our nation faced the prospect that tens of thousands of families and their children would turn up at more than 1000 childcare centres around the country and find the doors locked. Mums and dads would have been forced to make stressed decisions about what to do next. Who would stay home from work to look after the kids? Could the grandparents step in, and could they cope? What about the next-door neighbour? It could have been a nightmare but the looming disaster was averted as a result of urgent action by our government and its announcement of a package to keep all centres open in the short term. Then, to give people certainty about what would be happening in the new year, as early as

10 December, we advised that 720 centres were assessed as viable enough to continue to operate in 2009, only 55 were going to be closed and a further 262 would receive a limited further subsidy to enable continued operation in locations lacking alternative services.

No one wishes for crisis. But as the management saying goes, sometimes a burning platform is what it takes to secure big change. The ABC Learning crash forced us to rebalance and restructure Australia's childcare market. It was not a course of action we embarked on lightly. Maxine McKew and Tom Bentley were keen to see this moment used to bring profound change to the childcare sector. My departmental advice was to exercise caution: imagine the fallout if a failed private-sector venture was replaced with a failed not-for-profit one.

I inched my way to a decision rather than jumped. Finally, persuaded by the sophisticated approach taken by social-policy thinkers in Social Ventures Australia, Mission Australia, the Brotherhood of St Laurence and the Benevolent Society, as well as advocacy by Maxine and Tom, the government made a $15 million loan to enable their consortium to create Goodstart Early Learning, which acquired 650 of the former ABC Learning Centres. As a result, one of Australia's largest social ventures operates childcare centres that understand quality and the role of early learning in combating disadvantage.

Late in the life of the government I led we started to address the problem of wage rates in childcare. This workforce, predominantly women, do a skilled and difficult job for little reward. They suffer from the presumption that caring for children, 'babysitting', as women's work, is not that demanding and not that skilled. Truly addressing this will require their union to resource and prosecute a thoroughgoing and fair assessment of wage levels under the Fair Work equal-pay principles. But we did make a financial allocation to secure some improvement.

Despite our work in childcare and early education, there is more to do, especially in redesigning the way government payments work.

Any economist will rightly tell you that a subsidy is likely to distort the market and feed into a preparedness to charge increased fees. A better option for childcare would be a system-wide fee arrangement, where in exchange for the provision to centres of government funds a bargain is struck about cost relief to families and the future trajectory of fee increases.

As prime minister, ably assisted by the minister then responsible for childcare, Kate Ellis, I started work on this system-wide change, intending to bring it to fruition as an announcement for the 2013 election campaign.

I did not get to do that. But along with nurturing an appreciation of the importance of quality care and early learning, system-wide fee arrangements need to be part of the future.

Australians are infused with love for and loyalty to their children. Many go without to provide the best for their children; many work overtime or take a second job. Of course, costs for families matter, and many have to fight hard for every dollar of income. Even so, the focus of our national dialogue about childcare seems to shrink too quickly to mere dollars and cents.

At a national level, we are yet to fully absorb the lessons researchers are trying to teach us: every day in that young child's life is precious for their future ability to learn. Surely their paid care in those irreplaceable days should be of the best possible quality. Surely we should be prepared to do more to ensure it is. Surely too we should be prepared to do more to ensure our children are safe.

PROTECTING OUR CHILDREN

I grew up in an innocent, unaware age. Despite being in the city where the Beaumont children went missing, we did not live with a sense of danger. As quite young girls, Alison and I were allowed to walk to and from school, be at home by ourselves until Mum came back from work, and go to the local park without adult supervision.

We were lectured about not getting into strangers' cars. Even so, having got soaked, cold and muddy at our favourite haunt, Brown Hill Creek, on a day that turned unexpectedly rainy, my sister, two girl-friends and I accepted a lift home from a stranger. True to his word, that kindly man dropped us straight back to our door.

We didn't know about child sexual abuse. With adult eyes I look back on the dramatically changed and increasingly sexualised behaviour of a girl I knew who lived with her father after her mother died, and I wonder. But back then, the possibility did not – could not – occur to me.

Nowadays we realise that behind the façade of innocence, many children lived, and live, a life in hell. When Kevin Rudd delivered his magnificent apology, our nation faced up to the harm caused by the policies that resulted in the Stolen Generations. We also faced up to the harm and hurt caused to Forgotten Australians, former child migrants, when Kevin delivered the apology to them in November 2009. In 2013 I delivered the nation's apology for the shattering of lives through the practice of forced adoptions.

Over the period of these apologies, the incidence of sexual abuse of children was being uncovered. So was the fact that institutions, including Churches, had turned a blind eye, moving abusers on to other parishes rather than exposing them.

As early as 1998 and 1999, Queensland held an inquiry into child sexual abuse in institutions, leading to the creation of a $100 million redress fund. In 2004 South Australia held a Commission of Inquiry into Children in State Care to examine sexual abuse and death from criminal conduct between 1910 and 2004. A further inquiry was held into the abuse of children on the Indigenous Anangu Pitjantjatjara Yankunytjatjara lands in the north of the state.

In 2011, West Australian Premier Colin Barnett called for a special inquiry into child sexual abuse at the St Andrew's Hostel at Katanning. In Victoria, also in 2011, the Protecting Victoria's Vulnerable Children Inquiry chaired by Philip Cummins made a finding that 'a formal investigation by government into how to best address criminal abuse of children in Victoria by religious personnel is justified and is in the public interest'.[2] This led to the creation of a bipartisan Victorian parliamentary inquiry.

Then a crusade for change began in Newcastle. All the pain and suffering endured by so many came to be symbolised by John Pirona, a local man who had been sexually abused at school. As a result of the enduring trauma, he took his own life. By chance I was in Newcastle on the day of his funeral on 8 August 2012. In the course of a meeting with the editorial team of *The Newcastle Herald*, they explained the depth of mourning in their city for John and the determination to see justice for others who had been abused.

Detective Chief Inspector Peter Fox became a public voice for the Newcastle campaign to secure a royal commission into child sexual abuse. He wrote to Premier O'Farrell on 8 November 2012 and appeared on the ABC's *Lateline* program to put into heartfelt words his concerns as a police officer about Church cover-ups and obstruction of investigations. The premier promptly responded with the announcement of a special commission of inquiry, although its remit was immediately criticised as too narrow. Within days, the public call for a national royal commission became deafening. Over a weekend, I wrestled with the decision about whether to instigate one. I knew a royal commission would be publicly popular but I was disturbed that there was no path I could take that would not entail further pain for victims of child sexual abuse.

A royal commission would probe people's hurt. It would inevitably take a long time and cause frustration. While its findings would help guide the nation for the future, nothing it could ever do would take away all the pain.

Not having a royal commission though would feel like a further betrayal. People who had experienced so many doors being slammed in their faces when they tried to tell the truth, would once again experience the distress of another one banging shut. As a nation, new insights about how to protect our children could be denied us.

I thought about it deeply. I decided we should act and after a cabinet discussion, on 12 November 2012 I announced the creation of a royal commission into institutional responses to instances of child sexual abuse.

I spoke to Cardinal George Pell before doing so. I did not want the royal commission to be seen to be a witch-hunt into one Church, but rather to have the breadth it truly needed. The Opposition's bipartisanship avoided the royal commission being caught up in messy politics.

I wanted states to refer powers in a way which would enable the royal commission to have the maximum amount of authority possible. Almost all premiers were helpful but nervous about work already being done in their states being redone so we needed to work cooperatively through the issues.

Jenny Macklin, Nicola Roxon and I worked over summer to get the right team of people to be the commissioners. Wayne Swan provided some wise counsel along the way. It was not easy.

When I worked at Slater & Gordon, there was a young solicitor within the firm who was taking statements day after day from child sexual abuse survivors for a class-action claim being investigated. I remember how intensely psychologically wearing it was for her. I understood and respected the decisions of people who could not face spending years of their life immersed in evidence of so much pain. I was full of respect for those willing to serve.

I believe we assembled a first-class team and I wish them well as they continue their vital work.

On the day we announced the commissioners, I held a morning tea at Kirribilli House for advocates who had fought so long for a royal commission and survivors of child sexual abuse. I spent the morning with tears pricking my eyes.

The sun streamed, the scones were served, the harbour lay before us. A picture-perfect day. But the shadow of the past managed to lurk everywhere. In the pain of the man who held aloft a picture of his mother. He had been taken from her and abused in care. In the forthright descriptions of some about what had happened to them. In the words that trailed off mid-sentence from others. I knew we had done the right thing.

My early days as prime minister had been filled with damaging political leaks. Laurie Oakes won the prestigious Gold Walkley award for his reporting of those. In my final hours as prime minister, I hurriedly amended and signed a letter to *Newcastle Herald* reporter Joanne McCarthy, who in an exemplary example of a crusading journalist, fought for the royal commission. She won the Gold Walkley award for that work in November 2013.

The years in between gave me the opportunity to find ways to better educate and, through the work of the royal commission, hopefully to better protect our children.

Years of meaning and purpose.

16

Setting alarm clocks early

'I believe in a government that rewards those who work the hardest, not those who complain the loudest. I believe in a government that rewards those that day in, day out, work in our factories and on our farms, in our mines and in our mills, in our classrooms and in our hospitals, that rewards that hard work, decency and effort. The people that play by the rules, set their alarms early, get their kids off to school, stand by their neighbours and love their country.'

MY FIRST SPEECH TO THE NATION AS PRIME MINISTER

AS A PRIME MINISTER, THE LIFE YOU LEAD is necessarily very different from the lives of those you represent. But one thing I shared with millions of other Australians was setting my alarm clock early. I could wake up in Canberra at The Lodge, in a hotel room in Darwin or Hobart, Washington or Beijing. But wherever I woke up, my day started early.

A standard day began between 5 and 6 am. On a bad day, the mobile phone would beep me awake when the number four was still on the display. A day off would be letting myself sleep until after 7 am. It would be a day free from public commitments: unbroken time at the office or, even more deliciously, at The Lodge or Kirribilli. At the residence, work would be done but there would be no need to worry about how I looked. As a break from sitting at a desk, I liked to sit on the bed, mobile in easy reach, with the briefs to be read in piles around me.

Early mornings at The Lodge often included a session with a personal trainer named Tanya. As she put me through my paces – yoga, boxing, weights – we chatted about life. The sessions helped with more than just my physical wellbeing. On other days and in other places, I would try to walk or do some yoga in my room.

Next I scanned every newspaper available. At The Lodge the standard fare would be *The Australian*, the *Australian Financial Review*, the *Daily Telegraph* and *The Sydney Morning Herald*. For me and the government, the news was rarely good.

Once I'd absorbed the headlines I'd hit the shower, deliberately quelling any emotional reaction to them. Media negativity on difficult days was not easily washed away. But I treated it as a task to be done, in a sequence of tasks that would include the more energising and important: the policy work I cared about that mattered for the future, for the country I was trying to build.

If Tim was with me, we would briefly discuss what the day held. Often we did this while he blowdried my hair. His record for the earliest ever hairstyling session is 4.15 am!

Having exercised, read the papers, showered and had a light breakfast, I would get dressed. A routine task for most people, it was full of complexity for me. I have never been a girly girl, interested in fashion and make-up. I remember joking with a make-up artist once, after with one fluid stroke she applied eye-liner perfectly to me, that if I had tried to do the same I would have ended up with it on my cheek, in my hair and probably splashed on the wall as well. She laughed and replied she had been born wearing eyeliner. I most assuredly was not.

At the time I became deputy Opposition leader, my wardrobe and make-up routine was a simple one. I wore suits: a jacket and matching pants. I felt professional, comfortable and never had to run around replacing snagged pantyhose in the middle of a 14- or 15-hour day. I did not wear much make-up. It's lucky, I now realise, that during my teens I was forced to protect my fair skin. In summer I used to envy my tanned friends while I retreated under a tree, in long sleeves, wearing a hat. But avoiding too much sun has paid a long-term dividend for my skin and meant my make-up routine could be straightforward.

All that simplicity was soon replaced with complexity. Looking the same every day for a man – in a suit and tie, occasionally yielding to the regulation male-politician-goes-bush look of light pants, RM Williams boots, a blue blazer, an open-necked shirt and an Akubra hat – is fine. For a woman, that predictability would be frowned on as boring and dowdy.

For a long time I resisted the constant entreaties to wear more colour. 'Winston Churchill did not update the nation on the progress of the Second World War wearing canary yellow,' I would retort. 'Why do we think for women colour and being a leading politician go together?' Eventually I gave up my resistance. As deputy prime minister, I bought some items with more colour. As prime minister, a stylist routinely used by the Labor Party to assist key party figures, male and female, started helping me. A television professional, she offered good advice on what worked on screen and would bring a range of items to The Lodge for me to try on: my days of wandering through stores were over. To my surprise, I felt comfortable in white and in some of the brighter colours and could see how it lifted the on-screen image.

But the bright colours, because they are noticeable, date quickly. In my last period as prime minister, I sought some further advice and started again to wear more muted tones but not the simple suits of my past.

Shoes were less of a drama. Sensible shoes, with the occasional lash-out through online shopping to something more flamboyant, are my style. Much women's fashion seems curiously disempowering. Not for me the aspiration to be ultra-thin and totter on nine-inch heels. Even in my modest heels, I occasionally misstepped; when I see women walking on huge heels, my heart is in my mouth because I am so afraid they will fall. As for being ultra-thin, I have always savoured the pithy joke of a New Zealand comic, 'No, don't give me a whole vote, I couldn't possibly finish it.'

Acquiring the wardrobe was only the first step. Records needed to be kept on what I had worn when. You could not wear something too frequently or, heaven forbid, wear the same things two years in a row to the same event. My office, working with the staff at The Lodge, managed that burden.

Depending on whether or not I would be on television that day, I took one last step: make-up professionally applied. Preparing for a television appearance is a whole different thing for men and women. This was graphically demonstrated for me in the years I debated Tony Abbott on Channel 9's *Today Show* every Friday. For a spot filmed shortly after 7 am, I had to arrive at 6.20 am for hair and make-up. Tony would saunter straight onto the set around 7 am and someone would quickly powder him down so he did not look shiny and run a comb through his hair. I envied him those extra 40 minutes.

Historically senior male politicians have a staff member, usually a press secretary, who wields a comb, puffs some hairspray and pats them down with powder for TV doorstep interviews. Caterina, who did competitive salsa dancing as a hobby, was terrific at make-up and often helped me out. Mostly I relied on a network of professional make-up artists around the country; we saw so much of each other we became friends.

As prime minister, time is not for wasting. Make-up sessions were combined with briefings – usually from media staff. In my world, it was routine to have a press secretary, policy adviser and my chief of staff all yelling a briefing at me over the sound of a hairdryer being used to give already dry hair a final touch-up. I became adept at lip-reading: whoever needed to get across the most information had to be directly in front of me so I could see their mouths forming the words.

Despite all these novel demands on my prime ministerial time and the differences between the life I was leading and that of my fellow Australians, my focus remained on the stuff of everyday life for families around the nation.

Appearance is one thing, substance is another. That is true of economic statistics. Disappointingly the public dialogue about our economy tends to be simplistic: based around the economic statistics of the moment, with little depth about the context today or the challenges tomorrow. It is also beset by political game-playing. Governments always want to lay claim to everything good and distance themselves from everything bad. Oppositions want to create the reverse impression. This combination of game-playing and a blinkered take on context has consequences:

if economic statistics are poor compared with long-term trends, even if a government is being highly competent in managing the economy, it is likely to see its performance given low marks by the citizenry. Conversely a government that puts in a sloppy performance during a growth spurt will be given high marks.

The second half of the Howard Government was a period of good economic times combined with poor economic management. Infrastructure and skills needs were neglected. Government spending bloated, fed by a big expansion in vote-buying middle-class welfare. The vital debate about how productive a nation we could be was held hostage to an ideological crusade on workplace relations. Yet those days are remembered for buoyant job numbers and budget surpluses. The Liberal Party has too easily been able to claim the mantle of being expert economic managers, though in truth, the job numbers happened despite the economic management strategy of the Howard Government and the budget surpluses arose from strong revenue growth, not prudent budgeting.

Unlike the easy economic days in which Prime Minister Howard governed, Prime Minister Rudd faced the worst economic circumstances since the Great Depression. Almost overnight the government's economic strategy had to shift from managing a robustly growing economy, where inflation and interest-rate rises were real threats, to dealing with the risk of runs on banks and recession. The emergency response was not perfect but common sense tells us expecting perfection in a genuine crisis is not realistic. When bushfires rage, even the most competent emergency response workers can commit errors, despite the fact that they train and train to hone their skills for such circumstances. No training is available to a government or the public service on how to respond to global economic meltdown. The best you can do is look at past downturns and identify what seemed to make the best difference.

The Rudd Government did this, supported by able public servants. The economic strategy worked and Australia avoided a recession. Jobs and businesses were saved that would otherwise have been lost. Debt remained low and very manageable.

If we had not acted then, we would have seen more economic results like those of the December quarter 2008. In that three-month period our economy contracted by 0.9 per cent, the worst result since the recession of the early 1990s. In the year 2009, the first full year in which the world staggered under the weight of the GFC, our economy grew by 1.6 per cent while the economies of nations like Canada and the USA shrank. In 2009, our unemployment lifted to 5.8 per cent, while Canada's hit 8.3 per cent and the USA's 9.3 per cent. European nations staggered, with one in every four or five people out of work.

Even in 2013, as my period in office came to an end, the difference in our unemployment rates was stark. Australia's was at 5.7 per cent whereas Canada's was at 7.1 per cent and the USA's was at 7.5 per cent. Some European nations had gone backwards, with unemployment substantially higher than it was at the height of the GFC.

Admittedly there is always a debate about whom we should be comparing ourselves to. Our nation did come to the GFC without the debt burdens of many European countries, without the banking weaknesses of the USA, with a resource endowment like the one enjoyed by Canada but with the benefit of Asian, particularly Chinese, demand. But concluding that Australia's performance in the GFC is all about China and resources flies in the face of the facts. Without the Rudd Government's targeted and timely economic stimulus measures, Australia would have gone into recession. Without the provision by government of guarantees to our banks, they might have been crunched, despite their inherent strength.

Whatever comparisons are made, what lie behind the statistics are human stories. One image that lingers with me from the days of the GFC is a newspaper photograph of a young woman in Europe sitting precariously on a high ledge of a multi-storey building. She had lost her job, and until caring passers-by coaxed her back inside was intending to throw herself to her death.

The hurt of unemployment is not confined to the days of economic downturn. As a result of the recession of the early 1990s, in Australia some blue-collar workers never worked again. When the economy started growing again, they were left on the sidelines, viewed as too old and lacking modern skills. Yet the worst long-lived effect can be for young people. Disturbingly the evidence tells us that if a young person does not get that all-important first job within a reasonable time of completing study or training, this can create a life sentence of unemployment and underemployment, ensnared on the margins of society with no hope.

Among the effective things we did to respond to the GFC was a program to kick-start apprenticeship numbers so young Australians still had the opportunity to secure a trade qualification. After the 1991 recession, it took almost a decade for apprenticeship commencements to return to the pre-recession level but during the GFC we succeeded in sustaining apprenticeship numbers.

I came into the prime ministership in an economy viewed internationally as miraculous because of our performance throughout the GFC. But politically, the perceptions were completely different. Although Australians gave the government some credit for an economic plan that meant our nation dodged a bullet, they remained fearful about the world and their jobs. What was more, our economy had changed and none of it was to voters' liking. They watched with acute concern as the value of their biggest assets dropped. After years of growth in the real estate market, Australians were shocked to see growth in house prices limp along rather than canter. The value of their superannuation kept going backwards. Many Australians, even of modest means, have direct share investments. The news from the share market was all bad too.

Australians dramatically reeled in their spending and increased their savings. The savings ratio almost doubled to quickly reach around ten per cent of income and stayed there. Even as individuals and families pulled back their living standards and took to paying off their credit cards and mortgage or pumping money into their bank account, people hankered for everything to return to 'normal', which they identified as the economic conditions of the Howard Government years.

But those conditions had not been normal and they were not coming back. During the years of the Howard Government, our national savings rate fell below zero. It became common for people to buy a car, renovate their home, go on a holiday – funding this either on credit or, with property price rises, accessing through a mortgage extension the increased value of their home. It was not sustainable.

All of us in the Rudd Government found it hard to explain how problems in the mortgage market of the United States had lit a fuse to a bomb that then exploded through the world's financial system and economy. We tried saying how well Australia was doing compared with the rest of the world. But people's understanding of their standard of living and economic life is not based on comparisons with Spaniards or Canadians. They look at how things used to be or how they had hoped them to be. Basically people's plans for their future had been woven around a continuation of the pre-GFC economic days. The dashing of those hopes was painful.

The Opposition spun itself into this mix with a heavily poll-driven and deeply irresponsible strategy. The public had developed an aversion to debt. The Opposition shouted something it knew to be untrue, that the budget debt was all a consequence of Labor's 'waste and misman-agement', rather than the massive hit to tax revenues caused by the GFC and the need for economic stimulus. The biggest global economic event since the Great Depression was simply airbrushed from history. The Opposition then claimed the economic reputation of the Howard Government in a subliminal pitch that voting for them could somehow take you back to those economic times. It was a potent mix of fear-mongering and false hope.

Having inherited these economic and political circumstances, with no time or space before the election to explain to the nation the truth of our economic position and our path to the future, I adopted as my own the political strategy that had been the cornerstone of the May budget. The public service had advised Kevin and Wayne that because Australia had not gone into recession, the return to surplus could be accelerated by three years. As a way of inoculating against the Liberal waste and debt accusations, I proclaimed that the government would return to a surplus in 2013.

I inherited this political strategy but I certainly doubled down on it.

In going for this simple explanation, depicting surplus as the sole emblem of economic management, I made an error that came back to haunt me when projections about revenue radically changed. But what can be fairly said is during my prime ministership, we actively pursued policies to create jobs and saw over half a million created, around 460 a day, while millions were lost worldwide. Here in Australia, 41 jobs were created for every 1000 people, while in the United States, eight jobs were lost for every 1000 and Europe lost 12 for every 1000.

We managed the budget so it was on a path to surplus but were mindful of not slamming on the brakes so hard we risked smashing down economic growth and putting jobs across the economy at risk. We got that balance right. Plus we created the maximum space for the Reserve Bank of Australia (RBA) to take interest rates to record lows. The RBA sets bands within which it wants to see inflation kept. If inflation bursts out of those bands, it puts upward pressure on interest rates. Unlike any previous Australian prime minister, during my period in office inflation remained inside the target band.

We gained a triple-A credit rating from all three major global ratings agencies. We took women's participation in work to record highs. We oversaw an increase in labour productivity as fairness and decency at work was provided in new ways.

For my three years as prime minister, the OECD Better Life Index had Australia on top. New jobs, new opportunities, a better life.

JOBS

Despite the progress on multiple fronts, for many people in many parts of the country, things did not feel good. In fact, life felt hard and jobs seemed scarce. After forming government, beyond the 2010 election I kept trying to explain to Australians why our economy could rightly be viewed as a wonder by those overseas, even while our people could still be doing it tough. In doing so, I coined the term 'patchwork economy' to describe the different speeds and states of the economy in different parts of the nation and industries.

Our economy was undergoing deep structural changes. The crisis of the GFC had obscured some from view and others were intensified by the GFC itself. The rise of Asia as the economic powerhouse of the 21st century was reshaping our economy. Hundreds of millions of people in Asia were moving to cities and needed the resources we had to sell to build and power those cities. Prices for iron ore and coal reached record highs. The scale of the jump in prices was not generally appreciated across Australia but from 2005 to 2010, prices for thermal coal rose from A$74 to A$123 per metric tonne. Iron ore rose from US$28 per metric tonne to US$168.

Established Australian mines were making startling profits. Where there is demand and sharply rising prices, supply will increase. New mining projects were being approved and constructed. This resources boom was already profoundly changing our economy.

As deputy prime minister, I visited Karratha in March 2010 and stayed at the adequate and clean Best Western Karratha Central Apartments. It cost more than where I stayed the next night, which was at the upmarket Cable Beach Club Resort in Broome. The entire visit reinforced the oft-heard message that when the boom comes to town, you do not want to be a pensioner on the fixed income as the price of everything around you escalates. When the boom comes to town, you do not want to be the person trying to ensure the school has enough teachers or the hospital enough nurses or the police station enough officers because all these people can go and earn more working in the mine. You do want to be the person who owns the Best Western.

As well as driving some parts of our economy into warp speed, the resources boom drove a sharp escalation in our currency. Our dollar floats freely and around the world is viewed as a resources currency. When resources are going strongly, our dollar goes up in value.

Years previously, while travelling to the USA I had to surrender the best part of two Australian dollars in order to get one US dollar. Back then, if you had said out loud that in a decade our dollar would be more valuable than the US dollar, people would have checked you for signs of fever. Yet that is exactly what happened. From 48 cents US in April 2001, our dollar climbed until it got you one US dollar and ten US cents by 28 July 2011.

The Australian dollar had almost reached parity with the US dollar in July 2008 but the GFC saw it plunge to a low of 0.6122 US cents in October 2008. Generally, however, the GFC exacerbated the dollar's rise because, as a result of our superior economic performance, our currency came to be seen as a safe bet. In addition, while our interest rates were low, they were still higher than in many recession-racked parts of the world so investors wanted their money in Australia.

But while a strong dollar is good for some, it is bad for others. If you want to travel overseas, it makes everything cheaper and that makes you happy. If you are in the tourism industry in Australia, you are saddened when you see people going to Bali or Thailand or Disneyland for their holidays instead of the Gold Coast or Uluru or Tasmania. If you are buying imported goods, prices are lower and that makes you happy. For the economy overall, this has a dampening effect on inflation. But if you make something in Australia that competes against imports, you see your product undercut on price and sales plummet.

Selling Australian-manufactured goods overseas becomes very hard. Say you need to earn A$10 per item to make a profit; where you could once sell it in America for not much more than US$5 to get that return, with the dollar above parity, your customers will need to pay more than US$10, and doubling your price kills demand.

A student from Asia working out where to pursue their university education used to look at Australia as a cheap good-value destination. It would cost less of their local currency to study in Melbourne compared to Boston. An Australian dollar above parity switches that calculation around: they book tickets for Boston.

Around the country, the resources boom and the dollar created a patchwork. If you were in manufacturing in Kwinana in Western Australia or Elizabeth in South Australia or Altona in Victoria, you were doing it exceedingly tough. The Australian dollar was smashing your business model to bits. The same was true for tourism operators in Hobart and tropical Queensland. Wollongong could be doing it tough while mining districts in the Hunter saw explosive growth.

Those under the dollar's hammer were not only bleeding money today but did not know how to plan for the future. Everyone knew the dollar would moderate at some point, with the recovery of the US economy. No one could tell you when that would be. It is hard to hang on when you cannot calculate how long you will be hanging on for. Eventually the dollar started to moderate in April 2013, when it began to fall from US$1.0553 to a low of 0.8909 US cents in early August 2013.

During this period of a persistently high dollar, the terms of trade – what the world is paying us for what we sell compared to what we pay the world for what we buy – had been as high as anything since federation. While this increased our nation's income, the benefits were not being evenly spread, but rather doled out in lumps. From 2001 until mid-2007, profits in the mining sector grew by an average of 3.64 per cent per quarter compared to an average quarterly growth in profits across all other sectors of 2.33 per cent. However, from mid-2007 to September 2012, while mining sector profits continued to grow at just over three per cent, average quarterly growth in profits across all other sectors plummeted to less than one per cent.

Other structural changes were at work in our economy. The disadvantage of being unskilled continued to increase. There was less and less space in the economy for those who could not read, write, use a computer or produce a certificate to demonstrate a skill level. The continuing revolution in information technology, often referred to as the 'digital disruption', was changing business models as well as the way we live. Suddenly David Jones was not just competing with Myer. A shopping war opened up on many fronts: consumers could purchase anything from overseas online, a tempting proposition with the strong Australian dollar.

Unsurprisingly this brought into sharp political focus a debate about the GST. Domestic retailers complained about how unfair it was that there is no GST levied on overseas online purchases. But for the government, trying to tackle this problem has practical and political problems. Practical because the cost of inspecting parcels crossing the border to keep the system honest would be more than the revenue raised. Political because voters are consumers who love online bargains.

Through the term 'patchwork economy' I sought to convey the spatial effects as our economy restructured. I wanted the federal government to increasingly work with an understanding of space and of differences in communities.

We created local employment zones for those parts of the country really struggling with job shortages. We took jobs expos to those same locations to bring jobseekers together with employers. At its best,

Simon Crean's regional development work breathed life into regional economic plans.

Early in the life of the government, I commissioned Kim Carr, the Minister for Innovation, Industry, Science and Research, to develop proposals for ways to strengthen the capacity of Australian businesses to innovate, adapt and prosper in our changing region of the world. In 2008, as the responsible minister, Kim had updated the nation's approach to innovation policy and set objectives on better collaboration between researchers and industry. Australia is bad at this kind of collaboration, with around one in five large Australian businesses taking part in such collaboration, compared to around one in three large firms in, say, Germany.

Despite these identified objectives and increases in research funding, the government's support of innovation remained a jumble of programs without an overarching vision. Extra funding was not translating into change. Meanwhile the need for change was growing ever more acute as the resources boom and high Australian dollar were hollowing out our economy. I did not want Australia's future to be one where resources were our only strong suit. Where some parts of the country were places of plenty and other parts of our nation were left behind. I wanted us to emerge from the resources boom with a more diverse economy, not a less diverse one. Having witnessed Greg Combet's remarkable skills and intellect in handling the vexed debate about carbon pricing, in a ministerial redistribution on 14 December 2011 I demoted Kim and put Greg in charge of industry and innovation work. It earnt me Kim's enmity in the internal leadership wars but was the right decision to get a hard and vital policy job done.

Greg had also led the government's work to try and save the steel industry. Although affected by carbon pricing, what had really put steel-making into such a parlous state were years of underinvestment in new capital, which had caused inefficiency. This kind of problem could be tolerated when the dollar was low. A high dollar meant no inefficiency could be left unaddressed. The government's Steel Transformation Plan enabled the industry to survive and facilitated new investments in research and development, environmental improvements and in meeting the cost of restructuring operations. It saved jobs.

Greg's brief was to bust open what had become a circular debate about the future of our economy. For too long, participants in the economic debate had been busy punching straw men on the nose, pretending every policy issue was a contest between a free market and an industry subsidy view of the world. While all these blows were being traded, Australia had actually moved on. In truth, this debate was over. There cannot and never should be any going back on the modern open economy that the reforms of the Hawke and Keating era created for us. Rather the burning questions are more practical ones. How can Australian genius, holed up in our research institutions, break quickly and efficiently into the private sector. After all, we are the nation that invented wifi. Our problem is not a lack of brain cells, it is that innovation does not diffuse through our economy the way it does in powerhouse nations like Germany.

How, in this free-market era, can prosperity and opportunity be better spread to alleviate differences in our patchwork economy? The backdrop to this question was the sharp concern in the Australian community that mining companies looked overseas first for workers and suppliers. Inevitably some of that imagery was wrong.

The first time I visited Chevron's enormous Gorgon project on Barrow Island in the north-west, while scampering over hard dry dirt and rocks in my steel-capped boots, I ended up talking to a man employed on the project. His home was a few streets away from mine in Altona in Melbourne's west. We chatted about football and particularly the Western Bulldogs.

Clearly mining ventures sometimes went to extraordinary efforts in order to get the workers they needed from around Australia. But I knew from my own experience there were problems. Frequently I heard from highly skilled workers who applied to mining companies and never received the courtesy of a reply. Yet at the same time, these mining companies were in Canberra lobbying for better access to overseas workers.

In visits to workplaces in the likes of Kwinana and Rockingham in Western Australia, I would be told about lay-offs or a reduction in apprenticeship numbers because they could not get their foot in the door to tender to be a supplier to a mining company.

It just did not add up. I wanted answers to these difficult and pressing issues.

In February 2013, with Greg, I announced our policy response, The Plan for Australian Jobs. It built on and responded to collaboration between employers, unions and civil society through a Manufacturing Task Force set up to develop a shared agenda. For all the 'government at war with business' and 'class war' headlines, it was remarkable to see differences melt away and be replaced by common purpose when people were around a table. The Manufacturing Task Force had reported in August 2012 with thoughtful recommendations for change.

Our Plan for Australian Jobs policy backed Australian businesses to win more work at home by actively encouraging and requiring more Australian industry participation and local content. Through new laws, the Australian Jobs Act, we were determined to obtain a fair go for those businesses and their workers who wanted to get some of the vast amounts of work being generated by mining.

The plan also supported Australian businesses to win more work abroad by establishing up to ten precincts in Australia that would put researchers and businesses cheek by jowl, enabling the wonderful work of our scientists to flow into the hands of our businesspeople so our nation received the benefits of jobs generated through this new knowledge.

The third section of the plan helped small and medium-sized businesses to grow and create new jobs by providing growth capital for investment and expert advice.

The Australian Jobs Act was passed by parliament in June 2013, despite Coalition opposition. Through these many months of structural change in the Australian economy and the policy debate that ensued, the Opposition stuck to chanting three-word slogans, like 'no new taxes', a promise immediately ditched in government.

In 2013 too we tightened up the 457 visa system, which allows companies to bring in skilled workers for a temporary period if Australian workers are not available to fill the jobs. In May 2012, a scheme to bring in overseas workers for the Roy Hill project had blown up badly on the government. The process of consultation with relevant unions had not been well handled. In response, urgent work was done to create an online Jobs Board so that Australian workers looking for jobs had a place to register interest and employers had a place to look for workers. In addition, the board would give the government some harder evidence about whether or not company claims that they could not find workers were real.

Problems with temporary migration flared again in 2013. Unions, particularly the construction union, were identifying rorts where temporary visas were being used by unscrupulous employers to bring in foreign workers to exploit.

All this caused us to look again at the process and proofs required for 457 visas.

A survey showed 15 per cent of employers did not even bother to look for local workers. There were problems with jobs being dressed up in order to legitimise a claim that no local labour was available. A labouring job would be grandly described as being for a 'project officer', a waiter's job as that of a 'café manager'. Even more worryingly, it seemed deals were being made and money was changing hands, with 457 visa-holders paying to be taken on by the employer, who then exploited them. It was all done in the hope of turning their temporary visa into permanency residency in Australia.

I publicly spoke about the need to put Australian workers first in line for jobs and absolutely understood this was likely to strike a political chord. I was not naive about its potency.

But change was needed. Some of the criticism of my stance was understandable. After all, employers have traditionally campaigned for more and more discretion on these issues, not more and more regulation.

Some of it, particularly the suggestion that using the word 'foreign' to describe workers from overseas was offensive, was absurd. I watched with wry amusement as employer organisations who had sat quietly by while Tony Abbott had used the most inflammatory language possible about asylum-seekers, with its deliberate fanning of fear, now came out to criticise me.

Notwithstanding all this carry-on, we legislated for stricter requirements so employers seeking 457 visa employees would also have to be training local workers, better ensured there could be no undercutting of wage rates and enabled the workplace inspectors from the Fair Work agency to police the system.

As a result, the Australian community could be better assured that the 457 visa program was doing what it was designed to do and nothing more. I was unsurprised when Tony Abbott pledged to give business everything they wanted by saying that 'Under a Coalition government, section 457 visas won't just be a component, but a mainstay of our immigration program.'[1]

But behind this political skirmishing lies a profound national identity question. Our concept of ourselves has not been one of a guest-worker economy, where people come for a short period, never settle fully and leave again. Our great nation-building achievements, like the Snowy Mountains Scheme, were not built by guest workers but by locals and migrants who became Australians.

I hope our future too is of well-managed permanent migration, with short-term workers being here because of genuine skill shortages or as part of a thoughtful scheme to assist the most disadvantaged nations of our region, like the one we introduced to enable workers from the Pacific Islands to gain income and training. But realising such a future requires the nurturing of community acceptance of newcomers and population growth.

In the 2010 election campaign I distanced myself from the language of 'Big Australia' used by Kevin Rudd because I knew whatever was intended to be meant by that phrase, it was being heard as more unsustainable pressure on overstretched communities.

Under my government, even with the problems of patchwork economic pressures, we ran a sizeable immigration program by our nation's historical standards.

But I understood then, and believe now, that to maintain the best possible community consensus in favour of immigration, tolerance and multiculturalism, you need to respond to people's fears, and talk to them about the sustainability of their community and their nation.

Vitally you need to keep creating jobs so migrants are not viewed suspiciously as competitors for the limited number of opportunities available.

A currency higher than we have ever known it. A world still clawing its way back from the GFC. I governed in a time of strong economic pressures. Not every job could be protected but our actions helped save industries and maintain diversity in our economy. We kept more people in work, with the dignity that comes with it: the ability to make a life for yourself and your family.

I governed to maximise the number of jobs available and to create the economy of the future. Governing for today, while steering our nation to a stronger tomorrow.

DIGNITY

As well as being stronger, I wanted Australia's future to be fairer. The image of a patchwork helped explain the unevenness of our economy, but a much older patchwork of advantage and disadvantage was laid out across the country. Too many did it tough, eking out a life from one welfare payment to the next.

Years ago I met Kirsten Livermore at a function for Emily's List, the organisation founded by Joan Kirner to get more Labor women into parliaments around the country. Like me, Kirsten was standing for parliament for the first time in the 1998 election. Her electorate was Capricornia, based on the township of Rockhampton in Queensland, and she was fearlessly getting out and about asking for the votes of miners and workers in the beef industry. The two of us became firm friends. At her wedding in Barcaldine – where, incidentally, the Labor Party was formed – Kirsten memorably stepped behind the bar of the local historic pub and started pulling beers in her white wedding dress. But a phrase from her first speech to parliament also etched itself in my memory. In describing her life's journey she said:

> I was 11 when my father died. My mother found herself with the job of providing emotionally and financially for her three young daughters, the youngest of whom was only six. I have never forgotten the short trip from working class to welfare class, a trip that many Australians have shared, for whatever reason. It is a trip that no one in my family asked for but nonetheless had to endure.[2]

That evocative phrase 'the short trip from working class to welfare class' conveys a potential life sentence. Not just for adults but for children. The longitudinal study of Australian children reveals that joblessness begets joblessness, disadvantage begets disadvantage.

Even as we managed the patchwork pressures in our economy, I was determined to get people on the trip back to work and dignity and independence. As deputy prime minister I had commenced this journey when I created the portfolio of Social Inclusion. The aim was to join up what government was doing to assist those who were not fully included in our nation's life because of unemployment, ill health, disability or poor skills for speaking or reading English.

Our dependency ratio, the number of those not working compared with the numbers working, will grow as the Australian population ages and there are more long-lived retirees. The last thing our nation can afford in these circumstances is to have prime working-age adults who are capable of work out of the workforce and placing more tax burden on others.

At my insistence, the 2011 budget contained measures to move individuals at risk of long-term unemployment into training or work. Then almost 2.8 million Australians of working age were on income support payments. We targeted lone parents, teen parents, young people, under-35s receiving the Disability Support Pension (DSP) and the very long-term unemployed, and focused on local areas with high levels of disadvantage and joblessness.

There is broad diversity between and within these groups but the logic of our reforms was straightforward. In each case, people received better support for their efforts, such as keeping more of their income or getting access to better training and childcare places, in exchange for the acceptance of responsibility to actively pursue work and develop their own skills. Take the example of a young girl who becomes pregnant and leaves school to have and care for her baby. Income support is paid to her but she is at high risk of a life of unemployment. While her peers are studying, she is not. For that young girl, our reforms meant she would be required to work through a plan to learn and engage, not spiral into deeper and deeper isolation.

For people under 35 on the DSP, new participation requirements were designed to get them working to the maximum extent possible: DSP recipients could now work up to 30 hours per week and still receive the pension. Until then they had been reluctant to even try working because if they tried and failed, they would need to requalify for the pension. We also modernised the way disability is assessed for pension eligibility.

Ten disadvantaged communities around the nation received extra funding towards finding ways of improving the lives and employ-ability of those within that community. We further expanded income management so that in more places around Australia of concentrated disadvantage, welfare monies paid for the benefit of children were not being used to buy alcohol and cigarettes.

Employers were asked to give a go to a person with a disability or someone who had been long-term unemployed. Incentives were made available if they did.

We also ploughed money into literacy training and a workforce development fund designed to create opportunities for Australians in and out of work to develop new skills.

The 2011 budget changes reflected my belief in the dignity that work brings and the importance of children growing up in a home where someone works, and that includes the homes of single-parent families.

Our initiatives built on changes made by the Howard Govern-ment in 2006 to the Parenting Payment, the benefits paid to people out of the workforce raising children, most of whom are single parents, usually mothers.

The Howard Government moved single parents from Parent-ing Payment onto New Start, the unemployment benefit, when their youngest child turned eight. Although the New Start benefit came with extra support for a person with a child compared to an unemployed person with no children, it was less than the Parenting Payment.

However the Howard Government also decided on a slow phase-in. A single parent, on Parenting Payment at the time of the decision was 'grandfathered' and still able to stay on it until their youngest child was 16 years old. Indeed if they had further children, Parenting Payment would be paid until the youngest of those children turned 16.

There was persuasive evidence that those who did not get the benefit of the grandfathering and who moved to New Start demonstrated different work patterns.

We decided to draw a line so that for subsequent children, the new rules, which encouraged working, applied. Additionally those caring for teenage children would, on 1 January 2013, move to New Start. This change was designed to minimise the long-term differences between the benefits paid to parents in similar positions. It reflected our belief in the value of work.

To assist with the transition to employment, we changed the income rules so benefit recipients could keep more of the income and lose less of their benefit when they earnt it. More training and advice would also be offered to assist in finding pathways into work.

These changes created unease among welfare stakeholders and advocacy groups, but the overall commitment and direction of the package was welcomed. None of these changes meant I underestimated the struggle and pressures of bringing up children on your own. I have seen friends go through it. But if a single parent stays out of the workforce for many years, then a child grows up seeing no role model of employment and the adult risks never getting back into the workforce. For both the child and the adult, the result can be a life always lived on welfare. It was a tough-love approach, not a hard-hearted one.

We also needed the budget savings it garnered. The ongoing pressure on the budget meant that, in order to make all the new investments we wanted to in getting people into work, the money needed to be redirected from somewhere.

In 2012, in the throes of difficult budget discussions, we decided to go further by applying the move to New Start to everyone on the single-parenting payment with a child over eight years old. No more grandfathering of any kind. In a move that was fair, everyone would be in the same position from 1 January 2013. Everyone would also have the benefit of our more generous rules for keeping more of the income they earnt, which also started on 1 January 2013. In addition, from

1 July 2012, as a result of general changes we were making to the tax system, low-income earners would pay less tax.

These changes generated a saving of almost $700 million over four years. We were in a period of fiscal consolidation, a complicated way of saying that we needed to drive the budget to surplus as soon as possible and start paying down the debt incurred as a result of the GFC's hit to the budget.

In different budget circumstances, on fairness grounds, the measure may still have come under discussion but it is likely a broader reform proposition would have been funded, with more changes to the way working and benefits intersect, so that even more earnt income could be kept. This would have best accorded with my values of fairness and putting the emphasis on work.

When announced, the new rules hit with a thud. There was a sharply critical reaction from welfare advocacy groups and many in the Labor caucus. The rhetoric used created the impression that the government had cut benefits for every single parent, whereas what was actually happening was every single parent was now going to be treated in the same way, with their eligibility for payments defined by the rules established in 2006. Concurrently civil advocacy groups sensed a political opportunity to rev up the broader campaign on the rate of New Start.[3] This issue had been smouldering for more than a decade.

In 1980 the fortnightly rate of New Start and the rate of the single aged pension had been $6.45 apart. Over time, because New Start was only indexed to changes in the cost-of-living rate, not the more generous indexation rates derived from changes in average earnings for people in the workforce, the value of the two benefits diverged. Further the historically high pension rise delivered by the Rudd Government had not flowed through to New Start. So by 2012 the gap between the two benefits fortnightly was $205.60.

Welfare advocates were understandably concerned that unemployed people were being forced to live in poverty on $35 a day. The catch cry became, 'Could you live on $35 a day?' In a media stumble, Jenny Macklin suggested she could, which was interpreted as callousness. Ironically no one in my government had more empathy for people in need than Jenny.

But in their campaigning, welfare advocates were deliberately conflating the backstory on New Start and our changes to the Parenting Payment. No one raising children was in fact living on $35 a day, which is the rate of New Start for someone with no children. Extra payments were made for those raising children.

Of course, I appreciate that many in our community would like to see more generous benefits flow to everyone without work, whether or not they have children. But the decision for which my government should be rightly held to account is the one to make the rules consistent for all parents receiving benefits, rather than maintaining a different set of rules for those who were receiving payments before 2006. Of course, we should be judged too on our decision to deliver in the 2012 budget a supplementary allowance to New Start recipients, which was the single biggest increase to New Start ever.

Additionally, under both Kevin and me, Labor had made a number of positive changes to assist disadvantaged jobseekers. Everything from the design of employment services, to the funding of innovative social ventures which work to change lives, to initiatives for disadvantaged communities, to our schools, skills and training policies, to our childcare and early-education policies had been calibrated to work to alleviate disadvantage.

The Opposition, which had absolutely no intention of reversing our changes to Parenting Payment or of increasing New Start, cynically played the politics. Any student of Australian politics could have worked out that despite their tut-tutting in Opposition, in government their approach would be to roll back many of our policies designed to help those in need. Indeed in the 2013 election campaign Tony Abbott promised to abolish the New Start supplementary allowance.

In mounting a strong campaign, effectively against Labor, social welfare advocates were revisiting a political loop that hurts Labor governments. Expectations of Labor are always high. Any beneficial measure Labor brings receives a quick welcome and then is accepted as the new normal. The focus turns to demanding the next beneficial measure. When it comes to controversial change made by Labor, however, it is rarely weighed in the full context of everything done before but treated as a stand-alone measure. Conversely their expectations of Coalition governments are low. Small crumbs receive high praise. Indeed advocates fearing the worst express public gratitude on the announcement of a Coalition cutback to a Labor-inspired program if it is modest rather than severe.

Social welfare advocates are not alone in this. Universities, which saw enormous increases in their funding under the Labor government, took the same single-measure, single-campaign focus approach when the government needed to moderate the rate of growth of their funds for a limited period in order to support better expenditure in schools. This cargo-cult mentality towards Labor governments does not assist the progressive stakeholders in Australian society to build public support for and action towards sustainable long-term change.

Plenty of internal politics played out within Labor on the Parenting Payment changes. While many caucus members had legitimate concerns, Kevin's supporters used the decision to stir the internal pot. Kevin did not change the policy when he became prime minister.

With the pressure of an election looming and the fomenting of internal dissent, we did respond in the 2013 budget with modest measures to lift the amount of income those receiving New Start could keep if they worked. But much more policy work needs to be undertaken in relation to New Start and the plight of the unemployed than we had the time or budget space to do.

New Start is now serving two quite different groups: those who experience an episode of unemployment in an otherwise sound working career and highly disadvantaged jobseekers for whom New Start may well be the norm for the rest of their lives unless extraordinary efforts are made to assist them into work. Our nation should make those extraordinary efforts, but correlated with stringent participation and engagement requirements.

I would like to see better joining up of income support and training entitlements so working people have a kind of security, even as their working lives require of them more skills, more shifts in occupation, more flexibility. For a long time now, we have known that a job for life is a thing of the past, but our policy approach is still struggling to catch up.

Despite all the political problems, I believe my focus on work has eased the way of Australians taking the trip back from welfare class to working class. Between 2011 and 2013, the number of DSP recipients decreased by more than 10,000. By May 2012, more than 600 teen parents had plans to rebuild their life.

My expectation is that even our most controversial change will result in more children growing up in a household with a parent who works.

DECENCY

I passionately believe that work is the vital key to unlocking the life you want, but not work that strips you of your sense of self by harming you with unfair treatment. This belief is core to Labor's ethos. In a contest between working people and employers, we are hard-wired to favour working people. The Coalition is of a different view. Trade unions are viewed as a political enemy to be curtailed, even destroyed. In a contest between working people and employers they are hard-wired to favour employers.

Mostly life in our nation's workplaces does not play out as a contest. The relationship between employees and employers is one of shared interests and joint endeavour. Australians work hard and, in turn, overwhelmingly that hard work is valued, respected and fairly rewarded by employers. But there are times when conflict arises. Employees who tend to be in the weaker position compared with the power of the employer need someone in their corner to help them out. Occasionally, in the face of militant unionism, it is employers who are in the weaker position and need help from the law. Good workplace laws help to even the playing field, protecting the weak from exploitation by the strong.

Australians instinctively tend to share Labor's values of fairness and decency in workplaces. Politically the Coalition knows this but so deep-rooted are its beliefs that from time to time it cannot resist pushing them forward. One such occasion was the 1997–98 water-front dispute, when images were beamed into people's lounge rooms of senior Liberals almost dancing with delight as men wearing bala-clavas secured Melbourne's port after all the workers were sacked. It demonstrated how out of step the Coalition was with mainstream community opinion on the treatment of working people.

The introduction of the hated Work Choices in 2005 was another. Having won control of the Senate in the 2004 election, the Coalition could not resist the chance to enact its industrial relations vision. But in giving birth to Work Choices, the Liberals triggered the eventual death of the Howard Government because it offended long-held Australian values. Work Choices incited genuine fear; it effectively abolished the safety net and, for the vast majority of employees, any ability to mount an unfair dismissal claim. Employees could go to work and be presented with an Australian Workplace Agreement (AWA) that cut their pay and conditions. Should their employer cobble together some reason to sack them if they did not sign the AWA, no redress was available. Work Choices was also littered with provisions to stymie the work of trade unions.

After the 2007 election, as I undertook the repeal of Work Choices and its replacement with Labor's new Fair Work laws, I faced a much chastened Opposition. If you believed the public utterances, apparently Coalition supporters of Work Choices had become as rare as hen's teeth.

In Opposition, I had managed a delicate dance with unions to produce a workplace relations policy in the mainstream of the Hawke and Keating tradition. Under those Labor governments, our nation had moved away from having a centralised and inflexible system of conciliation and arbitration. For many years this system of going to the industrial umpire for almost everything had served the nation well. But the opening up of the Australian economy to the competitive forces of the world meant its rigidities were too much.

The new Labor way was to enable bargaining in workplaces so the focus of the system I wanted to create would also be bargaining.

As well as seeking the views of employers, I worked intensively with Greg Combet, then Secretary of the ACTU, on the architecture for the policy and all of its details. Greg brought to these discussions both his best thinking and his commitment to seeing a Labor government elected. As the driving force in the superb anti-Work Choices campaign, Your Rights at Work, his efforts proved pivotal to the election of the

Labor government in 2007 and to the creation of a campaigning culture in the union movement.

Greg never forgot who he was representing. He pushed the union case hard, seeking some things I was not prepared to give. I wanted a policy that was fair to all interests – employer, employee and union – and which could be defended as such. Between the two of us, it was a good-natured exercise, and our exchanges never became heated. I developed a profound respect for Greg's intelligence, his diligence and his vision for the future of the trade union movement. He knew, as I did, that this was Labor's opportunity to create a system that would endure for the long term. He took to teasing me about my penchant for naming everything 'Fair Work': the Fair Work Act, the Fair Work Commission. I was undeterred and have been pleased to see it settle in to the lexicon.

The policy document I produced, entitled 'Forward with Fairness', committed Labor to ending the divide between union and non-union collective agreement-making and proceeded from simple principles. That an employee has a right to join a union if they want to, and cannot be forced to join a union if they do not want to. That an employee who has chosen to be in a union has the right to be represented by that union in bargaining. Unions have a seat at the bargaining table if they represent an employee in the workplace.

Forward with Fairness was released in April 2007. Kevin had left this work to me but became concerned when, overtired after Labor's national conference, I slipped up in a John Laws interview. Over the phone, a softly spoken Laws enticed me into a silly sporting analogy: I said employers risked getting hurt if they were on the field in a political contest. *The Australian* went to town and accused me of threatening employers.[4] Kevin was understandably anxious about this and I was not happy about my misstep either. I apologised for my error and he understood.

In the lead-up to the 2007 election, it became necessary to build on the Forward with Fairness policy. Deliberately the policy had maintained a discreet silence on some questions, giving us time to assess how much more detail we needed to offer up before the election. With many employers mobilising politically against us, including a number paying for television advertising to buttress the Howard Government's over-the-top pro-Work Choices communications blitz, it became imperative to get a statement from someone on the employer side of the table that they could live with the Forward with Fairness policy.

There was no possibility of getting such a statement unless we addressed some of the particular issues in the resources sector, in which ultra-militant unionism had both prompted and aided a fierce employer backlash. Mining companies had worked hard to de-unionise, using AWAs to get there. The employees in question were well paid and not downtrodden. Resources companies feared being forced back into dialogue with unions.

The way our policy was structured, avoiding unions entirely was not an option but I worked with my staff to design a common-law contract provision for highly paid employees. It meant companies with no enterprise bargain in place need not fear the sudden revival of old awards that had provisions that prevented modern mining rosters and fly-in-fly-out work arrangements. Subsequently the Australian Industry Group said publicly that they could live with the proposed laws.

It irked me when journalists were spun a line by Kevin and his office that he had imposed this policy move on me. That was simply untrue. But I took it on the chin and did not complain.

Once we were in government, the policy words of Forward with Fairness needed to be translated into a comprehensive set of laws. Every detail and clause needed to be settled. To achieve this, on top of the usual cabinet processes I spent long hours collaborating with a business committee, a union committee, a tripartite body called the Committee on Industrial Legislation and a committee of my caucus colleagues. The process was onerous and entailed constant decision-making. But there was some fun to be had too.

I first made my name in parliament as the government's heaviest hitter in Question Time taunting the Opposition about its leftover Work Choices propaganda material. In desperation, the Howard Government had spent around $114 million in advertising trying to convince the Australian people its ideological bastard baby was really cute and cuddly. Controversially a senior public servant had fronted most of this advertising. But Work Choices paraphernalia also abounded: pens, mousepads, even sunscreens for car windows. When my department advised my office that the government had racked up costs of $110,000 to store thousands of these items and that such costs were still being incurred, I milked it in Question Time: a plague of mousepads was definitely to be feared. When you're playing in parliament for people to laugh at the Opposition and some of their own backbenchers join in, you know you're winning.

The Opposition did not wholly oppose the Fair Work laws. Julie Bishop, the Opposition spokesperson at the time, clearly wanted to defend some AWAs but was overruled by political hardheads. Nevertheless abandoning in a parliamentary vote something they loved and had fought so hard for as a government was painful for the Opposition.

To manage the contradictory forces of political pragmatism and ideological purity internally, they decided to take a stand around unfair dismissal laws and their application to small businesses. That meant that to get the laws through, I had to work in the Senate with the Greens and Senators Nick Xenophon and Steve Fielding, the latter a representative of the small conservative party Family First. It was good practice for the cajoling and persuasion skills I would later draw on so heavily in minority government. I remember sitting in the adviser's box, reserved for government staff, on the Senate floor for the final vote. There was tension in the air as the final Opposition amendment was put to the vote and there were an equal number of votes on either side. Fortunately tied means lost. Our Forward with Fairness Bill was through. I was backslapped and kissed by Labor senators and staff. Even Steve Fielding kissed me, though I didn't turn at quite the right time so he ended up kissing my ear. It was a good story to tell over a celebratory glass of wine later that day.

By 2010, the Fair Work regime was up and running and it has been widely accepted by Australians. Despite all the Liberal Party and employer claims of doom and gloom about our policy coming into the 2007 election, the nation is well served by our Fair Work laws. Working days lost to industrial action dropped to around one-third of those experienced under the previous government. And while workplace laws are merely one factor in the productivity of our nation, for the first time in many years, productivity has recently shown slight improvements.

In our modern economy, not everyone who faces exploitation at work is a traditional employee – the Fair Work Act did not address all issues. From my years as a solicitor at Slater & Gordon, I knew that those whom the law calls an 'independent contractor' or 'self-employed' can actually be the most exploited.

In 1987 the Clothing Trades Union won a new award provision which enabled it to follow up and prosecute those who mistreated outworkers, predominantly migrant women who sew clothing at home for piece rates. It was an immense privilege to collaborate with the union over my years at the law firm trying to trace and hold to account fly-by-night operators providing this work. I remember how satisfying it was to obtain the long-service leave owed to a woman who worked from home. The court found her to be an employee of long standing, even though the employer name on each of her tax group certificates was different. To avoid debts and accountability, her boss incorporated a new two-dollar shell company every year.

In that case, I appeared against a learned and stylish barrister who was definitely on his way up, Geoff Giudice. He served as the first president of Fair Work Australia. At the ceremonial opening, I stood at the bar table and delivered a submission wishing him well.

In another outworkers' case I worked on, the woman sewed silk blouses for an upmarket fashion label. The blouses were expensive in the shops yet, to my disgust, the women who made them were getting paid next to nothing. It felt especially rewarding, both as deputy prime minister and then as prime minister, to support laws through parliament that gave outworkers more effective protections.

The Labor Party also had a longstanding position of wanting to see a better deal for owner-drivers of trucks. These people are not employees and consequently Fair Work laws did not assist them. Despite being technically self-employed, essentially they are powerless. Historically many of the providers of work have set rates so low that a driver can only pay off their truck and make a modest living by working extraordinary hours. The resulting fatigue can kill, not only the driver but other road users.

The Transport Workers Union had long fought for a system of safe rates for truck drivers, ending the low rates behind unsafe driving practices. A simple concept but hard in implementation. The politics were tough too. While it is easy to sympathise with the plight of overstressed drivers and not want to share the roads with them, it is not as easy to accept that the price of goods transported may go up if drivers are paid more.

Over many years, the union had campaigned effectively, reaching out to conservatives on the safety issues and some state parliaments had passed safe rates laws.

As deputy prime minister, in July 2008 I started working towards a national system of safe rates and was pleased to see new safe rates laws pass parliament in March 2012.

Also in 2012, we introduced the most significant reforms to the Australian shipping industry for over a century, including protections for workers.

All of these extensions of fairness took considerable effort and political management. But the hardest fought changes were those relating to building workers.

In 1986, Labor governments, state and federal, had taken on those parts of the Builders' Labourers Federation that had become corrupt and rogue. This led to deregistration of the union, but while an organisation can be destroyed, a culture is harder to dismantle. That culture had infected the operations of the construction division in Victoria of the Construction, Forestry, Mining and Energy Union. In Western Australia too, big personalities with scant regard for industrial laws had come to dominate that construction division.

When the union movement was not quick enough to deal with this itself, the Howard Government responded with draconian laws that enabled secret interrogations of building workers. People could be gaoled for not cooperating. The body overseeing these laws, the Australian Building and Construction Commission (ABCC), was led by people on a crusade against unionism. To its discredit, the ABCC did not use its resources and powers to crack down on the real problems.

Rather it contented itself with terrorising workers for minor matters, like flying union flags on building sites.

Unions demanded of the Labor Party that the ABCC be abolished; they wanted no special body to enforce industrial laws in building. Nevertheless serious problems existed, and that would not have been a responsible course. As deputy prime minister, I initiated a review, led by Judge Murray Wilcox, to find a way through. It led to my announcement of a new building inspectorate which would keep coercive powers where needed. My approach was viewed as a sell-out by the union movement, but after the 2010 election campaign the changes were legislated. A sunset clause of three years applied, so the building industry had an opportunity to show that times had very much changed and coercive powers were no longer needed.

Although the traditionally male bastion of building was difficult to reform, progress was being made for women at work. Even though the Hawke Government made it unlawful for women to be paid less than a man for the same work, the pay gap hangs on. Across all sectors of the economy, it stands at 17.5 per cent. Partly this reflects male dominance of more senior, better paid positions. Partly it reflects the gender segregation of our workforce, with highly paid occupations like in mining disproportionately held by men. But it also reflects a persistent undervaluing of occupations that are viewed as women's work.

As deputy prime minister, I included in the new Fair Work Act an equal-pay provision with teeth, designed to sweep away the gender bias against properly paying 'women's work'. Under the old equal-pay provision, 16 separate applications for equal pay in various sectors dominated by women had failed. With the benefit of the new principle, the Australian Services Union brought the first test case for women working in the social and community services sector. In this sector women outnumber men by four to one. These workers assist families and children in crisis, work with the homeless, staff our women's refuges. But despite their having three-year tertiary qualifications, they were paid less than those in low-skilled occupations.

As a Labor government, we not only changed the law to bring about wage justice, we made an agreement about how we would assist the case and then made the tough budget savings necessary so more money to pay our share of the salary increases could flow to the organisations that receive federal funds and employ these workers. As a result, the Fair Work Commission awarded around 150,000 workers, most of them women, phased-in pay rises of between 23 and 45 per cent.

Our approach to the case was not a self-evident one. Naturally we always wanted the workers to succeed but there would have been some merit in a managed contest that allowed the Fair Work Commission to hand down a decision fully detailing the principles in this test case and the approach it would take to all future equal-pay cases. However, to ensure success and to give the government the maximum ability to influence the phasing in of the pay-rises, we went for a consent-agreement-style approach.

Since then, I have had the opportunity to meet these workers and to hear some of their stories. On more than one occasion, I was greeted with rapturous applause, even joyful tears. In fact, we should be applauding them.

For the nation, equal pay is continuing and unfinished business. As wonderful as it was to secure fair pay for social and community services workers, there remains much to do for heavily female occupations. Our government made a start for childcare workers and aged-care workers but the job is not finished.

I am proud that under the government I led, women's participation in work achieved its averaged highest ever level. Policies like better affordability for childcare, a sensibly constructed paid parental leave scheme, fair workplace laws and scrapping old distortions in the tax system, such as giving a tax break if women stay at home, do make a difference.

Even in my last few months as prime minister, we continued trying to extend fairness and dignity at work with new laws to deal with the scourge of workplace bullying and to extend family-friendly provisions. We also succeeded in extending provisions to enable unions to visit employees in workplaces. Too often, silly games are played to prevent unions getting about their legitimate business.

In a parliament where Labor lacked a majority, our track record of legislating for decency at work is remarkable. It is a source of personal satisfaction and I am proud to have worked alongside the trade union movement, as well as decent employers, in its delivery.

For my visit The Premier of the People's Republic of China held a ceremonial welcome at the Great Hall in Beijing, April 2013. (Luke Marsden/Newspix)

A North Korean soldier and I look at each other at the United Nations Command Military Armistice Commission meeting room in the village of Panmunjom, which separates the two Koreas. (AP Photo/Lee Jin-man, Pool)

Being welcomed by South Korean President Lee Myung-bak. (Alex Ellinghausen/Fairfax Syndication)

With Kate Ellis, helping out at the Adelaide Markets. (John Tass-Parker)

On a school visit with Jenny Macklin, talking to a young girl. (John Tass-Parker)

Staff Christmas party at The Lodge. Police, cleaners, political staff, attendants – gathered together. (John Tass-Parker)

And the requisite cricket match. (John Tass-Parker)

Working on the small plane, the Challenger. (John Tass-Parker)

With New Zealand Prime Minister John Key, his wife, Bronagh, and Tim in New Zealand. (Tom Battams)

Mucking around with staff and getting behind the camera this time. (John Tass-Parker)

What a press conference looks like from the outside. (John Tass-Parker)

Preparing to tape a video message in my office at Parliament House. (Denise Paton)

Herding premiers. Getting ready for a COAG press conference, April 2013. (John Tass-Parker)

Premier Barry O'Farrell signing the heads of government agreement to implement a needs based school funding system, 23 April 2013. (JP Preston)

With Aboriginal elder Alice Ngalkin, who was overcome with emotion at a native title ceremony at the Alice Springs Desert Park, June 2011. (Glenn Campbell/Fairfax Syndication)

Inspecting a building site in Brisbane with Wayne Swan and Mark Dreyfus, November 2012. (John Tass-Parker)

Attending the 19th APEC Economic Leaders' Meeting, Honolulu, November 2011. (Howard Moffat – AUSPIC/DPS)

With President Obama at the NATO Summit, Chicago, May 2012. (Howard Moffat – AUSPIC/DPS)

With the Queen at Parliament House, Canberra, October 2011. (Andrew Meares/Fairfax Syndication)

That speech, 9 October 2012. (Kym Smith/Newspix)

Hot and tired. Getting ready for a press conference on a trip to rural Queensland with Agriculture Minister Joseph Ludwig and staff. (John Tass-Parker)

The glam life of a PM. Briefing for a joint press conference with Ben Hubbard, Jay Weatherill, Jennifer Rankine and her granddaughter, Don Farrell and Annabel Digance. (John Tass-Parker)

Showing a visiting school group the PM's courtyard at Parliament House. (John Tass-Parker)

At Etihad Stadium with Barry Hall after a win by the Western Bulldogs, 1 August 2010. (Michael Klein/Newspix)

Campaigning in Western Sydney, 3 March 2013. (John Tass-Parker)

The day of the non-challenge, 21 March 2013, in a meeting with Paul Howes about forced adoptions. (John Tass-Parker)

I found out later that my speechwriter Michael Cooney started drafting a defeat speech on the day of the challenge that was not a challenge. (John Tass-Parker)

With Wayne Swan and Jenny Macklin on the day I first met Sophie Deane. (John Tass-Parker)

Coonabarabran Primary School, November 2012, on a visit with Peter Garrett. (John Tass-Parker)

Meeting friends in my office at Parliament House. (John Tass-Parker)

Setting up for a Sky TV interview on 26 June 2013 to call the spill on what would be my last day as prime minister. (John Tass-Parker)

Speaking to the media after my defeat in a party-room vote to former prime minister Kevin Rudd, 26 June 2013. (John Tass-Parker)

Entering the House of Representatives as backbenchers on 27 June, looking for our seats! Greg Combet, me, Wayne Swan and Craig Emerson. (Andrew Meares/Fairfax Syndication)

With loyal staff Jo Haylen and Michelle Fitzgerald, packing up the office. (John Tass-Parker)

The reputation of the trade union movement has been tarnished in recent times by some dishonest individuals. Just as corporate life brings us people like Eddie Groves, so union life has thrown up individuals who have been justifiably punished for their conduct. Nevertheless the union movement is also home to selfless decent Australians who continue to uphold many of the values that have made us the nation we are today. A nation that believes in fairness at work.

On many occasions I argued with trade unions. At the height of our disputation over what was to replace the ABCC, I flew to Brisbane to speak at the ACTU Congress only to be confronted with a sea of yellow: every unionist in the room was wearing a yellow T-shirt as a protest against my approach. But I have never shied away from engagement with unionists. I have attended ACTU Executive meetings and given as good as I got. Yet never have I doubted the vital role of trade unionism or the capabilities of most senior trade union leaders. In both the easier days and the many difficult days during my leadership, I felt common cause with and a sense of personal support from union leaders who were also trying to build a stronger and fairer Australia.

As prime minister, the worth of my work can be weighed by what was achieved for the working life of others: by the creation of jobs and the bringing to people of the benefits and dignity that can come with fair employment.

17

Getting ready

'Productivity isn't everything, but in the long run it is almost everything.'

NOBEL PRIZE-WINNING ECONOMIST PAUL KRUGMAN[1]

CABINET SITS IN A WINDOWLESS WOOD-PANELLED ROOM in the central spine of Parliament House, across from the prime minister's office. Before you enter it, you pass an alcove where you must surrender your mobile phone or any other electronic device you are carrying. Like all areas that need to be truly secure, the cabinet room is swept regularly for listening devices. Internet-connected electronic devices can be hacked and turned into listening devices; they are forbidden.

Seating around the table is done in order of seniority. As prime minister, you chair cabinet and sit in the middle of the side on your left as you enter the room coming from your office. The deputy prime minister sits next to you and across the table are the Senate leader and Senate deputy leader.

Ministers took to storing their cabinet documents on non-internet-connected iPads. It saved carrying around bulky lever-arch folders full of documents. Cabinet submissions deal with complex problems and can be lengthy. The first part consists of a summary and also the response to the proposal of senior public servants across departments. Those coordination comments do not substitute for political thinking and decision-making but inform it just the same.

Note-takers sit silently keeping the record. The Secretary of the Department of the Prime Minister and Cabinet sits at a small desk perched under a section of the bookcase that runs at head height around the room. Dr Ian Watt, a highly professional public servant I appointed as secretary, was always at risk of hitting his head when he stood up.

For our meetings, coffee, tea and small snacks were placed on tables at one end of the room. Bowls of nuts and jellybeans as well as pitchers of water were placed around the cabinet table in everyone's easy reach. The coffee in the urn was close to undrinkable and periodically someone would do a run to Aussies, the café in Parliament House.

The ministers who served on the Expenditure Review Committee (ERC) would put in the longest hours in the cabinet room, going line by line through the budget, hearing expenditure and savings submissions from other ministers. As deputy prime minister, I had done that, but as prime minister, I attended only the absolute crunch decision-making meetings. For Wayne Swan, Penny Wong, Jenny Macklin, Brendan O'Connor, Bill Shorten, Stephen Smith, Simon Crean and David Bradbury, the ERC, I knew what it was like to spend so long in the room that you could almost feel your bones flaking from vitamin D deficiency. One day is the same as another. It is sad when you work out Easter is almost upon you because hot cross buns appear as the snack in the room.

In cabinet meetings, I encouraged people to have their say. In debates, I tended not to speak early, knowing that would put ministers in a difficult position if they had a contrary view. They would not want to be seen to be openly challenging me as prime minister. I listened, summarising the perspectives and points for my colleagues at the end of the discussion. If there was division, I made the call about what would happen next: which view would be adopted or whether a compromise would be hammered out or the submission sent back for more work. If I felt strongly, then I would announce my view and effectively impose it on the room. But mostly, I wanted the team to work issues through together.

The ongoing internal campaign against my leadership meant that cabinet was more fraught than it should have been. Too much leaked.

From time to time there was pointed positioning within the room, obviously for later exploitation in internal leadership discussions. Is it nostalgia to yearn for something you never experienced, like the respite of a cabinet with the kind of solidarity shown for most of the Hawke and Keating era?

Despite the leadership divisions, there was unity of purpose around a number of the big things the government was trying to achieve. As Labor people, it was in us to seek to actively plan and shape the nation's future.

Some of the big things we needed to do to get ready for the future formed continuous threads through the Labor government Kevin led and the one I did. One was the importance of productivity to the wealth of our nation: how could we increase the amount of income generated as the work of Australians is combined with capital assets, like factories and the equipment used within them. According to the official Bureau of Statistics measure, productivity has increased year on year since 2006–07 by an average of 1.3 per cent. Whatever the increase, we were always hunting for more.

In this digital era, productivity depends so much on moving information more quickly than ever before so there was a great deal of enthusiasm throughout the government for the delivery of broadband around the country. Clogged roads, ports and railway lines diminish productivity as workers and goods move more slowly than they should. Across the government, everyone agreed we needed to build the nation's infrastructure. To these far-reaching decisions, I added my determination to build the nation's skills for the future: the more skilled the workers, the better the productivity.

As I governed, I focused on this productivity drive explicitly in the context of getting ready for the Asian Century, of having a plan for the days beyond the resources boom, when increasingly we would be living off our wits, knowledge and capabilities rather than our natural assets.

I was seized with the urgent need to get ready for that future and to make sure newfound opportunities and wealth would be fairly shared. That we would be stronger as a country and not leave anyone behind.

NATIONAL BROADBAND NETWORK

As I sat in the cabinet room, both as deputy prime minister and prime minister, I used to think about the other governments that had met there, the governments of Hawke, Keating, Howard. The big debates, the big personalities. During the days of my prime ministership, the cabinet was also home to some big debates and personalities. They do not come much bigger than Stephen Conroy.

Like me a migrant from the United Kingdom to Australia, Stephen is a man of strong opinions and sometimes dark moods. He can be incredibly funny and great company. A rarity in politics and in Australian life generally, he does not drink alcohol at all. That does not stop him dancing at parties. The harder it got for me in government, the warmer and more staunch Stephen was. I could not have asked for more support.

There are five great loves in Stephen's life, and his wife, Paula, and daughter, Isabella, top the list. The other three loves are the Australian Labor Party, the Collingwood Football Club and the NBN.

Stephen is no geek. His passion for the NBN is not the product of being the nerd in the high school computer club. It is the product of understanding the power of the NBN. The vision of what it can mean for our nation. But he does know the details.

In August during the 2010 election campaign, Stephen and I were standing at a media conference in Midway Point, Tasmania, after we had switched on the first release of the NBN. The press pack was a mixture of political journalists and some fresher faced technology specialists. After the political journalists went through their normal paces, I stood next to Stephen, and stood and stood as he answered at length technical question after technical question from the specialists. I could not suppress a smile when he sought to correct one: 'No, it's the upload, not the download.' He knew what he was talking about and he loved his portfolio.

Enough Australians shared his vision of faster speeds, economic benefits and health and education services provided at home for our broadband policy to be a material factor in winning the closest of election campaigns. Our broadband policy was pivotal in securing the support of

Tony Windsor and Rob Oakeshott for the government. Tony popularised the saying, 'Do it once, do it right, do it with fibre.' Both Tony and Rob understood the vision of an Australia without a digital divide. Where the richest and the poorest, the inner-city urbanite and those who live in the country have access to the same powerful technology at the same wholesale price. The spectre that the richer suburbs would see broadband roll out because commercial companies would know there would be enough customers to pay while the rest of Australia got marooned with the old technology would be eradicated forever.

In cost and scope, constructing the NBN is a bigger infrastructure project than the celebrated Snowy Mountains Hydro-Electric Scheme. But creating it was not just about fibre spooling out along streets. The law needed to be changed too.

The central problem for telecommunications in Australia was poor design of the market. Historically telecommunications provision had been done by a government monopoly. The Keating Government introduced limited competition into the market and the Howard Government overwhelmingly privatised the government-owned service provider Telstra. But there was insufficient thinking applied to what would happen in a marketplace where Telstra competed for customers while owning the copper network that brought telecommunications to homes and businesses around the country. Businesses trying to win customers off Telstra were in the perverse position of only being able to service those customers if Telstra did a deal to let them use the infrastructure or they could meet the cost of rolling out new infrastructure. Telstra could brutally wield the power that comes with such a dominant market position.

Labor's original vision for the roll-out of high-speed broadband was that private-sector players would be involved, specifically Telstra. But when the tender was put out to the marketplace, Telstra refrained from getting meaningfully involved.

The only alternative was for a wholly owned government company to get on and do the job. How to do this was comprehensively worked through at SPBC meetings. To ensure the market-design problem in telecommunications would be fixed, the Rudd Government announced plans to structurally separate Telstra into two different businesses: one that owned and operated the network and one that competed for customers. That way, all providers had fair access to the network and Telstra's retail arm did not get an unfair advantage from its ownership of the network.

Telstra has a loud voice in the Australian political scene and it was inevitable the government's approach would cause turbulence in its share price. So many Australians own Telstra shares, this was a political problem for the government. After a fraught period, in June 2010 the Rudd Government won through and reached a heads of agreement with Telstra on structural separation and the movement of its customers from the copper network to broadband. My challenge in late 2010 was to get laws through parliament to provide the legal underpinning of the Telstra deal and to create NBN Co, the government-owned entity that would create and run the broadband network. This was the first big test of the minority government. The Opposition had already decided its political strategy would be oppose, oppose, oppose. Its aim was to tear the government down. It was prepared to do anything to make parliament appear unworkable.

Actually securing passage in the House of Representatives was not the most difficult task. Unlike the Opposition, Tony, Rob and Bob as well as the Greens understood broadband. It was a different story in the Senate, where both Senators Fielding and Xenophon would wield the pivotal votes until 1 July 2011, when the senators elected at the 2010 election would take their seats and Labor with the Greens would have a majority. This curious sequence of our House of Representatives and Senate turnover is a product of our Constitution. It produces odd periods where senators like Steve Fielding, who know they have not been re-elected, continue to sit, while newly elected ones wait impatiently to start their term.

As was my practice throughout the minority government, in the House and the Senate, ministers conducted the front-line negotiations and kept me informed on their progress. Matters were referred to me if negotiations became stuck. I had a horror of negotiations becoming confused, where I was saying something, a minister was saying something else and potentially Anthony Albanese as Leader of Government Business in the House was putting forward a third position. Tight coordination across government of negotiating strategies was vital.

Fortunately for me, the government and the NBN, Senator Steve Fielding from Family First agreed to support the bills. An engineer by training, he had worked in telecommunications and understood what the government was trying to do.

Now we had to persuade South Australian independent Senator Nick Xenophon. Adelaide is a pretty small place so unsurprisingly I knew him from university. He is slightly older than me and was leaving the student political scene as I was coming into it. At that stage a Liberal Party person, Nick was infamously excluded from university for a period as punishment for stuffing a ballot box full of voting papers he had somehow procured. In adulthood, he had spurned the Liberal Party and become a crusader against poker machines. A wily operator and masterful manipulator of the media, Nick has created a public persona as the honest guy in politics. His electoral success seems assured for the long term.

The Opposition's fig leaf for opposing our laws was that the NBN had not been subject to a cost–benefit analysis. Already the NBN proposal had been subjected to much scrutiny, including an independent implementation study led by McKinsey & Company and KPMG and a detailed business case study of some 400 pages. We rejected their negativity and demand. However, Nick jumped on this line of argument and wanted special assurances about the viability of the NBN and particularly the release of the business case. Stephen Conroy had been resisting the release during parliamentary time, citing the document's complexity, the need for further briefings, and commercial sensitivities. He also believed it would be used by the Opposition to make mischief.

Nick had been negotiating with Labor's Penny Wong, another South Australian. But he also came to see me and I remember it vividly. It was a Tuesday, and the previous day I had arrived back in Canberra in time for Question Time after a physically punishing trip to a summit in Lisbon on Afghanistan. The round trip was completed in less than four days. On my return I felt fine but second-day jet lag kicked in and I felt weak as a kitten but still had to front up for the Labor caucus meeting and Question Time. Albo had moved heaven and earth to negotiate a pair for me on the Tuesday evening so I could go home earlier than the adjourning of the House at 10.30 pm. In a minority parliament, with every vote crucial, I had to vote too unless the Opposition agreed that they would have someone sit out of the vote as my pair.

But I did not get to enjoy the benefits of the pair Albo's efforts had procured because late into the night I was trying to persuade Nick to vote for the bills. We talked for some time and I put before him a proposal about the timing and manner of release of more information about the NBN, including the business case. He was enjoying this moment of power and wanted to keep going over details but his eyes told me he was going to accept the deal. In an unconventional negotiating approach I announced, 'Nick, I don't care how you vote, I'm going home. You can settle details with Penny if you want to vote with us.' I called it a night and called it right. He voted for the bills and our first big legislative victory was sealed. The way was cleared for the roll-out of the NBN.

A complex project of the size and scale of the NBN will inevitably encounter obstacles. So it proved. Getting contractors around the country to do the work took longer than first thought. Signing up workers who had the requisite skills was slower too. A new deal had to be reached with Telstra to get access to its pits and ducts so NBN fibre could be rolled out through this pre-existing infrastructure rather than building completely new infrastructure. The roll-out schedule slipped behind.

Some of Telstra's old ducts and pits were built in the era when asbestos was the construction material of choice. In May 2013, an order was issued for work to stop on some sections because of asbestos safety breaches, including potential exposure of workers and asbestos being left next to a primary school. A cautious approach was taken, as it should have been, given the horrible hazard asbestos poses for human health. Further delays in the NBN roll-out followed. The Opposition upped its campaign against the NBN and the media scrutiny was intense.[1]

In the roll-out of any huge construction project, there are always lessons to be learnt. This is true for government and for the private sector. But having been a participant in and student of the public debate about the NBN, it seems to me there are also some lessons to be learnt about the way major new government projects are discussed and analysed.

321

Delays in roll-out and issues with asbestos should of course be reported fairly and accurately. But modern media reporting, whether it is Australia's NBN or President Obama's health reforms and website, often fails to draw a distinction between a flawed vision and problems of implementation. Outside of government, it is accepted wisdom that projects, big and small, encounter problems. The home renovator who finds asbestos or the big developer with cost overruns. Neither means the renovation or the development were inherently bad ideas.

For established government programs, implementation issues are not reported as making the whole program a bad idea. In reporting a story about Medicare fraud by doctors, reporters do not conclude the whole of Medicare is a bad policy. But for new, visionary projects, any problems with implementation are used to besmirch the merits of the whole project. Obamacare was reported as fatally flawed because of website problems. The NBN was condemned by some because, really quite unsurprisingly, Australia's biggest ever public construction project has faced hurdles. At the same time as we read this type of reporting, we hear calls from the media and the community for more vision in politics.

There is a need for balance here between vision and accountability. One hundred per cent risk-averse politicians will never deliver our country the leadership it needs.

The NBN vision is absolutely right for our nation. Australia should not be left behind networked nations like the Republic of Korea. Country Australians should not be left behind their city cousins. Poorer Australians should not be left in a digital wasteland while richer Australians are fibred up for digital plenty. Rather our future needs to include a smarter, more dynamic, more productive economy. New ways of delivering services. New ways of connecting with each other and the best the world has to offer.

INFRASTRUCTURE

Anthony Albanese is another big personality. Brought up by his mother in public housing, he has been a fired-up warrior for Labor all of his political life. I have known him since he was 19, when he floated on the fringes of student politics basically in order to denounce it as a pastime for wankers. He wanted instead to focus on the real politics of fighting the heated factional wars in young Labor. He moved rapidly into adult politics, finding a mentor in Tom Uren. He was delighted when I insisted as prime minister on the government funding Tom Uren's proposal that all surviving prisoners of war be given pensions at the higher rate received by people with total and permanent incapacity. Some things the nation should just do.

Throughout my leadership, Albo supported Kevin. Indeed from the moment I arrived at the federal parliament, Albo and I were pitched against each other. Back then the national Left faction of the ALP, of which I was a member, was divided among the 'metalworkers' Left and the 'Ferguson' Left. Albo was the leading exponent of the factional group that enjoyed the support of the metalworkers' union. I had come to parliament with the support of Martin Ferguson.

While I thought factional politics was a nonsense, no longer about beliefs but all about patronage and power, as a newcomer I toed the Ferguson line. Albo and I were on different sides of Labor's various leadership contests. He supported Kim Beazley when I backed Simon Crean, Mark Latham and Kevin.

Anthony personally stuck with Kevin in 2010 and seemed to feel he had been locked out of the process and decision-making prior to me taking the leadership. Like the journalists of the press gallery, he struggled to accept that in that leadership contest there had been nothing to see until there was everything to see.

Despite that somewhat fraught history, Albo and I worked seamlessly together to keep the minority government going. He and exceptionally able staff in his office deserve loads of the credit for the government going full term.

Albo's critics believe that across many months, he played the role of double agent, running information gathered from his position at the centre of government to Kevin and his supporters in order to assist their cause. Albo would retort that he did his job exceptionally well, never abused my trust, but that I always knew that, should a leadership vote be held, he would vote for Kevin.

I suspect that the truth is a more complex, human story than either snapshot. For Albo, the years of my prime ministership would have been punctuated by difficult judgement calls, given the fundamental conflict between his role and his loyalties. Constant in-the-moment decisions about what to say, what not to say, to Kevin or to me. If I knew of every one of those decisions, I suspect I would be unhappy about a number of them. If Kevin knew of every one of those decisions, I suspect he would be unhappy about some of them too.

At one point, I did ask Albo to play peacemaker. Coming into the 2013 budget session, after the absurd and damaging non-challenge in March, I asked him to ascertain Kevin's state of mind, to see if it were possible to strike some arrangement whereby Kevin was an actual campaign asset for Labor.

In my perfect world, that would have meant Kevin agreeing not to stand at the next election but for him to campaign for Labor on the basis that he would serve a re-elected Labor government in a foreign affairs role, most probably as Australia's Ambassador to the United Nations. In Kevin's world, I imagined he might demand a return to cabinet or simply repudiate the approach. Regardless, all I ever heard back from Albo was a vague report that Kevin was unsure about everything. As it turned out, Kevin was not really quite that unsure about what he wanted to do next.

For Albo, this was the time when the conflict position he was in was too much for him to manage with fairness to both sides. But I will always be thankful that in the three years we collaborated so closely, Albo worked himself so hard to keep the government running and to keep building the nation. It took a toll on his physical health but he did not stop. He is a man incredibly suited to pursuing his love of 'fighting Tories'.

Together we were able to deliver on Albo's other great love: addressing our nation's increasingly desperate infrastructure needs, which were hampering productivity. Between 2007 and 2013, Labor built or upgraded 7500 kilometres of road; built or rebuilt 4000 kilometres of rail; and committed more to public transport infrastructure than all previous governments combined. Our big spend on infrastructure included some $60 million in national building programs for roads, rail and public transport infrastructure. In my last budget as prime minister, we also announced new funding to attract partnerships with the private sector, allocating funds to Melbourne's Metro, Brisbane's Cross River Rail and Perth's Light Rail. For major infrastructure projects, our government's commitments, combined with private-sector efforts, meant that by May 2013, total investment in infrastructure was 42 per cent higher in real terms than in the last year of the Howard Government, a proud achievement.

SKILLS

Broadband and bridges, road and rail. All keys to a productive future. But the most important key of all is expanding the capacity of the brains of our nation. It is the right economic choice and the right moral choice. As a Gillard girl, I certainly understood that.

My Uncle Terry, Dad's youngest brother, is the black sheep of the family. Not because he has failed to make a success of his life; in fact, he is the highest educational achiever of the seven children in the family. Because the older children were all working by the time he came along, the family was in a better position and he was able to stay at school. Dad spoke admiringly of how hard Terry hit the books. The effort was rewarded and Terry became a sought-after chemical engineer. He also became a Conservative and, consequently, the black sheep.

If you are Welsh, you are very likely to vote for British Labour. Or you might vote for the Welsh Nationalist Party because you believe in a free Wales, free from the 'yoke of English oppression'. If you were looking for a conservative alternative, you might consider going to the Liberal Democrats. Even in the most recent election in the United Kingdom, a bad election for Labour, with Gordon Brown losing power, the Tories ended up with only eight out of the 40 House of Commons seats in Wales. Sometimes Wales returns no Tory members to Westminster. The Tories have never held more than a quarter of the seats. So coming from a Welsh mining village, from the Gillard family, to end up a Conservative local councillor is quite something.

The issue that caused my uncle to renounce British Labour and embrace the other side of politics was selective schooling. He objected to Labour's policy of comprehensive schooling. He thought the only thing that gave bright working-class kids – the kind of child he had been – a chance, was selective education. Wales today is not home to any selective government schools.

While I do not agree with Terry's political decision, I understand his passion for education to be the change agent in children's lives. Like my uncle, I do not believe in holding the brightest children back in the name of providing education for all. Like my uncle, I value education for working-class and disadvantaged children as a passport to a better life. Like him, I know that journey, though mine was a far easier one.

While it is not explicitly articulated in the public debate, it is apparent that many people believe education should simply replicate the current social order. Children from the families that are most advantaged in our society should get the university degrees and enter the professions. Children from the most disadvantaged families should drift out of school to whatever low-level work is around. All the people in the middle should look at vocational education. This belief finds expression in the catchcry that broadening access to universities must mean standards are being lowered. The prejudice disguised behind this statement is that children from poorer families will not keep up and will drag standards down.

The Howard Government neglected university education, other than the political interventions of tying funding to employees being put on Work Choices contracts and lashing out at student unions.

For public consumption, it peddled the myth that universities were out-of-touch ivory towers.

Like their approach to schooling, the Howard Government took a divide-and-rule approach to post-school education. If you argued the case for universities, then somehow you were out of touch and did not understand the value of apprenticeships and trade qualifications. Liberal Party members spruiked the benefits of trade qualifications, while aspiring for a university education for their own children.

Labor in Opposition sometimes fell into the political trap that had been knowingly created and sounded like the only thing worth aspiring to was a university education.

Just as inter-sector competition in schooling obscures all the real issues, so does this inter-sector competition between university education and vocational education and training (VET).

The reality is that our economy in the future will need more people with university qualifications, more tradespeople and more people completing vocational courses. The imagined border between universities and Technical and Further Education Colleges (TAFEs) will become more and more riddled with holes. Our nation is already home to universities that pride themselves on their VET qualifications and TAFEs that graduate degree students. Many individuals have moved between the sectors. The VET student who decides to go to university and gets credit for the work they have already completed. The university student who, with a degree under their belt, sharpens a particular skill-set by then obtaining a VET qualification.

On becoming deputy prime minister, my message to the nation was to 'find your own path' to further education, skills and employment. Find what is right for you as an individual. It might mean becoming an engineer. Or a carpenter. Or an academic teaching philosophy. Or a hospitality worker. Choose your path, understanding the job prospects and mindful that your working life will bring change and retraining.

That message was about more than words; it was about ensuring our education system offered people opportunities and choices.

During the Howard era, our universities were starved of funds by the government. In response, many had gone heavily into providing education to full-fee-paying international students, meaning any shock to this market was going to push some universities to their financial limits. Another income-earner for universities was selling full-fee-paying places to Australian students, a policy introduced by the Howard Government. It is ironic that conservatives will tut-tut about more children from poorer backgrounds getting into university and reducing standards but are unconcerned about people buying their way in.

While funding was tight, red tape was everywhere. The federal government had set a cap on university places and then controlled the allocation of numbers. As Education Minister, I would literally have to sign off on a brief so that 20 or 30 places could be moved from a university that wanted to surrender them to a university that wanted to take them up.

Student unions had been strangled so they could no longer provide basic services.

At the same time, VET was struggling to adapt to the growing demand and new requirements of a 21st-century economy. The TAFE system was different in each state and territory; there was no coherent national picture. While there were many high-quality public TAFE institutions, their place in a more comprehensive system for skills and training was dramatically unclear. The service providers that emerged in parallel in the private sector were highly variable in their quality, too often opportunistic and short-term, with a sharp focus on revenue rather than long-term learning outcomes and quality.

Despite pockets of excellence, the whole VET sector, public and private, lacked the kind of comprehensive long-term partnership with employers that is vital to supporting a workforce that constantly updates its skills and contributes to the productivity and competitiveness of firms in all sectors. In 2008, I set out to reshape the learning opportunities available post-school, by reforming the lot.

To reform school funding, I relied on David Gonski's review panel to guide the way. For higher education, both universities and TAFE, I relied on a panel led by well-respected Australian educator Denise Bradley. It included an expert in vocational education, Peter Noonan, and a businessperson, Helen Nugent. Bill Scales served on both this panel and the Gonski one.

My guide in the selection of the panellists was my higher education adviser, Mark Burford. I had known Mark since the days of student politics. He too had been president of the AUS, serving before me and my immediate predecessor, Paul Carrick. Mark is also a South Australian and we had shared a student household before I made the journey to Melbourne to join the AUS. He is nicknamed Burf and when the government first invested money to assist universities to refurbish their capital, in his honour we called it the Better Universities Renewal Fund.

The Bradley Review team did an excellent job and deftly navigated the difficult currents of university vice-chancellor politics. Rather like

Labor's cabinet, university vice-chancellors tend to be big personalities. I have joked with them that higher education reform would be easier if *The Australian* stopped publishing the Higher Education Supplement on Wednesdays and there was less reason for public preening.

The review was presented to the government on 12 December 2008 and made public five days later. The government's main response to it was in the 2009 budget, where we made the fundamental policy changes and the funding commitment that created a new path for higher education in Australia.

In the lead-up to the budget, I had to fight for the funding needed to respond to the Bradley Review and start the journey of change in universities. Preparing a budget is never easy. At the end of all the long hours in the cabinet room, when the final revenue numbers and costings come in, the budget has to be locked down. The remaining final decisions must be made. By this stage, everything has been boiled down to a limited number of options.

My option for responding to the Bradley Review was on the table with a range of others. As the weeks wore on towards the budget deadline, its fate was uncertain. The package had been to the ERC a number of times and was either punted to later meetings or only vaguely discussed. Meanwhile the departments of Treasury and Finance were developing proposals to substantially cut my plans. Finance favoured new spending of less than $1 billion but the Bradley Review package would need to be at least $2 billion in size to credibly deal with reform. I was not at all confident of Lindsay Tanner's support as Finance Minister.

At the last ERC meeting before the budget, there was still no agreement. Thankfully Wayne suggested a ministers-only discussion in Kevin's office. I went in and fought hard, emerging with a $2.2 billion funding envelope.

I am particularly proud of our decision to unchain Australian universities, to enable them to define their own mission and educate more students. Specifically from academic year 2010 to academic year 2012, the changes moved universities in stages from a capped system of student places to an uncapped system. Universities could offer more places if they wanted to and government funding was made available per student enrolled. As a result of the new system, while students continue to compete for places, universities increasingly have to compete for students. In an uncapped system, a better run, better quality university can attract students who might be considering other universities. There is a reason to reach out to under-serviced country areas. The allocation of places by government no longer forces students into a pattern of enrolment.

The red-tape-bound system I inherited took a one-size-fits-all approach. But our universities are not all the same and the best future for them is not a uniform one. Some, like the Australian National University and Sydney and Melbourne universities, are institutions able to trade on and build their prestige. Their futures will not be in mass expansion in student places but teaching limited numbers of students well while engaging in comprehensive, world-leading research programs.

Other universities aspire to be big educators of undergraduates, including those reaching people who have traditionally been denied access to university education. The University of Western Sydney is a stand-out example.

James Cook University will continue to revel in being a university of and for its geographic place. With its main campus in Townsville, it leads the world in some tropical-research fields, including tropical medicine.

The University of Adelaide is a fine example of innovation, choosing to find the future by rediscovering the best of the past, with small-number personal-contact teaching models.

While our reforms allowed universities to grow to their own desired size, they also introduced a new focus on quality. In Australia, prior to our reforms, no one ever questioned whether an institution was worthy of the university label. We developed a new approach in which quality would be measured and more transparent. No one would be able to rest on their laurels and live off past successes. Everyone would be held to account in the same way we were holding schools to account for quality.

Regardless of each university's characteristics, I also insisted that the new system offer special rewards for getting students from poorer families into higher education. Money spoke, and more and more students of low SES were enrolled. More and more of them thrived once studying. A result destined to gladden my heart and my Uncle Terry's.

Labor addressed the two problems that had contributed most strain to university budgets. First, the Howard Government's indexation of university funding at incredibly low rates, so every year funding fell further behind the real running costs. Second, inadequate funding of research: cash-strapped universities had been dragging money away from teaching in order to maintain the search for new knowledge.

As a former student unionist, enabling student unions to once again provide services was a given.

In responding to the Bradley Review, we set two targets for the nation. We wanted at least 40 per cent of 25- to 34-year-olds to have attained a qualification at bachelor level or above by 2025. And by 2020, people from low-SES backgrounds would make up 20 per cent of university enrolments at undergraduate level.

As well as changing what happened within universities and thereby changing the shape of people's lives with that 2009 budget, from as early as 2008 the government was also changing the physical shape of universities and TAFEs through a dedicated capital-funding stream called the $3.7 billion Education Investment Fund (EIF). This was on top of BURF and the $1 billion distributed to universities and TAFEs for capital as part of economic stimulus.

I had the honour of opening some of these lighthouse projects. One was the Engineering Pavilion at Curtin University, applauded by the mining industry. From this state-of-the-art facility, many engineers of the future will graduate. I loved spending time with overexcited schoolchildren at the new Science and Technology Precinct at the Queensland University of Technology. In this multimedia wired-up showcase, a passion for learning will be sparked in visiting high school kids. Every Australian's life will be touched by what happens in new facilities like the Centre for Obesity, Diabetes and Cardiovascular Disease at the University of Sydney, the Peter Doherty Institute for Immunity and Infection at the University of Melbourne or The SMART Infrastructure Facility at the University of Wollongong. When the best brains are put with the right equipment and resources, the magic that is the birth of new knowledge can happen.

Over the budgets after 2009, challenges emerged not because our reform agenda was going badly, but because it was going too spectacularly well. Progress towards our goal of more Australians having at least an undergraduate qualification was happening more quickly than expected. In formulating each budget or each mid-term budget update, the departments of Treasury and Finance working with us would produce their best prediction of student-enrolment numbers. But the reality of how many students were going to university exceeded their predictions time and time again. By the end of my prime ministership, as a result of our changes full-time student numbers were at around 550,000 compared to around 400,000 over the final decade of the old Howard Government capped system. On these numbers, the 40 per cent undergraduate degree target would be easily reached.

At the same time, universities were responding to our incentives to enrol poorer, disadvantaged students enthusiastically and creatively. By 2013, these undergraduate enrolments had shot up to over 66,000 students, meaning the nation was likely to achieve our aspiration for 20 per cent of enrolments to be people who faced tough circumstances. Enrolments by Indigenous students also grew strongly.

With these statistics came costs, and internal pressure to reverse our commitment to the demand-driven model and revert to a more traditional, predictable capped approach to funding. The concerns expressed by Wayne, Penny and the other ERC ministers were legitimate. Theirs was the unenviable task of doing the detailed work to get the budget on a path to surplus as revenue continued to drop, while the government worked to better fund schools and create the NDIS.

As the architect of the reforms, had I not been prime minister, the reform agenda would probably have been trimmed considerably. Instead, to protect the reforms, for a limited time it made sense to slow the growth of university funding in order to help finance our initiatives for schools. A limited-efficiency dividend of two per cent in 2014 and 1.25 per cent in 2015 was imposed, yielding a saving averaging around $300 million per annum. There were also adjustments to student-income support arrangements and a cap placed on the tax deduction that can be claimed for self-education expenses.

These measures gave rise to vocal and violent opposition from universities and a hysterical and immature reaction from the National Tertiary Education Union. It was politically stupid to divert at this time to catcalling about a modest change rather than focusing on the risks a change of government in the 2013 election could mean for all of the new model and the huge new investments in universities.

In 2008 we had also begun the process of reforming the VET sector to better support the creation of the skills that individuals and our economy needed.

The key commitment on skills we brought from Opposition into government was the creation of 175,000 new training places, or Productivity Places. Once again, some of the risks with designing programs in Opposition, without the best access to advice, eventuated. The plan was underfunded and the training that could be offered for each place was of a lower level than really required to address our skills problem. Although I implemented this commitment in the best way possible, the profound work of reform lay in a different direction.

As with the approach taken to universities, I considered it prudent to define our goals. Following intensive work with state public servants in 2008, in a unique process that Kevin designed for working with state governments, targets were set and then endorsed by COAG: to halve the number of working-aged Australians without a Certificate III level qualification by 2020 and to double the number of working-aged Australians with higher level vocational qualifications, meaning a diploma or advanced diploma.

Australia's training system has many world-leading aspects. Our national system of defining skill levels is envied internationally. From lower level skills, which gain a Certificate I, to the highest vocational qualification of an advanced diploma, everything is capable of measurement and accreditation. But the task in today's world – and to get ready for tomorrow's – is to drive our people up the skills curve to higher and higher levels. The emphasis on Certificate III, which is an apprenticeship-level qualification, arose because this is the first level shown to make a genuine difference on employability and consequently offers solid prospects for getting and keeping work throughout life. The goal of higher level qualifications reflects the changing needs of the economy.

Agreement on reform directions was still needed after 2008. Consequently the skills agreement we entered into with state and territory governments – to start on 1 January 2009 – took a steady-as-it-goes approach.

To broaden the circle of advice so our nation could better understand its skills needs, a new body, Skills Australia – later to become the Australian Workforce and Productivity Agency – was set up. This entity transformed the debate on skills, largely because of the exemplary work of its chair, Phil Bullock, previously the Chief Executive Officer of IBM in Australia. Phil's appointment demonstrated the benefits of getting a smart outsider to the system to be a change agent within it.

In this journey of change, the government found willing partners in employers and trade unions. Images of warfare between employers and unions are more caricature than reality. There is no better example of collaboration than the work unions and employers did together on skills.

Ultimately the reform directions set for skills mirrored many of the aspects of change in universities. Growing the system while ensuring quality. A healthy dose of transparency. A focus on the disadvantaged.

Aspects of how university education is funded were borrowed and applied to upper level and more expensive qualifications via the spread of income-contingent loans. Previously if you wanted to study for a degree at a university, you could study now and pay later, whereas if you wanted to study an expensive high-level vocational qualification, you had to pay up front.

But beyond reflecting the reforms of universities, our changes specifically introduced an entitlement approach to vocational education, the sense and reality that as an Australian you are entitled to have your nation create a place for you to at least obtain a Certificate III qualification, given its ability to change lives.

It took us until 2012, but we were able to work through and agree this fresh approach with states and territories. By investing a new $1.75 billion, we secured agreement to an entitlement model, a new quality approach with a new regulator, a new transparency approach with the My Skills website and income-contingent loans for higher level qualification. Like universities, our changes specifically focused on better access for people from disadvantaged backgrounds.

Training and skills are certainly not just about what government does. Every day in workplaces around the country, people are being trained and developing new skills. Employers in real time know what skills their business and their industry will need next so we set up a National Workforce Development Fund, money to partner with employers on creating new opportunities for working people.

Encouraging progress was made. A report in October 2013 from the body that studies the effectiveness of COAG work showed that the number of working-age Australians who were gaining Certificate III qualifications had jumped by almost six per cent. Unfortunately the same report showed we are not on track to halve the number of Australians who have no qualifications.

Like all major reforms, you learn as you go. While the reform directions were right, greater effort is needed so more of our citizens have the chance of a life with the benefits of a life-changing qualification.

I was 15 turning 16 in 1977 when Fleetwood Mac topped the charts with a musical message that tomorrow will be better than today. It is a song of optimism I always liked. For individuals and nations, however, there is nothing preordained about tomorrow being better than today.

I do believe that for our nation our best days are yet to come. Not because we are born lucky but because we are smart enough to make our own luck and bend the inexorable changes of our age so that they serve our purpose. In government, that was my aim. Bending change, being ready for the future, so that tomorrow would be better than before. Stronger and fairer. Labor aimed high for the nation. So we always should.

18

Double trouble:
tax and the budget

'Can I say now a few thankyous, particularly to my colleague
Wayne Swan . . . He has been fantastic.'

MY FINAL SPEECH AS PRIME MINISTER

'Wayne Swan last night joined Paul Keating as the only
Australians to be named by banking magazine *Euromoney*
as the world's finance minister of the year. The Treasurer received the accolade for his judgment in steering the
Australian economy through the global financial crisis and
guiding a strong recovery.'

THE AUSTRALIAN, 21 SEPTEMBER 2011

I OFTEN WONDER WHAT DIFFERENCE IT WOULD HAVE MADE to my life
and to the Australian Labor Party if Wayne Swan and I had become
firm friends at the start of my time in parliament rather than only during
the days of government. Like every question you ever ask yourself about
changing the past, the only honest answer is, who knows?

Befriending Wayne never really seemed an option. He was a senior
figure of the national Right; I was in the national Left. He had a reputation as a machine man: he had cut his teeth in the ALP's head office
in Queensland and was schooled in the darker arts of campaigning.
I viewed myself as a policy person. To top matters off, at one of the first
Parliament House functions I attended, I overheard him insulting a
Victorian Labor identity who was a dear friend of mine.

Over the days of Opposition, Wayne, just like Albo, had always been on the other team during Labor leadership ballots. Indeed together with Stephen Smith he formed Kim's praetorian guard, while I supported Simon, Mark and then Kevin. But I should have looked more closely, thought more deeply.

If you sit next to Wayne, as I have done so often, above all you notice his hands. Tanned. Expressive. Around one wrist he wears a plaited leather band, something more associated with a hippie than a deputy prime minister. A surfer, a survivor in politics and of prostate cancer, a man moved by sentiment and substance, he proved to be deeper, more complex and much, much warmer than I ever expected.

What happened was not some sort of self-awakening but the need for support. We huddled together to survive the maelstrom that was Kevin's leadership.

As our political problems mounted in the second half of 2009, Wayne and I started doing something we had never really done before: spending time together. Just the two of us, talking about government and politics. Every discussion was about what we could do to get Kevin to settle down and deal with the issues we faced. None was about leadership.

But the bond that formed stood us in good stead during our time together as prime minister and deputy prime minister. Wayne's loyalty to me was exemplary. He never faltered in providing me political and personal support. He bore the weight of being Treasurer well, even though it was a burden made heavier because every prediction the departments of Treasury and Finance ever made about government revenue turned out to be wrong.

Politicians do not make up revenue figures, indeed budget figures generally. Rather, public servants in Treasury and Finance make careful predictions about how the economy will grow, what inflation will be, what unemployment will be and many other economic parameters that impact the bottom line. Every government decision – the ones that generate revenue, the ones that cause expenditure – is the subject of a public service costing.

Our 2010 election strategy had been to promise a return to surplus in 2013 as the best way of countering the Opposition's allegations of Labor waste and debt. In making this promise, I was relying on

Treasury and Finance figures. For complex reasons, reality did not live up to what the public service professionals had anticipated.

It is easy to be Treasurer when revenue is sloshing in and every public service prediction turns out to be too low. These were the happy circumstances that faced Liberal Treasurer Peter Costello in his last few years doing that job. In those days, Treasury was home to a specific team of officials whose job was to work out how to spend quickly at the end of each financial year because revenue was always rolling in well above predictions and the government did not want the surplus to look too amazingly high.

In contrast, post-GFC while Wayne was Treasurer, actual revenue was always less than predicted. Treasury and Finance had batteries of officials generating lists of painful cutbacks followed by even uglier options. Our late budget decisions were never about where to spend more; they were always about where to cut harder.

With these pressures aplenty and the need to fight Kevin's insurgency campaign, Wayne and I drew ever closer, sustaining each other through friendship and a penchant for gallows humour.

But more importantly, we never lost our shared sense of Labor's purpose. Together we made lasting changes to our nation.

BUSINESS–TAX TROUBLE

After defeating Kim Beazley, Kevin kept Wayne as Treasurer as a unity gesture. After every leadership change, in every political party, there is a need to reunite the team. By word and deed, to show that there will be no ongoing retribution against those who voted against the new leader. That they too have a stake in the future.

But despite Kevin's political embrace of Wayne, a mutual wariness characterised their engagements. Wayne was smart enough to know that Kevin was softly indicating to me, and I suspect also to Lindsay Tanner, that come a Labor victory, I could be Treasurer if I wanted to. A piece published in the now-defunct political magazine *The Bulletin*, just before the 2007 election, speculated about me becoming Treasurer. With a media frenzy brewing, Kevin publicly verified that Wayne would be Treasurer. That suited me fine; I had my eye on Workplace

Relations, Employment and Education, portfolios that matched my passions.

The relationship between Wayne and Kevin was at its best during the GFC and the structuring of our emergency response. With things so desperate, nothing else mattered above pulling the economy through.

There was neither the time nor space for personality issues. But after the crisis abated, difficulties re-emerged.

With only a quick heads-up to Wayne, Kevin announced on *The 7.30 Report* a root-and-branch review of the tax system. John Howard did something similar, announcing the Goods and Services Tax (GST) without much warning to his side. His subsequent election win was so narrow he spent part of election night telling his family to prepare for the worst electoral news. The Howard tale contains a salutary lesson: the politics of tax is always diabolical.

Wayne received the Henry Tax Review report just before Christmas in 2009. He found himself landed with a ticking time bomb, not because of any ill will from panel members, but because the politics of tax is so thorny. Kevin took almost immediately to criticising Wayne for his management of the review process – for not ensuring the report was more politically palatable. How this was supposed to be achieved when Kevin had called for a thorough review and the panel was both strong-minded and independent was never made clear.

When Wayne released the report on 2 May 2010, he released an accompanying list indicating the recommendations he rejected outright and the ones that were under further consideration. One recommendation left on the table was that 'the current resource charging arrangements should be replaced with a uniform rent-based tax legislated for and administered by the Australian government'.[1] The recommended tax rate was 40 per cent.

To have a profits-based tax for resources was a proposal of both economic merit and diabolical politics.

Economics has many complexities but some principles stand out clearly. One of those is that a diversified economy with many sources of strength will always be more resilient than an economy overly reliant on one sector, one customer. It is the economic equivalent of the old saying, 'Do not put all your eggs in one basket.' Another is that taxes that rise and fall with profitability are more efficient than flat taxes.

Historically for onshore metal and mineral resources, tax arrangements are flat and inefficient. State governments levy volume-based royalties, which remain the same per tonne whether prices for coal or iron ore are sky high and huge profits are being made or prices are bargain-basement low and the tax is discouraging new investment.

In contrast, for the offshore petroleum industry, Australia has a successful profit-based tax. In 1987, the Hawke Government introduced the Petroleum Resource Rent Tax (PRRT). Craig Emerson, as an adviser to the Resources and Energy Minister Peter Walsh and then to Bob himself, had designed it. It has served the nation well ever since, collecting more than $20 billion in revenue and is widely accepted by the industry.

In responding to the Henry Tax Review, it seemed intellectually self-evident to embrace the goals of economic diversification and more efficient, profit-based taxation on resources. But a profit-based tax arrangement for onshore resources was always going to be more complex to achieve legally and politically than the PRRT. Offshore exploration and development is under the sole jurisdiction of the federal government. Onshore has traditionally been the province of the states.

While the federal government had power to legislate, such action would be resented and resisted because of state-based parochialism: the sense that the minerals do not belong to the nation, they belong to West Australians or Queenslanders. The political ground was particularly fertile for an our-state-comes-first campaign because of ongoing disputation about the distribution of the GST, which is levied nationally but distributed to states. Indeed pivotal to John Howard's GST reform agenda was giving states the benefit of a tax that would increase in value over time and assist in meeting the growing demands on their budgets. Many Australians, if they stopped to think about it at all, would assume their state gets the GST that is paid on goods and services sold in that state. This is not true and never has been.

GST is distributed to states on a complex formula that has launched a thousand arguments. At the base of the formula is a population share but it is adjusted to reflect the levels of advantage or disadvantage in a state or territory. It reflects the principle that no matter where an Australian lives, they are entitled to a similar standard of service delivery in vital areas like health, education and policing. Consequently places like Tasmania, South Australia and the Northern Territory receive more than their population share would dictate because these are economically weaker and more disadvantaged parts of the nation. But the formula also means, depending on the ups and downs of the economy in different parts of the nation, that money can be redistributed among the stronger states of Queensland, New South Wales, Victoria and Western Australia. Politically this can be rough.

There are other federal government money flows to states and territories apart from the GST. Once again controversially, if the federal government agrees to give a particular state a lump of money, say for a major infrastructure project, that is taken into account and leads to a recalculation of the GST distribution.

As the resources boom took hold and these principles were applied, Western Australia was receiving less and less of a share of GST monies. A persistent state government campaign fed the perception that Western Australia was being ripped off. It fell squarely into the long-standing WA political tradition of blaming everything on Canberra. It slipped their minds that for most of the years of federation, taxation monies had flown from the prosperous eastern states to subsidise an undeveloped West. Regardless the stage was set for a state-based campaign against a profit-based tax in mining.

Second, the mining companies were always going to resist fiercely. The mining industry boasted some of the smartest players in the business elite. Women like Catherine Tanna of BG Group and Ann Pickard of Shell had my admiration as they worked to change the face of the industry. Don Voelte of Woodside, Roy Krzywosinski of Chevron, the gentle Sam Walsh of Rio Tinto and the ferociously intelligent Marius Kloppers of BHP-Billiton would sit down and seek to work issues through. But no one likes paying more tax.

Then there was the 'boys' own' underside. I certainly encountered it at the 2010 annual Minerals Council dinner in Parliament House, while representing Prime Minister Kevin Rudd. The disputation over the Rudd Government's proposed Resources Super Profits Tax (RSPT) was raging, so it was always going to be like entering a lion's den. As the guest of honour, I was one of two women seated at the head table. Keeping me company was my chief of staff, Amanda Lampe. Dinners in the Great Hall at Parliament House follow a predictable pattern: three courses come and go and you are offered white or red wine. At this dinner, at a hand signal from the Chief Executive Officer of the Minerals Council, Mitch Hooke, a tray of what looked to be rum and Coke was brought to the table. A glass was dutifully put in front of every man except Marius Kloppers, who declined it. Neither Amanda nor I was offered one.

The two of us exchanged a look and afterwards uproarious laughter about this rudeness. For the record, like Marius I would have said no. Even now, I do not know which was worse, the embedded sexist assumptions or the sheer stupidity of this kind of treatment directed at the second most senior political leader in the country.

At the first Minerals Council dinner I attended as prime minister, the rudeness continued, with the then Chair of the Minerals Council, Peter Johnstone, introducing me for my keynote speech as 'the current prime minister of Australia'.

At its best the minerals industry produces innovative leaders and at its worst produces macho throwbacks and people so reflexively anti-Labor they have ceased to think.

My instinct on the RSPT was that our political agenda was already so complex and so crowded that we did not need another fight. But I understood the economic need to better tax mining and to use the proceeds of that tax to provide relief to other parts of the economy. Wayne's proposal was not just to design better functioning arrangements for mineral resources taxation, it was about dealing with the effects of the minerals boom on Australia's wider economy. For the patchwork economy, the revenue would provide tax relief to companies in other sectors by cutting the company tax rate, provide additional relief to small and medium-sized businesses, grow our pool of national savings through more superannuation and invest in infrastructure in those fast-growing parts of the nation where the boom had come to town.

Two questions stared us in the face: should we embark on this fight and how could we win it? Agonisingly meeting after meeting of the SPBC passed without those questions being squarely addressed. I distinctly recall a meeting where Kevin spent hours on a modest proposal from Chris Bowen to increase Sydney's attractiveness as a financial services centre. We never got around to the RSPT. As the meeting concluded, Jim Chalmers, Wayne's talented chief of staff, sank his head into his hands in frustration. Rarely have I seen such a dejected-looking figure at a meeting table. I patted his shoulder.

Determined to prevent leaks, Kevin did not want ministers outside the SPBC consulted. Had there been a better internal process, the insights of others on the structure of the tax, the management of the stakeholders and the public communications strategy would have been invaluable. I am imagining Craig Emerson on the technical issues, Martin Ferguson on industry insights, Gary Gray and Stephen Smith on the West Australian politics.

As the days ticked down until the budget and the political space for manoeuvre contracted, more public servants were consulted and Wayne was instructed to test people's views outside government.

At some point a non-decision always becomes a decision. Kevin procrastinated his way into the RSPT.

Looking back on my one-to-one discussions with Kevin in this period, I suspect he was hoping I would start arguing forcefully against the RSPT because of the political risks. Then he would be able to go to Wayne and say that, thanks to my carrying on, the government could not proceed. Unbeknown to Kevin, by then Wayne and I had forged too close a partnership for those games to work. My political gut was churning but I knew the decision was right for the nation and I thought Wayne had been put too far out on a limb for the government not to back him in.

When the tax was announced, all hell broke loose. It became immediately apparent that the model of the tax recommended by the Henry Tax Review was flawed. The model meant in a downturn, the government would write cheques for major mining companies as losses were sustained. Industry executives just did not believe this would ever actually happen.

It also became apparent that Premier Barnett in Western Australia was going to say something different publicly to what he had apparently said to Wayne and Kevin privately.

But worse than all of that, the industry decided to go straight into a pitched public battle. Whether it was the macho culture, the anti-Labor bias, too much money at their disposal, a belief that in an age of 24/7 media the only way to create change was through television advertising, I do not know, but their campaign hit the government hard. As we reeled, there was no systematic decision-making about what to do next. Indeed in the final days of Kevin's leadership, Wayne was highly anxious because Kevin was working, without consultation and effectively aided by only one staff member in his office, on a plan to settle an agreed mining tax with Andrew Forrest of Fortescue Metals. Andrew, more commonly known as Twiggy, is a self-made billionaire, who to his credit has now devoted himself to philanthropic work, particularly a campaign to end the scourge of modern-day slavery. But at this stage, along with Gina Rinehart, he was the most public face of the campaign against the tax.

Fortescue's business model is different from that of others in the mining industry. Wayne was worried Kevin would give too much away to get a political settlement and that something specifically designed for Fortescue would be a dreadful fit for the rest of the resources sector. Wayne also feared the design of the tax would be badly distorted in order for Kevin to claim the headline rate had not changed from 40 per cent. Kevin had made it clear he thought a reduction in the headline rate would be too humiliating for him.

After Kevin's leadership came to an end, there was some speculation about the role the RSPT played in his demise, even suggestions of a cloak-and-dagger plan by the resources industry to overthrow him, including false claims about leadership polling being shown to me by mining representatives. The truth is much simpler. Once again, to his colleagues, Kevin appeared to not be coping when political pressure rose.

After I became prime minister, I needed to fix the mining tax and allow the government to move on to other issues. Within a very short time, a principles-based agreement on the new MRRT was reached. Everyone committed to a process to work through all the details. This commitment was delivered upon by us creating an Implementation Working Group headed by Don Argus.

The headline rate of the MRRT was 30 per cent but with a 25 per cent extraction factor reduction. In reality it was therefore a 22.5 per cent tax that applied to mining profits reduced by various allowable deductions. Wayne and I were not above playing the politics of being able to claim a higher headline rate.

The agreement ended a war but created ongoing problems, some of our own making. To negotiate quickly, the representatives of the mining industry I invited into the process were the big players: BHP-Billiton, Rio Tinto and Xstrata. The other players who were potentially liable for the tax complained bitterly that they had been locked out of the process and that the agreement did not take their needs into account. My choice of a small, selective process was the right one, even though it meant opposition to the tax continued in some quarters. An agreement would never have been struck quickly had there been large numbers of participants; minute by minute, everything would have leaked. In any event, I had invited into the room the taxpayers who would pay around 90 per cent of the tax. Others had the ability to participate in the Argus process.

Nevertheless we made an error in not more aggressively seeking to dispel the image that the long-lasting dispute between the government and the 'smaller' miners was one with plucky little guys: the MRRT as announced only applied to coal and iron ore businesses earning $50 million or more in profit a year. Such companies are not small. The tax as legislated increased this amount to $75 million or more a year, as the result of an agreement with Andrew Wilkie. Consequently the tax applied to just over 300 businesses.

A bigger error, which was undoubtedly our fault, was the ambiguity in the hastily drafted agreement concerning the complex intersection between the MRRT and state-based royalties. The upshot was that states could increase royalties and, as a federal government, we would need to compensate mining companies for the amount of the increase. For states it was a political free pass to more revenue. For us, it was an unpredictable cost.

Then, in a sickening repeat of other budget problems, the revenue projections for the tax were never realised and the gap was big. The tax as agreed was supposed to raise $3.7 billion in 2012–13, $4 billion in 2013–14 and $3.4 billion in 2014–15. By the 2013–14 budget, these projections were down to $200 million, $700 million and $1 billion respectively.

Revenue going down when prices and profitability went down was exactly the way the tax was supposed to work, and in mid-2012 prices did tumble more sharply than expected.

In addition, the real value of the tax was going to be realised when the mining boom reached its third and final stage. As I explained in speeches as prime minister in 2011 and 2012, a mining boom is best understood in three phases: investment, when new money flows into new projects; construction, when all those new projects are built; and the decades-long production phase, when projects have come online and ore is being pulled out of the ground.

But while the dividends from the MRRT were going to peak in the phase three future and be paid for generations to come, the immediate failure to raise the revenue predicted was both concerning and politically embarrassing. Wayne was especially disturbed by how this dramatically dropping revenue related to the assurances he had been given by mining companies during the negotiation process about revenue generation.

Lastly and most bizarrely of all, the Liberal Party, allegedly the pro-business party in Australian politics, voted against the tax cuts for other businesses. The legislation to impose the MRRT got through the parliament with the support of the Greens and the independents. But the Greens would not support the associated measure to cut the company tax rate. This was the economic diversification side of the MRRT, the use of more tax being paid by the strongest sector of the economy to finance tax relief to businesses in other sectors. After railing against the evils of our minority government having an agreement with the Greens, the Coalition under Tony Abbott got into bed with the Greens to destroy a tax cut for every company paying tax. The Coalition was also critical of better tax arrangements for small businesses when they buy new assets; however, we succeeded in getting this through the minority parliament despite their opposition.

Approaching the 2012 budget, in the face of this negativity from the Opposition, I advocated internally for repackaging the company tax cut into new benefits for Australian families raising children, including single-parent families and those who were students or unemployed. I knew this would be opposed by Australian business but, while there had been hard campaigning by business against a tax on mining, there was no hard campaigning against the Opposition's antics, which were denying businesses the tax cuts we wanted to deliver. Had the business community, their advocates and conservative media commentators gone in hard against the Opposition for blocking a tax reduction for business, their resistance would have crumbled. The legislation would have gone through and tax relief would have followed.

Faced with the political oddity of the Coalition wanting business to pay more tax than a Labor government and a business community responding softly, I worked with Wayne, Penny and Jenny to design and deliver the Sharing the Benefits of the Boom package for the benefit of millions of Australians.

The concept of the MRRT was right for the economy. The community embrace of the concept actually strengthened over the life of the government I led. But the politics was always sour.

Sour initially because at the point the RSPT was announced, the huge stresses on the rest of the economy flowing from the high dollar had not yet manifested. The evidence of the need for better taxing super-profits and using it to assist with diversity in the economy was not yet before people's eyes.

Sour because the case for change was never able to be punched through.

Sour because the implementation, particularly the problems with revenue and the treatment of state-based royalties, played into the spin that the government was not working competently.

Sour because it fed perceptions the government was engaged in a war on business. From my perspective, there was never any such war.

I treated the businesspeople I met with courtesy and respect. They found my office door open and the person inside willing to listen.

Under the government I led, businesses were able to make their way as economic growth continued, employment continued to grow and productivity grew. As our budget was triple-A rated and inflation was right where the RBA wanted it. As we invested in broadband and skills.

While I was prime minister, a businessperson looking anxiously at the economic statistics would have seen in a month like August 2012 that Australia had its gross domestic product growing at 4.3 per cent, inflation at 1.3 per cent, unemployment at 5.1 per cent and mortgage interest rates were below seven per cent. Finding another time in Australian history when Australia's Gross Domestic Product (GDP) growth was four per cent or more, inflation was 1.5 per cent or less, the unemployment rate was 5.5 per cent or less and the standard variable mortgage interest rates were seven per cent or less, means going back to the March quarter 1964. The world had lost JFK a few months earlier, the Beatles were soon to visit Australia, the Melbourne Football Club would go on to win the VFL Grand Final, Donald Horne published *The Lucky Country* and Robert Menzies was prime minister. It was a long time ago.

At the time that I secured support for Labor as a minority government, I agreed to Rob Oakeshott's proposal that a tax summit be held. I never viewed this as a big decision-making exercise, given the government already had a full agenda, including on tax. But properly gestating new ideas to make our tax system more efficient and fairer takes a long time so I thought it could play a useful role in creating a broader, richer public discussion. It also fitted with the kind of approach I chose to use regularly of reaching out to business to participate in discussions that embraced as well trade unions and civil society representatives. Time after time as I took that approach, I was struck by the dichotomy of meeting savvy, engaged businesspeople with coherent and thoughtful views on public policy issues, and the blundering around of the Business Council of Australia (BCA) as the peak big-business lobby group.

Throughout my political career, I came to know and respect intelligent people at the BCA like Melinda Cilento, who served as their Chief

Economist and went on to be a co-chair of Reconciliation Australia, as well as serving on company boards. It seems to me after she left in 2010, the BCA lost its intellectual rigour.

During the lead-up to the tax summit, which was held on 4 and 5 October 2011 and brought together 180 business representatives, unions, civil society and policy experts, the BCA started campaigning for an increase in the GST in order to fund a reduction of the company tax rate. As floated, it was ill-thought through both politically and technically. What was being airily suggested was that individuals and families could take a two or three or five per cent cost-of-living hit so companies that pay CEOs millions and make billions of dollars of profit could pay less tax. The kindest comment about the proposal was that it was naive. A blunter comment would be that refusing to actively support a company tax cut funded by the booming mining industry and instead asking for one to be paid for by a GST rate hike imposed on everyday Australians, including the disadvantaged, is driven by the wrong values.

In the Great Hall of Parliament, the summit started with early discussion of this proposal. The BCA advocates got smashed in the debate. One of the figures leading the case against was the ACTU Secretary Geoff Lawrence. While steely in his resolve, Geoff is quietly spoken and his demeanour is gentle. No one would describe him as a firebrand. Yet in this debate he came out the clear winner.

Despite such differences, I retained hopes of working with the business community on tax policy, as did Wayne. Our goal was to challenge the business community to share responsibility for finding realistic ways to advance and fund further reductions in business taxation. Consequently out of the Tax Forum we formed the Business Tax Working Group, with the aim of looking 'at reforms that can increase productivity and deliver tax relief to struggling businesses in our patchwork economy and develop a set of savings options within business tax, such as broadening the base and addressing loopholes or unnecessary concessions'.[2] In our continued push for genuine outcomes, we enlisted the expertise of leading lights from the business community. Despite Chris Jordan, the Chair of the Board of Taxation, doing a wonderful job in chairing this group, its work fell short of expectations.

Partly hopes were dashed when the negativity of the Opposition and the business community's failure to campaign meant I had to take a one per cent decrease in the company tax rate funded by the MRRT off the table.

Another factor was that the business community faltered when pushed to the hard task of identifying savings within the complex world of business taxation in order to fund a company tax cut. It proved easier to point to another taxpayer, like individual Australians, to bear the cost rather than at each other.

We did enact some of the recommendations that helped repair holes in the company tax base but more does need to be done on taxation. The fundamental reform task will need a better budget environment, processes that help garner bipartisan support and a more mature approach from organisations like the BCA.

TAXING TROUBLE WITH REVENUE

As these debates about taxation were being pursued, the budget revenue environment was degenerating.

In financial year 2010–11, the government emerged from the GFC with a net debt of $85 billion. The vast majority of it arose because revenue collapsed during the GFC, rather than being the result of expenditure on economic stimulus. The impact of policy expenditure decisions between May 2008 and May 2009, which covers the period when economic stimulus was announced, was around $97 billion. During the same period, the hit to the budget bottom line from GFC-induced changes to the economy, including the punch-down of tax revenue, was around $173 billion.

As economic activity in Australia went sharply backwards for one quarter and then slowly forwards, companies were making less and paying less tax. In addition, during the days of the GFC many individuals worked shorter hours. Pleasingly employers did not react to the economic shock by going for redundancies. A lot kept their people on but reduced overtime or otherwise reduced hours, meaning less personal income tax was paid.

Property prices stopped rising, and in some parts of the country went backwards, while share prices fell, affecting capital gains tax.

But the revenue effects persisted and persisted in a way not predicted by Treasury. To be fair to Treasury, it was hard to predict something that had never happened before.

The approach of the government to this revenue shock was a conventional economic one. First, our policy was to let the budget's automatic stabilisers do their work: complicated economist language for saying that you do not intervene with the natural tendency of the budget to do the right thing to support the economy. Put crudely, as the economy strengthened and revenue returned, it would be saved not spent, to help get the budget to surplus. Our second approach was to drive towards surplus by making prudent savings. Third, we committed to offsetting major new expenditure with new savings, which is the approach we took for our longer-term new expenditures on school funding and disability.

But collapsing revenue kept hurting the budget bottom line and the government's economic credibility. The high dollar not only hurt many businesses, it hurt the budget.

Explaining this to the Australian community was not easy because understanding it required an appreciation of the difference between measuring the growth in our GDP, basically what our economy generates in nominal terms, and measuring it in real terms. By the time I was talking on television about the very unusual fact that growth in Australia's nominal GDP was below growth in Australia's real GDP, I could almost hear Australians watching and joking with one another, 'Whatever!' or 'Shoot me now' and changing stations. Nevertheless this weird and wonderful economic fact was a cause of many budget miseries.

My best shorthand description of this problem was that real GDP growth is the growth in the volume of the economy. The actual activity in the economy includes real things like the quantity of infrastructure we build, how many tonnes of coal are dug up, how much beef is produced. Nominal GDP growth counts this growth in volume and it also counts growth of the prices of all these things. Our real GDP was growing solidly but prices were growing at a slower rate than expected. As a result, nominal GDP growth for the financial year 2012–13, the year we had planned to come to surplus, was significantly slower than was forecast and nominal GDP growth for future years was revised down.

The difference between the first prediction and the revised one was big. At budget time 2012, nominal GDP growth was forecast by the professionals at Treasury at five per cent. It ended up being two per cent. This reflected prices falling for coal and iron ore faster than expected. Normally an economist would expect that would cause our dollar to fall. But it did not. Our economic strength compared to the rest of the world gave the Australian dollar a desirable status and people wanted it. Even though our interest rates were low, the rates of many countries post the GFC plummeted to nearly zero, so returns in Australia still looked good.

This rule-breaking combination of low prices for exports and a strong dollar, meaning low prices for imports, fed the divergence between the growth in real GDP and nominal GDP.

As I said to the nation in April 2013 as I tried to explain this effect:

This has never happened for such a long period in the whole half a century and more of the National Accounts.

. . . But for the budget bottom line, it's a very meaningful fact – because, naturally enough, companies don't pay tax on volume, they pay tax on value, which is driven by price.

The Pharaoh might have kept one-fifth part of the grain from the field but the Tax Commissioner collects in dollars and cents.

So even if the economy is growing as much as expected, when prices are growing much less than expected, tax grows much less too.[3]

This fall in revenue of around $12 billion dollars in financial year 2012–13 and its feed into continuing deficits until 2016–17 shattered Labor's claims to budget management. It fed the Opposition's preposterous claims of a so-called budget emergency, that there was a spending problem rather than a revenue one. The facts told a different story to their puffed up rhetoric. Under the Howard Government, in which Tony Abbott and Joe Hockey served as ministers, by 2004 the share of the economy taken in tax reached a peak of 24.2 per cent, making that government the highest taxing in Australia's history. By the start of 2013, this was down to around 21 per cent. Put another way, if my government had taken the same share of the economy in tax, then the 2012–13 budget would have had a large budget surplus as its bottom line.

It suited the Opposition to pretend that the deficit arose from too much spending rather than a revenue shock. Of course, each year there is a natural growth in spending. More people become aged pensioners, health care costs go up, family payments are indexed. This natural growth is not evidence of a budget crisis. It is not appropriate to put dire language around the costs of the new programs we introduced either. These were being financed by hard fought-for savings. Indeed from the 2011 budget through to the 2013 budget, including the decisions taken in mid-year updates, our government announced savings worth $126 billion. New spending decisions during the same period amounted to $67 billion.

A particular spotlight was understandably put on our big new expenditures on schools and to create a national scheme for people with disabilities. Less understandable were the frequent misstatements or assumptions that these policies were unfunded. For the next decade, new expenditure on schools was supported by making savings in areas like family payments and by moderating the rate of growth of university funding. Business tax loopholes were closed and the new revenue went to schools. Also for the next decade, new expenditure on disability care was financed by reducing the tax breaks for superannuation benefiting those on higher income, cuts to the private health insurance rebate and a new levy on tax payers. All these difficult decisions meant that to meet the projected costs of these two vital new reforms, there would be no need to go looking for more budget dollars until around 2023.

A big government was not the problem either. As smarter commentators pointed out consistently, government spending in Australia was low compared to other countries. In fact, the second lowest of advanced Western economies. Only the Swiss and the Koreans were spending less. The actual track record of the government on budget management is a world away from the then Opposition's critique or what has sunk into popular memory.

The Rudd Government did the right thing stimulating the economy during the absolute crisis of the GFC. The government I led did the right thing in finding hard savings to drive the government back towards surplus and to fund nation-changing programs for our children and people with disabilities. In fact, in 2012–13 the government presided over the biggest real reduction in spending in Australia's history, edging out of first place the Hawke Government's savings in 1988–89. For each of the budget years that I was prime minister every single dollar spent on newly created programs was matched with a dollar saved. Growth in budget spending was contained below two per cent.

There are some who will no doubt argue that we should have gone for more savings earlier. However no one can cogently argue that additional savings made in 2011 could have been the difference between deficit and surplus in 2013. The revenue write-downs were simply too large.

In addition, it should be a source of wonder that we got as many hard savings through a hung parliament as we did. We were advantaged in 2013 by the Opposition quietly supporting our savings in the parliament, even while criticising them in the media. By then Joe Hockey and others were no doubt thinking they were likely to get elected and they might as well have Labor wear the odium of as many hard savings as possible. That soft support is not an approach the Opposition would have taken in its fever to force a new election in 2011.

Beyond doubt, I erred in making the budget surplus for a nominated year the symbol of everything about our economic management. But a fair reading of the government's record of budget management shows us taking a competent and prudent approach. That is a tribute in particular to Wayne Swan, Penny Wong and, in the last period of government, David Bradbury. The savings we made reflected Labor values of shielding those in the most need. We took good decisions to means-test the private health insurance rebate, to pause the growth of family payments at higher income levels, to abolish the baby bonus, to wind back tax breaks that encouraged people to artificially pump up the kilometres driven on company-supplied cars.

It is a budget record and a set of savings choices which I am sure will come to be viewed more positively as time passes.

19

Our atmosphere

'Alan, you emailed me and asked how things are going . . .

In . . . January . . . I talked about me (and consequently the government) having lost definition in the public mind and needing to rebuild that definition. I think the realistic status report is that this is still a huge problem for me and us. I don't think the public have settled on a fixed adverse view of me – I think we still have a window to get an integrated image of me through but the window is diminishing. I have stuck pretty doggedly to the narrative I laid out for you in January. But this has been overlaid with the carbon tax, she lied debate, in a way which is damaging . . .

'I think this probably would have been painful but capable of being handled and lived through if it wasn't exacerbated by the Kevin problem. Kevin's malice knows no bounds. . . . I am absolutely convinced he was the leak in the campaign and every day he calibrates his media to tear at me on character questions. The last week has been particularly diabolical with him deliberately setting up a narrative on carbon pricing that he is honest, I am not; he believes, I don't really. And then my failure to slap him down generates "she is weak" as the image . . .

'On everything else my analysis is as follows:

'There are things that will get a bit worse before they get better but we can make them get better.'

EXTRACTS OF AN EMAIL SENT TO ALAN MILBURN AND JOHN FAULKNER, MONDAY 11 APRIL 2011 8:18 PM

A s THE PRESSURE GREW and the distorted views of Kevin and his cardinals appeared in the newspapers almost every day, a public commentary developed about whether or not I truly understood the depths of the political problems the government and I faced. Common claims were that I was 'in denial' or 'delusional'. But I always understood the problems and was striving to find the solutions.

Clearing time for strategic thinking about your own political position is incredibly hard when you are required to front for all the demands on a prime minister's time. Quarantining real time, when you are fresh not exhausted, and finding meaningful chunks of time, not 15 minutes here or there, was exceptionally challenging. I struggled with this and so did my colleagues. Labor people have such a work ethic for doing the things that matter for the nation that setting aside time for political strategising almost feels like an indulgence.

In order to reflect and think, I needed solitude. Despite having been the most public of figures, I am not someone who feeds off the energy of the crowd. I refresh by spending time in my private space, either alone or with Tim.

It is a regret that I did not reach out much more often, to seek out other perspectives. With my packed work diary, doing more reaching out would have come at the cost of the limited remaining time available to me to rest and recover. I should have been more disciplined about carving the extra time out.

But in that meagre time, I would write for myself and then share with a limited circle of others my views on our strategic and tactical problems. Alan Milburn was included in this group, as was John Faulkner. Wayne Swan was also constantly in this dialogue with me.

In my email to Alan and John of 11 April 2011, I predicted that things would get worse before they got better. Periodically my office briefed to journalists the same message, using the expression that I was 'playing the long game'.

My email expanded on that as follows:

First – the carbon debate. I think we can get there with a package with the Greens. The debate will continue to go fairly badly for us until we can get the household assistance figures out there but then I think we can turn it around a bit. And the real turnaround will come when we are post implementation after 1 July 2012. While Abbott is profiting now, I think he has three problems long-term for his scare campaign. First, he is hysterical every day. There is no sense of building up in his campaign. Once you've claimed the world's going to end a hundred times in a row, then it's hard to know what you do next, and that's where his campaign is. Second, he has made a huge error committing to repeal the legislation if it gets through and take the assistance back. And third the arms and legs of his 'people's revolt' are actually climate-change deniers and fringe political types. This has already cost him once with the sexist signs at the rally and I think it will again.

Second – the Gillard Government. As I indicated in January, one of my problems is I am fixing the wreckage of the Rudd Government rather than clearly governing as the Gillard Government. I am increasingly satisfied we will tell a new story about participation and opportunity from the budget which will be Gillard Government rather than Rudd leftovers. It will be tough – a tough sell, a tough process through caucus – but it will be about my values so that's good.

I was right in my belief that 1 July 2012, the start of carbon pricing, would be a pivot point. This was always my belief, from the 17 days in which I negotiated to form the minority government through all the dark days of the carbon pricing debate. When people can judge for themselves through their own direct experience, they will. The hysteria of the fear campaign was going to crash into the hurdle of truth.

And it did feel good to be stamping out my own agenda of work and opportunity, and the email reflects that. The days of government gave me the space, notwithstanding the leftover political problems, to inject my own policy passions, my own sense of purpose, into the heart of the government.

Ever the optimist in a pretty bleak political world, I included some better news for Alan and John in the email:

In other good news (yes, it's a difficult world where you classify as good news the things that will get worse before they get better but could get better):

My office is being pulled into better shape but there is more to do, particularly on the media/messaging side. The reality is we need a communications strategy that gets us around the print media and Canberra press gallery. We aren't there yet but I think we now have the capacity to get there . . .

We have a new good National Secretary – George Wright – non-factional and competent. My pick.

The NSW Government is gone and at the moment they seem too tired in NSW Labor to truly kill each other so it is remarkably quiet.

The Indies are going okay and I am not predicting any short-term problems with their support.

I shared blunt words like these with Alan and John because I respected them and their advice – each for different reasons. In Australian politics, there are many people with whom you can talk tactics, the day-to-day management of political problems. Plenty of people who, in a sophisticated way, can work out how to run over the top of bad news stories with a big, shiny new government announcement, so the journalists run after what is glittering and only give the briefest of attention to what is not. There are also a number of people who can read polling and craft a message that will hit home. Thankfully within the Labor Party there are not only tacticians and developers of the message but great policy thinkers who can develop change agendas that matter. But among this rich jumble of skills and attributes and luminaries, far, far less common are people who can lift their eyes from the day-to-day tactical decisions, media management, message development, policy design, and look at the far horizon and think strategically. Who can truly answer the question for the whole of a government, of a political party, of a political movement: where do we want to be in a year, two years, three years' time. What should we be doing now to define in the minds of the voters the values we stand for and the ground on which the next election will be fought and the one after that?

Alan is one of those strategic thinkers. Plus he had the wonderful benefit of being able to bring fresh eyes from the outside. If you are in the centre of politics, in the middle of the whirlwind, then it can be much harder to get a sense of the entire picture. From the United Kingdom, Alan could contribute the unique perspective that only comes with distance.

John I relied on for other reasons. He can think strategically but what was so important about his contribution was his rich, deep experience in the heart of Australian politics, including the many times he has been on the leader's plane, at the core of strategy during election campaigns. I leant on John until it became evident he was backing away from me. Initially I thought that was only because of his slow retreat from public life which would end with his resignation from the Senate.

But there was more to it than that. John was always deeply troubled by the leadership change in 2010, even though he was frequently and directly exposed to Kevin's flaws. He told me a story about how he once came to Canberra because, as prime minister, Kevin had asked to meet with him. The meeting was moved from the first agreed time and John stayed overnight in Canberra. It was rescheduled a few more times, requiring further lengthening of his stay. He ended up missing a family birthday party. He accepted that this consequence would not have been obvious to Kevin, who would have asked staff to keep reorganising his diary without understanding the implications for other people. But it was a good example of the ripple effect of constant churn at the centre and John's frustration with it.

But John worried about what changing the Labor leader in government meant for the ALP's ongoing culture as he agonised over more general party reform issues in the context of the review I asked him, Steve Bracks and Bob Carr to do after the 2010 election campaign. He became increasingly frustrated by the pace of Labor's progress on internal reform.

Later I came to see that, in part, this sense of estrangement between us reflected the fact that he would support Kevin if a ballot was held. John is a very proper person. He was never a combatant on Kevin's behalf, but I felt he ceased to provide any active bolstering of my leadership. To this day I do not really know why.

Back in April 2011, I was keen for his and Alan's views. I concluded my email by saying:

> So, any Milburn or Faulkner insights welcome.
> And when you have finished offering your views on the future of social democracy, the future of Australian Labor and the future of the Gillard Government, feel free to get engaged with the biggest problem – what should I wear to the Royal Wedding!

Fortunately neither of them took up my invitation to play fashion consultant.

When I wrote this email, I could not have imagined that even after both the end of my prime ministership and a change of government, it would still be fair to say about the politics of carbon pricing that things will get worse before they get better. It is inevitable that our nation will have an ETS that puts a price on carbon because it is the best way to make our contribution to tackling climate change, a challenge the world has known about for decades now.

As long ago as the 1960s and 1970s, the first scientific conclusions were being drawn about climate change. The Hawke Labor Government started to respond to this science over two decades ago and the Keating Labor Government signed on to the United Nations Framework Convention on Climate Change (UNFCCC), the first global treaty responding to the science, at the 1992 Earth Summit in Rio de Janeiro, in Brazil. In December 1993, the 50th country ratified the UNFCCC, bringing it into force.

Initially the election of the Howard Government did not bring a dramatically different approach to that pursued by Hawke and Keating. Australia continued to participate in the international process. In 1997, ahead of the UNFCCC scheduled meeting, the Howard Government created the Australian Greenhouse Office and adopted a two per cent national target for renewable energy generation.

The UNFCCC meeting produced the Kyoto Protocol, an international climate-change agreement which was the fruit of two years of negotiations. It included specific targets for reductions in greenhouse gas emissions from 2008 to 2012. It also included a commitment to create a global carbon market, so countries that were going to reduce their emissions by more than their target could sell their right to emissions to a country that was going to exceed its target.

Australia was seen as having secured a large and controversial concession in the drafting of the protocol, enabling land use and forestry changes to be counted in emissions reduction. The Howard Government's Environment Minister, Senator Robert Hill, was enthusiastic about the agreement, including the global emissions trading, heralding it as a win for the environment and Australia.

Australia signed the protocol in April 1998, along with 20 other countries. In May 2002, Japan and the European Union ratified the Kyoto Protocol, bringing the number of ratifications to 55, the trigger point needed to bring it into force. Despite international pleas for Australia to follow suit, John Howard announced that Australia, despite being a signatory, would not ratify it.

While the Kyoto Protocol was coming to life, climate change was not an issue featuring strongly in Australia's domestic political debate. It did not burst into popular consciousness until Al Gore's Academy Award-winning movie, *An Inconvenient Truth*, brought the science fully and understandably to public attention.

In Australia, the message of the movie was absorbed by our citizens as they watched drought ravage our land. The two, the climate change message and the drought, combined in people's minds into one big scary thought about what the future could look like. The popular campaigning for action to address climate change was suddenly everywhere. Television shows like *Sunrise* were running campaigns to 'cool the globe'.

The call for our nation to ratify the Kyoto Protocol became louder and louder. Suddenly the politics swung from there being no real downside to the Howard Government's failure to ratify the Kyoto Protocol to it becoming the emblem of why John Howard was really yesterday's man.

The Howard Government sought to mitigate this political effect. Prime Minister Howard devoted a major speech in the lead-up to Australia Day in election year 2007 to the announcement of a

$10 billion Murray Darling Basin Plan. Despite the eye-catching figure, this did little to address community concern nor the political problem. Polling conducted by the prestigious Lowy Institute found that Australians saw climate change as:

> the most important threat Australians face from the outside world and tackling it ranks equal first as Australia's most important foreign policy goal (together with protecting Australian jobs). Of all goals, international and domestic, tackling climate change is as important to Australians as improving standards in education, and more so than improving the delivery of health care, ensuring economic growth and fighting international terrorism.[1]

At this stage of the political contest, John Howard would often argue that ratifying an international agreement does not magically fix things. On that he was right, but the public debate stayed on Kyoto rather than moving to a more detailed consideration of the mechanism for reducing the amount of carbon and other greenhouse gases our nation generated.

However, the Howard Government was working on the right mechanism and by May 2007 was in possession of a report on emissions trading generated by a task force chaired by the Secretary of the Department of the Prime Minister and Cabinet, Dr Peter Shergold. By the time of the 2007 election, both the Liberal Party and the Labor Party were promising to create ETSs.

Both had plans to cap the amount of carbon dioxide our economy could generate measured in tonnes. Despite Tony Abbott's later foolish claim that carbon dioxide is an odourless, weightless gas, it does have a weight and can be measured. In our domestic political debate, carbon dioxide was referred to publicly as carbon pollution or just carbon.

With a cap set, permits to release a tonne of carbon dioxide would then be issued. A market for the buying and selling of permits would spring into existence and the market would set the price. A business that generated carbon would need to buy permits in order to release it. The price of the permits would be set by demand and supply: how many businesses were chasing the limited supply fixed by the cap.

Depending on the price, it might prove cheaper for a business to change its processes so it generated less carbon and had less need to purchase permits.

Free permits would initially be issued to businesses that needed help because their competitors were overseas and not subject to a carbon-pricing scheme.

Over time, the government could tighten the cap so the economy generated less carbon. Less permits would be available, the price would go up and the substitution of alternative, more carbon-efficient technologies would be accelerated.

In short, both parties stood for a market-based approach to carbon pricing, the introduction in Australia of a version of the kind of ETSs which were operating in more than 30 countries around the world.

From the public debate, it was virtually impossible to see this point of unanimity.

For Kevin, with his pitch to be the fresh and safe alternative prime minister, the politics of climate change broke well. He, unlike Howard, seemed to understand the future. He, unlike Howard, would ratify Kyoto.

When Kevin and Penny Wong attended the 13th UNFCCC meeting in Bali, just after Australia ratified Kyoto, they were received as heroes. What we did not know then was that the easy days of the politics of climate change would soon be coming to an end. What we did not know then, and what would have seemed so unlikely at that point, was that a policy that had bipartisan support, an ETS, would become the flashpoint partisan issue of the decade.

In 2008, Lowy Institute polling found Australians still anxious about climate-related issues. But the same polling showed that 'There was a decline in the perceived urgency of the need to address global warming and the willingness to pay to tackle the problem, but a solid majority remains in favour of immediate action even if this involves significant costs.'[2]

This pointed to the shape of things to come. The politics did not go bad immediately, but it did go bad.

Bad around the question of cost. While the focus on Kyoto had suited Labor, it meant Australians had not grappled with the idea that there are costs involved in reducing carbon. Meanwhile electricity bills were skyrocketing for other reasons, considerably worsening perceptions of cost.

Bad around the international negotiations, when the UNFCCC meeting in Copenhagen, which had been built up to mean so much, looked so shambolic.

Bad around the issue of urgency. When the drought broke, relieved Australians no longer felt the same pressure for action.

Bad as the context changed. The attention of Australians, which had been so much on climate change, dramatically moved to economic survival as the GFC hit.

And most unbelievably of all, bad around the acceptance of the science.

Australians, almost without exception, react rationally and well to scientific findings. Scientists tell us that sun exposure causes cancer. People wear hats, use sunscreen. Even those who like to be tanned do not justify their tanning by saying the science is wrong, they merely accept the risk and play mental games with themselves to bolster their self-belief that cancer will never hit them.

But with climate science, sensible conduct has been overwhelmed by the campaigning of eccentrics, not only here but in other nations.

The campaigners against the science cannot even advance a credible theory about why scientists around the world and in overwhelming numbers would conspire together to try and persuade the world of something that is not true. Would they do that to increase research funding? Can anyone really argue that? It is not as if the science of climate change has somehow persuaded the governments of the world to create scientific nirvana where research funding is always in plentiful supply. Scientists continue to struggle for funding the way they always have.

How would they do that? Can anyone truly believe that from the 1960s to now, a vast conspiracy has been knowingly faking data and falsifying results, and remained undetected for decades?

It is so ridiculous. Yet if you pick up the newspapers, listen to the radio, watch television, you find the views of non-scientists and conspiracy theorists arguing loudly against climate change. Disturbingly this has impacted on public opinion.

Being able to analyse how the politics turned bad can be done in hindsight. At the time, with no line of sight to many of the the obstacles ahead, the Rudd Government got on with the work necessary to create an ETS. I was not directly involved in that work as deputy prime minister. Already I had a back-breaking workload. I was automatically on every cabinet committee, but as we formed government, I took the decision that trying to be involved directly in climate-change policy, as well as everything else, would not be physically possible. Occasionally, when specifically asked to do so, I attended the cabinet sub-committee dealing with climate change.

In April 2007, Labor premiers and chief ministers provided political support to federal Labor's climate-change agenda by commissioning Professor Ross Garnaut, a leading Australian economist, to review the impact of climate change on the Australian economy and to point to a future direction. Ross is both opinionated and persuasive. He has a fine mind and brought his intellect to bear on this task. His final report, published in September 2008, recommended that Australia adopt an ETS covering as many sectors of the economy as possible, to achieve emissions reduction at the lowest overall cost. It concluded that a 'transitional' period of fixed prices for carbon emissions permits was acceptable.

By 15 December 2008, official government policy was for a CPRS, with a medium-term target range to reduce emissions by at least five and up to 15 per cent below 2000 levels by 2020 and a long-term goal of 60 per cent below 2000 levels by 2050.

On the surface, the process seemed methodical. Behind closed doors, however, problems were emerging. Kevin had decided to run over the top of the cabinet sub-committee dealing with climate change. Decision-making on carbon pricing had been centralised to what was referred to internally as 'the troika', meaning Kevin, Penny and Wayne. I did not seek to be included. In creating the troika, Kevin had cut his prime suspect for being a leaker of cabinet discussions, Martin Ferguson, out of the loop. As Resources and Energy Minister, Martin was necessarily on the cabinet sub-committee but Kevin wanted Martin excluded from decision-making. This distrust of Martin also explains why he was kept at arm's length during the early discussions of the RSPT: grandly ironic considering Martin's subsequent support for Kevin to return as Labor leader.

While the existence of the troika guarded against leaks, it had other negative consequences, like narrowing the number of minds engaged in decision-making about policy and political strategy. It also allowed Kevin to easily dictate on a whim the location and timing of meetings and how papers were prepared for them, including whether or not the public service would be involved. Slowly but surely, Penny and Wayne found it harder to get adequate time with Kevin to work through such a complex policy, the politics of which was continually worsening.

In May 2009, the government announced that the implementation of the scheme would be delayed by one year from a start date of 1 July 2010 to 1 July 2011, a move designed to appease business concerns about the scheme starting while the economy was still shaky because of the GFC.

At the same time, in a move designed to appease environmentalists who would be disappointed by the delayed start, the government committed to a new upper-end target for Australia in the year 2020. Instead of our sights being limited to at most a 15 per cent cut in emissions, if an ambitious global deal was reached to stabilise carbon pollution in the atmosphere at 450 parts per million, then Australia would play its part with a 25 per cent reduction.

This announcement was linked to international negotiations and the prospect of a global agreement at Copenhagen in December 2009. It also reflected the increased confidence brought to the international process by the election of President Obama.

Looking back, both decisions seem breathtakingly naive. The delay in the start date had the potent political side-effect that the 2010 election campaign could become about whether or not carbon pricing should go ahead.

Hyper-partisanship in the USA and global realpolitik meant optimism about the ability of the Obama administration to price carbon and the likelihood of a comprehensive deal at Copenhagen were misplaced.

But as the months of 2009 passed by, Kevin anticipated big things at Copenhagen: he would make a difference; he would go there with the CPRS legislated, able to point to Australia's action on climate change as he participated in the global debate.

Unfortunately none of that eventuated.

The CPRS was defeated in the Senate in August 2009 by an unholy alliance of the Greens, independents Xenophon and Fielding, the Liberals and the Nationals. The decision by the Greens to vote against it was unprincipled. They failed to put the national interest above their tactical political interest, insisting instead that they had reservations about the way industry was being assisted and the degree of ambition in the target.

After the CPRS was first defeated, the Greens may have fancied that they could force amendments on the government. But every calculation made by them was tone deaf to the emerging new political reality that support for action on climate change was waning. Every calculation was also blind to the injury to the national interest, which lay in getting the legislation through and bringing certainty to the economy.

Kevin had not approached the Senate vote with a systematic negotiating plan for brokering the CPRS through and had not met face to face with the Greens leader, Bob Brown, to discuss it. But the Greens would have voted the same way no matter what Kevin did. They wanted to look purer than Labor in the eyes of environmentally aware voters.

That meant that when the government brought the CPRS back to the Senate, it would only get through if a deal was struck with the Opposition. Its leader, Malcolm Turnbull, was personally in favour of an ETS and had led the Howard Government to that position as its Environment Minister. Penny Wong was deployed to meet with the Opposition's Ian MacFarlane, to see if a bipartisan deal was possible.

It was at this point that Penny asked to see me.

Penny is not an outwardly emotional person. I have seen her fully in tears only once – sitting in my office, across the desk from me, when she advised me not to stand in the June 2013 ballot that made Kevin prime minister again. She said it would be 'easier', to which I somewhat acidly replied, 'You mean easier for you, Penny.' While we disagreed vehemently on that occasion, as deputy prime minister and then prime minister, I was among Penny's supporters, and admired her abilities and cool head.

To see her in 2009, in the throes of the second parliamentary debate on the CPRS, with tears welling up was a major shock. She revealed that she was simply at her wits' end because even as she was doing the negotiations with the Opposition's Ian MacFarlane, she did not know whether her political instructions from Kevin were to get a deal or to crash the prospects of a deal. She did not know whether Kevin's call on the politics was to get carbon pricing through with bipartisan support and neutralise it as a political issue or what he actually wanted her to do was to give the appearance of a good faith negotiation but to ensure no deal was reached, so he could then go and fight for carbon pricing at the next election.

The two strategies were like chalk and cheese. Was it in the national interest to get a negotiated scheme done, with the political stability of having the support of the parties capable of forming government, or to hold out for Labor's vision of the scheme? As to the politics, would it be in Labor's interests to get carbon pricing done and move on? Or was carbon pricing likely to attract public support and be a positive defining political issue for Labor at an election?

Kevin was obviously equivocating on, indeed hiding from, such a profound decision. What he had been engaged in was a public strategy of hectoring and humiliating Malcolm Turnbull, who had spectacularly misfired with the political attack that came to be known as 'Utegate'.

In June 2009, Turnbull foolishly contended Kevin had to resign as prime minister because of wrongly seeking a government benefit for an individual who had donated an old ute to his election campaign. The allegations came from a Treasury officer with a mental illness. Turnbull had been deceived, had not done basic checking and had shot himself in the foot.

Under his leadership, his colleagues had seen the Opposition record their best primary vote in opinion polling since the 2007 election and Labor's vote trended down for ten straight weeks. But the same polls recorded a plunge in voters' satisfaction with Malcolm of 40 per cent immediately after Utegate, while the Opposition's vote trended down and the government's trended up. Recriminations and regrets would have been reverberating within the Opposition.

Undoubtedly Kevin felt he was entitled to return political fire, given he was the focus of Turnbull's aborted attack. But making that fire about climate change only made sense if your political strategy was driving towards carbon pricing being an in-contest election issue. If your strategy was to get a deal, then Turnbull, weakened by Utegate and facing increasing division within his own party on the science of climate change and emissions trading, needed propping up. A political hug, not an attack. Letting him have 'a victory' on some of the amendments to the legislation so he could sell the deal to his political party.

As Penny held back tears, I swore in frustration and then decided to do everything necessary to force proper discussions and government decision-making on our climate change strategy. I worked with Penny and Wayne, lending my political weight to them. Urgent discussions with Kevin did result and we all resolved to try to get a deal. In fact, Penny did succeed in striking one by conceding to the Opposition that more assistance would flow to industry under the scheme.

But the political winds on climate change and putting a price on carbon had shifted in the wider community and Tony Abbott, the self-described political weathervane, had sensed the shift. He used that shift to become Opposition leader, to overwhelm the wounded Malcolm Turnbull and to see off Joe Hockey. Tony Abbott was elected to the Liberal leadership on 1 December 2009 and the Senate rejected the CPRS legislation again on 2 December. Indeed the Opposition voted against, even though the legislation now included the amendments Penny and Ian MacFarlane had agreed.

Under its new leader, the Opposition went from divided but mostly rational on carbon pricing, to united and irrational almost overnight. Many of the leading lights of the Opposition, who had publicly and volubly supported a price on carbon, now executed a policy u-turn without so much as a glance over their shoulder. In a debate that came to turn so much on questions of political honesty, these acts of dishonesty towards their own beliefs by so many in the Liberal Party have gone largely unrecorded and uncommented upon.

Kevin and Penny were already in Copenhagen when Turnbull fell and the amended CPRS failed. After discussions with them and Wayne, I announced as acting prime minister that the government would put the CPRS legislation back to the parliament and give the Liberals 'one more chance' to support it in February 2010. I verified that the ETS proposal the government now stood for was the one agreed with the Malcolm Turnbull-led Opposition.

Meanwhile in Copenhagen, the global politics of climate change appeared to be spinning out of control. Heartbreakingly, especially for Kevin, the Copenhagen negotiations were beset by problems, including between the United States and China about the nature of the commitment, squabbling about whether the outcome of the conference would be a political agreement or a legally binding outcome, disagreement within the G77, the negotiating group of developing nations, and the hostile leak of a version of the agreement text while the conference was in its early stages. Both Kevin Rudd and Penny Wong played an important role in saving the negotiating process from complete collapse.

In the end, a political agreement was brokered at a meeting between President Obama, Chinese Premier Wen Jiabao, Indian Prime Minister Manmohan Singh, Brazilian President Luiz Inacio Lula and South African President Jacob Zuma. The agreement articulated a commitment by its signatories to keeping global temperature increases below 2 degrees Celsius and invited every nation to put forward its own commitments to reducing emissions by the end of January 2010.

The agreement was loose enough to heighten the uncertainties and tensions that were already running through the Australian community on carbon pricing and the pictures on television from Copenhagen were overwhelmingly images of chaos.

When Kevin returned from Copenhagen, he was physically exhausted and also broken in spirit. Worried, I talked about how low he was with one of his most senior staff members. Perceptively he said that the two of us were dealing with what happened at Copenhagen as a domestic political problem, admittedly a large one, there to be managed. In contrast, Kevin was grieving it as an international failure. Our response was practical, his was emotional.

But that understanding did not help with our immediate problem: whether or not to call the 2010 election early.

While the politics of climate change was shifting and memories of the government's good performance in the GFC were being submerged by concerns about debt and waste, these trends had not yet peaked. There was every reason to assume both were going to get worse across 2010. The turbulence in the Opposition and its election of an unpopular man as leader gave Labor a political opportunity. An early election had merits on all these counts.

John Faulkner talked to me and was all for an early election. Karl Bitar was for it too. He started putting the campaign machine on a war footing. Wayne war-gamed it through in his own mind and came down strongly in favour. In these discussions I sat back. I could see the merits of an early election but kept looking at Kevin and wondering whether he was in the right shape to fight it. These were doubts I did not share.

Kevin went through a few pretty disjointed motions for considering an early election. One was a meeting in Sydney on 23 December 2009 of the PSG, where Wayne, John, Karl and Mark argued their position. Karl presented the results of polling he had commissioned to test the question of an early election. He concluded that Labor would win but not increase its majority. He also advised that a February election was best if Labor was sticking with the CPRS. Contained in the polling were messages that were not pleasant to hear. The end of the year for the government had not just been about the CPRS. Voters were irritated with Kevin and the government because hospitals had not been fixed as promised and increasing numbers of asylum-seekers were arriving.

Karl's report told us that carbon pricing was not breaking the government's way. It spelt out that the public did not understand it and thought the government was not really trying to explain it. This made them suspicious of why the details were being hidden. Perversely, when we spoke of compensation for the flow-through effects in people's general cost of living because businesses paying a carbon price would seek to pass some of the cost on, for many this was the first time they realised tackling climate change had a price tag for them. Overall, carbon pricing was a key reason people were moving their votes to the Liberals and a key reason others were moving their vote to the Greens.

But the very good news was that we had a healthy primary vote, Kevin had a commanding lead over Tony Abbott as preferred prime minister and many voters thought the Opposition was not ready to govern.

The meeting ended inconclusively, with staff asked to do further work on options. At the meeting, I had been relatively quiet and had kept to myself my misgivings about whether Kevin was in the zone to fight an election.

On 4 January 2010, at Kevin's invitation, I met with him at Kirribilli House. I remember the summer sun, the sparkling harbour and the political discussion. His office had been working on sequencing documents, basically a grid showing all of our clustered and difficult political issues and how they could play into 2010, an election year. Kevin and I talked about this and about the prospects of an early election. From the uncertain, almost offhand way he raised it, to everything else about the discussion, I was left with the clearest of impressions that he neither wanted to nor was in the right state to go out and fight an election.

I had a choice. I could press Kevin and try to get him to say yes to an election. Or I could try to bolster his spirits by affirming to him we should not have a February election and see if, in the weeks that followed in early 2010, I could help him get into better form. I chose the second, non-confrontational course.

I believe I made a major political error; I also believe that had I tried the former option, I would have failed.

Had I, against my expectations, succeeded, and we had gone to an election then, I think we would have won it but it would have been heart-stoppingly close.

If we had been campaigning in February, then the closure of the foil home insulation program, followed quickly by the shut-down of the whole scheme, would have been a dominant and powerfully negative campaign issue.

Second, I believe my concerns about Kevin's state would have been proved right with a very ill-disciplined campaign. It was around

January that Kevin was described to me by a senior staff member in his office as being in 'funksville with no map about how to get out'. Basically he was adrift, having staff take all his meetings, with no plan for the year and no apparent ability to put one together. If we had called an early election and been campaigning in this period, then Kevin might have been re-energised by the momentum of the campaign. But what if he had continued in this inertia? It is debatable whether he would have coped. Nevertheless I believe voter perceptions of Tony Abbott and Liberal disunity at that point would have been enough to just carry us through.

If we had gone to an election and won, hindsight tells me that Kevin's leadership would have continued down the path of disintegration. In the period 2010–13, the same hard decision I made in 2010 would at some point have confronted me. But I would not have ended up in a leadership crisis situation in an election year.

Whatever my views, by 11 January Kevin must have been clear enough with his key staff that he did not want a February election that they felt confident to convey that message. Alistair Jordan, his young, incredibly hardworking and decent chief of staff, certainly conveyed that message by email to Karl Bitar, nominating April as the possible window for the election.

In this summer period, the contrast between a drifting prime minister and an Opposition leader with the bit between his teeth could not have been sharper. Tony Abbott announced his climate-change plan, the only merit of which was the focus group-driven title, 'Direct Action'. Essentially, he started the con job on the Australian people that tackling climate change and meaningfully reducing carbon emissions could be done at no real cost by measures such as tree planting.

Post Copenhagen, Kevin had insisted that the government investigate moving from carbon pricing to such a plan. It was researched by political staff in his office. Wayne, Penny and I worked together to dissuade Kevin from this course because the plan was obviously policy nonsense. Abbott also announced the formation of a Border Protection Committee, playing on our political weakness about asylum-seeker boats. He announced his opposition to the Wild Rivers Legislation, a Queensland state government act which had proved divisive. In case this made him look too anti the environment, he also vowed to take over the Murray Darling Basin if elected.

While the policy work underpinning these announcements was shamefully inadequate, the political gains were solid.

At Kirribilli House in the summer of 2008–09, Kevin wrote a manifesto about greed and the excesses of capitalism. In the summer of 2009–10, he was supposedly planning what to do in 2010 and how to sequence the government's major reform agendas. Instead, he emerged with a children's book, co-authored with Rhys Muldoon, the comedian and media personality.

This was no antidote to the government's political problems. Rather it caused many who cared about Labor's fortunes to shudder as it reinforced the perception of an increasingly aloof and out-of-touch leader. Kevin had aided Tony Abbott's political positioning, not countered it.

Kevin was also not associated in any way with the biggest government move in this period, the launch of My School. Both he and his office underestimated its impact and he never sought to really engage with it.

At some point in this period Kevin must have decided to delay the CPRS. I was not aware of it at the time, but Karl Bitar was told confidentially by Kevin's office that he had decided to delay it and that urgent focus group work needed to be done to inform how best to execute this decision.

Karl immediately conducted such focus groups in Brisbane and briefed Kevin on the findings on 12 February 2010. Karl says that in this discussion and in others surrounding it, he was crystal clear with Kevin that any sudden backflip would seriously harm how Kevin was viewed by the Australian people. He suggested such a move could only happen in a dramatic moment, where the nation's attention was focused and people would be more likely to absorb Kevin's reasons for the change.

Karl's view was that the legislation should be brought again to the parliament and when it was inevitably rejected again, at that point Kevin should announce to the nation he had accepted the political reality and he was moving ahead with a new plan, including further action on climate change through other mechanisms until carbon pricing could be secured. Kevin did not ask to speak to Karl directly again on this matter.

Not knowing any of this at the time, along with others, I continued to debate internally what we should do next on our ETS. By this stage a decision was overdue. Kevin was not campaigning on carbon pricing but Tony Abbott was kicking goals with his own messages. The Liberals' approach became clearer with each passing week as they sought to exaggerate and demonise the economic and cost impacts of emissions trading. The Opposition had endorsed the government's emissions reduction target of five per cent by 2020 and claimed that their policy would achieve it. The fact that no expert of any significance was prepared to endorse this claim did not stop them making it. At this stage, Australia's business community, which has a long-term strategic interest in sensible, informed public policy debates, should have gone flat out on the absurdity of the Liberals' plan but it pedalled softly.

Working with one of Kevin's staff, Penny, Wayne and I provided views about what the government should do next on the CPRS. An options document was prepared. I drafted and advocated what was nicknamed 'the bipartisanship option' because it essentially delayed the introduction of an ETS until there was bipartisan agreement.

Two decided views informed it. First, Tony Abbott was getting away with political murder and no weight was being placed on his shoulders. Second, we were not just losing the public debate, the government was effectively not showing up. Kevin, post Copenhagen, had not been campaigning on carbon pricing and in my judgement he was simply not going to run out hard for the CPRS. This plan was criticised internally as putting Tony Abbott in too much of a decision-making role but that was the point. My assumption was that underneath the façade of Coalition unity, there were still bruises and sore spots from their divisive leadership contest. As a newly installed leader, Tony Abbott was managing this by being all things to all people. To some audiences he sounded like a climate-change sceptic. To others, he would assure that the Opposition endorsed the government's target. I wanted him to feel the blowtorch of having to answer these questions precisely, not with platitudes. Specific answers might shake something loose from inside the Coalition.

I was prepared to put my position forcefully and hoped to squeeze a decision, any decision from Kevin. Whether my position was accepted or rejected, what I wanted to see more than anything was an end to our political drift.

Instead the weeks dragged from January into February, March into April, with no decision made. By then, Kevin had immersed himself in health reform and was touring the country talking to administrators, doctors, nurses and other health workers in hospitals. What eventually brought him to a decision was the impending budget. The CPRS had massive budget impacts: businesses would be buying permits and billions of dollars of revenue would come in; households would receive compensation and billions of dollars of revenue would flow out. Wayne needed to know whether the CPRS would appear in the budget with a start date of 1 July 2011. In the past, budget documents had been printed then pulped and redone overnight on the eve of the budget. Understandably Wayne wanted to avoid such midnight mayhem.

Meetings with various attendees whirred and blurred. A decision had to be made. Key discussions occurred in the days of 9 April to 12 April, a Friday to a Monday, in Brisbane. Such was the volume of backlogged SPBC business that it met on the Sunday and the Monday. On the Saturday, a PSG meeting occurred. I had flown up late on the Friday night and could not stay for all of Monday's meeting. I joined sections of it by telephone from Canberra. Wayne recalls going to Kevin's home for a dinner over this weekend, with Penny and Lindsay also attending. I was not there.

In all of the meetings regarding the fate of the CPRS, to the best of my knowledge, none of the politicians in the room knew that earlier in the year Kevin had conveyed a decision to Karl Bitar in favour of delay. All options under consideration had Labor maintaining its support for pricing carbon through an ETS. I stuck with my bipartisanship plan. Another delay option was dubbed the 'international option': the reason for delay was the state of international negotiations and the trigger for the start of the CPRS would be progress in them.

Penny and Lindsay opposed delaying the scheme. Wayne was in favour of delay of the CPRS but not my strategy for explaining it. That did not faze me. Above all, we needed a decision and I distinctly remember saying in a meeting what I had said to Kevin personally: if your call is that we go and get our stack hats on and get out and fight this thing, then let's go. But we cannot keep drifting.

At the Brisbane SPBC meeting, while I was in the room, Kevin asked ministers to outline their positions. Kevin did not crystallise a decision to be minuted but it was apparent that he was heading to the CPRS coming out of the budget. There was an inconclusive discussion about how to explain this change of policy. Across all the discussions Kevin was more attracted to the international option. However, at the meeting, no political plan was formalised for dealing with the announcement.

The formal decision to take the CPRS out of the budget was minuted at an SPBC meeting in Canberra on 21 April.[3]

On 27 April 2010, Lenore Taylor, a journalist then working at *The Sydney Morning Herald*, reported that the cabinet had postponed the introduction of the CPRS for at least three years and that its implementation costs and projected revenue had been removed from the budget.

Lenore was one of the few journalists in the Canberra press gallery who deeply understood and had followed all the complexities of the CPRS. She wrote that the ETS had been 'shelved for at least three years in a bid to defuse Tony Abbott's "great big new tax" attack in this year's election campaign.'[4] Somewhat ironically, her article also contained the following sentence:

> A poll by the Climate Institute think tank released yesterday showed those trusting Mr Rudd most on climate change fell from 46 per cent last year to 36 per cent in April, and the proportion of voters believing there was no difference between the two leaders rose from 37 per cent to 40 per cent over the same time.[5]

That kind of polling was about to get a whole lot worse. The leak had terrible, damaging effects and demanded a response from the government that clarified our position. But both its timing and its nature made a credible response more difficult, and Kevin did not rise to the challenge. He was visiting a hospital in Penrith as part of his ongoing advocacy for national health reform and dealt with this huge political crisis amid responses to a range of questions during a media conference. His explanation focused on the fact that global progress had been slower than expected and on the withdrawal of the Opposition's support for carbon pricing. He said:

> Climate change remains a fundamental economic and environmental and moral challenge for all Australians, and for all peoples of the world. That just doesn't go away for the simple reason that it's not in the headlines. Therefore, the practical question is this. Our current actions delivered through until the end of the current Kyoto commitment period, which finishes at the end of 2012 – the critical question then is what actions postdate 2012, and the decision that we've taken as a government is that that provides the best opportunity to judge the actions by the rest of the international community before taking our decision about the implementation of a Carbon Pollution Reduction Scheme from that time on.[6]

Clear as mud. His responses did not provide sufficient explanation of what had happened, where the government stood or what our future commitment to carbon pricing might look like.

There were glaring, negative repercussions for the Labor government in the media and in the wider community. Everyone criticised our lack of courage and consistency. Kevin's poll numbers dropped dramatically, and voting intentions showed support for the Labor government falling sharply.

Almost immediately internally, and then over the next few years publicly, Kevin peddled spin that I was the one who forced him to drop the CPRS. Peter Hartcher, as usual, spoke for Kevin when he wrote, 'Gillard was determined to stop Rudd proceeding with the scheme.'[7]

Admittedly I was fed up to the back teeth with his procrastinations on carbon pricing, taxing mining, health reform, asylum-seekers, our political strategy, our plan for government and I let that frustration show. But I consistently told him that if the call was to fight for the

CPRS as the key election issue, then I was ready to fight. Kevin was an incumbent prime minister, capable of conduct that could reduce highly competent people to a quivering, tearful mess. The suggestion he was too weak and cowering to stand up to me if he wanted to is absurd.

While Lenore Taylor's leak and its political aftermath were dramatic, other pressures meant that the focus of attention internally was quickly driven onto the need to decide and resolve other issues: the 2010 budget, including the RSPT, the government's response to the Henry Review, and before even that, the COAG health negotiations.

In June I inherited the mess that was the politics of carbon pricing. In my first press conference as prime minister, I stated:

> It's my intention to lead a government that does more to harness the wind and the sun and the new emerging technologies. I will do this because I believe in climate change. I believe human beings contribute to climate change and it is most disappointing to me, as it is to millions of Australians, that we do not have a price on carbon, and in the future we will need one. If elected as prime minister, I will re-prosecute the case for a carbon price at home and abroad. I will do that as global economic conditions improve and as our economy continues to strengthen.[8]

This was a commitment of principle, as well as a conscious political decision. I worked with cabinet on our approach to carbon pricing and the political problems we were in. Cabinet agreed with me that we needed to find ways of taking the Australian community back through the whole reform case, what climate change was, how humans were causing it through carbon, why emissions trading was the best solution, what was happening internationally. We had to find a policy approach for the 2010 election which preserved our commitment to carbon pricing, took practical steps to combat climate change and left open the final policy design and implementation until we had better persuaded the broader community.

This broad political aim prompted the election policy commitments in the 2010 campaign, including the Citizens' Assembly, a policy to encourage older, more polluting cars to be taken off the road, an investment to help renewable energy generators to access the electricity grid, tougher environmental standards for coal-fired power stations and a carbon farming scheme through which farmers could earn income from reducing their carbon emissions.

In our preparation for the campaign announcements, we planned to focus on climate change towards the end of the first week of the campaign, consistent with a thematic approach in which we would talk about a particular policy area over several days and make specific, often modest, individual policy announcements one at a time.

The climate-change announcements were anchored by a long speech that I gave at the University of Queensland on 23 July 2010. In it, I explained that the Labor government maintained its long-term commitment to carbon pricing and explained some of the challenges of implementation in the absence of cross-party support. In our media management, we took a very standard approach of 'dropping' part of the speech to the newspapers while saving some of the content so it would be fresh on the day. A drop is an embargoed release. The journalist accepts that the contents cannot be run earlier than in the morning version and online equivalent of the newspaper. Drops are often done selectively to favoured journalists to maximise the potential of a good run. In campaigns, they are given frequently and distributed liberally to obtain as much momentum as possible.

The excerpt I authorised for release that day included the commitment to create a Citizens' Assembly, a public consultation process in which a representative group drawn from the wider community would meet and work through, in detail, the issues involved in carbon pricing.

As I said in the speech, the proposed assembly would not decide the government's policy but it would provide an important marker of the progress of the debate. The idea behind it was precisely to create a process through which Australians from many different walks of life could have the time and the factual support to be able to think through everything about climate change. Such a process, if it was impartially conducted and well covered by the media, would result in more people concluding that an ETS was the best long-term approach, and that it could be implemented without causing real damage to the Australian economy or their cost of living. It was a commitment to a deeper, better structured discussion.

While I was part-way through my speech, the room was invaded by noisy environmental protesters. Dramatically one was tackled to the ground by a police officer. I did my best to just keep on delivering the speech despite the atmosphere of anxiety and discord.

The subsequent media response to the Citizens' Assembly announcement was universal, comprehensive condemnation and derision. Every media organisation dismissed it as a gimmick – a cynical and superficial attempt to offload responsibility for taking the policy decision on carbon pricing. Newspapers devoted pages to spelling out why it was not the way to go and how ridiculous the idea was of engaging a group drawn from the public in this kind of exercise.

The following day, at the announcement of the program to provide cash incentives for the surrender of old, high pollution-emitting cars, the criticism of the climate-change policy continued.

Within a few days of the media downpour, opinion polls showed that public did not like the idea either, amazingly enough. I absorbed this, internally grimacing; now I can refer to it with a wry smile.

During the 2010 campaign, I suggested to Garry Linnell, then editor of the *Daily Telegraph*, that the newspaper should sponsor a new format of town hall meetings. One hundred swinging voters drawn together to see and question the contending leaders. Garry latched on to the idea and on two separate nights Tony Abbott and I appeared at Rooty Hill. The events were televised live.

Such events are now a campaign staple, every moment analysed and re-analysed by commentators. The meetings are reported as if the fate of the election campaign can turn on every word, and undoubtedly a very good or very bad performance by a leader can make a difference. Yet the very same journalists who now live and breathe for such events were pillorying the idea of a Citizens' Assembly.

In the years since I have joked with journalists, 'What kind of idiot proposes getting 100 Australians to discuss hard political issues, like climate change?' They all laugh, enjoying the apparent self-deprecating reference to the assembly. Then comes my punch line: 'Me, when I suggested an election forum at Rooty Hill!' At this point the journalists realise my joke is on them.

We did not exactly sail through our early campaign events, it must be said. Every campaign event is 'advanced', that is, checked out ahead of time by a staff member who, among other things, figures out what the televised pictures will look like. After I took over being prime minister so suddenly, a new team was hastily put together and there were teething problems with some roles, including advance. A more experienced team would never have put a climate-change speech in an open-air venue at a university. It was really begging for protesters.

Another error occurred at our event about replacing high-polluting old cars. The television coverage had me in the foreground and the prime ministerial car, with the licence plate C1, in the back. That was begging to be sent up.

Some errors were all mine. The policy to replace high-polluting cars, dubbed 'Cash for Clunkers', was a dog. In a policy sense, what it best illustrated was the problem with trying to reduce emissions in a cost-effective way by so-called direct action methods. It also high-lighted the risk of trying to get policy work done for the election from a standing start.

In the newspaper drop of my climate-change speech, I should have substituted for the Citizens' Assembly some of the more policy heavy content, like the work on pollution in power stations. Having the assembly as the stand-out policy made it a bigger target and everything else was obscured.

But some things I could not control. For the first week of the campaign, the Abbott team was in many ways missing in action because they had not been ready for the announcement of the election. As a result, the media trained all their focus on me and my team. What they picked up on was the apparently controlled and boring nature of our campaign. Commentary began cropping up about spin and stage management, about our rationing of announcements, along with crit-icism of our approach of providing one event and set of pictures for each day.

This provides some context for the wall-to-wall hostile reaction in the media to our proposed Citizens' Assembly. A misinterpretation quickly took hold that the proposal was to give control of climate-change policy to a group of randomly selected citizens. But it was also a reaction to the perceptions of spin, of message control and of weakness in the face of a difficult policy decision.

As the campaign moved into its fourth and fifth weeks, carbon pricing became more prominent again. The Coalition started running ads essentially saying a carbon tax was coming. Of course, a carbon tax is not an ETS. In the consumer world, we are familiar with taxes on products with proven undesirable consequences like tobacco and alcohol. Taxing increases price and reduces consumption. There is no doubt that increasing the tax on tobacco over time has had an impact on smokers' behaviour. A carbon tax would take a comparable approach to carbon dioxide: a business would have to pay the tax for each tonne of carbon dioxide it released. Undoubtedly having to pay a tax on something that a business used to do for free would cause a rethink and many would reduce their tax liability by adopting more environmentally friendly processes. But a carbon tax is not a market-based mechanism. The government, not the market, fixes the amount paid per tonne. In addition, with a carbon tax, a government cannot predict with certainty the amount of emissions the economy as a whole will produce. There is no way to set an economy-wide cap.

Both are prices on carbon. One a tax, the other a cap-and-trade ETS. At no point had the Rudd Government or I ever contemplated enacting an ongoing carbon tax.

To get emissions trading going, government can set the price as the market starts. The first version of the CPRS considered by the parliament in May 2009 had a one-year fixed price of $10 per tonne. During the vexed CPRS process, such a fixed price had not been commonly referred to as a carbon tax.

As the 2010 campaign was moving into its final stage, *The Australian* had a front-page story about my final messages to the electorate. Headed 'Julia Gillard's Carbon Price Promise', the first words of the article read, 'Julia Gillard says she is prepared to legislate a carbon price in the next term.'[9] In the interview, I had given a clear answer that I ruled a carbon tax out but not an ETS. Earlier in the week in an interview on Channel 10, I had given half the answer, saying, 'There will be no carbon tax under a government I lead.'[10] I did not give the other half. This is what was spun into my 'carbon tax lie'.

If at any time since they were uttered I could have taken those words back, then I would have done so in a flash. They were twisted and turned to dreadful political effect against me. But I did not lie. I had never intended a carbon tax and did not introduce one.

Had the government been re-elected with a majority, then I would have carefully started to prosecute the case for an ETS to do the campaign job that had been left undone at the end of the Rudd Government. A Citizens' Assembly would have been one part of that process. But I would have conducted around the country what worked for me so well during the campaign: face-to-face meetings with voters on serious policy questions.

Would I have been able to make enough political space to introduce and get through the parliament an ETS during the government's term from 2010 to 2013? I doubt it. But I thought patient explanation needed to be given a chance.

After the election resulted in a hung parliament, it was clear to me from my discussions with the Greens that at least in Parliament House there was going to be new political space in which to work through an ETS.

From the earliest discussions I realised that the Greens, on the issue of emissions trading, were no longer going to play the politics of protest. It was obvious from their demeanour but I could also read the politics.

The politics of protest works for the Greens against a majority government, particularly a Labor one. They can argue the purist position, valiantly lose and then go to their constituency saying, 'We can only overwhelm this evil old party if you strengthen our hand and vote in more of us.' From the start, I felt they rightly sensed that the politics of a minority Labor government, if one was formed, would work out differently. If they failed on an issue as important as climate change, when a Labor government needed their vote in the lower house and they had their best representation ever in the Senate, their constituency might well conclude that the Greens would never be capable of success. Gough Whitlam famously said only the impotent are pure.

In the post-election days, I found a new take on his wisdom: pride in purity easily becomes the ignominy of impotence.

For myself, in those hard days after a campaign redolent with treachery, I was determined to form government, but not at any price. I needed momentum. I needed the Greens to sign up to give it to me. I sensed the policy opportunity that would come if – instead of a Labor government hitting a Senate gridlock, as had happened under Kevin – there was a different process and attitude from the Greens, which enabled an ETS to get through.

The agreement Wayne and I signed with the Greens simply said:

That Australia must tackle climate change and that reducing carbon pollution by 2020 will require a price on carbon. There-fore the Parties agree to form a well-resourced Climate Change Committee which encompasses experts and representative ALP, Greens, independent and Coalition parliamentarians who are committed to tackling climate change and who acknowledge that reducing carbon pollution by 2020 will require a carbon price. The Committee will be resourced like a Cabinet Committee.[11]

In our private discussions I had gone further and said that if we could reach agreement then I would legislate it during the parliamentary term, provided agreement could be struck quickly enough so that the scheme was up and running on 1 July 2012. In doing so, I bet my future, the government's future, on two things. First, that I could get the Greens to accept a workable scheme. Second, that if an ETS started and people lived with it, then opposition would fall away.

My instinct in the run-up to the election had been to engage in community campaigning to create enough political consensus to force a gridlocked Canberra to act. The opportunity that presented after the election was the other way around: to use the unexpected possibility of enough consensus in Canberra to get a scheme through, the very existence of which would create community acceptance of the scheme.

Getting to an ETS involved a novel process. Cabinet committees are the preserve of governments. I created one, the Multi Party Climate Change Committee (MPCCC), which included the government, the

Greens, Rob Oakeshott and Tony Windsor, along with the outside experts Ross Garnaut, Rod Sims, an expert in the electricity sector, Will Steffan, a climate scientist, and Patricia Faulkner, an expert on the community impacts of policy. It first met on 27 September 2010.

In spite of considerable outside political heat and fire, the committee applied itself thoroughly and well. A set of principles was agreed and released. The details of legislation were talked through. Greg Combet worked unbelievably hard and incredibly competently to get it all done. The hours and effort harmed both his health and personal life. But he did not complain. Instead he showed what it means to truly put the nation's interests first.

Throughout the process he was consistently pessimistic about the chances of the Greens accepting a practical workable scheme. Every time we spoke, he mentioned the need for a plan B, should negotiations falter and the Greens walk away from the process and the government. Ever the optimist, I believed the Greens had too much skin in the game. My prediction to Greg was always that the Greens would do the deal and then close to the election split to the left away from the government and campaign for changes to the scheme that they had helped create.

Ultimately this did happen, with Christine Milne announcing at the National Press Club on 19 February 2013 that the Greens were withdrawing from their agreement with the government.

But back in mid-to-late 2010, the concession by the Greens that made everything else possible was agreeing to park the issue of the target for emissions reduction. While the government had an unconditional target of cutting emissions by five per cent compared with 2000 levels by 2020, the Greens advocated a much higher target of 40 per cent compared with 1990 levels. Arguing about the targets would have taken us in a never-ending circle. The government would never have agreed to a target high enough to win the Greens approval. We would not countenance a target which would force business into a rapid, dislocating adjustment. This had been the stumbling block to any real meeting place between the Rudd Government and the Greens on the CPRS.

Our government and the Greens agreed to effectively side-step this argument. The ETS would be designed with a three-year fixed-price period, with the price sufficiently high so that it would start changing behaviour enough to put the nation on a path to the government's minus five per cent target. During the fixed price period, a climate commission of independent experts would make a recommendation to government on the future target and therefore the cap when the scheme moved from the fixed price to the market set price. Under the model, we retained government as the decision-maker on whether or not to accept this advice but there would be transparency and parliamentary debate. Consequently the model was for a two-year longer fixed price than the CPRS as agreed with Malcolm Turnbull.

With the vexed question of the targets put on ice, then the details of the scheme could be worked through. Step by step, piece by piece, the ETS and companion policies took shape. Greg consulted with business and rightly insisted on good shielding arrangements from the full effect of the carbon price for businesses that compete globally. He worked painstakingly through the support necessary to the electricity sector to ensure continuity of supply. Tony Windsor focused on the advantages that could flow for farmers from changing their land practices and storing more carbon in the land. He also focused on how the food processing industry could be assisted in the transition to a lower carbon future. Rob Oakeshott focused on biodiversity and the intersection between our soil, our water and our atmosphere. The Greens wanted to see more invested in the science and commercialisation of renewable energy.

Compared to the CPRS, the ETS that emerged had more scope for ambition in emissions reduction targets and a greater focus on renewable energy, with more help available to businesses to innovate.

In addition, I insisted that the scheme contain a major tax reform measure. The household assistance was to be distributed through the mechanism of tripling the tax-free threshold, the amount people could earn before paying any tax. This meant not only that dollars went to low- and middle-income earners but that our nation was changing the equation between work and tax. Work, on which I put a high personal value, would now return more to those at the lower end of the income scale. It would make it much more rewarding for a welfare recipient to move into some casual or part time-work. The approach I demanded took a million people out of the tax system. They went from paying tax to paying no tax.

Within the MPCCC room, people listened to each other with respect. Out of the room, the hard bargaining was conducted. Greg did the first-instance bargaining with Christine Milne and I negotiated the too-hard basket with Bob Brown. In this process I relied heavily on Ian Davidoff, who led my policy staff. He played a pivotal role in the negotiations to get an agreement, just as he had done throughout the long 17 days during which we formed the government. His policy reach and intuitive feel of what was needed to get everyone over the line were indispensable.

Personally I got on well with Bob Brown. He and his partner, Paul, dined with Tim and me on more than one occasion and we enjoyed their company immensely. Bob often showed genuine concern for my wellbeing, behaviour you would expect from an uncle looking after his favourite niece but not from a politician dealing with another politician from a different political party. In many ways I liked him but I was never beguiled. He could be as hard as nails in the interests of his political party.

It was self-evident he was coming to the end of his political career. He would tire easily, could not put in the hours I did. But the fact he was in legacy mode, I thought made him far more likely to want to see legislation get through.

The final deal was done by Bob and me in a series of meetings in my office. The discussions were cordial but tense.

I have jokingly described the prime minister's office as like living inside a gumnut. It has a great deal of modern wood panelling which, in the right light, can throw off a golden glow. The furniture for the office, picked when Parliament House was first opened in 1988, is very much a product of its era. Four large, semi-circular orange chairs are the strongest feature of the room. When Labor was in Opposition we lampooned John Howard for putting these chairs in storage and bringing out green Chesterfield ones. After a few weeks of working in the prime minister's office, I could see what had motivated him.

Sitting in these chairs, Bob and I did our bartering, including the question of the starting price. The Greens had initially said the starting price should be $60 per tonne of carbon dioxide. They fell back to $40 per tonne. On my side of the table, I was determined to have a price that would take us seamlessly to the likely price when the cap-and-trade scheme started fully. At this point, our Australian scheme could link with other schemes, including the world's largest, the European Union scheme.

International linking was important because it meant that the price being paid for releasing carbon by Australian businesses would converge with the price being paid by businesses overseas. It also meant that the transition in the Australian economy, which is so highly carbon intensive, could be worked through more gently with access to overseas reductions to make up our target. Indeed there was a full circle back to the concept Liberal Senator Robert Hill spoke so enthusiastically about after the Kyoto meeting. Economies with excess emissions like ours could buy carbon permits from economies that were going to fall below their emissions targets.

Given the international linking, you needed to project a starting price that would take you to what the EU price was likely to be in 2015. We accessed the best Treasury advice to work out the figure. I got Bob down to $23 per tonne and that was in the right zone according to Treasury. We shook hands. The deal was done.

The Eurozone crisis, which caused so many problems for the global economy and so much anxiety at the G20, also bit hard into the credibility of this starting price. What I could not have foreseen was that European carbon markets would be so volatile and the price would plummet as low as 2.63 Euros. It made the political task of selling our ETS harder.

The legislation passed both houses of parliament on 8 November 2011. When I introduced the legislation, I spoke about the judgement of history in the following terms:

There is a reason votes on legislation in this House are recorded. There is a reason these matters are decided in an open vote. It is so every member in this place can be judged. Judged on the decisions they make here . . . judged on where they stand on the great issues of our national debate. Judged by every Australian. Judged now . . . judged in the future.

Because the final test is not: are you on the right side of the politics of the week or the polls of the year? The final test is: are you on the right side of history? And in my experience, the judgement of history has a way of speaking sooner than we expect. To newer members of this place – and I see some in front of me – I say, just ask those more senior members who sit opposite. Ask those who voted in this House against Medicare in 1983. How smart did that look in 1984? Ask those who voted in this House against universal superannuation in 1992. How smart did that look in 1993? Ask those who voted for Work Choices in 2005. How smart did that look in 2007?

Yes, the judgement of history comes sooner than we expect. And the demand for policy leadership comes hard on its heels. Nothing hard ever gets easier by putting it off. And if you do not do what is right for the nation then you should not be in this parliament. It is time to deliver the action on climate change we need. It is time to do what is best for Australian families, what is best for future generations, what is best for this country.[12]

Those words still ring true today.

When the bill passed the parliament, there was a spontaneous round of congratulations along the front bench. It might not have been politically smart because it enabled the Opposition to characterise us as self-absorbed, but it was human. We had fought extraordinarily hard to see this moment.

I kissed a number of my colleagues on the cheek. Kevin then loomed alongside me proffering his hand. I knew, and suspect he did too, that whatever happened next would be the picture used by all the media. If I only shook his hand, having kissed other colleagues, I thought that would be the subject of commentary. I kissed his cheek. The front page of the *Daily Telegraph* the next day was almost wholly devoted to that photo, described as a kiss of death. It was another spectacular example of trumped up leadership carry-on overwhelming proper reporting of something that mattered a very great deal to the nation: the creation of its first ever ETS.

*

The ETS started on 1 July 2012. Inevitably it was a highly complex arrangement. Over 200 million permits needed to be issued. Around $2.5 billion distributed to business in free permits and other assistance to help with the transition. $1.5 billion distributed to households. What has not been publicly credited was that such a big structural change to our economy was implemented without a hiccup.

I went campaigning and so did Tony Abbott. He took a short break from campaigning to go overseas on holidays. Then I punched through with a message about the real drivers of high electricity prices, like the huge investments in poles and wires, some of which would not be necessary if there was a better structured energy market, and announced my intention to work through COAG to make a difference to them. By the start of August, I could feel the heat going out of carbon pricing. The world had not come to an end as the community had feared. Community attitudes were settling. The scheme was working well.

The ALP's pollster, Tony Mitchelmore, told me that before 1 July 2012, the only thing anyone would talk about in focus groups was the carbon tax. After a few months of carbon pricing being in operation, he found himself having to prompt a discussion in a focus group: no one spontaneously mentioned it.

Underneath all the frenzy associated with this comprehensive reform, the track record of the ETS is a particularly good one. The cost of living impact was a little bit less than was predicted and so the household assistance worked as it should. In the first 12 months of the scheme, emissions from electricity generation reduced by more than six per cent. Significantly the generation of electricity in the national electricity market by brown coal, which is a more emissions-intensive fuel, decreased by more than 12 per cent. At the same time, cleaner sources of energy became much more popular. Hydro-electricity grew by 33.8 per cent and other renewables by 8.9 per cent. The economy and employment kept growing. Not one of the horror scenarios sketched by the Tony Abbott-led Opposition came true.

I won my two huge political gambles. The first bet was a leap of faith that the Greens would cut a deal, which they did even though our scheme was in some aspects a more conservative one than the CPRS.

I also bet that if Australians lived with carbon pricing, their concerns would fall away. Time after time I was told that it was not possible to get a scheme up and running by 1 July 2012. But I insisted and won that bet too.

So why was the politics so miserable?

First and foremost, I compounded my error in the election campaign of not qualifying my statement, 'There will be no carbon tax under a government I lead', by conceding the use of the incorrect term 'carbon tax'. Religiously in my media appearances I referred to our plan as putting a price on carbon. I did not go around every day saying 'carbon tax' but I did not fight the characterisation.

The circumstances help explain but do not excuse it. In politics, time is a precious commodity. I caught Greg's sense of urgency about the need to launch the principles to guide the development of the carbon pricing scheme which had been agreed with the Greens, Windsor and Oakeshott. Greg was desperate to launch them so that he could start the intensive process of sitting with business and working all the details through. My office and I had not war-gamed as comprehensively as we should have the approach to the press conference. By getting on with it rather than holding back, I erred. Whether the war-gaming would have made a major a difference I cannot be sure, but I should have given myself the time.

But even with more time, I may well still have fallen for the classic political error of basing today's tactics on yesterday's problem.

What was at the forefront of my mind was the 'don't say billions' debacle that engulfed Kevin and Wayne immediately after the delivery of the 2009 budget. Kevin had decided that during the budget sell, neither he nor Wayne would use the word 'billions' after stating the budget deficit. The strategy totally backfired. It became a media game that went on for 13 days until eventually Kevin said the magic words. He and the government looked ridiculous.

Scarred by that experience, I visualised days of the media badgering me to say the words 'carbon tax'.

Craig Emerson was of the view we should not concede the language of carbon tax, that we should make it plain that it was not one. Greg and I have different memories of his argument at this time. He was certainly arguing that one of the reasons Kevin had failed with the CPRS was that he never came clean with the Australian people and explained things like the price effects for consumers. Greg wanted to be clearer and fight on the substance. My recollection is this extended to him arguing that we should not get caught up in a word game.

But while recollections vary, the political responsibility for the error is absolutely mine. Craig was right, I was wrong, It is the worst political mistake I have ever made, and I paid for it dearly.

Doing a joint press conference with Rob, Tony and the Greens to announce the carbon pricing principles was misconceived too. It was a critical demand from the Greens. I have never been a big pomp and ceremony person. The prime minister's courtyard is routinely used in good weather for prime ministerial press conferences. By convention, ministers do not use it without the prime minister but are regularly invited to appear with the prime minister to provide extra detail on whatever is being announced. For me, standing in the prime minister's courtyard with politicians who were not members of my political party to make an announcement did not seem like allowing an intrusion into a sacred government space, but this was the way it was portrayed in the media. My sense was it was better to give the Greens this token and save up credit for the negotiation of the real issues in the scheme. In that, I made the error of thinking in modern politics that substance should come before spin. For all the complaints by the media about spin in politics, many journalists actually thrive on it. They do not have time for the substance. Spin, tragically, has never been more important, and I did not put it number one.

Even with the carbon tax and courtyard errors, the politics could have been recovered in a more balanced environment. But everything was spiralling out of kilter. The media coverage of putting a price on carbon was in large part hysterical and just plain wrong.

For example, I awoke on 5 May 2011 to a shrieking headline in *The Australian* reading, 'Westpac Joins the Carbon Revolt'. The only revolt that had been joined was *The Australian* against the truth. Nothing in the article justified the headline, absolutely nothing. Before 9 am that same day, Gail Kelly, the Chief Executive Officer of

Westpac, had gone on radio to debunk the story. What *The Australian* should have done the next day was publish a retraction on the
front page of the same size and scale. Instead it included a small story
on page two.

The tabloid newspapers were in on the act too. Day after day there
were big beat-ups about price impacts that contained no reference to
the fact that more money was going to be in people's pockets as a result
of tax cuts and benefit increases. Their venom was not just saved for
the government. Award-winning actress Cate Blanchett was vilified
as 'Carbon Cate' because she appeared free of charge in an advertising campaign funded by environmental groups and in favour of
pricing carbon. The attack against her was mounted on the basis that
she was wealthy and out of touch. National Party Senator Barnaby
Joyce's florid quotes in the article included: 'If you really care, how
about you give some money to help people meet the increased costs
they are about to face . . . Instead of sticking "I care" bumper stickers
on their Mercedes four-wheel drives, they should get out and talk to
people who are forced to eat No Frills [brand food] because they can't
afford anything else.'[13]

Of course, this News Limited tabloid smash-up piece failed to
explain that millions of low-income Australians were going to end up
better off.

This bias and silliness was catching and percolated throughout
the media.

As it all ran crazily on, Wayne Goss, the former Queensland
premier, remarked to me that it amazed him watching the media that
there were absolutely no rules when it came to the treatment of me.
Other leaders had endured harsh media, but there was always some line
that would not be crossed, some sense of respect for the office that set
a boundary. I was the first prime minister he had ever known not to be
afforded that respect.

How much of this is a general loss of manners by the modern
media, how much was the special circumstances of the minority parliament, how much was driven by some from my own side treating me
with disrespect, and therefore freeing others to do so, how much is
gender? I do not know. But it all combined to give aid and comfort

to Tony Abbott's campaign. It became routine for the Leader of the Opposition to run the nightly news with grabs like, 'This is a toxic PM with a toxic tax.' Really?

Abbott's ruthless playing of the politics of personality overwhelmed a true focus on the policy. The media's sensationalism overwhelmed the reporting of the facts. Nevertheless, once our scheme started, the Australian community just got on with living with a price on carbon. Fear of the change started to fall away.

Out of all of this, some principles for the future stand shining and true. First, climate change is real and the world needs to reduce its output of carbon dioxide. Second, our country has an obligation to act and should be an active contributor to the further shaping of global reduction targets, including our own. Third, our nation should reduce carbon in the cheapest way possible, and that is via an internationally linked ETS. Four, an ETS is a better mechanism than a carbon tax. That's why I legislated one.

I understood the political and policy rationale of Kevin Rudd and the Labor team announcing in the lead-up to the 2013 election that the fixed price period would be shortened. I had considered this with Greg, Penny and Wayne.

We too saw it had some merits as an election announcement. It would not have been an antidote to the 'she lied' claim, and given the potency of that claim, there was understandable political nervousness about me going back to policies on carbon. There was also merit for me in being the custodian of the status quo on carbon pricing, given how much quieter the reaction had been since the scheme started.

Greg was also concerned about legal concerns from the business community with long-run forward contracts having factored in the legislated price for three years.

But for a new leader, it was a proposition of merit that needed to be argued for on the basis of the policy superiority of more quickly getting to a cap and trade scheme. It was foolish for the Labor Party at that time to put the reason for shortening the fixed price period as a cost of living issue. That was conceding the central argument at the heart of Tony Abbott's negative campaigning. Carbon pricing in Australia has not caused a real cost of living issue.

Despite all the general and sexist abuse, all the ugliness of the carbon pricing debate, I am proud of what was achieved. Ironically no prime minister has ever fought harder for a big reform and yet I constantly faced allegations that I did not truly believe in carbon pricing.

I was grateful I did not fight alone. Rather I fought alongside the extremely able Greg Combet as minister and the talented Mark Dreyfus as parliamentary secretary. As with all things, Wayne and other good colleagues went hard in the battle to win through.

Penny retained her passion for seeing the reform through. Around the time the legislation was passed, she said to me wistfully that she sometimes wondered what could have been had Kevin supported her the way I supported and worked with Greg. Perhaps history could have been so very different.

Many Labor members around the country fought courageously for carbon pricing, even under the most intense political heat.

Emissions trading will be a part of our nation's future. It is inevitable.

I will enjoy living to see the day when I can have conversations with young people about putting a price on carbon where they will look at me with wonderment in their eyes. 'Was anybody really ever opposed?' they will say. And I will smile and say, 'Let me tell you about the old days.'

20

Our water, our land

'He set off for the Mackay Fish Market, where he was invited to fillet a barramundi. Abbott, by now in full Action Man mode, not only wielded the filleting knife but decided to sink his teeth into his work. "Is this sashimi-grade?" he asked the fisherfolk. "Nope," he was told. But there was no stopping him. The Opposition Leader chewed on a raw fillet.'

TONY WRIGHT'S OBSERVATIONS FROM TONY ABBOTT'S
CAMPAIGN AGAINST MARINE PARKS,
THE SYDNEY MORNING HERALD, 28 JULY 2010

WHEN I WAS INVOLVED IN THE STUDENT MOVEMENT, as a young political activist, it was progressives who took to the streets, protested, sought signatures on petitions. Liberal Party supporters, conservatives, would have died before they engaged in protest politics. But in contemporary politics, in Australia and in countries like the United States, the shrillest, most mobilised pursuer of protest politics is the radicalised Right.

In the carbon-pricing debate, the climate-change deniers have out-campaigned the voices of reason. The Liberal Party embraced protest politics, even though its leading members had sat at the Cabinet table in John Howard's government and adopted emissions trading as policy. This new-found protest culture enveloped the Liberal Party on the issue of marine parks and the Murray Darling. The real-world circumstances confronting forestry in Tasmania were ignored.

The denial of science, the over-inflated false claims, the dismissal of any fact that does not fit the story are all worrying trends that deserve greater analysis and commentary. The merits of our environmental reforms will withstand the scrutiny.

OUR WATER

It was John Howard who started the process of taking what has worked on land, the concept of parks, into our oceans. It was one of the commitments of his 1996 election campaign. To deliver on it, in 1998 the commonwealth, state and Northern Territory governments committed themselves to establishing a national system of protected marine areas by 2012. In October 2005, the Howard Government announced the process for doing this under federal environmental law. Like parks on land, this was not a concept about an all-encompassing locking up that kept humans out. Some areas would be kept pristine and some would have mixed use, including commercial and recreational use.

In government, when Labor moved to complete Howard's vision, the Liberal and National parties embraced the politics of irrational protest.

It is natural for people to fear change and recreational and small-scale fishers were understandably concerned about what marine parks would mean for them. Tony Abbott deliberately stoked this fear during the 2010 election campaign by suggesting that in a marine park, a family would be unable to go out in a small boat, a tinny, and throw a line over. Of course, this was a lie but the campaign was an effective one.

As with carbon, the dishonesty of the campaign run by the Abbott Opposition was gobsmacking. The federal government's powers for our oceans only start three nautical miles, meaning 5.5 kilometres, from land and end 200 nautical miles, or 370 kilometres, out to sea, at the outer limit of the exclusive economic zone. Overwhelmingly people wanting to fish recreationally stay closer to shore and, as a result, would not be affected in any way. As observed by Senator Joseph Ludwig, a laconic Queenslander with ministerial responsibility for fisheries, if a person went that far out in a tinny, their problem would not be marine park regulations, it would be that they were never going to make it back to shore.

People were also told that our commercial fishing industry would be devastated. In fact, expert assessments showed that only around one per cent of the total annual value of Australia's commercial fisheries would be displaced and Tony Burke announced a $100 million package to assist industry to adjust.

Once again, despite a hysterical campaign against, it fell to Labor to complete this reform. Starting in May 2011, Tony Burke methodically released for wide consultation draft commonwealth marine reserve network proposals for five different parts of the ocean. There was then a 90-day public consultation period for each region, including 245 public and stakeholder meetings. Over 56,000 submissions were made on the draft proposals. The final proposal, released in February 2012, was for the Coral Sea, which would be the world's largest marine protected area. Painstakingly management plans dealing with uses of the parks were then released and consulted upon.

The final plans, reflecting more than 65,000 public comments, were tabled in parliament in March 2013. In June, true to negative form, the Opposition tried to have the plans disallowed. We were victorious by one vote.

Australia now has the largest network of marine protected areas in the world, covering 3.1 million square kilometres. People are still enjoying the fun of fishing.

We also needed to call on our courage to stare down Opposition negativity on saving the Murray River. For me, growing up in South Australia, the River Murray was an intrinsic part of my world. As a teenager, I used to holiday with a school friend at her family farm outside Loxton. The river then was a place for fun, for picnics and boat rides.

But in my home state the river is also a source of life. Not just the life given to fruit and other agricultural produce but a source of life to Adelaide itself. Around half of Adelaide's drinking water comes from the Murray. In times of severe drought, that percentage rises. During the severe drought of the early 1980s, I remember filling the bath with water so brown it was debatable whether you would emerge from it cleaner or dirtier. At that stage, 90 per cent of the water was coming from the Murray. South Australians feel the unfairness of living on what is left after the upstream states have grabbed more than their share of the water.

During the millennium drought of 2000–10, which was a catalyst for community anxiety about climate change, sand-bearing tidal action clogged up the mouth of the Murray; its lower lakes were in danger of turning to acid. But the politics of changing water use to ensure environmental sustainability for the river had proven diabolically hard over decades.

As long ago as 1994, COAG had agreed to do something comparable to emissions trading but for water: to create a water market. Historically a farmer's entitlement to land and water use was bundled together. The aim of the reform was to separate the entitlement to water, to price water properly and to determine entitlements to the use of the water.

As with carbon, the price and the ability to sell an entitlement to water use would encourage the adoption of water-efficient practices. A cap was needed – again, like carbon – and an interim one was struck and came into effect on 1 July 1997 for New South Wales, South Australia and Victoria.

Just like carbon, the facts and the politics of being seen to be doing something on an issue of such national importance drove the Liberal Party in government, but in Opposition, cheap populism took over. Instead of assisting with a major reform, the Coalition members hunted the politics. Consequently in upstream states everyone was promised that water would not be taken away from them and in South Australia promises were made to get water back into the river.

To get the job done and defeat this kind of beguiling nonsense required resolve. Doing the job meant understanding that those who want to use water have voices to raise and a clear view of the amount of water they need.

The loser in this process can be the silent river. To remain healthy it needs a sufficient flow of water to keep the river mouth open. The quantity of water needed to do that was not really known prior to the work of our government, even though efforts had been made to increase environmental flows.

The first big step was taken in 2002 when the Howard Government and the Labor governments of New South Wales and Victoria agreed to fund projects that would save water and allow more to flow down both the Snowy and Murray Rivers. By July 2004, there was an agreement that $500 million would be spent over five years buying water and returning it to the river. Under the Rudd Government, the Murray-Darling Basin Authority was created in 2008: the first single inter-governmental body to assume responsibility for the planning and management of the Murray-Darling Basin. It had only taken over a hundred years since Federation to recognise that a river system that crossed state boundaries need to be viewed and managed as a whole, not in competing pieces.

In the 2010 election campaign, I committed to accepting the expert advice of the Murray-Darling Basin Authority and buying back water each year at the levels which would be detailed in its forthcoming report. The banner headline in the *Adelaide Advertiser* read, 'River Queen: Gillard Will Buy Enough Water to Save Murray'.[1] The Opposition did not make a comparable commitment.

On 8 October 2010, shortly after our minority government was formed, the Murray-Darling Basin Authority released a document which was described as a guide on its thinking about the plan for the Murray-Darling Basin. This document was a stage along the way to developing the final plan. It was open to consultation, with all the public information sessions scheduled for October and November. The guide said the aim of the Authority was to put between 3000 and 4000 gigalitres of water back into the river system, which would mean water allocation cuts for irrigators.

The public consultation process degenerated into heated public meetings, demonstrations and public burning of copies of the plan. People were turning up in their thousands. The pictures being beamed around Australia showed near violence and people in real distress.

Tony Burke figured out what had gone wrong. The authority's work was governed by the Water Act, which charged the authority with putting a plan together that weighed the environmental, economic and social effects. To the government that meant everything had to be on the table and considered. The authority, and particularly its Chair,

Mike Taylor, had been putting the environment first, without due regard for the jobs and the people. The guide had not appropriately considered people's needs and they had responded with rage.

For hard issues on which politicians are seen to dither, it is common for a call to go up that the matter should be put in the hands of experts, people who can cut through without worrying about the election cycle. This argument has many merits but its flaw is that it is impossible for politicians to outsource political risk. The aggrieved will always lay their claims at the feet of government. So it was with the guide. People were not protesting against bureaucrats, their protests were against the government.

Tony pushed hard the government's view of what the Water Act required, even getting advice from the most senior lawyer in the country, the Solicitor General. The legal advice backed the government's view and by 7 December, Mike Taylor had resigned from his post.

But the anger in regional Australia and the damage from the loss of trust continued. Fortunately Tony Windsor's special abilities came to the fore. Tasked by Simon Crean to lead a parliamentary committee to inquire and report on the Murray-Darling Basin Plan, he did a wonderful job of reaching out, absorbing anger and getting people talking about a way through. In this work he was very well aided by his Deputy Chair, Sid Sidebottom, a dear friend of mine, deservedly known for being gentle, funny and very able. Tony Windsor's parliamentary committee reported on Thursday 2 June 2011. The government overwhelmingly accepted the ideas.

Meanwhile the indefatigable Tony Burke was organising new leadership for the authority, sourcing a more detailed scientific analysis and properly ascertaining people's needs.

The fresh scientific analysis made an appreciable difference. Rather than looking at whole river flows, the basin was analysed piece by piece to work out what was necessary to restore the river to health. Between more detailed modelling, the use of a full range of data sources and making the most of innovations and efficiencies in water management, it was shown that significant environmental gains were achievable that were compatible with better social and economic outcomes. For instance, the new basin plan could secure sufficient environmental flows with 1000 gigalitres less water than the previous plan prescribed.

Tony released a draft plan detailing this new approach on 28 November 2011. It proposed that 2750 gigalitres per year be returned to the river system over a period of seven years. While there were further intergovernmental processes to be worked through, this would be the figure.

Two political problems emerged. First and unsurprisingly, the plan disappointed those who had campaigned for higher water figures. Jay Weatherill, the Premier of South Australia, had constantly stated that to meet the needs of his state, more than 3000 gigalitres were required. In careful and productive discussions, this gap was bridged by assisting with water-saving infrastructure works in South Australia.

Second, we needed to get the plan adopted by the parliament.

To implement the plan, legislation was needed to create a special account with which to buy water. In addition, the plan would be dead if either house of parliament passed a disallowance motion. The moment had come where the Opposition had to strike and stick to one position. The easy days of different members of the Opposition taking different positions to court constituencies at odds with each other were coming to an end. Rumours swirled that there would be splits in their ranks.

In late 2012, there was a messy debate about disallowance of the plan, with three members of the Opposition in the House of Representatives voting with Bob Katter and Adam Bandt for disallowance. However the rest of the Opposition voted with the government. Fortunately reason continued to prevail and the Opposition voted with the government to get the legislation through in 2013.

For our waters, our rivers and our oceans, even in the face of the new conservative politics of protest, we succeeded. But we were also to face a major challenge with policies on our land.

OUR LAND

When I wrote out my purpose as prime minister, if I had also listed the issues I did *not* want to confront, the vexed debate about Tasmanian forests would have topped it. For me this issue was associated with

Mark Latham crashing our vote in the 2004 election. During that campaign, Mark phoned me on the eve of his announcement to end logging and protect more of Tassie's forests. Right away, I sensed it was both the wrong policy and bad for us politically. 'Don't do this, Mark,' I pleaded. But he was not to be dissuaded. The announcement proved a turning point for Mark and an unhappy election outcome followed.

From the moment of my call with Mark, I viewed the issue of Tasmania's forests as political kryptonite. I was not intending to touch it. But I was given no choice. In 2010, amazingly, the combatants in the forests wars started to lay down their arms. Given how long the industry and the unions had been fighting the environmentalists, this was a truly amazing turn of events.

The trigger for the process was the decision by Gunns, the most visible and notorious of Australian forestry operators, to exit from native-forest logging. Its new business model would be about plantation timber and the proposed pulp mill at Bell Bay, near Launceston. This change threatened to make the whole native forest industry unviable. As logging volumes collapsed, the surrounding supply chain of contractors and hauliers would go too. Not only were the livelihoods of timber employers and workers jeopardised, the Tasmanian state government-owned body, Forestry Tasmania, was vulnerable. It needed reliable contracts for wood supply and export in order to meet its state-legislated quotas. Loss of production or revenue would push its business further into the red, directly threatening the state budget.

In reality the restructuring of the forestry industry in the years before 2010 had already shaken out many of the jobs that once existed. The high Australian dollar was now heaping pressure on. Meanwhile environmental campaigning in many places around the world meant forestry products without high-level environmental certification were on the nose.

The Gunns-generated crisis, coming on top of everything else, was enough to motivate industry and the unions to stop fighting and start talking. Environmentalists too wanted a part in consensus-building. While the exit of a big private logging firm from Tasmanian forests looked like a step forward for them, it brought fresh threats to some of Australia's oldest trees and habitats. A hostile government and a desperate industry might turn to any and all customers for wood products, stripping forest and selling wood chips at rock-bottom prices and desolating the environment in the process.

First meeting in November 2010, this group of employers, unions and environmentalists tentatively came together, sensing the opportunity to end a decades-old dispute. Together they hammered out a statement of principles. Then they asked the government for help to get their discussions through to the next stage. We responded by appointing well-known former union leader Bill Kelty as an independent facilitator. The chance of achieving a bargain that lasted was emerging.

Industry needed, above all, a long-term guarantee of timber supply that would not be contested by environmentalists. That would allow businesses to proceed with certainty, knowing both that wood was available for them and that the wood taken would be certified by environmentalists as from a sustainable source. This was key to unlocking international markets.

The environmentalists wanted more areas protected from logging in the future. Specifically they sought the extension of World Heritage status to new areas, including many of the most iconic sites in Western and North-western Tasmania, like the Styx Valley and Butler's Gorge.

Impediments to consensus were evident. As a matter of practicality, as the industry struggled with its own viability, areas with mature, high-quality timber were increasingly the most profitable ones but these were also the areas that conservationists were most likely to be determined to protect. As a matter of psychology, after decades of conflict, trust was in short supply. Everyone had a war story of perfidy by the other side.

In the past, attempts to reach agreement had come to nothing and governments had stepped in and imposed an outcome. I was not going to do that. When the Kelty work was presented to us and to the Tasmanian Government, with the report then tabled in the Senate on 5 April 2011, it asked for governments to become directly involved in finalising an agreement. I recognised that we had to play a supporting role but I was not going to let the industry, unions and environmentalists off the hook. They had to shape the long-term outcome through a methodical, step-by-step, process. To facilitate this, studies were commissioned, including analysis and modelling of various scenarios for forestry and its economic, social and environmental impacts.

But time was in short supply. The industry was withering. It was vital for all parties, meaning industry, unions, environmentalists and both governments, to agree about what to do next. Should the whole process keel over, there would be mutually assured destruction: both job losses and no new environmental protections.

During the weeks after April, discussions between advisers, signatories and stakeholders intensified. I joked with both Tony Burke and Tom Bentley that they had gone to live in Tasmania.

Hoping that my very presence would be a catalyst to winding up the discussions, I arrived in Tasmania for a weekend visit on 23 July 2011. It was classic shuttle diplomacy, and I was ferried back and forth between the groups but worked intensively with Premier Lara Giddings and Deputy Premier Bryan Green. Forestry Tasmania was a committed protagonist in the conflict and was plainly a barrier to trust and commitment. It kept secret the detailed information only it had about logging schedules. This was a deliberate tactic to frustrate the negotiations.

The interim heads of agreement I signed on 24 July with the premier broke through this barrier by creating an independent verification process to report on sustainable timber supply requirements and recommend which areas to protect in permanent reserves. Professor Jonathan West, an expert trusted by all sides, would oversee that process. It also provided for a minimum volume of future wood supply of 155,000 cubic metres and a minimum protected forest area of 430,000 hectares.

Some money was made available to help those suffering as their jobs were lost or their businesses folded. In addition, resources were made available for work Simon Crean was overseeing to assist with diversifying the Tasmanian economy so there were new sources of jobs and growth. But the big money in the agreement would only flow if the parties came to a final, lasting agreement.

On 7 August, I was back in Tasmania to sign a more detailed interim agreement, one that built on the 24 July document. In this agreement, the commitment to protect 430,000 hectares from logging was expressed more firmly. I accepted that holding the environmentalists in the process required giving them greater certainty. Some industry representatives within the talks acknowledged that too but others inside and outside the negotiations went on the attack.

Bob Brown sensed a political opportunity. He had criticised the interim agreement basically because he had no significant role in negotiating it. The environmental groups involved and the state-based Greens members of parliament were not jumping to his command. Now that industry was agitated, Bob went out and praised the agreement and thereby incensed industry even more.

Accusations followed that Lara and I had capitulated to political pressure from him. Nothing could have been further from the truth. Instead, the episode demonstrated how players on both sides of the argument, including those who had not played a direct role in creating the outcome, were trying to use it to maximise their own political positions. This was most certainly true of the federal and state Liberals, who were trying to pretend nothing in the world had changed and any issue with forestry only arose because of Labor meddling.

Fortunately, during this difficult period, significant industry players – some of the last remaining employers of forestry workers – indicated their determination to see the agreement work. These businesses understood that the timber industry in Tasmania genuinely hung by a thread because of the new requirements in international markets to show that timber had high-level environmental accreditation, a visible demonstration that the wood was sourced in a way that was conflict-free. The intervention of these businesses helped rebalance the process and kept it moving.

But then came a bombshell.

Professor Jonathan West's verification report, released on 23 March 2012, came as a brutal shock to all. Almost everything anyone believed about forestry in Tasmania turned out to be wrong. Previously employers, union officials, environmentalists all had at the tip of their tongue commonly understood figures about how many coupes of trees – a coupe being the area foreseen for harvesting in a particular year – were potentially available for logging. The dispute was about how they were to be divided between forestry and conservation. It was now revealed that Forestry Tasmania had been fudging the figures. This state government agency had effectively gone rogue and over-committed in contracts. Even in a no-change scenario, Forestry Tasmania had sold the right to harvest more wood than was really available.

For everyone who had spent so much time and energy blueing about how to slice the pie, it was devastating to find out the pie was actually smaller. This created a crisis of confidence for the process and forced the local politics back into a negative cycle of blame and recrimination. It put the state government in a difficult position because it owned Forestry Tasmania. Jonathan West came under attack in a stereotypical case of shoot the messenger.

Miraculously the commitment by the signatories to the agreement to negotiating an outcome did not evaporate. Rightly Tony Burke insisted that governments would not impose an outcome as that would only lead to failure of the agreement; previous agreements had failed that way. At every stage I was saying amen to that approach.

Negotiations dragged on as the parties bargained about the reduced number of coupes. Finally, just when agreement seemed close, Forestry Tasmania updated its data to show that even less wood was available. The industry, unions and environmentalists absorbed this second blow and persisted.

But by 10 August 2012, an impasse had been reached over whether conservation groups could give up any more forest areas for protection or industry groups could give up any greater volume of secure supply. Tony Burke, Bryan Green, advisers and signatories worked through the night to find a way to rescue the agreement. In the early hours of the morning, both sides signalled their willingness to shift further but it was not going to happen soon. Ministers Burke and Green later announced to waiting media that an agreement could still be weeks away. The work continued and came back to an impasse, once again over the gap between volume of supply and reserve area.

On 27 October 2012, after another deadline failed to bring agreement, Tony Burke stated publicly that he was now deeply pessimistic about the prospects of an agreement. He added that this time, in the face of unresolved conflict, the federal government was not going to impose an outcome and thereby allow any of the participants to escape responsibility for its impact. Neither was the federal government going to fund an open-ended subsidy to the timber industry.

The statement sent a shock through the players, particularly the different industry players, who were struggling to find a common position. Realising all government assistance could be lost was the circuit-breaker, and a fresh compromise was brokered. It was based on 137,000 hectares of guaranteed sawlog supply and 395,000 hectares of forest protection. If the rest of the agreement was successfully implemented, more areas would be reserved in the future.

On 22 November, the 11 signatory organisations signed up to this deal. What many would have thought was impossible, an accord between industry and environmentalists on logging in Tasmania, had been achieved. Much of the credit for this achievement needs to be given to Jane Calvert, the leader of the Forestry Workers Union. I have known her a long time. She is smart and principled, passionate about protecting workers and their jobs; she commands respect. She used those characteristics to hold the negotiations together. Don Henry, the Chief Executive Officer of the Australian Conservation Foundation, also showed resolve and the ability to forge a common position across disparate environmental groups. Amended legislation, which enacted the signed agreement, passed the lower house of the Tasmanian Parliament. That left one last hurdle, the unpredictable upper house of the Tasmanian parliament.

The 15 members of this chamber are mostly independent, not subject to any party line. Many wanted to play politics and pretend to those fearful of change that they could stop it happening. This was an act of cruelty because life would never again go on as it had in the past, even if the legislation failed.

Frantic preparation, advocacy and discussion ensued and former adversaries from the forestry conflict combined forces to seek ways to persuade a majority of the upper house that it was in the community's interest to end the conflict with this deal.

It came agonisingly close, but fell short of a majority by one vote. Instead the legislative council referred the whole package to committee to examine it again in the year of 2013, thus avoiding having to make a decision and creating fresh opportunities for opponents to continue attacking the deal.

Throughout the process, Tasmanian federal Labor MPs remained steadfast and conscientious in supporting the need for an agreement and seeking to reflect and represent the needs of their electorates. This was particularly difficult for Sid Sidebottom and Dick Adams, whose electorates included many local people who depended on forestry and wrongly thought change would go away if the agreement failed. Their courage in doing so became clear when the campaign against the agreement became a factor in Dick and Sid losing their seats in September 2013.

Finally, on 30 April 2013, the Legislative Council passed amended legislation supporting the agreement. The amendment made the creation of full reserves conditional on the industry achieving Forestry Stewardship Council certification, the necessary environmental certification to access international markets.

The legislation was condemned by Green politicians, including Bob Brown and Christine Milne, but that had no impact.

In a sign of the growing importance of the agreement to the industry's future, the Chair of Forestry Tasmania made a strong statement of commitment to ceasing logging inside the newly nominated World Heritage areas. On 24 June 2013, the World Heritage Committee placed 170,000 hectares of forest under World Heritage Protection. In late August 2013, the Tasmanian Legislative Council voted nine to five to support the passage of a reserve order to formalise the protection of the extended World Heritage Area.

During all of this work, the Liberal and National parties played the role of saboteur. It is a credit to all those involved in the process of agreeing and legislating change in forestry in Tasmania that they did not buckle under this pressure. Premier Giddings and Deputy Premier Green showed great fortitude.

Without Tony Burke's outstanding input, all the effort would have come to nought. He has a fine mind for policy and a knack for bringing out the best in people.

In the vital areas of climate change, water, marine protection and forestry, our government pursued needed, constructive reforms while the conservative side of Australian politics became the worst kind of protest politicians, those full of complaint and bereft of real answers.

21

Caring for each other

'What the image shows, for me, is a real connection between two people – my daughter and the former PM. You see, Sophie has a radar for people. She doesn't discriminate. She can tell whether or not they're being genuine with her; if they are she loves them right back. That's what this picture is all about.'

THE FATHER OF SOPHIE DEANE, TALKING ABOUT THE
PHOTO SOPHIE TOOK OF ME. SOPHIE IS A YOUNG GIRL,
A KEEN PHOTOGRAPHER, WHO HAS BUT IS NOT
DEFINED BY HER DOWN SYNDROME

I FEEL LIKE I GREW UP WITHIN AUSTRALIA'S HEALTH SYSTEM – not that I was unwell. Once our family moved from the cold climate of Wales to the hot climate of South Australia, there was no bad recurrence of my previous respiratory issues. What I mean is that Mum and Dad worked within the healthcare system and I was immersed in the stories and experiences of both of them.

Mum was a cook at Sunset Lodge Eventide Home, a Salvation Army-run aged-care facility for women. She prepared afternoon tea and cooked the evening meal for the around 80 women who ate in the central dining room. The infant school I attended was on the same major road, Unley Road, and the primary school I later enrolled in was within walking distance. Mum arranged with the Salvation Army brigadier who ran Sunset Lodge to slip out and collect Alison and me from school each afternoon. We would hang out at Sunset Lodge until Mum finished work in the early evening and then go home.

There is a three-year age difference between Alison and me and once she was old enough, she was allowed to go home by herself. Many afternoons, I'd sit on one of those stools that doubled as a set of steps for getting things off high shelves and read while Mum worked. But those afternoons were also times of fun and learning. Being migrants, we had no extended family in Australia, no grandparents, no aunts or uncles or cousins, and the women of Sunset Lodge – many of whom were active, hale and hearty – became substitute grandmothers. As a child I always had women making a fuss of me, reading to me, helping me colour in, playing cat's cradle, helping me knit.

It seems unimaginable now but women moved into Sunset Lodge when they were still very able-bodied. Some had cars and drove. A number lived at Sunset Lodge for more than a decade. As a teenager, I returned to Sunset Lodge for my first part-time job: setting the tables for the evening meal and helping serve the food. On Saturday mornings, I spent three hours peeling vegetables. I was proud of the little yellow pay packet that contained my meagre weekly earnings.

I didn't often go to Glenside Hospital, where Dad worked for well over two decades, but constantly heard stories about it – and witnessed it change. It opened its doors to the mentally ill in 1846 and once, while looking for something at the back of a cupboard in one of the oldest sections, Dad found a pair of thumb screws! By Dad's day, the treatment of mental illness had come a long way from those horrors but change was still needed.

The job advertisement Dad responded to invited applications from people who wanted to be either prison guards or psychiatric nurses. The jobs overlapped because Glenside had a secure ward for criminals with mental illness. When working there, in Z ward, Dad had access to a firearm.

Dad had previously carried a gun – he'd been a night-time security guard at the head office of the Savings Bank of South Australia. With it, he was issued with a single bullet. One of his standard jokes was that if ever confronted by a gang of bank robbers in the dead of night, he would have shot one, thrown the gun at the second and then run. Fortunately no such dramatic incident ever occurred.

With every passing year, the hospital became less regimented and more open. When Dad first started, he was issued with a suit as his uniform, to be worn with a shirt and special tie. The colour of the tie designated what level nurse you were. By the time Dad left, he was wearing casual pants and a T-shirt to work. The locks had gone too, and when we went to pick Dad up, it was impossible to tell by looking who was a doctor, who was a nurse and who was a patient.

In the era before deinstitutionalisation, Glenside was home to people with Down syndrome and intellectual disabilities. A few times, as children, Alison and I joined in ward parties where we would play games like chasey or hide-and-seek with residents 20 or more years older than us.

As a consequence of these experiences, I grew up with no real fear of difference. I do not pretend some special virtue and was not above using the standard schoolyard taunts of my era. But if confronted by someone with an intellectual or physical disability, I never felt fear or the need to look away, which I know is a common reaction.

Working in government on creating the NDIS, improving all of health care but particularly aged care and mental health, felt like coming full circle.

BETTER CARING – DISABILITY

I still cannot explain where the tears came from. On 15 May 2013, as I prepared to go into the House of Representatives chamber to introduce the bill to increase the Medicare levy and partially fund our new way of supporting people with disabilities, I felt businesslike. I knew it was a big day, one with a real sense of achievement attached to it.

Parliamentary days offer little quiet; neither is there time for reflection. There is always the next thing to do and then the next.

Until I rose to speak, I had been in work mode, getting things done. Then it hit me. A wave of unforeseen emotion. A wave that brought with it unasked for tears.

I struggled to keep going with the speech, to not dissolve further.

It is so unlike me.

414

Wayne teased me when I sat down after finishing the speech, saying he would have had his money on Jenny Macklin crying, not me. A deeply caring person, tears spring readily to Jenny's eyes. If anything, I am known for being at the other end of the spectrum: the woman made of titanium, hard as nails. As prime minister, the cladding, the ability to hold emotions at bay and get on with it was an asset. But on this occasion, feeling deeply, crying easily and getting on with it were all one and the same thing.

Our nation needed this moment of change, this new way of embracing people with disability. It was worth shedding a tear for and it had certainly been worth fighting for. And a fight it was. Predominantly a fight against political stasis.

For decades better support for people with disabilities had been one of those issues where politicians all said something sympathetic but the profound reform job remained undone. There was always something more urgent, more politically pressing, apparently more important.

Projections are that 2.3 million Australians will have a high level of disability by 2030. Any one of us could be among that number. An accident, a degenerative illness is all it takes.

Our nation and our people have long been held in a vice of rising need and a failing system. Despite the investment of more financial resources by state and federal governments, Australians with disabilities and those who cared for them found themselves without the help they needed.

In the words of the 'Shut Out' report put together by the National People with Disabilities and Carer Council in 2009:

The disability service system was characterised as broken and broke, chronically under-funded and under-resourced, crisis driven, struggling against a vast tide of unmet need. Services were unavailable or infrequent, unaffordable or of such poor quality as to be of little benefit. Respondents felt that more effort went into rationing services than improving them. Many said that the system is characterised by a one-size-fits-all approach that offers very little choice or flexibility. Programs and services were built around organisational and system needs rather than the needs of clients. In a democratic country as wealthy as Australia, many found it absolutely unacceptable that they are unable to access the support and services required to achieve even a basic quality of life.

In the lives of people with disability this was experienced as a sense of pain and neglect. The child who could not get access to services and therapies that could maximise their abilities for the future. The teenager, moving from childhood to adulthood, stuck with a package of assistance that did not respond to their needs. The adult who could not work without the availability of support services. The parents who feared death, not for themselves, but because no one would be left behind to care for their adult son or daughter with a disability.

As a local member of parliament, it was common to find desperate families banging on the door of your office, needing respite, needing help. One of my staff members, Myra Geddes, who had worked in the office of a state minister responsible for disability services, told harrowing stories of mums and dads leaving their child at local disability support offices or not collecting them from respite services because the parents were on the brink of breaking down and needed recovery time.

Against this background of bubbling community anxiety, it is unsurprising that creating a new approach, an NDIS, was one of the ideas discussed at the 2020 Summit, held in the first year of the Rudd Government. Not that the concept was newly conceived at the summit: plenty of advocates had spent years campaigning for change.

The case in essence was a simple one. Someone who acquired a disability through a motor vehicle or at work would be covered by one of the state-based public insurance schemes. That person would have options and choices about their care. The insurance scheme would meet the costs of all necessary reasonable support. People in these schemes would not be told things like, *The only time someone can come to assist you to shower and dress is late in the afternoon, a couple of times a week.* Or, *Sorry, but there is no more funding and you have missed out on the care you need.* Yet people born with a disability or who acquired it during their life in circumstances where there was no insurer, frequently heard such disheartening words.

Advocates rightly said that no matter how a person gets a disability, our nation should ensure that there is a funding body that conducts itself like the best of the insurance bodies and flexibly, fully meets needs. Yes it was a persuasive argument, a simple concept. But to make it happen was big, complex, costly and nation-changing. Nevertheless, as a government, we shifted it from the too-hard basket into the in-tray and then got it done.

A number of things had to converge. There needed to be an agitator within government who harried people into seriously thinking about the proposal. Bill Shorten was that person. He became the Parliamentary Secretary for Disabilities and Children's Services on his election to parliament in 2007.

I have known Bill for years. When I was a partner at Slater & Gordon, I used to do the first-round interviews for articled clerks. Victoria had an article-clerk interviewing season. Applications would come and firms would compete for the best of the potential articled clerks as the articled clerks competed for the best of the jobs. Bill applied to Slater & Gordon.

Even before the interview, I knew of Bill as an up-and-comer in the Right faction of Young Labor. Because Slater & Gordon was more closely aligned with the Left, I asked Bill why he had applied. He explained his tendency to do the opposite of what people expected. Because everyone in Young Labor expected the victorious activists to be from the Left, he had taken the less expected course, joined the Right and still come to dominate. He seemed attracted to doing the same in his preference for law firms.

I enjoyed his cheeky demeanour, was impressed with the spirit of endeavour that seemed deeply ingrained in him and said in the interview, 'We should offer you a job.' Bill later took up a place with Maurice Blackburn, a law firm more traditionally associated with the Right. This time, the more conventional approach appealed to him. Mercifully all of this factional labelling of law firms has since broken down. It was always pretty silly.

On his entry into parliamentary politics, Bill was surprised to be made Parliamentary Secretary for Disabilities and Children's Services, areas in which he had no real prior experience. He came to see me, unsure what to make of it. I said it was an opportunity to develop new skills and show another side of himself. Everyone knew he could win through in factional politics, everyone knew he had legal skills, an understanding of the economy and labour law. Now he could show his abilities at something beyond the stereotype.

Bill did more than I was urging. He actually fell in love with the policy area and the possibility of making change for so many Australians leading such difficult lives. His passion and enthusiasm brought the need to do the big reform to the centre of the government's thinking.

At the 2010 election campaign it was a pleasure and a privilege to meet with hundreds of people with disabilities and their carers to announce a re-elected Labor government would move to the next stage and ask the well-respected Productivity Commission to report on how an NDIS could be created. At this time, as Bill's ministerial career took him in other directions, the proposal needed a seasoned minister with the intellectual capacity to make change happen. Jenny Macklin stepped up and shepherded the idea into a start-up, putting in hundreds of hours of the most disciplined and thoughtful work. Jenny has few rivals when it comes to public policy capacity and she drove the proposal home.

Our first task as a re-elected government was to make good on our election promise and have the Productivity Commission report. The terms of reference for the inquiry were issued in February 2010.

The Productivity Commission grew out of a body called the Industry Commission, established in 1990 to provide the government of the day with independent expert reports on matters of importance to the nation. In practice, if something is running big in the media and a government is uncertain what to do about it, announcing the matter has been referred to the Productivity Commission can be enough of a response to get the government through the media cycle. When the report comes out months, sometimes years, later, it can be quietly shelved.

Promising a Productivity Commission inquiry is also a staple for an Opposition. It means all they need is a few policy platitudes and that commitment to appear determined to act.

But our reference was not this kind of political manoeuvre. We genuinely wanted to get to grips with how to build a better system.

On 31 July 2011 we received the report and I released it on 10 August. The Productivity Commission had provided a rigorous, detailed examination of the unmet need and the type of national scheme that could work best. Now came the most difficult aspects of making the scheme a reality: designing it right so it provided individual support over a lifetime, based on the costs of care, and getting it agreed, implemented and funded with states and territories.

The Productivity Commission did not even try to identify how the scheme should be financed, suggesting only that the funding could come from general revenue. In releasing the report, having investigated an NDIS, I promised we would have one.

The commitment I made was for a change that would require agreement with all the states and territories. A commitment that would require every government to put in more money. A commitment to build the biggest way of responding to need since Medicare. There was understandable nervousness internally on taking on such a big challenge when we would also be changing forever the ways schools were funded. Both would be colossal new expenditure items at a time of constrained revenue. There was a strand of thought that we should choose one and shelve the other.

I was never prepared to choose. Our nation needed both, and while it would require hard budgetary savings, our nation could afford both. Budgets are about choices. I was prepared to face judgement as a prime minister, as a government, on the hard choices we would make to put our children's education first and to treat people with disabilities decently.

We not only decided to act but to act quickly. On 30 April 2012, Jenny Macklin and I announced that the NDIS would launch in 2013, a year ahead of the timetable recommended by the Productivity Commission, in up to four launch sites. In the 2012 budget we committed $1 billion to the launch of the NDIS in a limited number of sites.

This added momentum to the negotiation with state and territory governments about the full roll-out of the scheme. By this stage, my COAG experiences had proven the adage that work expands to fill the time available. Create a deadline and the system can move quickly. Give the system years, and years will be taken. Apart from a deadline, a great motivator is competition. Specifying that there were a limited number of launch sites was meant to spark some competitive tension about who would get a launch site and who would miss out.

Now having fired the starting pistol and mustered the determination to win through in the hard world of commonwealth–state negotiations, to guard against potential failure we needed momentum for change from the community. State leaders had to feel political skin was at risk. The vital final ingredient that made an NDIS possible was the new professionalism of the disability sector in its approach to campaigning.

The sector has always had its earnest advocates, doing their best to influence decision-makers. What Bill Shorten understood was the high degree of power the sector could wield if it came together and really flexed its campaign muscle. During his time as parliamentary secretary, he had spoken frankly to the sector about this, galvanising it. That latent power became increasingly well understood by advocates and under the leadership of a seasoned campaigner, former NSW Labor politician John Della Bosca, it came alive in the Every Australian Counts campaign, launched in January 2011.

The campaign, assisted by Jenny, organised photo opportunities with political leaders and children with disabilities. Premiers and chief ministers participated in one such photo opportunity on the way into a COAG meeting. Inside, Victorian Premier Ted Baillieu remarked to me such events only increased expectations. I thought, *Exactly. That's why we are going to keep corralling you into them.*

When COAG met on 25 July, after our $1 billion budget announcement, agreements needed to be struck for sites. Unless we could secure a trial in a major geographic site, and with the participation of one of the bigger states, the NDIS could be viewed both politically and organisationally as a failure. The Labor states of South Australia and Tasmania agreed to launch arrangements for children and teenagers, and the ACT Labor leader agreed to a geographic launch site.

But the politics with the conservative states was gridlocked. I needed to get an agreement from one or both of the two conservative states most likely to sign on, New South Wales and Victoria. Barry O'Farrell and Ted Baillieu had created a big conservative states pact. Intent on sticking together, both refused to meet the financial benchmarks I was outlining for participating in a launch site, benchmarks consistent with those agreed in South Australia, Tasmania and the Australian Capital Territory.

As the COAG meeting became bogged down, I invited both of them to my office and outlined the deal again and gave my analysis of the politics. From Barry's eyes, I sensed he got the political problem coming his way. If he did not sign up for a launch site that day, he would be publicly positioned as heartless in the face of the needs of people with disabilities. Ted could not read the politics; he was obsessed by the detail. He kept bringing me back to a diagram he had drawn about aspects of the funding. As the discussion dragged on, Barry was increasingly moving uncomfortably in his chair. But Barry kept his word and stuck with Ted. New South Wales and Victoria left COAG having not signed on for a launch site.

Together Jenny and I waged war about their failure, describing it as letting politics get in the way of helping people with a disability. Within a few days, the resistance crumbled. Both Barry and Ted agreed to sign on for geographic launch sites – in the Hunter region in New South Wales and the Barwon region in Victoria.

On 29 November 2012, I introduced into parliament, dry-eyed, the NDIS bill, which created the framework for the launch and set out eligibility criteria.

As 2012 drew to a political close, Barry O'Farrell was locked in negotiations to be the first state to sign on for the full scheme. He had lived through the adverse consequences of holding hands with Victoria and was not intending to do so again. Rather he was positioning for the political prize of being the first mover. Barry's attitude meant doing the deal was full of technical and financial, but not political, complexity. He and I were able to announce we had reached agreement on 6 December 2012.

At the COAG meeting that followed there was a certain conservative state coolness to Barry. Everyone knew that the most populous state in the nation signing on meant the only way this was going to end was with everyone signing on. All that remained was the order of sign-up and the various arguments put to try and explain any delay in doing so. Each subsequent agreement felt to me like a victory. Every time, I had another opportunity to celebrate with people with disabilities.

But the problem of finding the money was as hard as the negotiations, in many ways harder.

On the eve of every Canberra COAG meeting, the prime minister hosts a dinner for state and territory leaders. Over its life, COAG has met in other parts of the country. Deliberately I stopped this and held the meetings in Canberra: there is a reason footy teams prefer to play at home. I was not about to surrender the home-ground advantage. It also ensured I could host the dinner at The Lodge.

At COAG dinners, I am told, John Howard liked to talk cricket. Instead, with only the leaders in the room, I preferred to talk frankly about the hard issues and complex politics. Bringing together leaders for an intimate dinner, when you are from different political parties and have often been at each other's throats, can be awkward. But at its best, people took the opportunity to leave some of their party politics at the door and get to know each other as people. The observed convention was that the discussions were confidential.

Political leaders are often not the best with punctuality. Packed diaries, media commitments, dozens of calls to return – leaders tended to drift in over the course of half an hour. As their car pulled up on the gravel driveway, I would greet the arrival at the front door of The Lodge, usher them in through the green- and glass-paned wooden doors and ask them to sign the visitors' book.

Had we not confined our dog, Reuben, out the back, he would have assisted me in welcoming the guests. He had learnt that when a particular bell sounded, a car was approaching, and would bolt to the door, tail wagging furiously. On a few celebrated occasions, Reuben found a way through to the dining room and went on to test which visiting dignitary was soft enough to give him a tidbit.

After the entry welcome was done, I would have leaders gather in what is called the morning room to stand and mingle. When the complement was assembled, I would invite everyone to the dining room, which as a matter of tradition is resplendent with 'PM'-inscribed everything.

PM is decoratively carved into the back of the dining chairs, it is etched into the glasses, it is imprinted on the crockery and on the place mats. A three-course dinner would then be served, with the serious discussions tending to start after main course and continue through dessert. Irrespective of any political heat and rancour, at the end of dinners, premiers and chief ministers often asked me to sign the formal menu card for them as a keepsake. The more enthusiastic would have everyone at the dinner sign their menu card.

At dinner prior to the COAG meeting on 25 July 2012, Queensland's Campbell Newman made the suggestion that everyone at COAG should back me to raise a levy on income to pay for the full cost of the NDIS. For all levels of government, revenue was tight and the long-range costs of improving schools and disability care were formidable. It was rational to look for new revenue sources. It was also smart to try to get the federal government to foot the whole bill. Some of the Labor premiers made approving noises about Campbell's suggestions. Tellingly Barry and Ted effectively sat the discussion out.

Campbell compared his proposal to the levy I had struck to help finance the rebuilding of Queensland after the devastating natural disasters. It was not a good example of an appeal for a nonpartisan accord. Tony Abbott had ferociously opposed the levy. Shock-jock rantings chorused that if I could not get it through, it was the end of my government. It had played into the ongoing instability image about the government, even though I assembled the votes and it was passed.

Nothing about this discussion solved the issue of money. From the moment Campbell started to speak, I smelt a rat. I thought a political game was being played, rather than a genuine offer being made. I talked about how the premiers' agreement would not carry the Opposition and it would end up being as partisan an issue as far too many others.

On the following Saturday, my suspicion was confirmed when Peter Van Onselen, writing for *The Australian*, not only had chapter and verse of this discussion but also details of what was served for dinner at The Lodge. That was the last time menu cards were placed on the table for COAG dinners.

At this point, the Tony Abbott-led Opposition was being bipartisan about creating an NDIS, which we renamed Disability Care. However, the Opposition made no contribution to the policy discussion. Its only suggestion was to establish a bipartisan parliamentary committee to oversee the scheme. It was a clever ploy because it sounded nice but it would never work in practice. A parliamentary committee could never manage the intergovernmental negotiations to establish the scheme and the hard task of financing it. My expectation was that bipartisanship would continue to be Abbott's pledge on the benefits of the scheme, but that the Opposition could well go sharply partisan on the ways of funding it.

At the time of this COAG dinner, my intention was to fund the federal government's share of the new money necessary for Disability Care through savings in other policy areas. Although it would be painful and hard, I thought it was doable. I also wanted to avoid the political liability that would come from advocating another tax. The government was already in the most bloody of fights about what was generally referred to as the carbon tax and the minerals resource rent tax. I imagined a new tax for disability would become the next frontier for the Opposition's hard campaigning.

However as revenue continued to get downgraded, it was apparent that the government could not responsibly fund the NDIS and schools in the long term without a new revenue source. After much discussion, a simple increase in the Medicare levy to provide a stream of funding for disability services was determined to be the best way to go. Politically I was wary of being seen to have backflipped and to be striking a new tax. To get through the politics, I announced the extension to the Medicare levy and said I would seek a mandate for it at the next election. Then I braced myself for the next iteration of Tony Abbott's 'great big new tax' slogan.

To my surprise, he challenged me on 1 May 2013, shortly after my announcement, to bring the legislation to parliament immediately. Bizarrely, having yelled at me across the parliament – so many times that I had lost count – that I was dishonest or toxic or both because I would not immediately go to an election on the 'carbon tax', on this occasion Tony Abbott decided no election was necessary. It was obvious by this stage that the Opposition was in major difficulties with its own budget position. It was determined to use the language of budget emergency but had no plan for big savings, indeed repudiating many of ours. It was also spurning the revenue from carbon pricing but had conceded by this stage that it would keep much of the expenditure. Clearly a speedy calculation was made within the Opposition that it was better to forgo another scare campaign and see the revenue from the levy flow in than make its bad budget position worse.

So after Tony Abbott challenged me about the increase to the Medicare levy with the words, 'Now, if she's fair dinkum, why not do it in this parliament? We've got a month of parliament left after budget week, why not get the legislation into the parliament, deal with it in this parliament, so then we can get on with the job of building the kind of National Disability Insurance Scheme that all Australians would like to see?'[1]

My response was, 'If the Leader of the Opposition is prepared to support this half-a-per-cent increase in the Medicare levy to fund Disability Care, then I will bring this legislation into parliament immediately.'[2]

One day later, Tony Abbott offered conditional support on the basis that the increase in the levy would not be permanent and would be removed once the budget was back into strong surplus and the policy could be funded without it; a small political twist to complete the agreement with me while preserving his argument about Labor and taxes.

With our strong savings and the now agreed increase in the Medicare levy, the hard task of funding Disability Care was done.

Throughout the wrangling, I did not learn anything new about politics. The COAG negotiations and the public campaigning went very much in accordance with my expectations. Campbell Newman's leaking and positioning, while distasteful, was in keeping with the political tactics I saw played out around me so often.

What I did learn, or perhaps more accurately what I was reminded of, all those years after my experiences in Glenside, was the dignity and courage of Australians with disability.

The joy of children like Sophie, who took my photo in Melbourne, or Sandy, who gave me a card in Queensland.

The unbelievable capacity for love that drives the parents who care for sons and daughters who cannot communicate, or walk, or do all the things they thought would be natural and inevitably learnt by their child.

The love given to the teenage boy who cares for his mother and sister but kicks them when his inability to communicate drives him from frustration to anger.

The love lavished by a dad on his daughter, an adult woman, always at risk because her childlike wonder means she hugs and kisses strangers.

The fact that some tears, in the most unusual of circumstances, are really happy tears.

BETTER CARING – MENTAL HEALTH, AGED CARE AND DENTAL CARE

In conceiving and creating Disability Care, we proudly made history. But it was not the only area in which history was calling. In Opposition, I served for an extended period as Shadow Minister for Health. With my father's work in my mind, I spent many of those days in Opposition thinking about what could be done to improve mental health care.

Since Dad's nursing days, the entire world had changed in the field of mental health. Deinstitutionalisation had taken people from lives of seclusion and regimentation back into the community. Unfortunately a policy with the right intentions had not been backed with the right resources and for too many, this newfound freedom translated into days whiled away in decrepit and unsafe rooming houses. For too many families, the stress of care was beyond them. Many of these problems would be targeted by Disability Care, and the record investments the Rudd Government had made in addressing homelessness were also helping.

The science of mental health care was changing too. It was becoming clearer that many of the most profound mental illnesses have their onset in adolescence or young adulthood. If intensive treatment could be provided in this period, then it could make a difference for all of the rest of life.

Suicide statistics continued to be depressingly high. Clusters of youth suicides – the heartbreaking instances when, in a particular area, suicide seemed to be catching – saddened and puzzled.

In this period, I came to know Pat McGorry, later named Australian of the Year. A brilliant mental health practitioner and advocate, he had developed some world-leading models of care. Heartbreakingly his approach was being taken up with more alacrity around the world than in Australia.

Something had also changed in the community's approach to mental health. For many years, mental illness had been viewed as shameful. People would not speak of their own mental wellbeing. The families of the mentally ill would come up with a cover story about what was wrong with their loved one. Physical illness was viewed as an act of God, with no blame attaching. Mental illness was viewed as evidence of personal failure, of a lack of self-discipline. But mental illness was moving out of the shadows into the mainstream. It was both pleasing and surprising, in the community meetings I would conduct as Shadow Minister for Health, how often someone would raise their hand and then speak frankly about their own battle with mental illness.

Out of these experiences, I distilled a mental health policy for launch during the 2004 election campaign. It was the first time a party contending for government had had a specific mental health policy launch, with a day's media of the campaign directed towards it. On 28 September 2004, I brought Dad to the Adelaide launch of the mental health policy. He was behind the scenes with me in the preparation meetings for the event with Mark Latham; John Faulkner, who was on the road with Mark; and media and policy advisers.

A few days later, the Howard Government also announced a policy, making the 2004 campaign a turning point in how political parties approached mental health.

But while we were in government, there remained much to do to meet need. The Rudd Government started delivering the two types of facility integral to the McGorry approach. One was called headspace, and consisted of centres which created a welcoming and supportive environment for young people with concerns about their mental wellbeing. In tight budget circumstances, in the 2010 election campaign

I released another mental health policy, which included an announcement of the locations for ten more headspace sites. However the landmark feature of the policy was not this incremental progress but a $277 million investment in suicide prevention, which included support for Lifeline. This amazing volunteer-based organisation provides a sympathetic ear and the support necessary to talk people in absolute crisis out of killing themselves. By this stage the Opposition had also embraced the McGorry model. With no pressure for their budget numbers to add up, their election promise was financially larger.

After forming minority government, I was determined that in my first budget as prime minister, the nation would take a big leap forward on mental health. The government, heavily relying on the work of the Minister for Mental Health, Mark Butler, delivered a $2.2 billion package. Among a range of new services, we brought funding up to include 90 headspace centres and we funded twelve of the second type of facility that is key to McGorry's approach. These are the Early Psychosis Prevention and Intervention Centres for young people with intense mental health needs.

Budget discipline meant closing an underperforming program and directing the more than half a billion dollars of savings to these more effective new services. Inevitably that caused a kickback but our policy was taking the nation in the right direction.

Dad was very pleased to see the budget announcements. Even as he drew towards the end of his long life, he still cared about helping the mentally ill.

Twelve months later, Mark Butler also generated a package of aged care reforms.

Aged care had well and truly been relegated to the too-hard basket. Everyone knew the system was desperately in need of reform. Everyone involved in politics also knew it was a perilous policy area and any proposed change easily generates swift protests and hard-fought battles. The Howard Government had floundered in the reform of aged care because the politics was too tough.

Understandably, given the risks, the Productivity Commission was used to guide reform. The inquiry initiated during Kevin Rudd's leadership was delivered under mine in August 2011.

Politically difficult solutions were found by the Commission for hard reform questions. The aged-care sector was not keeping up with growth in demand, offering limited choices for older Australians and finding it hard to attract a qualified and steady workforce.

Mark worked patiently to build an agenda for change. In April 2011, the government announced the modernisation of aged care with a suite of measures that did not put a substantial new impost on the budget and taxpayers.

While the final package settled upon required individuals to make more of a contribution to the costs of being cared for in their old age, the politics did not explode on us. Partly it was because the package was cleverly designed, with a fair means test and a cap on how much anyone would be required to contribute in a lifetime. The political hot button issue of the treatment of the family home was sidestepped: its value was excluded from the means test.

Partly it was because everyone in the sector now knew the status quo was broken, people were ready for change.

Partly, I suspect, it was because the package was launched on Friday 20 April 2012 and on the following day the James Ashby allegations against Peter Slipper exploded in the *Daily Telegraph*.[3] The Opposition had its guns trained on Peter Slipper and through him, the government, rather than on the aged care package.

The benefits of the package were also tangible. We increased the number of care packages available, to help more people get care in their homes and in residential aged care. We enabled people to have more choice about the kind of care they received than ever before. At that pressurised point in a family's life, when it is time to confront an older relative moving into care, we gave families more time to make decisions and different ways of making payments.

There are few things harder than watching your mother or father go from being strong and vibrant to confused and frail. Everything about it hurts. Nothing government can do can ease that. But we did make choices about care wider and the process easier.

As prime minister, I went back to Sunset Lodge. I talked to both staff and residents. For those who devote so much time and attention to caring for our elderly, we entered an aged-care workforce compact to better pay and support them.

When I met with the residents, it was abundantly clear that while parts of Sunset Lodge looked the same as in my childhood, the clientele is very different. So much more in need of personal care. For the generations to come of older Australians, who will need help, we made a difference.

When I was Shadow Minister for Health, one of the main things I talked about around Australia was dental care, both a rich and poor cousin of our health-care system. Anyone my age, like me, has gruesome stories to tell about fillings cracking, root canal work and implants. I am glad that children today grow up with far better teeth thanks to fluoridation and better care.

When my friends and I swap colourful dentist-chair stories, the complaining is just as likely to be about the cost as the pain. While we can afford it, millions of Australians cannot. As Shadow Health Minister, I found myself inspecting the mouths of many pensioners in need of dental care, who really wanted me to understand the problem.

The Howard Government hit those reliant on public dental care hard when it abolished the Commonwealth Dental Health Program, making dental health services solely the responsibility of state and territory governments. As a Labor government, we restored this payment.

But I am pleased that under my leadership we did more. Tanya Plibersek oversaw a blitz to clear waiting lists and worked hard to come to an agreement with the Greens on new ways of supporting dental care. Once again, money was redirected from a Liberal government-designed scheme which was under-performing, to a better approach for children and those in real need.

HEALTH REFORM TO LAST

In each of these reform areas, we were guided by a Labor approach that bears all the hallmarks of Hawke and Keating. A ruthlessness about cutting under-delivering programs in order to put money into more effective approaches. A preparedness to means-test and target where necessary, for example our means-testing of one of the fastest growing areas of health expenditure, the private health insurance rebate. A focus on properly functioning markets. Compassion for those most in need. An understanding that caring for each other is the obligation of each of us.

But my need to engage with the complex question of health reform went further and deeper. I inherited from Kevin health agreements that were not going to last. In Opposition, Kevin had astutely identified that people wanted big changes in health. The most visible face of that was the seemingly perpetual problems in hospitals. The overcrowded emergency waiting rooms. The delays for elective surgery. The so-called and cruelly described bed blockers, meaning older Australians who ended up staying in a hospital bed because there was nowhere else for them to go.

As Shadow Minister for Health I had considered all these issues. The years of the Howard Government were characterised by the aggressive promotion of private health insurance and a declining federal government share of hospital funding. That meant, compared to need, there was scant money to support hospitals. Dramatically it also meant a long-term viability problem for state governments. As health-care costs continued to grow and the share picked up by the federal government fell, states increasingly shouldered the burden. With the expenditure needed in health growing faster than state revenue, fast-forward the clock a couple of decades and entire state government budgets would be consumed by funding health care. Forget about having police forces or schools. In such a nightmare scenario, there would be big state budget deficits, dramatic increases to taxes in their narrow taxation base or the slashing of health care.

On top of money problems, there were alarming structural problems. In broad terms, the federal government funded primary care through Medicare. It also funded aged care. States and the federal government both funded hospitals, but states ran them and had the political liability for them. It was therefore relatively easy for the federal government to cut doctor training numbers or not increase aged-care beds as the burden would end up in hospital emergency departments or beds. More likely than not, it would be the State Minister for Health who would get the blame.

To fix the problem between the aged-care system and the public hospital system, in Opposition I worked with experts to design a new approach. Announced during the 2004 election campaign and called Medicare Gold, it was politically popular albeit poorly understood by commentators and even some Labor colleagues. It was a measure to ensure that one level of government handled the health-care bill for older Australians, thereby ending the spectre of older people being left in acute-care hospital beds, the most expensive in the health-care system, while cheaper and more appropriate aged-care places were not funded.

In Opposition, Kevin promised health reform and a potential takeover. In government, with Nicola Roxon as Health Minister, he first commissioned a report from an expert Commission chaired by Dr Christine Bennett. Presented to government in June in 2009, it was a quality contribution to policy development. Following it, on 7 December 2009 at the COAG meeting in Brisbane, the states agreed that national health reform would be a central priority for 2010.

On 3 March 2010, Kevin and Nicola announced the government's approach to health reform to be taken to COAG for agreement in April 2010. The reforms included creating a national network for health and hospitals that would make what was happening in health-care transparent and would impose tough new standards about treatment, like how long someone could wait in the emergency department.

The element of the package that would in many ways be the most powerful reform driver was paying Local Hospital Networks for the work they did, with the amount to be paid calculated at an efficient price. Instead of receiving a big bucket of money, a hospital would get money for each activity, say a hip replacement, at an efficient price. If the hospital was being less than efficient, it would end up in financial trouble if it did not lift its game and because of the new transparencies and standards, everyone would know about the problem.

A new approach to primary care was also promised so that all the practitioners in a geographic area would be better able to work together to coordinate care. Every community would have a Medicare Local to serve this purpose.

Kevin promised that the federal government would move from being a Howard Government-style bit player in hospital funding to being the dominant funder. The sting in the tail was that the federal government, in order to end up taking 60 per cent of the funding responsibility for public hospitals, would claw back from the states one-third of the GST revenue currently distributed to them. Because health-care costs grow more quickly than GST revenues, this would alleviate long-term financial burdens for the states.

But understandably, state governments baulked at losing revenue. Many people were suspicious that it was creative accounting so that the federal government could claim it was the dominant funder.

Getting to the point of announcing this package had been a nightmare. Publicly Kevin had been seen to consult around the country by going to hospitals day after day. Behind the scenes, he had worked chaotically on potential reform proposals, unable to decide what to do, procrastinating about whether to go to the 2013 election with a referendum question asking Australians if they wanted to have the federal government take over health care. Technically the advice was clear: a referendum is unnecessary. The federal government already had the power to take over hospitals, should it choose to do so. To put a referendum question was no simple matter; no preparatory steps had been taken, and we were already too short of time to do them. Kevin was angling to be seen to keep his word on a takeover of hospitals and to play out the politics. For a long time he did not recognise that the politics would consist of people shrieking, 'Spin over substance!' And so it all played out, with hundreds of pages of briefing documents asked for at the last minute, urgently prepared and then never read, and meetings called for at extraordinary times that never properly proceeded. Advisers had to do things like work all night on 23 December 2009 so Kevin could have a health-reform document delivered to him Christmas Eve, to read on Christmas Day. The work was done. It seems the reading was not. Certainly no feedback was given on any timetable that would have respected the urgency of the request for the work.

On Valentine's Day 2010, a Sunday, advisers were told to be at The Lodge, only to be excluded from a ministers-only meeting at the last minute. Instead of receiving profuse apologies and being sent home, they were left for hours. The wait was so excruciatingly long and boring they took to playing a game with stones out in The Lodge grounds. Eventually someone managed to procure a ball and at least the game improved; their treatment did not.

I viewed my role in this as helping Nicola to drive Kevin to a decision. The prevarication wore everyone down. Nicola's persistence, stoicism and dedication to getting the work done were nothing short of amazing.

COAG met to consider Kevin's health-reform proposals on 19 and 20 April 2010. By then, the debate was playing out publicly in a way that meant it would be damaging for Kevin if he was perceived to be unable to get a deal. Happily, with some changes to the way funds flowed from the federal government to states and territories, all the Labor premiers and chief ministers accepted the deal. I was personally responsible for getting the most reluctant Labor Premier, John Brumby, to agree.

The last crucial discussion was held in my office and advisers worked through the final documents with me. By then Kevin's knowledge that he needed a deal and resentment that the politics was not playing out better for him had tipped over into an unwillingness to work through the final details. But the deal was done, although Liberal Premier Colin Barnett had refused to sign, saying, 'I wasn't going to be one of those premiers that just fell over like bowling pins. That's what happened; they just fell over one after the other.'[4] Premier Barnett repudiated any approach that had implications for GST paid to states.

While it was not totally apparent at the time, Premier Barnett's refusal contained the seeds of the undoing of the agreement. The Opposition leaders in Victoria and New South Wales, Ted Baillieu and Barry O'Farrell, later backed in Premier Barnett. Barry was fully expected to be elected in March 2011; Ted's future, to be determined at the November 2010 election, was viewed as less assured. Nevertheless he emerged victorious. In his first press conference as premier, Ted Baillieu committed to re-examining the health agreement signed by Premier Brumby. From that moment, it was obvious that whether I liked it or not, my first COAG meeting as prime minister would be about redoing health reform and this time getting it done properly.

However even without this change of government in Victoria and the expected change in New South Wales, I believe the agreement would have unravelled. This became clear when one Labor premier said frankly to me that everyone viewed the targets for the amount of time spent waiting in emergency departments as unachievable in the timeframes specified. Basically getting the federal government to put in more money to deal with the problem of rising costs was worth signing on for, even while knowing the targets would need to be revised later.

If I was going to secure an agreement for the nation, I had to get Western Australia in the tent. Early in January 2011, I travelled to the west and met twice with Premier Barnett. I knew the GST arrangements would need to be re-cut to get his support. As I found out, he was also very wary of Local Hospital Networks with community involvement in their leadership. He equated this to re-enlivening local boards for hospitals. He explained that boards of local community representatives had not worked, particularly in the regional centres of Western Australia, where there was a narrow range of people from which to choose. A political price had been paid getting rid of these boards. He was not prepared to revisit that past.

Nicola and I consulted quietly and thought all the problems through. My Director of Policy, Ian Davidoff, who had worked with Kevin on the earlier reforms, brought his powerful intellect to bear on finding a solution. We put together a new plan that would keep the key reform elements of transparency, efficiency pricing and national standards. It would also keep Local Hospital Networks and the new primary-care structure, Medicare Locals. The federal government would also put more money into health but rather than have a merry-go-round with the GST, states would keep their GST and the federal government would be an equal partner in the rapid growth of health-care funding. This would take the federal government from a 45 per cent share of the growth in hospital costs in 2014 to a half share in 2017. From then on, federal and state governments would be equal partners.

The deal I put on the table contained a promise to bring forward $200 million in incentive payments for states meeting emergency and elective surgery targets while threatening that the $16.4 billion in growth funding available under the deal by 2020 would be denied if states did not sign up. This package was endorsed by cabinet before I took it to COAG.

During that cabinet discussion, Kevin expressed deep unhappiness that the new deal was a 50:50 split and that his plan of being the dominant funder was not being pursued. In reality, the amount of new federal government money was close to the same until 2020, but the percentages had changed because state government GST was not being retained by the federal government. But Kevin wanted the package to be true to his rhetoric of 'dominant funder'. Having made this point, he then left the meeting. The door banged loudly behind him and this became the subject of media reporting.

There were claims and counterclaims about whether Kevin shoved the door in a show of rage or the handle slipped from his hand and it just closed loudly. Whatever the truth, the reaction in the room to the manner of Kevin's exit was mirth, particularly when Craig Emerson took a dollar coin from his wallet, threw it on the table and said, 'Here, add that, and now we're the dominant funder.'

The states came to Canberra showing much more antipathy than for the last COAG meeting with Kevin. Effectively Labor states thought they had done the right thing by the Labor government and, thanks to events in between, looked like they had done a dud deal. I had sympathy for this view but also was alive to a fundamental inconsistency: the states were advocating a relaxation of the waiting targets because the ones signed up to had been unrealistic.

You know you have your work cut out for you at a COAG meeting when the only person in the room supporting you is the leader of the Australian Capital Territory. After I outlined the new deal, only Jon Stanhope was with me.

Over the course of a day, through one-on-one discussions and with plenty of time with only leaders in the room, I talked people around. As part of getting to a deal, I agreed to convene an expert panel to review and revise the targets, to get states off the cleft stick of having signed up to targets that could not be achieved. Perseverance, indeed bursts of belligerence during the discussions, paid off. I left the room with a deal; everyone was prepared to sign up. Major health reform –

a more efficient approach, an end to the spectre that state government finances would be broken by health-care costs – had been achieved.

It was Kristina Keneally's last meeting. Everyone, including her, knew she would not be back, that the election would be lost. Not that she would ever have said it, of course. I was very admiring of how well briefed she was under such circumstances, how active she was in the discussions, how determined she was to do the best deal for New South Wales. It was a deal her successor, Barry O'Farrell, accepted.

As with any COAG reform, there was much work to do to have the final agreement in all its details prepared and the backing legislation passed through the parliament. But the substance of health reform was achieved once and for all on that day.

Unfortunately, with all arrangements involving politicians, there are always those prepared to play cheap politics. The money that flows from the federal government to states and territories for hospitals and many other areas is paid for in advance. To do anything else would cause a cash-flow crisis. Inevitably that means for things relevant to the calculation of how much money flows, like population data, estimates are relied on. This happened for the health agreement and, in accordance with a method agreed by all governments, adjustments were made to population figures based on the best available estimates by the Australian Bureau of Statistics. The Victorian Government queried the resulting figure. Because the adjustment for the 2012–13 financial year did not favour them, Premier Newman and Premier Napthine, who had replaced Ted Baillieu as Liberal leader, claimed that the federal government had cut funding arbitrarily and that they had no option but to pass the changes on immediately to hospitals. In Victoria, the *Herald Sun* jumped on board. The political and media claims that we were cutting health in Victoria by $107 million and in Queensland by $103 million[5] were a crock and indicative of conduct that simply undermines real reform.

Given the politics of election year, we engaged in a political fix and gave each of them more money. But true reform is not about the cheap politics and the fixes. It is about what matters for the community.

A doctor in your community when you need one. Your care coordinated so you are treated as a person not a collection of body parts. Care for your mind as well as your body. Being able to eat without dental pain. A hospital that has reasonable waiting times when you genuinely need the emergency department. An efficient system that costs you no more as a taxpayer than it should. Information about your health-care system available to you in a form that makes sense. Care when you are aged. Support if you have a disability. Our health reforms.

22

The party problem

'. . . we do have a responsibility always to renew ourselves and our organisation. I look forward to the debate in December in Sydney.

'I am determined that we have a fair dinkum Labor Party conference, not an American-style convention. I want there to be debates, I want there to be votes, I want there to be surprises.'

SPEECH TO CHIFLEY RESEARCH CENTRE, OLD PARLIAMENT
HOUSE, 16 SEPTEMBER 2011

PAGES AND PAGES OF NEWSPAPERS, magazines, books and blogs are devoted to the question 'What's wrong with the Labor Party?' It is a perpetual question in search of an unknowable final answer. A political party of reform is always going to be a political party of change, including change to itself. Maddeningly there will never be a time that Labor believers can shout, 'It's finished, it's perfect.' The work of building and rebuilding Labor will never be done. Each new generation will need to renovate our political party, one of so much proud history, to make it ready for a new age.

While the ceaseless round of internal repair jobs and extensions are done, Labor members will have plenty of advice shouted from the sidelines. It is burnt into our media culture to think only Labor needs change. Little is ever reported about the Liberal Party's need for reform. Every public argument that is put about the challenges that face Labor can also be put about the Liberal Party. Both face the tensions and contradictions that come from serving twin constituencies.

In a crude snapshot, Labor seeks to embrace both upper-income professionals who mobilise around social causes and invest their hopes in Labor or the Greens and the more traditional constituency of outer-urban and regional working-class voters, who if they desert Labor vote Liberal, National or for whatever third option is highly visible at that point. In the 2013 election this was the Palmer United Party.

The Liberal Party also seeks to serve twin and potentially warring constituencies: the economic elite, including business, which champions much smaller government and much larger immigration numbers, and the more traditional, conservative voter who is anxious about mass migration and sees a role for government in supporting families and older Australians.

Both Labor and the Liberal Party have seen their parliamentary members become embroiled in corruption scandals. Both have suffered from poor preselection choices, often done over the heads of local party members. While many would cite too much union influence in Labor, there is less commentary about the heft of unrepresentative groups like anti-choice abortion law campaigners within the Liberal Party. Both face the challenge of growing and holding membership as political party engagement through in-person local party meetings becomes less attractive.

What is true for the Liberal Party is even truer for the National Party, which faces a crisis between the image it tries to present to local members and communities and the policies it votes for in Canberra.

But while the paucity of public debate around the problems of the Liberal Party may frustrate Labor believers, our task is to tend to our own change agenda.

The right place for the Labor Party to renew itself is at its national conference. This meeting of elected party delegates and trade union representatives is the Labor Party's chief decision-making body. Elected delegates fly from all over Australia to debate Labor's platform and rules. The Labor Party platform is important. It is not a manual for government but a statement of values and aspirations towards which Labor governments should work. The rules of the Labor Party matter too. They govern how easy and attractive the party is for people to join, the method by which candidates will be preselected, the way disputes within the party will be resolved. All that means that when it is good, national conference is a place to hothouse ideas and agree new directions. When it is bad, it is a place for screaming matches between factional leaders on things no one in the community cares about. When it is at its worst, it is a lifeless beast of no debate, no ideas, with everything controversial swept under the carpet. I inherited a situation where for good and bad reasons, the last two Labor national conferences had been at their worst.

The 2007 national conference was held in April, when the election was just around the corner. For electorally pragmatic reasons, everyone worked hard to ensure the meeting came across to voters watching snippets on the news as that of a united, determined political party. There was no real debate. For the wrong reasons, the 2009 national conference was also inert.

Kevin, as prime minister and Labor leader, distanced himself from the conference. He did have Private Benjamin Ranaudo's funeral to attend while the conference was in progress but his approach was not purely dictated by the necessary demands of his diary. Kevin was determined to make sure that he minimised, and was seen to minimise, his attendance at national conference.

With an instruction to keep everything quiet, he delegated the management of national conference to me, aided ably by his staff and mine, as well as key ministers. All debates were to be prevented.

The kind of discussions the Labor Party needed about its policies and on its own rules and processes were all put into suspended animation. Consequently delegates were bored and felt irrelevant. To anyone watching, it looked like Labor had no passion or purpose.

As prime minister in the lead-up to the 2011 national conference, I wanted the Labor Party to show some life. I deliberately set the conference early so electoral considerations would not stifle all debate. I wanted a vibrant debate about our modern purpose, steps forward in democratising the ALP and a resolution of debates postponed for too long, like the one about same-sex marriage. In all this, I saw my role as acting as a guide not an imposer of my views. It is common for Labor leaders to receive advice that the best way to define themselves in the public mind is to have a war with the Labor Party and win it.

There are times leaders need to have such wars. Tony Blair and his fight to modernise British Labour is possibly the best example. But this political advice now is so ubiquitous that it has spawned the stuff of caricature. Labor Premier Peter Beattie's tactic of pushing himself up in public esteem by beating up the Labor Party is now past its use-by date. Everyone gets the trick so the magic is gone. Even worse, this manoeuvre privileges short-term gain while inflicting the longer term pain of diminishing Labor itself. I tried to weave a line between demanding leader and cheerful facilitator, but I wanted everyone to hear the drumbeat; it is about purpose.

Everyone now knows of the many flaws of New South Wales Labor in government. What is less recognised is that the heart of the problem was lack of purpose. New South Wales Labor ended up not knowing what it was in government to do. The vacuum was filled by the most naked self-interest.

Of a different nature was the lack of defined core purpose at the centre of the Rudd Government. While I was prime minister, the best of my colleagues in the parliamentary party understood my sense of purpose and with them I was able to lead a government of conviction. But, in my view, the Labor Party more broadly was adrift from a clear sense of purpose, which – together with good parliamentarians and thinkers in the union movement – I hoped to revitalise.

In September 2011, in an effort to put a spotlight on purpose, I gave a speech to the Labor faithful at Old Parliament House. In that building, history is all around you. In that speech I tried to fuse the aspiration of individuals today to have the power to make choices about and have control over our lives, to the traditions of collective action that are at the core of the Labor Party and trade union movement. I talked about using collective strength so that we all shared and supported each other in the face of life's risks, like illness and disability. I spoke of using collective strength to better share opportunity, through education, fair employment, the ability to start your own business. It was a little reported speech.

It was a much better speech than the widely reported one I gave at national conference itself, which flared a controversy because it referred to Labor governments past but not the Rudd Government. The people who helped prepare and proof the speech, and I, were simply not seeing everything through the prism of me in comparison to Kevin. Unfortunately though, rather than thinking about purpose, concentrating on the future, tackling the challenges of government, too many people were gripping that prism. I should have been smart enough to pick the problem. It was definitely my fault.

But my greater regret is not having the time or the space to successfully act as the midwife for a new, modern and accepted definition of purpose for the Labor Party. My time in office was too short and the environment in the ALP too polluted by leadership instability to get it done. This remains core work for the Labor Party as part of its next revival. Of course, the antiquated socialist objective in the party's constitution, which defines our purpose as 'the democratic socialisation of industry, production, distribution and exchange' should be replaced. The difficult question is with what.

In effect, the Labor Party needs a collective process to do the equivalent of what I did at Alan Milburn's urgings as leader: to write down, indeed boil down, a definition of and dedication to purpose. The temptation will be to make it all-things-to-all-people pap. It will be hard but vital to resist this course.

Democratising our own processes remains core work too. As prime minister, I successfully pressed for national conference to adopt a growth target of 8000 new members in 2012, supported by community outreach work and lower fees for new recruits, especially the young and poorly paid. In addition, new structures were created to revive Labor's connection to activists within communities, the kind of volunteers who keep schools, sporting groups and environmental clean-up campaigns going. This work embraced getting union members, not union officials, involved individually within Labor. Pleasingly the goal of 8000 new members was achieved.

The door was pushed open to direct party member voting on who represents the rank and file at national conference and to involving Labor supporters in preselections, by trialling community preselections, or primaries, in some seats. This suite of reforms did not go far enough for some and went way too far for others. However it was the biggest round of change to Labor's rules since 2002, when Simon Crean as Labor leader, forced through a reduction in trade union representation at Labor's decision-making bodies from 60 per cent to 50 per cent.

Of course, more needs to be done and I believe the 2011 changes point the direction forward, but to achieve greater change, Labor needs to cut through a circular debate. The party is consistently hectored, sometimes by the conservative commentariat, sometimes from within, to sever its ties with the trade union movement and empower the membership. In my view, this is both wrong in principle, given the Labor Party's purpose, and misconceived in practice.

Labor rightly conceives its purpose as the party for working people and their families. Spurning organisations of working people that even in the modern age comprise 17 per cent of the workforce, meaning 1.75 million people, is anathema to that purpose. This is particularly so when severing ties with the millions would leave Labor governed by rank and file members currently numbered at 45,000; those members are overwhelmingly in older age brackets and generally to the left of the centre of community opinion.

A simple switch to 100 per cent empowerment of the membership would give our nation a less, not more, representative Labor Party. The risk would be that Labor's own internal structure then drags it left-wards, beyond the bounds of sensible policy and electoral acceptability.

If party membership suddenly burst into the hundreds of thousands, then of course this risk would be lessened. But in an age of so many competing priorities for individual time and attention, even with the most open and democratic structures possible, it is unlikely such size and reach into the community mainstream will be achieved. Even if it was, it would be foolhardy and wrong in principle to exclude the voice of organised labour.

But that voice needs to be heard fresh and direct. The obvious reform direction, and one I support, is maintaining the partnership with the trade union movement but having trade unions represented at Labor decision-making bodies by people actively elected from their membership.

Trade unions should ask their members on joining whether they want to be affiliated with the Labor Party. The clout of individual unions within Labor should be based on the number of its members who say yes. Those who do should vote in regular ballots for national conference delegates and the state-based equivalents as well as for any trade union component involved in preselecting Labor candidates.

Trade unionists so elected would sit in these decision-making bodies alongside Labor Party members elected by the rank and file party membership. Effectively no one would participate in decision-making without having specifically canvassed for votes and support. Trade unions would have an incentive to proselytise within their membership for Labor in order to encourage people to belong.

The adoption of direct voting for Labor's federal leader energised the party membership base after the 2013 defeat. For this, Kevin Rudd should be thanked. But careful stewardship is now required to ensure this reform works for the long term.

I hope that for many decades my party does not face another circumstance where a Labor leader overwhelmingly loses the confidence of his or her colleagues. But if it ever happens, then the answer is not stasis, with the leader hiding behind artificially high majorities for change and too cumbersome procedures.

Additionally political dynamics will necessarily mean that the more familiar people become with direct election of the leader, the greater the temptation for political smarties to find ways to manipulate and manage it. What needs to be avoided at all cost is any bias in the system to participants with money and resources. To avoid the process becoming corroded, it will need to be periodically reviewed.

Then, if the reform directions I support were adopted, the question of the role of trade union members who have actively signalled their desire to be affiliated with the Labor Party will need to be thought through. It is hard to argue that a childcare worker who is a member of a union and has ticked the box to become involved in the party is less connected with community opinion or more easily manipulated in voting than a long-time party member who originally came to be a Labor member via a factional stacking operation.

But some of the most complex questions are not rules-based, not structural. These are the cultural questions, the way in which Labor colleagues treat each other and perform as a team. If poor conduct is rewarded internally, then it is very likely there will be more of it. Through returning Kevin Rudd to the leadership in 2013, Labor grandly rewarded the very worst of conduct. The message sent was clear. If a group of people put themselves above the party and are prepared to do anything, including trashing a Labor government, to achieve their aims then they will win through. Now Labor has to confront the hard task of re-engineering its internal culture so that the quiet doing of hard yards for the team is explicitly recognised and valued while showy, self-interested behaviour is repudiated.

The Labor Party I inherited not only needed a greater sense of purpose and democratisation but the resolution of simmering tensions on issues not discussed in a meaningful way at the 2007 or 2009 national conferences.

The issue that was most explosive at national conference while I was prime minister was that of same-sex marriage. At Kevin's request, at the 2009 conference, I convened the high-level discussions that put a lid on claims for Labor to adopt civil unions for gay couples as its policy. Problems deferred fester, they do not resolve.

By 2011, civil unions were no longer the demand. The debate had raced on to amending the Marriage Act so it no longer defined marriage as the union of a man and woman. The fight had also moved on to abolishing the conscience vote for same-sex marriage so every Labor parliamentarian, regardless of their religious or personal beliefs, would be required to vote yes.

This canter to a new and harder line position partly reflected developments in community opinion. It seemed that across the Western world, the push was on for same-sex marriage. But partly it reflected the age-old problem that slamming a lid on a political cauldron means it will boil all the more furiously.

The opportunity in 2009 to move to a progressive position that could have been broadly, but not unanimously, supported across Labor was lost. Definitely I would have supported it and in the 2010 election campaign, where so many doubts were legitimately raised about Tony Abbott's ability to deal with modernity, it would have been a useful point of political differentiation. But by 2011, it was obvious same-sex marriage would be carried as Labor's substantive position. I worked to facilitate the debate we should have had earlier and ensure passions did not run so high that the conscience vote was lost and Labor was forever split on the issue.

I am well aware that my personal position of not supporting an amendment to the Marriage Act to permit same sex-marriage looks odd given who I am and the life I live. My views are not that same-sex marriage is too radical. If anything, the vision is not radical enough.

In the feminist era, in which I cut my political teeth, marriage ceremonies were viewed as redolent of the yesteryear stereotypes of women. A father gives his daughter, dressed in white, to her husband so she can love, honour and obey. Our reaction in the early 1980s would have been 'Spare me! Can't we imagine a future of equality better than that?'

The gay rights movement of that era would also have been horrified. They were trying to forge a new way of living, not mimicking current social norms. To this day, one friend of mine is known to joke that the best thing about being a lesbian is that it got her out from under her family's expectations about marriage and children.

I acknowledge that my vision of a nation that has marriage, as we have traditionally known it, and an equally valued but different way of solemnising the lifetime commitments for both heterosexual and homosexual couples is not going to be realised. Marriage is winning out and has won the support of most but not all of the gay rights movement.

While my own reasoning and position were undoubtedly idiosyncratic, I nevertheless created the space for Labor to have the debate and resolve it. The outcome, having the flexibility of a conscience vote while having a substantive position in favour of same-sex marriage, makes sense for a progressive political party in today's environment.

In time, Australia will adopt same-sex marriage. When it does, the 2011 debate at Labor's national conference will be historically viewed as the first decisive step forward. The next decisive and necessary step will be the adoption of a conscience vote by the Liberal and National parties.

Within Labor forums and publicly, same-sex marriage is discussed as a dual constituency issue for Labor, one where our progressive and blue-collar bases pull in different directions. I suspect this is abating and will lessen further over time. To the extent many traditional working families think about same-sex marriage at all, I suspect it is with an increasingly benevolent live-and-let-live outlook.

The far sharper dual constituency issue is asylum-seeker policy. Many progressive activists want a compassionate approach, which they define as not viewing unauthorised boat arrivals as a problem and offering permanent protection, meaning residence and then citizenship, to those found to have valid refugee claims. Labor's more traditional blue-collar constituency is unnerved by unauthorised boat arrivals and draws a straight line from too many asylum-seekers to too much pressure on things like local roads and various services. While wrong, it is widely believed asylum-seekers are the recipients of generous amounts of government welfare support. This constituency is for punitive action: often, whatever it takes to stop the boats.

During the days of my prime ministership, I felt somewhat wearily that the asylum-seeker issue had been with me always. John Howard skilfully rode the political momentum that can be created around asylum-seeker issues at the 2001 election. Coming after the terrorist shock of 9/11 and in the atmosphere of fear that it created, Howard took a hairy-chested political approach and deployed our elite military forces to stop a Norwegian freighter, the *Tampa*, from bringing rescued asylum-seekers to our shore. Working people, so-called Howard battlers, rewarded the Liberal Party with their votes.

Labor went along with Howard's approach but was electorally punished. Progressives viewed this as an abominable sell-out and voted for the Greens. Many in Labor's traditional constituency sniffed an apparent lack of sincerity in Labor following Howard's lead and voted Liberal.

After the 2001 election, in a crazy brave move, I volunteered to be Shadow Minister for Population and Immigration. Policy-wise I wanted to craft a position that we could genuinely support as a Labor Party and stick to, whether the media story of the week was one that provoked compassion in Australians, like a child being hurt in a detention centre, or one that hardened Australian hearts, like asylum-seekers escaping detention. I recognised this as the challenge that would make or break me in the eyes of my colleagues and the media. Either I would succeed and be viewed as a serious, substantive person for the future or I would fail and be severely set back in my political career.

I crafted a policy that was entitled 'Protecting Australia and Protecting the Australian Way'. Its title and contents were meant to demonstrate that Labor understood why Australians craved orderly immigration, that we as a nation should seek to discourage asylum-seekers from making dangerous journeys by boat but that we should demonstrate fairness and compassion to those in genuine need.

I formed the view that the approach favoured by much of the progressive constituency, including the many emotional party members who called me disgusting in consultation meetings because I did not quickly agree with them, was naive. It ignored that people-smuggling is a transnational crime and that money was being made by unsavoury people. It failed to recognise that, unavoidably, there was a limit to the numbers of boat arrivals Australians were prepared to tolerate. Also it meant turning a blind eye to the risks of people dying at sea. But most disturbingly of all, it extended compassion to those within our line of sight, while our view of the millions waiting in refugee camps unable to move further was obscured by the horizon.

My policy was viewed by progressives as hard-line. It retained first-instance mandatory detention, albeit in more hostel-style accommodation for families, once first-instance health, identity and security checking had been done.

The policy included a temporary first-instance visa so that if conditions stabilised in a refugee's home country, then at the end of that visa they could be returned home. If conditions had not stabilised, then permanent protection would be granted.

This differed from the Howard Government arrangement whereby someone found to be a refugee could only ever get a three-year visa, so they would never be able to be a citizen or sponsor family members to join them.

It also kept offshore processing on Christmas Island, which was excised from Australia's migration zone. My dream was that the processing of claims could be done there quickly, following the approach taken in refugee camps by the UNHCR so that there would be no difference in acceptance rates.

With the benefit of hindsight, aspects of this policy seem naive. Because of the High Court's judicial activism on refugee and asylum-seeker issues, running a UNHCR-style processing system free from judicial review on Christmas Island would have been impossible.

Within Labor, I had to fight for this policy. Carmen Lawrence resigned from the Shadow ministry in disgust over its adoption. A cross-factional but predominantly Left-aligned group called Labor for Refugees fought it at national conference in 2004. Prior to the conference, I attended the national Left caucus and moved for adoption a motion consistent with my policy. I did not get a seconder. Finally someone seconded so it could be a valid motion. Everyone then voted against it except me.

At the national conference itself, my preferred resolution was carried in a tight vote after an emotional debate. Some Left colleagues, like Martin Ferguson, did vote with me.

As arrivals slowed under the Howard Government and I moved on to other portfolios, within Labor the debate was kept quiet internally by the use of language with a more compassionate flavour. This was the case at the 2007 national conference. By then, the efficacy of Temporary Protection Visas (TPVs) as a deterrent was open to question; support for those visas was dropped from the platform.

While Kevin decided to send the hardest of messages on the day before the 2007 election by saying he would turn boats around, in reality Labor had allowed some complacency to creep in. Early in the life of the government, the Immigration Minister, Chris Evans, implemented Labor's promised policies and closed the offshore processing centres in Papua New Guinea and Nauru. The government also ceased to issue TPVs.

In calendar year 2007, the last year of the Howard Government, five boats arrived, with 148 asylum-seekers on board. By 2009 that had grown to 60 boats and 2726 asylum-seekers.[1] The people-smugglers were definitely testing us. This illegal business advertises for clients in places of desperation around the world. A change of government in Australia and the end of the so-called Pacific Solution would have been trumpeted by people-smugglers. 'Go now' would have been the message.

As a government, we needed to respond to this provocation effectively and with substance. Otherwise the numbers of asylum-seekers would keep growing. Politically the prospect of ever more boat arrivals was already costing us. But for a mix of more and less understandable reasons, we failed to tackle this problem head on.

In part, managing the GFC consumed so much time and energy that for a number of months, there was really not a minute spare. The volume and complexity of the rest of our agenda also gobbled decision-making time. But in some measure, this failure to respond also flowed from Kevin's leadership style and reluctance to work through issues in a measured and systematic way.

Then this hardening policy and political problem flared up into a devastating one courtesy of the *Oceanic Viking* fiasco. There was no mix of factors here. This was a crisis entirely of Kevin's making.

Notified on a Saturday morning in early October 2009 that an asylum-seeker vessel was in trouble, Kevin perceived it as a golden media opportunity in Australia to look tough and decisive. He also believed it would send a message of deterrence up the people-smuggling pipeline, demonstrating that asylum-seekers could not assume they would end up in Australia. In government, Kevin was a procrastinator in the face of big strategic decisions but the hunger he showed in Opposition for good media stories was with him still. Without consultation with his Foreign Minister, Stephen Smith, or his Immigration Minister, Chris Evans, he dispatched the *Oceanic Viking* to rescue and return the asylum-seekers to Indonesia.

Chris was watching his son play sport when he received a call from Kevin's office to inform him that this was happening. Immediately he contacted the secretary of his department, Andrew Metcalfe, who uttered the prescient words, 'Minister, they won't get off the boat.'

Had advice been sought properly, Kevin might not have embarked on a strategy that generated positive attention for a few days and then was a disaster for a month. After painful weeks went by, with the government looking impotent, a deal was cut that had the asylum-seekers leave the boat.

By the end of 2009 and into election year 2010, Opposition leader Tony Abbott was making political hay with his promise to 'stop the boats'. Images of the asylum-seekers' laundry on the railings of the *Oceanic Viking* had made the Labor government look too weak to stop anything. On into 2010, there was no truly substantive government action on this critical political issue. A suspension was put in place on the processing of asylum-seeker claims from Afghanistan in the hope this would make a difference to arrival numbers. It did not.

In March, Kevin left me to chair a meeting of SPBC at which Chris Evans presented the critical need to move asylum-seekers from Christmas Island to detention on mainland Australia. The numbers on Christmas Island were now too big to cope with and the situation was a potentially violent one.

According to Kevin's office, his inclination was to knock back Chris's request. The asylum-seekers in question were part of the cohort whose claims were not being processed and Kevin had said publicly these asylum-seekers were not going to be brought to the mainland. Chris is a quietly spoken, capable and thoughtful man. Written all over his face was real anxiety and distress. I thought to myself, *If this issue is not resolved appropriately he will resign*. Wayne sensed the same thing and passed a note to me saying, 'Give him what he wants'. Flouting Kevin's wishes, SPBC agreed with Chris's plan.

This experience pushed me into looking for fresh policy answers to the issue of asylum-seeker boat arrivals. At my urging and with Kevin's consent and participation, a committee of ministers set to work on making a return to offshore processing, particularly through an approach to Timor-Leste to host a detention centre.

On the night I challenged him for the leadership, despite his role in seeking to resume offshore processing, Kevin sought to parade progressive views on asylum-seekers by saying, 'We will not be lurching to the Right on the question of asylum-seekers'.[2] It was a hollow statement.

As prime minister, I decided to own the ministerial group work and sought to implement a return to offshore processing, first through a failed bid to have a processing centre in Timor-Leste and then in Papua New Guinea. Working with Chris Bowen, I wanted to move further and implement an arrangement whereby any asylum-seeker who came by boat would never be able to settle in Australia. With the utmost care, a group of cabinet ministers – including senior Left ministers and most particularly Brendan O'Connor – Chris and I collaborated to secure caucus acceptance of a deal with Malaysia that achieved precisely that. It was an incredibly big and difficult step for a number of individuals who had passionately opposed offshore processing under Howard. In many ways the majority attitude of Labor caucus on this question speaks of its maturity, its ability to change its mind and embrace new solutions when required.

But no maturity was shown by the Opposition, who fought the necessary legislative amendments, to give the government the ability to process asylum-seekers offshore. Previous governments had this legal power but it was removed by the High Court in a decision on the Malaysia arrangement in September 2011, against the expectations of those advising the government. Instead of agreeing to give our government the same range of options that the Howard Government had at its disposal, the Opposition flung itself into a unity ticket with the Greens, who did not believe in offshore processing at all.

Indeed it took until August 2012 – following my decision to create an independent expert committee comprising Angus Houston, a former Chief of the Defence Force; Paris Aristotle, an expert in refugee matters; and Michael L'Estrange, a foreign policy specialist – to get legislation through the parliament that empowered the government I led and future governments to process asylum-seekers offshore. The courage of these three individuals in being prepared to step into such a fraught political debate in order to try and resolve it was admirable. I had known Paris personally for a long time and marvelled at his perseverance in doing work to support survivors of torture and trauma. Angus I had come to hold in the highest regard as he led defence. Michael I did not know well but he was fearless in putting the national interest first. However, even with these new laws passed, we needed the Opposition's political consent to new offshore places and, in a hypocritical move, that consent was limited to countries signatory to the 1951 United Nations Convention Relating to the Status of Refugees. As a result, we were never able to implement the agreement with Malaysia and send a big shock up the people-smuggling pipeline. All this partisanship sent a 'game on' message instead. Arrivals by asylum-seekers peaked in 2013, with 20,587 asylum-seekers arriving on 300 boats.[3]

In addition to finally securing the reinstatement of offshore processing, I continued to work with ministers and through our National Security Committee on new answers. The work gained even more intensity in the second half of 2012 and the first half of 2013 as asylum-seeker numbers kept rising despite offshore processing getting underway.

Consequently, now with Brendan as Immigration Minister, we went on a hunt for nations that would be willing to not just have a processing centre but offer a permanent resettlement place to any asylum-seekers found to be refugees. Effectively we were trying to move the Malaysia agreement to another nation. Unfortunately we were unable to do so.

It is a credit to Kevin Rudd and those who worked with him, such as Richard Marles, that on his return to the prime ministership they were able to secure such a deal. It would be interesting to know whether these discussions were pre-seeded in anticipation of his return. But whatever the process, it worked, and asylum-seeker boat numbers plummeted. In the fortnight before the election on 7 September, there was only one boat arrival in each week. This seems to vindicate the view that I, Chris Bowen and others within government took, that the Malaysia arrangement, if implemented, would have stopped the boats.[4]

For the Labor Party, the force of this vexed history must be absorbed. There are no limits on what the Liberal and National parties will do to prevent a Labor government dealing with asylum-seeker policies. The Coalition simply and brutally views it as in its political interests to have boats arrive under a Labor government.

With Labor now in Opposition, the painful realisations we came to in government about how hard it can be to deter unauthorised boat arrivals cannot be lost. Rather at every level in the party, including at national conference, the lessons need to be absorbed so that Labor never again succumbs to a moment of complacency or fails to show the policy agility necessary.

Opposition can be a time of renewal and reflection or else of indulgence and flabby thinking. Even worse, like the most dreadful of national conferences, it can be a time of inertia. Every good poll, every stumble by the government can be received internally as a compelling reason to not deal within Labor with any hard questions. To stay quiet, to keep the focus on the failing government.

But a bedrock truth is that there is rarely a shortcut back to government. Voters will only feel they have political permission to vote Labor if it has articulated its sense of purpose, modernised its identity as a party and thought intelligently about the lessons of government.

Blunt negativity worked for the conservatives in 2013. But the downside of the Coalition getting a shortcut back to office because of Labor's internal instability has been on display in their poor performance as a government. The hard work necessary in Opposition to settle what you intend to do in government was sidelined in favour of slogan-driven negativity. The holes are now showing.

I sincerely hope my much-loved Labor Party will have the fortitude to use the days of Opposition to not only defend fairness but to extend its sense of purpose and its own democratic practice. Of course, I will be cheering it on.

EPILOGUE

What now?

'In a blinding flash
I see the years go by
Memories twisted around
Somebody's finger
Behind me now
Oh but I still remember
Do you see what I see?'

HUNTERS AND COLLECTORS

STEVE BRACKS LAUNCHED his successful 1999 Victorian state election campaign in Ballarat with the Hunters and Collectors song 'Do you see what I see?' blaring. I remember being amazed and delighted by the choice.

He ended his run onto the stage with a ferocious man-hug of Kim Beazley, the federal Labor leader, who had introduced him. Steve ended his run onto the government benches with unexpected success on polling day, a further win in a by-election and negotiation to form a minority government. Jeff Kennett, the apparently unbeatable premier, had been humbled.

For John Brumby, the Victorian Labor leader Steve Bracks had overthrown, the surprisingly good result on election night in 1999 provoked mixed emotions. Still bruised from being deposed as leader, it now seemed likely he would end up on the government benches again thanks to Steve's popularity and campaigning.

I had served as John's chief of staff, leaving him in order to contest the 1998 federal election and become the Member for Lalor. But once a chief of staff, always a chief of staff, so when he finished being a commentator on the television election night coverage, it was me John rang. We spoke for ages, both of us sipping red wine as we did so, but the real taste in our mouths was that intricate bittersweet flavour which is the essence of politics.

During an altogether different election, the 2013 federal election, there was no pumping rhythm, no election cliffhanger. Instead there was a dreadful campaign and a devastating loss. My over-riding emotion was sadness. For our nation. For Labor. For Kevin. And yes, from time to time, for myself.

In the days since, while writing this book, I have often heard the refrain 'Do you see what I see?' in my head, a deft encapsulation of what I wanted to achieve through my words. I hope they have helped you see not only the world I lived in as prime minister but the vision of our nation I was working towards. Stronger and fairer.

In my life after politics, I continue to think about policies and programs to better our nation beyond those I worked on in government. Thinking about public policy is an addiction I could not break even if I tried.

Spending time with my infant great-nephew, Ethan, I see the wonder of growing and learning, of the development of human capacity, which I cared so much about as prime minister. But being with him leads me to thinking about the world he will inherit, about the equity or lack of it that exists between my generation and his. Some of this is caught in the periodic federal government statements about what financial burden our nation's suite of tax and social policies will put on the shoulders of the taxpayers of tomorrow. But tomorrow's Australia will also be fundamentally shaped by how sustainably we have lived. By how degraded our soil, our water, our seas are. By how much carbon we emit. Why shouldn't our nation's periodic intergenerational reports account in rigorous detail how heavy our footprints are on this land, which we hold in custody for future generations?

My family's experiences have taught me to think about ageing and how important it is to die at the right time in the right way. Health economists can chant the painful statistics about how much money is spent on care in the last year, indeed the last few weeks, of life. Behind this expenditure lie stories of heroic and sometimes invasive efforts to do everything possible to sustain life even though that is not necessarily what the patient may have wanted.

This is a process an individual can seek to control by leaving specific instructions. My father did that but many people do not. Even if they do, such wishes can be countermanded by a family member.

Death is perhaps life's most uncomfortable subject. In our ageing Australia, I feel it is time to regularise and mainstream discussion of death. As we age, we will all intersect regularly with the superannuation or old-age pension systems or both. As part of these systems, I now believe it should be compulsory to consider and complete the kind of advanced-care directive that will spell out our wishes. Of course, people should be free to choose maximum intervention or any other option. Their wishes should not be able to be countermanded by anyone. I understand I am prescribing a grim task. But silence about death is not the answer. Across the course of human history, ignoring it never has, and never will, make it go away.

As I muse about this and other public-policy problems in our world, I worry about the conduct of democratic debates in today's Australia, where we have more information coming at us than ever before but with less accuracy and more bias. Even with today's plethora of online information and social media, the reporting of Australia's political news is still dominated by the traditional media players in one of the most concentrated media markets in the world. The newspapers come out, the early-morning workers in the news rooms of radio and television stations compose their bulletins based on what they read. A biased or inaccurate newspaper story quickly becomes a biased or inaccurate radio and television story.

This concentration of our media may grow even more intense as Fairfax, the owner of *The Age*, *The Sydney Morning Herald* and *The Australian Financial Review*, is forced by the market to embrace a new business model of solely online publication.

News Corp Australia, particularly its national newspaper, will undoubtedly carry on, irrespective of the real market dynamics.

Newspapers started their lives as rich men's vanities. It seems that at this end stage of their life cycle, they are the vanities of rich people once again.

Already, even without further concentration in ownership, the world of fact is a poor cousin to the world of opinion. Factual errors are not corrected at all or in any way adequately. Substantive debates are infantilised or distorted. If you complain individually then you will be the subject of payback. The bullying culture of sections of our media establishment would be right at home in the school playgrounds of yesteryear.

The media's preparedness to argue for freedom of the press waxes and wanes. When one media outlet is berated by government, the other media outlets join in. They see a competitor being given a beating and want to land their own blows, rather than defend it as an example of the free press at work.

Undoubtedly our media reforms were poorly handled. Frustration took too much hold. But there is a need for a genuine and effective model of media self-regulation, which means someone harmed by false reporting can complain and get a remedy, free of the fear of retribution.

I am pleased new technology has brought some entrants into our market and I regularly write for one of them, *The Guardian*. But I hanker for a ubiquitous culture of transparency, the media doing what it demands of others. Sources of information where any fact cited that turns out not to be true is corrected as soon as possible with equal prominence. Publications capable of fostering and sustaining deep-thinking policy discussions. Where every journalist publishes all the information you need to know about them to assess their perspectives as they publish their articles. Their pecuniary interests, whether they are a member of a political party, whether they ever worked in a political position.

A publication that gives the reader a regular stocktake of what stories it did not publish or did not pursue and why. A publication that only extends the benefits of off-the-record quotes or views appearing in print to sources that truly would face some persecution or payback, not people who are using a cloak of anonymity for their own reasons. I suspect I will have to dream on.

But I do hope that people of good will and good ideas, including my political party, will find ever more effective ways to work around the strictures of the traditional media and engage directly. I hope people do find ways through the cacophony to authoritative sources of news and information, places for ideas and dialogue. Perhaps the very volume will cause people to become more searching and selective.

Of course, I am still a passionate barracker for Labor and will do everything across the remainder of my life to see the election of Labor governments, federal and state.

The Asian Century continues to unfold, with its world of promise for us. I still want us to seize every bit of it that can enrich us as a nation for the future. That will be the work of the next federal Labor government, as will be renewing the fair go Australians crave.

In the days since being prime minister, I have set about building a new life for myself beyond politics but with the same sense of purpose that has always driven me. At the centre of my life now is work on education. By chairing the board of the Global Partnership for Education, the only multilateral world body solely dedicated to education, I can make a personal contribution to enabling children in the poorest of nations to access the life-changing power of a good-quality education.

As a Distinguished Senior Fellow at the think tank Brookings in Washington, I am able to play a role in the global policy struggle with the many complex parts of actually providing a good-quality education to all. How do we measure quality globally? How do we scale up good approaches that are working? How do we sustainably finance education? How do we make sure the poorest, the girls, the children with disabilities and those in conflict zones do not get left behind: out of school and out of hope?

My life has brought me back to the University of Adelaide, so I have the opportunity to be amazed and delighted by our nation's young people. It is a full life and it sustains me, as do Tim, my family and my friends.

Now, having left political life, having faced its stresses, used its opportunities to make change, I am not haunted by regrets or doubts. Emotions do continue to be mixed. I live many of my days still knowing the taste of bittersweet. But the sweet, as always, is by far the stronger.

I used to spend my political days after delivering each big new policy, saying to myself, *What next?* Right now, for me, I know what is next. More life to live. More work to do. The same sense of purpose to drive me on.

NOTES

1: Becoming the first
1 Department of the Prime Minister and Cabinet, briefing provided to Hon. Julia Gillard, 2014
2 Ibid.
3 Kevin Rudd, transcript of opening remarks to the National Climate Change Summit, Parliament House, Canberra, 31 March 2007

3: A campaign sabotaged
1 'National Nine News', 8 August 2010
2 Julia Gillard, transcript of press conference, Brisbane, 7 August 2010

4: Minority government
1 Michael Gordon, '. . . and then there were three', 4 September 2010, accessed 9 August 2014 at brisbanetimes.com.au

5: The enemy within
1 Barrie Cassidy, 'Leadership tussle: Rudd circles, Gillard stumbles', The Drum, abc.net.au/news/2012-02-17/cassidy-leadership-tussle/3834486, accessed 21 July 2014
2 26 June 2013

6: The curious question of gender
1 'Strange silence on Gillard status', The Australian Financial Review, Rear Window, 27 September 2013, Joe Aston (ed.)
2 Q and A, 'Politics and porn in a post-feminist world', ABC1, 19 March 2012
3 dailytelegraph.com.au/news/national/julia-gillard-spread-eagled-as-she-fell-after-losing-her-shoe-on-a-visit-to-new-delhi-in-india/story-fndo2j43-1226497905553, 17 October 2012, accessed 23 July 2014
4 'John and Kevin: Men with feet and mouths of clay', Malcolm Farr, Daily Telegraph, 25 July 2007
5 'At home with Julia', ABC 1, 4-part series screened during September 2011
6 'Barren behaviour', The Australian, 4 May 2007, accessed 9 August 2014 at www.theaustralian.com
7 Paola Totaro, 'Gillard's first appearance on international stage as PM', The Sydney Morning Herald, 4 October 2011, accessed 10 August 2014 at www.smh.com.au

8 Anne Davies, 'Bligh a white light beside the cool, coiffed Gillard', *The Sydney Morning Herald*, 13 January 2010, accessed 9 August 2014 at www.smh.com.au

9 Bridie Jabour, 'Julia Gillard's "small breasts" served up on Liberal Party dinner menu', *The Guardian (Australia)*, 12 June 2013, accessed 9 August 2014 at www.theguardian.com

10 Alison Rehn, 'Abbott's no means no gaffe', *Daily Telegraph*, accessed 9 August 2014 at www.dailytelegraph.com.au

11 Transcript, joint doorstop interview, 25 February 2011, accessed 9 August 2014 at www.liberal.org.au

12 David Farley, speech delivered at Invigorating Agriculture conference, Adelaide, 2 August 2012

13 House Hansard 26 June 2013, accessed 9 August 2014 at http://parlinfo.aph.gov.au

14 Jonathan Swan, Dan Harrison, 'Rudd ends speculation of another tilt', *The Sydney Morning Herald*, 22 March 2013, accessed 10 August 2014 at www.smh.com.au

7: Resilience

1 Tony Abbott, transcript of doorstep interview, Sydney, 26 January 2012

9: Fighting a war

1 Julia Gillard, House of Representatives Ministerial Statements: Afghanistan, 19 October 2010

10: The 1961 kids

1 Paul Osborne, 'US forces get the nod – new defence deal', *The Courier-Mail*, 16 November 2011, accessed 9 August 2014 at www.couriermail.com.au

2 President Obama, Parliament House, Canberra Australia, 17 Nov 2011, accessed 21 July 2014 at www.whitehouse.gov/the-press-office/2011/11/17/remarks-president-obama-australian-parliament

11: Australia in the Asian Century

1 www.abc.net.au/news/2010-10-05/foreign-policy-not-my-thing-says-gillard/2286744

2 Department of Foreign Affairs and Trade, briefing provided to Hon. Julia Gillard, 2014

3 Sid Mayer, 'China deal the cornerstone of Gillard's Asian Century', *The Australian*, 10 April 2013, p. 1

4 gaiwaterhouse.com.au/gaisblog.gai-waterhouse-diary-monday,-254,25 April 2011, Gai Waterhouse Racing, Gai Waterhouse Diary, accessed 2 June 2014

5 Quoted in Michelle Grattan and Ben Doherty, 'PM's visit opens new chapter with India', www.smh.com.au/federal-politics/political-news/pms-visit-opens-new-chapter-with-india-20121018-27tvd.html, 19 October 2012, accessed 9 August 2014

12: Respected in the world
1 Dennis Shanahan, 'Europe won't be "lectured" by Julia Gillard, EC chief Jose Manuel Barroso has said', *The Australian*, 19 June 2012, accessed 10 August 2014 at www.theaustralian.com
2 Simon Benson, 'Why Gillard looks like a European Bloc-head', *Daily Telegraph*, 22 June 2012, p. 13

14: Our first Australians
1 George W. Bush, speech to the National Association for the Advancement of Colored People's 91st Annual Convention, 10 July 2000, accessed at www.washingtonpost.com/wp-srv/onpolitics/elections/bushtext071000. htm on 21 July 2014
2 'Northern Territory Emergency Response Report of the NTER Review Board', Commonwealth of Australia, October 2008, p. 8
3 Julia Gillard, House of Representatives Ministerial Statements: Indigenous Affairs, 4 House of Representatives Canberra, 9 February 2011
4 Senator Nova Peris, First Speech, The Senate, Canberra, 13 November 2013

15: Our children
1 Max Liddell et al. 'Investing in our future: An evaluation of the national roll-out of the Home Interaction Program for Parents and Youngsters (HIPPY)', Department of Education, Employment and Workplace Relations, August 2011
2 'Protecting Victoria's Vulnerable Children Inquiry', State Government of Victoria, January 2012, vol. 2, p. 330

16: Setting alarm clocks early
1 Tony Abbott, 'The Coalition's plan for more secure borders', address to the Institute of Public Affairs, Melbourne, 27 April 2012
2 Kirsten Livermore, Governor-General's Speech: Address-in-Reply, 23 November 1998
3 For example, Brotherhood of St Lawrence, 'Towards a fair and decent social security system: Submission to the Senate inquiry into the adequacy of the allowance payment system for jobseekers and others, August 2012, www.bsl.org.au
4 Patricia Karvelas, 'Gillard fuels business anger', *The Australian*, 1 May 2007, p. 1

17: Getting ready

1 Gemma Jones, 'Get set for rorts', *Daily Telegraph*, 10 May 2011, p. 1

18: Double trouble: tax and the budget

1 'Australia's Future Tax System: Final Report, Part 2: Detailed analysis, Chapter C: Land and resources taxes', Commonwealth of Australia 2011, *see* taxreview.treasury.gov.au

2 Wayne Swan, media release no. 123, 12 October 2011, accessed on 29 July 2014 at www.ministers.treasury.gov.au

3 Julia Gillard, address to Per Capita Reform Agenda Series, Canberra, 29 April 2013

19: Our atmosphere

1 Allan Gyngell, 'The Lowy Institute Poll 2007: Australia and the World, Public Opinion and Foreign Policy', Lowy Institute for International Policy, 2007, p. 3

2 Fergus Hanson, 'The Lowy Institute Poll 2008: Australia and the World, Public opinion and foreign policy', 23 September 2008

3 Department of the Prime Minister and Cabinet, briefing provided to Hon. Julia Gillard, 2014

4 Lenore Taylor, 'ETS off the agenda until late next term', *The Sydney Morning Herald*, 27 April 2010

5 *Ibid.*

6 Kevin Rudd, transcript of doorstop interview, Penrith, New South Wales, 27 April 2010

7 Peter Hartcher. 'Great procrastinator takes reins of inaction on climate change', *The Sydney Morning Herald*, 24 June 2010, p. 9

8 Julia Gillard, transcript of press conference, Parliament House, Canberra, 24 June 2010

9 Julia Gillard, interview on 'Ten News' with Deborah Knight and Bill Woods, 16 August 2010

10 Paul Kelly & Dennis Shanahan, 'Julia Gillard's carbon price promise', *The Australian*, 20 August 2010

11 The Hon. Julia Gillard MP, The Hon. Wayne Swan MP, Senator Bob Brown, Senator Christine Milne and Adam Bandt MP, The Australian Greens & The Australian Labor Party ('The Parties') – Agreement, Canberra, 1 September 2010

12 House Hansard, Tuesday 13 September 2011, p. 9851, accessed 10 August 2014 at http://parlinfo.aph.gov.au

13 Brenden Hills, '"Carbon Cate" Blanchett tells Aussies to pay up over carbon charge', *Daily Telegraph*, 29 May 2011, accessed 10 August 2014 at www.dailytelegraph.com.au

20: Our water, our land

1 Mark Kenny, 'River queen: Gillard will buy enough water to save Murray', *Adelaide Advertiser*, 10 August 2010, p. 1

21: Caring for each other

1 Tony Abbott, transcript, Joint Doorstop Interview, Casterton, Victoria, 1 May 2013, accessed on 29 July 2014 at liberal.org.au

2 Richard Willingham, Jonathan Swan and Dan Harrison, quoting Julia Gillard, *The Sydney Morning Herald*, 1 May 2013, www.smh.com.au/federal-politics/political-news/pms-challenge-to-abbott-on-disability-scheme-20130501-2irx5.html

3 Steve Lewis, 'Speaker rocked by sex scandal', *Daily Telegraph*, Saturday 21 April 2012

4 Colin Barnett, as quoted by Amanda O'Brien, 'COAG ended up like Labor meeting: Barnett', *The Australian*, 22 April 2010, p. 7

5 www.news.com.au/national/breaking-news/federal-govt-cuts-funds-to-qld-hospitals/story-e6frfku9-1226582404209

22: The party problem

1 For historic boat arrival numbers see www.aph.gov.au/About_Parliament/Parliamentary_Departments/Parliamentary_Library/pubs/rp/rp1314/QG/BoatArrivals

2 Kevin Rudd, press conference, Canberra, 23 June 2010

3 www.aph.gov.au/About_Parliament/Parliamentary_Departments/Parliamentary_Library/pubs/rp/rp1314/QG/BoatArrivals

4 Ibid.

ACRONYMS

ABC	Australian Broadcasting Corporation
ABCC	Australian Building and Construction Commission
ACTU	Australian Council of Trade Unions
AEU	Australian Education Union
AFP	Australian Federal Police
AGSRC	Australian Government Schools Recurrent Cost
ALP	Australian Labor Party
APEC	Asia-Pacific Economic Cooperation
ASEAN	Association of South-East Asian Nations
ATSIC	Aboriginal and Torres Strait Islander Commission
AUS	Australian Union of Students
AWA	Australian Workplace Agreement
B20	International Business Community Meeting at the G20 Summit
BCA	Business Council of Australia
BER	Building the Education Revolution
BURF	Better Universities Renewal Fund
CHOGM	Commonwealth Heads of Government Meeting
COAG	Council of Australian Governments
CPRS	Carbon Pollution Reduction Scheme
DMZ	Demilitarised Zone
DSP	Disability Support Pension
EAS	East Asia Summit
EIF	Education Investment Fund
ERC	Expenditure Review Committee
ETS	Emissions Trading Scheme
G8	Group of Eight Leading Industrialised Countries
G20	Group of 20 Major Economies
GDP	Gross Domestic Product
GFC	Global Financial Crisis
GST	Goods and Services Tax
IED	Improvised Explosive Device
IMF	International Monetary Fund
ISAF	International Security Assistance Force
MPCCC	Multi Party Climate Change Committee
MRRT	Minerals Resource Rent Tax
NATO	North Atlantic Treaty Organization
NBN	National Broadband Network

NDIS	National Disability Insurance Scheme
NPT	Treaty on the Non-Proliferation of Nuclear Weapons
NSG	Nuclear Suppliers Group
NTER	Northern Territory Emergency Response
OECD	Organisation for Economic Co-operation and Development
PRRT	Petroleum Resource Rent Tax
PSG	Political Strategy Group
RAAF	Royal Australian Air Force
RBA	Reserve Bank of Australia
RMB	Renminbi
RSPT	Resources Super Profits Tax
SES	Socioeconomic Status
SPBC	Strategic Priorities and Budget Committee
TAFE	Technical and Further Education College
TPV	Temporary Protection Visa
UN	United Nations
UNESCO	United Nations Education Scientific and Cultural Organization
UNFCCC	United Nations Framework Convention on Climate Change
UNHCR	United Nations High Commissioner for Refugees
VET	Vocational Education and Training
VFL	Victorian Football League
WTO	World Trade Organization

ACKNOWLEDGEMENTS

My life has encompassed many varied experiences but I have never written a book before. At every stage of this adventure, Random House has offered the right mix of encouragement and practical support, while always respecting my need to tell *My Story* my way. My thanks go to Gabrielle Coyne for her leadership of an incredible team and to Nikki Christer for her friendly encouragement and savvy insights as editor. To Anne Reilly, who has lived and breathed this work, put simply, you are a legend. Thanks also go to Meredith Curnow for her fresh eyes and suggestions. All those who went to the index first to see if their names were included will join me in thanking Alan Walker for his efforts.

At Random House, the marketing team, like the editorial staff, are high-quality, dedicated professionals. My thanks go to Brett Osmond and to Karen Reid.

Leaving the prime ministership, I took with me hastily packed boxes and a jumble of memories. Straightening all this out takes effort and it would need to be done whether or not a book was being written. In all this work I have enjoyed the amazing support of Bruce Wolpe, Marielle Smith, Nina Gerace and Michelle Fitzgerald. Thank you for all your continuing work on my behalf and your friendship, which is so very dear to me.

Marielle is owed a special expression of gratitude. Over and above anything required of her during her working day, she has intelligently and patiently assisted me in the creation of this book. My most sincere thanks for all your help, Marielle. When I am next confronted by someone pessimistic about the future of the Labor Party, I now have access to the very easy retort, 'There is every reason for optimism when we can attract young people of the calibre of Marielle Smith.'

A very big thank you as well to Tom Bentley, who extended his work with me in government to undertaking research for this book. In all the work we have done together, Tom has combined his huge brain with his generous spirit. I am so very grateful.

To try and get all the details right in this book, there was an incredible amount of work needed to chase down source material. Thanks go to Philippa Battersby and Ciannon Cazaly for their work hunting down some of the needed information.

A number of former colleagues and staff have provided very valuable feedback on sections of this book and I thank them all. I pay a special tribute to those who read the whole of the manuscript at different stages: Craig Emerson, Nicola Roxon, Wayne Swan, Ian Davidoff, Ben Hubbard and Sean Kelly. A particular thanks to Amit Singh for his efforts.

When I first decided to write this book, I was well advised by Ian Robertson of Holding Redlich. Thank you, Ian, for helping me take the first steps.

Heartfelt thanks go to my family, who have heard week by week about my progress. Thank you to my mother, Moira, my sister, Alison, my niece, Jenna, her husband, Damien, my nephew, Tom, and his girlfriend, Laura. In particular, thanks for understanding the very many times I had to say, 'Sorry, too busy, I'm writing', despite moving to Adelaide to be closer to you. While my great-nephew, Ethan, cannot read yet, for the record let me reaffirm my statement in my last speech as prime minister that 'I intend to be the most meddlesome great-aunt in Australia's history'.

Last but by no means least, loving thanks to Tim for his words of encouragement and the endless cups of coffee.

I have been well supported in every way in writing this book. Even Reuben the dog played his part, sleeping at my feet and quietly keeping me company as I wrote.

While thorough research work has been done and every effort made to ensure the book is accurate, any errors are my responsibility.

I hope my words inform, provoke, intrigue and amuse.

INDEX

Note: Page numbers in bold type, e.g. **80–85,** indicate the most detailed discussion of the topic. Photographs and captions are identified by Plate numbers.

2GB (radio station), 56
7.30 Report (ABC TV), 25, 61, 339
9/11 (11 September 2001), 105, 146, 448
11 September 2001 ('9/11'), 105, 146, 448
457 visas. *see* visas
2020 Summit (2008), 416

A

A New Tax System. *see* goods and services tax (GST); tax reform
Abbott, Tony: election (2010), 40, 44, 46, 56–58, 61, 63, 65–68, 92, 373–76, 382–83, 392, 398–99, 446; election (2013), 302; in Howard Government, 353; as leader of the Opposition (2009–13), 15, 38, 50, 55, 71, 74, 88–90, 110–11, 123–25, 162, 234, 262, 267–68, 283, 295–96, 346, 358, 363, 378, 396, 423–25, 452; leadership transfer from Turnbull (2009), 79, 107, 370, 372; personality, 106, 113; as prime minister (*see* Abbott Government (2013–)); slogans, 46, 50, 294, 455
Abbott Government (2013–), 82, 268, 294, 296, 302
ABC. *see* Australian Broadcasting Corporation
ABC Learning, 273–75
ABCC. *see* Australian Building and Construction Commission
Aboriginal and Torres Strait Islander Commission (ATSIC), 226, 229
Aboriginal Australians. *see* Indigenous Australians
ABS. *see* Australian Bureau of Statistics
academic circles, 174
ACT. *see* Australian Capital Territory
Act of Recognition, 234
acting prime minister, Gillard as, 27–28
ACTU. *see* Australian Council of Trade Unions
Adams, Dick, 96
Adelaide, SA, 26, 39, 123, 144, 221, 276, 320, 400, 427, Plate 3, Plate 18; Hills, 216; University, 240, 320, 330, 460

Adelaide Advertiser (newspaper), 402
ADFA. *see* Australian Defence Force Academy
adoptions. *see* National Apology on Forced Adoptions
advertising and market research, 18, 30, 34, 50, 263, 307–8, 344. *see also* public relations
AEU. *see* Australian Education Union
Afghanistan: asylum-seekers, 18, 452; soldiers killed in, 21, 55, 144, 148–53, 161; Uruzgan Province, 147–48; war & strategy in, 10, 102, **144–53,** 156, 158–59, 161, 166, 320, Plate 16
AFL. *see* Australian Rules football
AFP. *see* Australian Federal Police
African Americans, 155–57
The Age (Melbourne newspaper), 62, 81, 458
aged care, 141, 144, 312, **428–30,** 431. *see also* older Australians
ageing population. *see* older Australians
agriculture, 20, 61, 184, 213, 400–401, Plate 27. *see also* irrigation
AGSRC. *see* Australian Government School Recurrent Cost (AGSRC) index
Ahmadinejad, Mahmoud (President of Iran), 181
aid. *see* overseas aid
aides. *see* staff (ALP)
air force. *see* Royal Australian Air Force (RAAF)
air travel, 8, 26, 47, 50, 75, 94, 97, 142, 144, 146–47, 152, 198, 221–22, 241, 253, Plate 20. *see also* international travel
Al Qaeda, 150, 153
Albanese, Anthony, 21–22, 64, 75–76, 111, 319–24, 337
alcohol, 53, 57–58, 96, 101, 127, 154, 166, 243, 297, 299, 317; Indigenous people, 225, 230–31
Alice Springs, NT, 226, Plate 23
Allen, John R (General), 148
ALP. *see* Australian Labor Party
Altona, Vic, 290, 293, Plate 6

Index

Australian dollar, 48, 173, 175–77, 261, 289–92, 296, 347, 405. *see also* exchange rates

Australian Early Development Index, 269

Australian economic conditions & policy, 10–11, 37, 134, 137, 166, 198, 200–202, 204, 287–90, 292, 298, 317

Australian Education Union (AEU), 253–54, 256, 258, 263

Australian Federal Police (AFP), 27–28, 45, 54, 123–25, 143

The Australian Financial Review (newspaper), 66, 97, 281, 458

Australian forces. *see* Australian Defence Force (ADF)

Australian Government School Recurrent Cost (AGSRC) index, 264–65

Australian Greenhouse Office, 361

Australian Greens. *see* Greens

Australian history. *see* history

Australian identity & values, 36, 135–36, 139–41, 143, 160, 175, 186, 207, 215–17, 220, 223, 233, 317; cultural cringe, 202; work, 280, 296, 305, 313

Australian Industry Group, 307

Australian Jobs Act, 294

Australian Labor Party (ALP). *see also* trade unions: caucus (*see* caucus); constituency, 440, 448–49; consultants, 18, 47; culture, 89–93, 317, 360–61, **439–55**; democratisation, 441, 443–46, 455; disciplining misbehaving members, 77; election campaigns, 12, 32–35, 37–47, 49–50, 134, 257; elections (federal), 53–54, 57–58, 78, 243, 372 (*see also* elections (federal)); electorates (*see the names of electorates, e.g.* Lang); factions, 7, 23, 95–96, 117–19, 170, 235, 323, 417–18, 441, 445, 450 (*see also* 'faceless men'; Left factions; Right factions); focus group polling, 10; foreign policy, 146, 164; foundation, 297; Gillard's career in & loyalty to, 116–20, 127, 460; government role, 245; governments (*see* Australian Labor Party (ALP) governments); instability, 2, 22, 44, 47 (*see also* Gillard Government); Jewish community, 207; leadership (*see* Australian Labor Party (ALP) leadership); loyalty, 77, 83, 86, 89, 95, 128, 130; members of parliament, 1, 19–20, 79, 85, 90, 100, 127–28, 175, 206, 235–38,

242 (*see also* caucus); membership, 443–45; minority government (*see* Gillard Government (second)); national conference, 187–88, 306, **439–43,** 445–47, 450, 454–55; national executive, 237–38; national secretary, 13, 19, 66, 117, 236, 359; in Opposition (*see* Australian Labor Party (ALP) in Opposition); organisation, 128; polling, 33 (*see also* polls (public opinion)); premiers, 18, 29, 58, 103–5, 117, 129, 169, 223, 251, 423; preselections, 41, 59, 119–20, 235, 237–38, 443; president, 58; prime ministers, 97 (*see also the names of prime ministers*); purpose & values, 92, 94, 304, 316, 322–24, 338, 354, 357, 359, **439–55**; rules, 444–45; senators, 308, 320; staffers (*see* staff (ALP)); state governments, 420; state parliaments, 128; student movement, 206, 240; women, 297, Plate 7; Young Labor, 75, 116, 323, 417

Australian Labor Party (ALP) governments, 92–93, 140–41, 195, 231, 267–68, 302–3, 311–12, 317, 324, 385–86, 440, 443, 446, 460. *see also the names of prime ministers and premiers*

Australian Labor Party (ALP) in Opposition (1996–2007), 83, 90, 92, 117, 244, 337, 389; education policy, 262, 270, 273, 326; Gillard as deputy leader, 27, 102, 281; Gillard as Manager of Opposition Business, 5; Gillard as Shadow Minister, 225, 426–27, 430–32, 448; Indigenous affairs, 228; industrial relations, 305–6; leadership (*see* Australian Labor Party (ALP) leadership); refugees & asylum-seekers, 450–51

Australian Labor Party (ALP) in Opposition (since 2013), 93, 267, 454–55

Australian Labor Party (ALP) leaders (*in chronological order):* Beazley as leader (1996–2001 and 2005–6), 5, 160, 323, 337–38, 456; Crean as leader (2001–3), 32, 83–84, 323, 337, 444; Latham as leader (2003–5), 5, 44, 323, 337; Rudd as leader (2006–10), 38, 42, 57, 83, 87, 107, 232, 323, 337, 344; June 2010 election of Gillard (unopposed), 39, 79, 81–82, 84, 86–87, 89, 107, 170, 323, 360, 374–75, 380, 446; September 2010 election of Gillard (unopposed), 79, 170–71,

individual contracts. *see* industrial relations

Indonesia, 115, **177–81**. *see also* Bali; asylum-seekers, 16, 192, 451; Bali bombings (*see* Bali); economy, 204; president (*see* Yudhoyono, Susilo Bambang)

industrial relations (labour), 284, 295, **304–13**. *see also* Australian workplace agreements; independent contractors; unfair dismissal laws; waterfront dispute; workplace or enterprise agreements; conflict, 304–5, 308; contracts (*see* workplace or enterprise agreements); department (*see* Education, Employment and Workplace Relations, Department of); enterprise agreements (*see* workplace or enterprise agreements); Gillard's interest, 339; House of Representatives committee, 242; Howard Government, 4, 137 (*see also* Work Choices); minister, 7, 47, 339

industry, 114, 180, 297. *see also* live animal exports; services sector; Combet as minister, 94, 292; Kim Carr as minister, 292; subsidies, 293

Industry Commission, 418

industry protection. *see* tariffs

inequality. *see* egalitarianism

infant mortality: Afghanistan, 147; Indigenous Australians, 225

inflation, 284, 288, 290, 337, 348

information technology (IT), 291

infrastructure, 141, 166, 284, 316, 318, 321, **322–25**, 331, 341, 343, 404

innovation, 292–93, 330

Insiders (ABC TV), 36, 45

insulation program, 259, 373

intelligence agencies, 59

interest rates, 48, 196, 200, 284, 288–90, 348

intergenerational report. *see* Charter of Budget Honesty

international affairs. *see* world politics

international aid. *see* overseas aid

International Court of Justice, 182

International Criminal Court, 202

international economy. *see* world economy

international law. *see* border protection; world politics

international meetings. *see* meetings

International Monetary Fund (IMF), 198–201, 203

International Security Assistance Force (ISAF) (Afghanistan), 147–50, 161;

Chicago summit (2012), 149, Plate 24; Lisbon summit (2010), 149, 154

international students in Australia, 186, 290, 327

international travel, 162. *see also* air travel; overseas visits

International Women's Day, Plate 14

Internet, 291, 314, 458. *see also* Fuel Watch website; Grocery Watch website; My School website; My Skills website

interpreters, 190

interviews. *see* media

investment, 292, 294, 325, 346

Investor State Dispute Settlement provision, 189

iPads, 149, 314

Iran, 181

Iraq, 59, 152

iron ore, 166, 173, 289, 340, 345

irrigation, 402

ISAF. *see* International Security Assistance Force

Islam, 178, 181; Muslim community in Australia, 208, 210

Islamic extremism, 179. *see also* 9/11; Al Qaeda; Bali

Islamic schools, 179

Israel, 205–10

IT (information technology), 291

Italy, 115, 200, 202

J

Jackson, Sharryn, 56

James Cook University, Qld, 330

Japan, 15, 154, 172, **182–85**, 192, 196, 218, 362, Plate 12

Jenkins, Harry, 75–76

Jews, 50, 206–9, 211

jobs. *see* employment

Jobs Board, 294–95

John Forrest High School, Perth, WA, 256

Johnstone, Peter, 342

joint party meetings. *see* Coalition

Jones, Alan, 105–6, 122

Jones, Barry, 239

Jordan, Alistair, 374

Jordan, Chris, 349

journalists. *see* media

Joyce, Barnaby, 395

Judaeo-Christian heritage, 207. *see also* Christianity; Jews

Index